# THE GUINNESS BOOK OF

# AIRCRAFT

## Records Facts and Feats

# THE GUINNESS BOOK OF

# AIRCRAFT

## Records Facts and Feats

## MICHAEL TAYLOR & DAVID MONDEY

CANOPY BOOKS
A Division of Abbeville Press
New York

Editor: Paola Simoneschi
Design: Stonecastle Graphics Ltd
Picture Editor: P. Alexander Goldberg

First published 1992 in the United States by
Canopy Books, a Division of Abbeville Press, Inc.,
488 Madison Avenue, New York, N.Y. 1022

First published in 1970 by Guinness Superlatives Ltd
    Second edition 1973
    Third edition 1977
    Fourth edition 1984
    Fifth edition 1988 by Guinness Publishing Ltd, London
    Sixth edition 1992

ISBN 1-55859-419-1

# Contents

Introduction                                7

Balloons and Airships                       9

Rotorcraft                                 40

Parachutes, Kites and Gliders              63

Civil Aviation and Route Proving           73

Air Warfare and Military Aviation         130

Research, Experimentation
    and Spaceflight                       206

Valour and Achievement                    220

Index                                     241

*Northrop B-2 'flying-wing' strategic stealth bomber taking on fuel, the most expensive aircraft built at a cost of approximately $776 million each for the first 15. (Northrop)*

# Introduction

If proof was ever needed that aviation history is still being made, it came as this sixth edition was being prepared. Almost every aspect of flying has been touched by the events of 1991, reflected in the many new entries to be found throughout this book.

Who, in 1990, would have believed that the old record of 674 passengers carried by an airliner would – or could – be bettered? Yet in May 1991, it wasn't so much 'bettered' as smashed! The old record had been created out of emergency, when it became necessary to airlift the 306 adults, 328 children and 40 babies from cyclone-torn Darwin, Australia, in 1974. It was a perceived necessity to accelerate the evacuation of the Falasha people from Ethiopia that led to the new record, by the removal of fittings from an El Al Boeing 747, the installation of 760 seats with their armrests folded so that six persons could occupy every four seats, and the eventual lift-off of 1084 people on one flight, the figure rising to 1087 with three on-board births. Such a number appears to steal some of the thunder from manufacturers who are currently planning a new generation of 800-seat airliners.

Achievements in other spheres have been no less dramatic. On 26 May 1991, Soviet cosmonaut Musa Manarov returned to Earth after 175 days in space, accompanied by another Soviet and Helen Sharman, the first British astronaut/cosmonaut. Although only launched into space twice, Manarov's accumulated 541 days has, nevertheless, broken all records for time spent in space, his previous year-long mission (1987–88) having been the longest in history. In a very different mode of transport, in January 1991, the remarkable duo of Richard Branson and Per Lindstrand added to their 1987 historic transatlantic balloon crossing by traversing the Pacific in a vast 2.6 million cubic feet hot-air balloon, the largest ever built and flown.

On the military front, the Gulf War provided the backdrop for many historic facts and feats. In the largest airlift in history and the longest fighter self-deployment, coalition forces became so vast that air power alone made the outcome virtually certain. Here, unique stealth aircraft and 'smart' weapon technologies were used in abundance to keep civilian casualties to a minimum, although television coverage made it seem that the ratio of conventional 'iron' bombs released to smart weapons of super accuracy was far from the actual

93 per cent iron to 7 per cent smart. It was undoubtedly the capability of precision weapons that captured the attention of TV audiences. Yet, the great changes in Eastern Europe during the past few years and the newly granted self-determination for countries that had formerly been part of the Soviet Union, have thrown into question the ongoing need to spend huge sums on new and even more advanced weapons.

Many of the new facts to be found in this sixth edition relate to earlier periods of aviation history, in an ongoing endeavour to improve the book and vary the entries where appropriate. It has only recently come to notice that the first heavier-than-air aircraft to be built in quantity for sale was an Otto Lilienthal glider, in 1895, although the Short Brothers are still credited with establishing the first production line for aeroplanes in 1909. It is also to our many correspondents worldwide that we owe a number of entries. These often come from the relatives of the aviators involved and we offer our thanks to them. So, if an enthusiast wishes to know who and what aircraft recorded the first ever double crossing of the Atlantic in a single day, or details on thousands of other historic firsts, facts and feats, the answers are here.

Virgin Otsuka Pacific Flyer's capsule and remaining fuel tank on their side after landing at about 800 ft per minute. (Thunder & Colt)

# Balloons and Airships

The principle of lighter-than-air flying was not new to the 18th century, even though many consider the experiments of the French Montgolfier brothers in the late 1700s as the origins of flight. The fundamental understanding of why a body can float in liquid or gas goes back more than 2000 years to the work of the Greek mathematician Archimedes of Syracuse. Archimedes, best remembered for his discovery of how a body immersed in a tub of water apparently lost weight equal to the weight of the water it displaced, realised that the same principle applied to gas, and he is credited with the design of a (impracticable) flying crystal sphere in about 250BC.

The invention of the barometer in the 17th century gave some scientific credence to the first recorded design for a lighter-than-air craft. Francesco de Lana-Terzi envisaged a four-sphere airship, the idea being that the thin copper foil spheres (with air extracted to create vacuums) would weigh less than the volume of displaced air, thereby making them float if not tethered to the ground. Great interest was expressed in de Lana's concept, but many of the contemporary 'doubters', including some involved in rival heavier-than-air experimentation, proved more able to demonstrate the impossibility of de Lana's craft than to propose practical alternatives. However, the demonstration of an air-pump by Otto von Guericke in 1654, was further proof of its scientific basis, but of course other problems in the design were insurmountable. For example, how to make the spheres thin enough to save weight, yet strong enough to withstand outside air pressure.

The first successful demonstration of a model hot-air balloon was made by another Jesuit priest, Bartolomeu Laurenço de Gusmão, who was born some fifteen years after de Lana's design was published. However, de Gusmão was not above making his own errors of judgement, and in 1709 had also shown drawings (and may have even constructed a model) of an intended full-size aircraft that coupled an ornithopter with a balloon sail or parachute, known as the *Passarola*.

More significant than even de Gusmão's model hot-air balloon to the future of lighter-than-air flying was the isolation of 'inflammable air' by English scientist Henry Cavendish in 1766. The gas, later named hydrogen by Lavoisier, offered the key to manned flight and could be manufactured in quantity by an expensive process of chemical reaction; ironically the inventors of a practical gas-holding craft (the balloon), Frenchman Étienne and Joseph Montgolfier, chose heated air as the lifting agent produced by the combustion of solid waste, though the first hydrogen balloon took to the air very soon after.

Due largely to the Montgolfier brothers' experiments in Paris, 1783 is viewed by historians as the foundation year of manned flight proper. Remarkably, the inherent dangers of carrying a 'bonfire' suspended below the balloon's envelope did not dampen the determination of the aeronauts that actually flew the man-carrying Montgolfier balloons. It is interesting to note that while the name Montgolfier is well remembered, the names of the men who piloted the balloons and thereby were exposed to the greatest dangers during these early flights are not generally known.

In what must have seemed great ingratitude at the time, while the Montgolfiers prepared for a demonstration to the Académie des Sciences in Paris, that organisation raised a public subscription to assist balloon research and gave it to physicist Professor Jacques Alexandre César Charles. He was to develop a hydrogen balloon, and to buy quantities of iron filings and sulphuric acid to manufacture gas.

The possible perils of fire producing hot air as the lifting agent divided opinion between this and the use of combustible hydrogen gas, the latter having the added benefit of offering the possibility of longer duration flights. History records that hydrogen won the day, though the safety of modern fuel cylinders, burners and flame-resistant fabrics such as Nomex have once again made hot-air ballooning an important aspect of the aviation scene.

A surprisingly short time elapsed before tentative ascents gave way to daring feats. This is particularly surprising when it is considered that the aeronauts were launching themselves into the unknown, at a time when fear of the sky still persisted. But complacency led to tragedy and two such daring flights ended in the first deaths of men and women aeronauts. The first men to lose their lives did so while attempting to cross the English Channel in a combination hot-air/hydrogen balloon, less than two years after the first manned ascent. The first woman aeronaut to die in a ballooning accident had been viewing her own firework party from the vantage point of a hydrogen balloon. In both cases the hydrogen gas ignited.

Few appreciate the scale of ballooning in the 19th century, for pleasure, sport, serious experimentation and observation. From the 1860s balloons filtered into military service, aided in the case of America by the Civil War. This war heralded three innovations that greatly enhanced the usefulness of balloons in military service. On 18 June 1861 the first telegraph message was transmitted from a tethered balloon to the ground, so opening the way for proper air-to-ground communications. The second innovation was the invention of the field-mobile hydrogen gas generating plant, using a process of dilute sulphuric acid reacting with iron and the gas purified by lime. The third was the adoption of a coal barge to transport and tow balloons, so introducing the aircraft carrier. However, the first major balloon operation took place between 1870 and 1871, when the defenders of Paris eluded the surrounding Prussian army by using hastily fabricated balloons to carry from the besieged city despatches, letters, persons and carrier pigeons. This operation led to the deployment (by the Prussians) of the first purpose-designed wagon-mounted anti-aircraft guns.

When it is appreciated that the period between 1895 and 1914 is termed 'the Golden Age' of ballooning, it becomes clear that this form of flying apparatus can claim a far longer period of continuous prominence than is the case for heavier-than-air machines. Moreover, the great interest in hot-air ballooning of recent years has brought ballooning close to the forefront of sport flying for a second time.

Modern balloons are still subject to the whim of the wind. It was this helplessness that first prompted early pioneers to use propellers and rudders to achieve propulsion and directional control. Attempts to navigate basically spherical balloons by such means lasted far longer than is often supposed, and it is well documented that the Swedish scientist and engineer, Salomon August Andrée, fitted 845 ft² (78.5 m²) of sail to a mast, foresail and jibs on his balloon *Ornen* prior to his ill-fated 1897 North Pole flight. Successful directional control was gained with the invention of the airship (correctly dirigible), which moved away from a spherical envelope but was far larger and much more expensive to construct. Despite greater control, early airships appeared to suffer many accidents which, with cost and size, partly explains why the balloon remained popular. Nevertheless, prior to 1915, with development and a great increase in size, the airship was regarded as the most comfortable and safe form of air travel, one suited to commercial operation, and the most destructive vehicle of war devised by man.

The last few years have seen some of the greatest exploits by balloons in the history of aviation, with both gas and hot-air craft crossing oceans and attaining unprecedented sizes. Records for distance and speed have been broken, and plans are still afoot for a round-the-world attempt.

In the field of airships, Britain's Airship Industries went into receivership in 1990, with Slingsby Aviation taking over the type certificates and manufacturing equipment for the civil Skyship 500 and 600. AI's half share interest in Westinghouse Airships of the USA, which is developing the Sentinel 5000 as an airborne early warning airship for the US Navy, has been taken over by its former US partner, Westinghouse Electric Corporation.

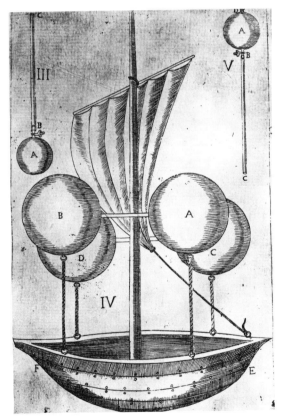

Drawing of de Lana's lighter-than-air craft, with four rope-tethered copper foil spheres intended to provide lift.

# BALLOONS

## Firsts:

**The first recorded design for a lighter-than-air craft** was attributed to the Jesuit priest Francesco de Lana-Terzi. Dated 1670, this comprised a wooden boat hull for three to four people, lifted into the air by four rope-tethered copper foil spheres from which the air had been extracted to create vacuums. A central mast with square sail was to provide propulsion and a hand-carried oar was to give directional control.

**The first successful demonstration of a model hot-air balloon** took place on 8 August 1709 in the Ambassadors' drawing-room at the Casa da India, Lisbon, in the presence of King John V of Portugal, Queen Maria Ann, the Papal Nuncio, Cardinal Conti (later Pope Innocent III), princes of the Court, members of the Diplomatic Corps, noblemen and courtiers. The balloon, made and demonstrated by Father Bartolomeu de Gusmão, consisted of a small envelope of thick paper, inflated with hot air produced by 'fire material contained in an earthenware bowl encrusted in a waxed-wood tray' which was suspended underneath. The balloon is said to have risen quickly to a height of 12 ft (3.5 m) before being destroyed by two valets who feared it might set the curtains alight. Suggestions that Gusmão became airborne later in a full-scale version of the balloon, although documented, cannot be substantiated.

**Hydrogen was first isolated** in 1766 by the English scientist Henry Cavendish, who referred to it as 'inflammable air' or Phlogiston. The Royal Society was told of the gas, which is much lighter than atmospheric air.

**The first person to demonstrate successfully the lifting properties of hydrogen gas** was Italian Tiberius Cavallo (1749–1809), when in 1781 he filled soap bubbles with hydrogen gas and released them. Further attempts to 'fly' bladders filled with hydrogen gas were unsuccessful.

**The first model hot-air balloon demonstrated by Joseph Montgolfier** was a silk bag, which rose to the ceiling of a lodging house at Avignon, France, in November 1782.

**The first balloon to ascend, capable of sustaining a weight equivalent to that of a man** was a hot-air balloon made by the brothers Joseph and

Étienne Montgolfier (1740–1810 and 1745–99 respectively). This balloon, calculated as being able to lift 450 lb (205 kg), was released on 25 April 1783, probably at Annonay, France, rose to about 1000 ft (305 m) and landed about 3000 ft (915 m) from the point of lift-off. The balloon had a diameter of about 39 ft (12 m) and achieved its lift using hot air provided by combustion of solid waste (probably paper, straw and wood) below the neck of the envelope.

**The first public demonstration by the Montgolfier brothers** was given in the market place at Annonay on 4 June 1783, when a small balloon of about 36 ft (11 m) diameter, constructed from linen and paper, rose to a height of 6000 ft (1830 m). This balloon travelled more than 1 mile (1.6 km) before landing.

**The first free ascent by a hydrogen-filled balloon (unmanned)** was made on 27 August 1783 from the Champ-de-Mars, Paris, when Jacques Alexandre César Charles (1746–1823) launched a 12 ft (3.5 m) balloon. It was filled with hydrogen that Charles had manufactured and was capable of lifting 20 lb (9 kg).

The balloon drifted for 45 min and came to earth at Gonesse, 15 miles (25 km) from Paris, where it was promptly attacked by a frenzied mob of panic-stricken peasants, who destroyed the 22 000 ft³ (620 m³) rubber-coated silk envelope.

**The first living creatures to become airborne under a balloon** were a sheep, a duck and a cock which were lifted by a 41 ft (13 m) diameter hot-air Montgolfier balloon at the Court of Versailles on 19 September 1783 before King Louis XVI, Marie-Antoinette and their Court. The balloon achieved an altitude of 1700 ft (520 m) before descending in the Forest of Vaucresson 8 min later, having travelled about 2 miles (3 km). The occupants were scarcely affected by their flight nor by their landing.

**The first known award for an aviation feat** was the Order of St Michel presented to the Montgolfier brothers by King Louis XVI after the balloon demonstration of 19 September 1783.

**The first man carried aloft in a balloon**, and therefore **the world's first aeronaut**, was François Pilâtre de Rozier. On 15 October 1783 he ascended in a tethered 49 ft (15 m) diameter Montgolfier hot-air balloon to 84 ft (26 m), the limit of the restraining rope. The hot air was provided by a straw-fed fire below the fabric envelope and the balloon stayed up for nearly 4½ min. Interestingly, the honour of being the first aeronaut had nearly gone to two criminals who, as proposed by King Louis XVI, might have gained their freedom by volunteering for the flight. After protests by de Rozier, he was given the opportunity to become airborne instead.

The first men carried in free flight by a balloon, the first pilot and passenger, and the first men to make an aerial journey were de Rozier and the Marquis d'Arlandes, who rose in the 49 ft (15 m) diameter Montgolfier balloon at 13.54 h on 21 November 1783 from the gardens of the Château La Muette in the Bois de Boulogne. These early aeronauts were airborne for 25 min and landed on the Butte-aux-Cailles, about 5½ miles (8.5 km) from their point of departure, having drifted to and fro across Paris. Their maximum altitude is unlikely to have been above 1500 ft (450 m).

The first public demonstration of a balloon in England was made by Italian Count Francesco Zambeccari on 25 November 1783, when an unmanned hydrogen balloon of some 10 ft (3.05 m) diameter was released in the Honourable Artillery Company's training ground in London. The balloon finally alighted at Petworth, Sussex.

The first men to be carried in free flight by a hydrogen balloon were Jacques Charles and one of the Robert brothers. The Robert brothers had been responsible for producing rubber-coated silk material, ideal for retaining the gas, and indeed had helped construct the balloon for the attempt. They ascended from the gardens of Les Tuileries, Paris, at 13.45 h on 1 December 1783, in a balloon

28 ft 2 in (8.6 m) in diameter before a crowd estimated at 400 000. The craft landed 27 miles (43 km) distant, near the town of Nesles. This flight can be said to have heralded the beginning of the end for the early hot-air balloon, having achieved a greater distance than was possible with the Montgolfier type.

The first reference to using a movable horizontal winged surface as a method of controlling balloons is attributed to David Bourgeois, in 1784.

The first unmanned hot-air balloon experiments in Germany were conducted by a monk, Ulrich Schiegg (1752–1810), at Ottobeuren in January 1784. Earlier still, at the end of the previous year, balloon experiments had begun in the Netherlands, though by whom is not clear.

The first unmanned hot-air balloon to be released in the United Kingdom was that constructed by an Irishman named Riddick. It was flown on 4 February 1784 from the Rotunda Gardens, Dublin.

The first manned balloon ascent in Italy was made on 25 February 1784, when Chevalier Paolo Andreani and brothers Augustin and Charles Gerli ascended in a Montgolfier balloon from Moncuco, near Milan.

Left  Living creatures first take to the air in a balloon on 19 September 1783. Less than a month later man first flew.

Right  François Pilâtre de Rozier and the Marquis d'Arlandes undertook the first aerial journey on 21 November 1783, in a Montgolfier hot-air balloon. Note in this illustration that the ropes attached to the poles for captive flights hang loose. (Science Museum, London)

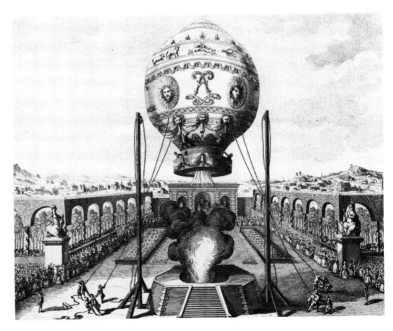

**The first manned balloon flight in the United Kingdom** was made on 15 April 1784, when Mr Rosseau and a ten-year-old drummer boy took off at 14.00 h from Dublin, Ireland, for a 2 h flight. They eventually landed at Ratoath. This marked also **the first occasion music was played from an aircraft,** as the boy beat a tune on a drum for at least an hour of the flight to indicate their position to the crowd below.

**The first women to ascend in a balloon** (tethered) were the Marchioness de Montalembert, the Countess de Montalembert, the Countess de Podenas and Mademoiselle de Lagarde, who were lifted into the air by a Montgolfier hot-air balloon on 20 May 1784 from the Faubourg-Saint-Antoine, Paris.

**The first woman to be carried in free flight in a balloon** was Madame Thible, who ascended in a Montgolfier with Monsieur Fleurant on 4 June 1784 from Lyon, France. The balloon, named *Le Gustav,* reached an altitude of 8500 ft (2600 m) in the presence of the King of Sweden.

**The first manned balloon ascent in Austria** was made on 7 July 1784, when Austrian J. Stuwer ascended from Vienna.

**The first Scottish aeronaut** was James Tytler, who made a balloon ascent from the Comely Gardens, Edinburgh, on 7 August 1784. However, he is better remembered for making an ascent in a home-made Montgolfier-type balloon on 25 August, this time from the city's Heriot's Garden. He is believed to have attained an altitude no greater than 500 ft (150 m).

**The first aerial voyage by a hydrogen balloon over Great Britain** was made by Vincenzo Lunardi of Lucca, an employee of the Italian Embassy in London. On 15 September 1784 he ascended in a 'charlière' (hydrogen balloon) from the Honourable Artillery's training ground at Moorfields, London, and flew northwards to the Parish of North Mimms (today the site of the village of Welhamgreen), Hertfordshire, where he landed his cat and jettisoned ballast. This caused him to ascend again and he finally landed at Standon Green End near Ware, Hertfordshire. On the spot where he landed stands a rough stone monument on which a tablet proclaims:

Let Posterity know
And knowing be astonished!
That
On the 15th day of September, 1784
Vincent Lunardi
of
Lucca in Tuscany
The first Aerial Traveller in Britain
Mounting from the Artillery Ground
in London
And traversing the Regions of the Air
For two Hours and fifteen Minutes
in this Spot
Revisited the Earth.
On this rude Monument
For ages be recorded
That wonderous enterprize, successfully
achieved
By the powers of Chymistry
And the fortitude of man
The improvement in Science
Which
The Great Author of all Knowledge
Patronising by his Providence
The inventions of Mankind
Hath generously permitted
To their benefit
And
His own Eternal Glory

**The first English aeronaut** was James Sadler who, on 4 October 1784, flew in a home-made Montgolfier-type hot-air balloon of 170 ft (52 m) circumference at Oxford.

**The first application of a propeller to a full-size man-carrying aircraft** was recorded on 16 October 1784, when Jean-Pierre Blanchard added a small hand-operated six-blade propeller to the passenger basket of his balloon. As a means of propulsion it was, of course, completely ineffectual.

**The first English aeronaut of a hydrogen balloon** was also James Sadler, who ascended in such a craft from Oxford on 12 November 1784.

**The first aerial crossing of the English Channel** was achieved by the Frenchman Jean-Pierre Blanchard, accompanied by the American Dr John Jeffries. On 7 January 1785 they rose from Dover at 13.00 h and landed in the Forêt de Felmores, France, at approximately 15.30 h, having discarded almost all their clothes to lighten the craft *en route.* Their balloon was hydrogen-filled.

**The first attempt to cross the Irish Sea by balloon** was made by Richard Crosbie on 19 January 1785. Before a crowd of tens of thousands of onlookers, he set off in his hydrogen balloon from Ranelagh Gardens, Ireland. After a good start to the journey, Crosbie decided to postpone the actual sea crossing as darkness was setting in. He eventually landed safely at Clontarf. On 12 May the same year Crosbie made a second attempt at the crossing, but on this occasion the hydrogen balloon only just managed to lift off from the Dublin Barracks and was soon at rest again.

**The first woman to ascend in a balloon in England** was Frenchwoman Mlle Simonet, who flew with Jean-Pierre Blanchard from the Barbican on 3 May 1785.

**The first aeronauts to be killed while ballooning** were François Pilâtre de Rozier and Jules Romain, who were killed while attempting to fly the English Channel from Boulogne on 15 June 1785 in a composite hot-air/hydrogen balloon. It is believed that, when hydrogen was vented from the envelope, the escaping gas was ignited, and the balloon fell at Huitmile Warren, near Boulogne.

**The first British woman to travel by balloon in Britain** was Mrs Letitia Anne Sage, who ascended in Lunardi's hydrogen balloon from St George's Fields, London, on 29 June 1785. Lunardi, who had proclaimed that he would be accompanied by three passengers (Mrs Sage, a Col Hastings and George Biggin), discovered that his balloon's lifting power was not equal to the task. Rather than draw attention to the lady's weight (by her own admission, she weighed more than 200 lb [90 kg]), he stepped down from the basket with Col Hastings. The balloon eventually came to earth near Harrow, Middlesex, where the two occupants were rescued from an irate farmer by the boys of that famous school.

**The first manned balloon ascent in the Netherlands** was made on 12 July 1785, when Frenchman Jean-Pierre Blanchard ascended from The Hague.

**The first manned balloon ascent in Germany** was made on 3 October 1785, when Frenchman

*Richard Crosbie's final bid to cross the Irish Sea, 19 July 1785, ascending from Leinster Lawn. (National Library of Ireland)*

Jean-Pierre Blanchard ascended from Frankfurt-on-Main. Other European nations in which he made the first balloon ascent include Switzerland.

**The first manned balloon ascent in Belgium** was made on 20 November 1785, when Frenchman Jean-Pierre Blanchard ascended at Ghent.

**The first use of the word 'hydrogen'** for the 'inflammable air' used in balloons was made by the French chemist Lavoisier in 1790.

**The first free flight by a balloon in the United States of America** was made on 9 January 1793 by the Frenchman Jean-Pierre Blanchard, who ascended in a hydrogen balloon from the yard of the old Walnut Street Prison, Philadelphia, and landed in Gloucester County, New Jersey, after a flight of 46 min. Among the vast crowd who turned out to witness this event were the President, George Washington, and four future presidents of the United States: John Adams, Thomas Jefferson, James Madison and James Monroe.

**The first use of a man-carrying balloon in war** (tethered) was in June 1794, deployed by the French Republican Army at Maubeuge, Belgium. On 26 June, during the battle of Fleurus, Capt Coutelle ascended in the balloon *Entreprenant* to make an aerial reconnaissance of the enemy, Coutelle had been sent to Maubeuge by the Committee of Public Safety but, on arrival, had nearly been executed as a spy by an officer of the French Army whose job it was to ensure that soldiers did not desert the fighting ranks. Both balloon companies attached to the Army were disbanded five years later.

**The first balloon ascent on a horse** is generally believed to have been made by Frenchman Pierre Testu-Brissy, ascending from Meudon on 16 October 1798.

**The first man to survive the destruction of his hot-air balloon while in flight** was R. Jordarki Kuparanto who, on 24 July 1808, baled out of a Montgolfier balloon that had caught fire. Luckily Kuparanto had taken the precaution of ascending with a parachute as part of his equipment.

**The first aerial crossing of the Irish Sea** was accomplished on 22 July 1817 by Windham Sadler, son of James Sadler, the first English aeronaut. His journey took him between the Portobello Barracks and Holyhead, Wales.

*In tethered flight above the battling armies, Capt. Coutelle of the French Republican Army makes the first ever aerial reconnaissance during the Battle of Fleurus, 1794. (Royal Aeronautical Society)*

*James Sadler, the first English aeronaut, as engraved for the Dublin Magazine. (National Library of Ireland)*

**The first woman aeronaut to be killed in a flying disaster** was Madame Blanchard, widow of the pioneer French aeronaut Jean-Pierre Blanchard (who had died after a heart attack, suffered while ballooning, on 7 March 1809). Madame Blanchard was killed when her hydrogen balloon was ignited during a firework display at the Tivoli Gardens, Paris, on 7 July 1819.

**The first aeronaut to record 100 flights** was undoubtedly the Englishman Charles Green (1785–1870) who, on 14 May 1832, ascended in a balloon for the 100th time, on this occasion from the Mermaid Tavern, Hackney, London. Green was the pilot of the *Great Nassau Balloon* during Robert Cocking's parachute descent of 24 July 1837.

**The first long-distance voyage by air from England** was made during 7–8 November 1836 by a hydrogen balloon named *The Royal Vauxhall Balloon*, crewed by Charles Green, Robert Holland MP and Monck Mason. They ascended from Vauxhall Gardens, London, and travelled 480 miles (772 km) to land near Weilberg in the Duchy of Nassau. The balloon was subsequently renamed the *Great Nassau Balloon*.

**The first joint-stock company associated with ballooning** was the Aeronautic Association, for which 4000 £2 shares were offered to the public in 1837. Expected to realize a profit of up to 200 per cent, the Association intended to construct the largest balloon to date, for 'promoting geographical surveys of some of the remaining undiscovered tracts of the globe, the first attempt to be directed to the unexplored regions of Africa'. The venture was unsuccessful.

**The first recognized design for a kite-balloon**, intended to be tethered to the ground and shaped to derive stability in high wind conditions, is generally attributed to the Frenchman Louis Godard, though another Frenchman, Abel Transon, expounded similar ideas much earlier, in 1844.

**The first British aeronautical magazine** was *The Balloon or Aerostatic Magazine*, published for the proprietors by B. Steill and edited by Henry Wells (pseudonym for Henry Tracey Coxwell). Priced 6d, the first edition of this monthly magazine appeared on 1 August 1845 and lasted just four issues.

**The first balloon bombing raid** was carried out on 22 August 1849, when Austrian unmanned hot-air balloons were launched against Venice. These caused little damage, despite each carrying a 30 lb (14 kg) bomb and time fuse.

**The first balloon flight over the Alps** was made between Marseilles and Turin on 7 October 1849 by M. F. Farban.

**The first hydrogen balloon ascent in Australia** was achieved on 29 March 1858 from the Cremorne Gardens, Melbourne, in a balloon named *Australasian*. This was flown by two men named Dean and Brown.

**The first photographs taken from a tethered balloon** were the work of Frenchman Félix Tournachon (1820–1910), better known as Nadar, in 1858.

**The first long-distance balloon flight in America** was made on 2 July 1859 by John C. Wise, John La Mountain and O. A. Gager, who covered 1120 miles (1800 km) from St Louis to Henderson, New York.

**The first telegraph message transmitted from the air** (and then relayed to the President of the United States) was keyed out by an official telegraph operator who accompanied the flamboyant showman Thaddeus Sobieski Constantine Lowe, during a tethered demonstration flight in the balloon *Enterprise* on 18 June 1861.

**The first American Army Balloon Corps** was formed on 1 October 1861 with a complement of 50 men under the command of Thaddeus S. C.

Lowe who, following his demonstration flight, had been made Chief Aeronaut of the Army of the Potomac. The Corps had originally five balloons, the *Constitution, Intrepid, Union, United States* and *Washington*. Two more, the *Excelsior* and *Eagle*, entered service early in 1862. They were used for reconnaissance and artillery direction. The Corps was disbanded in mid-1863, almost two years before the end of the American Civil War.

**The world's first aircraft carrier** (defined as a waterborne craft used to tether, transport or launch an aircraft) was the *George Washington Parke Custis*, a coal-barge converted during the American Civil War in 1861 under the direction of Thaddeus S. C. Lowe for the transport and towing of observation balloons. The *G W Parke Custis* entered service with General McClellan's Army of the Potomac in November 1861, towing balloons on the Potomac River for the observation of the opposing Confederate forces.

*Inflation of the Civil War balloon* Intrepid. *(US Air Force)*

*USS* George Washington Parke Custis *on the Potomac River near Budd's Ferry, below Mount Vernon, in November 1861, deploying the balloon* Washington *to make a reconnaissance of the blockade. (US Navy)*

*Intrepid*, one of the five original hydrogen balloons of the American Army Balloon Corps, was deployed for observation during the Battle of Fair Oaks in the Civil War on 31 May and 1 June 1862. On 11 December one of the balloons was used by the Corps to assist in the crossing of the river Rappahannock, probably the first time a balloon had been used in connection with crossing difficult terrain.

**The first military use of balloons in an international war outside Europe** was by the Brazilian Marquis de Caxias during the Paraguayan War of 1864–70. This atrocious conflict, which committed the combined forces of Brazil, Argentina and Uruguay against landlocked Paraguay, brought total disaster to the latter nation whose dictator, Francisco Solano López, ordered mass killings among his own people in a savage attempt to compel them towards victory. In the event Brazil occupied Paraguay until 1876; of about 250 000 Paraguayan male nationals before the war, only 28 000 survived in 1871.

**The Prussian Army** formed two lighter-than-air detachments in 1870, with the assistance of Englishman Henry Coxwell. These were deployed during the Franco-Prussian war (see below).

**The first major balloon operation** was carried out during the Franco-Prussian War of 1870–1.

The Prussian Army had surrounded Paris and had cut off the city from the rest of France. Inside the city were a few skilled balloonists and material for balloon-making. In an attempt to get despatches out of Paris, Jules Duruog ascended in a balloon on 23 September 1870. He flew over the Prussian camp and landed at Evreux three hours later. He was followed by Gaston Tissandier, Eugène Godard and Mangin, who were all fired on. Meanwhile, inside Paris other balloons were being made from available material and sailors from the French Navy were being trained as pilots. Balloon ascents carried on until 28 January 1871, by which time 66 flights had been made, carrying about 110 passengers in addition to the pilots, 2½–3 million letters, and carrier pigeons to fly back to Paris with despatches. In mid-October 1870 a chemist, M. Barreswil, suggested the use of microphotography to allow each pigeon to carry a large number of messages. On 18 November **the first official pigeon post** was introduced between Tours and Paris. This microphotography system was reintroduced during the Second World War as the Airgraph service, coping with large volumes of forces and civilian airmail.

**The first crossing of the North Sea** was made from Paris, France, on 1 November 1870 in the hydrogen balloon *Ville d'Orléans*. The 774 mile (1246 km) journey ended at Blefjell in Norway.

**The first attempt to fly across the Atlantic** in a hydrogen balloon was made by John Wise in 1873. Sponsored by the *New York Daily Graphic*, the attempt had to be abandoned after only 41 miles (66 km) following an accident.

**The first practical development of balloons in the British Army** dates from 1878 when the **first 'air estimates'** by the War Office allocated the sum of £150 for the construction of a balloon. Capt J. L. B. Templer of the Middlesex Militia (later KRRC(M)) and Capt H. P. Lee, RE, were appointed to carry out the necessary development work. Although Capt Templer was thus the **first British Air Commander** and an aeronaut in his own right (and the owner of the balloon *Crusader*, which became the **first balloon used by the British Army** in 1879), the **first two aeronauts in the British Army** were Lt (later Capt) G. E. Grover, RE, and Capt F. Beaumont, RE, who had been attached as aeronauts to the Federal Army during the American Civil War from 1862. The **first British Army balloon**, a coal-gas balloon named *Pioneer*, cost £71 from the £150 appropriation and had a capacity of 10 000 ft$^3$ (283.2 m$^3$). It first flew on 23 August 1878.

**The first military use of a man-carrying balloon in Britain** was that by a balloon detachment during military manoeuvres at Aldershot, Hampshire, on 24 June 1880. A balloon detachment accompanied the British military expedition to Bechuanaland, leaving on 26 November 1884 and arriving at Cape Town on 19 December. Another accompanied the expeditionary force to the Sudan, departing from Britain on 15 February 1885.

*British Army balloon at Frensham in 1890. (RAF Museum)*

**The first kite-balloon used in army manoeuvres** was designed by August von Parseval, a German officer, and Bartsch von Sigsfeld, and used by the German Army in 1897.

**The first attempt to carry out an exploration of the Arctic by free balloon** was made on 11 July 1897, when Salomon August Andrée and two companions took off from Danes Island, Spitzbergen. Their 160 000 ft³ (4531 m³) capacity balloon had a sail attached to a complicated arrangement of drag ropes, with which it was hoped to steer the craft. Nothing was known of the explorers' fate until their bodies were discovered on White Island, Franz Josef Land, on 6 August 1930.

**The first American pilot to be shot down in war** was Sgt Ivy Baldwin, Army Signal Corps. In 1898 America and Spain went to war and Baldwin successfully persuaded the Army to deploy a balloon for observation. During the Battle of Santiago, Cuba, Baldwin ascended and gave important information on Spanish troop movements. Seeing the tethered balloon, Spanish troops opened fire on the envelope and it dropped into water, causing only slight injuries to Baldwin. He died in 1955.

**The first ratified altitude record for balloons** was that achieved on 30 June 1901 by Professors Berson and Suring of the Berliner Verein für Luftschiffahrt who attained a height of 35 435 ft (10 800 m). At the time of this record's ratification there was much controversy with those who still firmly believed that James Glaisher had achieved a height of 37 000 ft (11 275 m) on 5 September 1862; as instrumentation to confirm this altitude with any chance of accuracy did not exist at the time, ratification of the Berson and Suring record was upheld; this record remained unbroken for 30 years (although exceeded on a number of occasions by aeroplanes). Berson and Suring's record was beaten in 1931 when the Swiss physicist Prof Auguste Piccard, carried in a sealed capsule suspended beneath a balloon, made **the first balloon flight into the stratosphere** with an altitude of 50 135 ft (15 281 m). In the following year he increased this to 53 153 ft (16 201 m). On 11 November 1935 Capt Orvil Anderson and Capt Albert Stevens of the USA attained an altitude of 72 395 ft (22 066 m) in a balloon in which they ascended from a point 11 miles (17 km) south-west of Rapid City, South Dakota, and landed 12 miles (19 km) south of White Lake, South Dakota.

**The first official balloon race in Great Britain**, organized by the Aero Club, took place on 7 July 1906. Seven balloons competed, taking off from the grounds of the Ranelagh Club at Barn Elms, London. Winner of the event was Frank Hedges Butler, accompanied by Col J. C. and Mrs Capper.

**The first international balloon race**, and also **the first of the balloon races for the Gordon Bennett Trophy**, attracted an entry of 16 balloons. Flown from the gardens of the Tuileries, Paris, on 30 September 1906, it was won by Lt Frank P. Lahm of the US Army who covered a distance of 402 miles (647 km) before landing at Fylingdales Moor, near Whitby, Yorkshire.

Without doubt, the Gordon Bennett contest for a trophy and an annual prize of 12 500 francs, presented by the expatriate American James Gordon Bennett, became the most famous international balloon event.

**The first international balloon race in Great Britain**, on 30 May 1908, began at the grounds of the Hurlingham Club, Fulham, London. Thirty balloons competed, representing five European nations.

**The first National Balloon Race** held in America was won by John Berry and Paul McCullough on 5 June 1909. Their distance covered was about 378 miles (608 km).

**The first operational use of intercontinental bomb-carrying balloons** was made on 3 November 1944, when the Japanese initiated an assault on the United States. An ingenious constant-altitude device was intended to ensure that the balloon remained aloft in the prevailing jet stream which carried the balloons 6200 miles (9978 km) across the Pacific Ocean. Each carried a payload of one 33 lb (15 kg) anti-personnel bomb and two incendiary weapons. More than 9000 of these balloons were launched, and it is estimated that approximately 1000 completed the crossing. Because of a self-destruct device, there were only 285 recorded incidents as a result of their use, and only six persons are known to have been killed by them.

**The first ratified altitude record for a manned balloon of over 100 000 ft (30 480 m)** was achieved by Maj David G. Simons, a medical officer of the US Air Force, who reached an altitude of 101 516 ft (30 942 m) on 19–20 August 1957 in the 3 000 000 ft³ (84 950 m³) balloon *AF-WRI-1*. He took off from Crosby, Minnesota,

Above   *Japanese rubberised silk balloon floating across the Pacific Ocean in late 1944, carrying a 33 lb anti-personnel bomb and incendiary weapons. (US Army)*

*Major David G. Simons sitting inside the compact gondola before take off. (US Navy)*

*AF-WRI-1 rises from an abandoned iron mine in Crosby, Minnesota on 19 August 1957, taking Maj Simons to an altitude of 101 516 ft (30 942 m). The mine pit was used to prevent surface winds tearing the balloon's polyethylene fabric on launching. The envelope, some 280 ft (85.3 m) long at lift off, swelled to a diameter of about 200 ft (61 m). (United States Information Service)*

on 19 August to gather scientific data in the strato-sphere and landed at Frederick, South Dakota, the following day.

**The first hot-air balloon record to be ratified by the FAI**, a height of 9770 ft (2978 m), was achieved by B. Bogan in the USA on 13 September 1965.

**The first crossing of the Swiss Alps by hot-air balloon** was achieved on 21 August 1972 by Cameron A-140, crewed by Don Cameron and Mark Yarry. The flight was from Zermatt, Switzer-land, to Biella, Italy.

**The first hot-air balloon World Champion-ships** were held at Albuquerque, New Mexico, USA between 10 and 17 February 1973.

**The first transatlantic crossing by a gas balloon** was achieved by Raven *Double Eagle II*, crewed by Ben L. Abruzzo, Maxie L. Anderson and Larry M. Newman. This achievement, made between 12 and 17 August 1978, established absolute world distance and duration records for gas balloons of 3107.62 miles (5001.22 km) and 137 h 5 min 50 s respectively, of which the duration record remains unbeaten.

**The first non-stop balloon flight across the American continent** was achieved by Fred Gorrell and John Shoecroft in the helium-filled balloon *Superchicken III*. Launched from Costa Mesa, Los Angeles, California, on 9 October 1981, a landing was made on Blackbeard's Island, Georgia 55 h 25 min later. The distance covered was 2515 miles (4048 km).

**The first transpacific crossing by gas balloon** was achieved by *Double Eagle V*, between Nagashima, Japan, and Covello, California, USA, during 9–12 November 1981. (See also Longest.)

**The first solo balloon crossing of the Atlantic** was completed by Col Joe Kittinger in the 105 944 ft³ (3000 m³) helium balloon *Rosie O'Grady* between 14 and 18 September 1984, flying from Caribou, Maine, USA to Savona, Italy. The 3543 mile (5700 km) journey took 86 h.

**The first transatlantic crossing by hot-air balloon** was achieved by *Virgin Atlantic Flyer*, crewed by Richard Branson and Per Lindstrand. The flight began at 0410 hours (local time) on 2 July 1987 from Sugar Loaf, Maine, USA, and the balloon first alighted near Limavady, Northern Ireland, on 3 July, regaining altitude after being dragged some 150 ft (46 m) but finally alighting in the sea approximately 1650 ft (500 m) off the coast.

**The first balloon flight from Britain to the USSR** was achieved in October 1990 by the Cameron combination helium/hot-air balloon Roziere R-60.

**The first transpacific crossing by hot-air balloon** was achieved by the Thunder & Colt *Virgin Otsuka Pacific Flyer*, crewed by Richard Branson and Per Lindstrand. The flight began at 3.47 (UTC) on 15 January 1991 from Miyakonojo, Japan, and ended at 17.02 (UTC) on 17 January in North West Territories, Canada. Flight duration was 46 h 15 min. (See also *Largest*, *Fastest* and *Longest*.)

## Largest:

**The largest hot-air balloon constructed by the Montgolfier brothers, and the third-largest hot-air balloon ever** was the *Flesselles*, which reputedly had a capacity of some 812 980 ft³ (23 000 m³). Flown on 19 January 1784, it carried seven passengers, including Joseph Montgolfier and Pilâtre de Rozier.

**The largest balloon ever built** was constructed by Winzen Research Inc, Minnesota, USA, with an inflatable volume of 70 000 000 ft³ (2 000 000 m³).

**The largest non-rigid kite-balloon ever constructed** was built by the French Aerazur company in the 1960s, with a volume of 529 720 ft³ (15 000 m³). This and others were employed for tests in the atmosphere of nuclear weapons.

**The largest number of hot-air balloons to ascend from one site** was 128 in one hour, during the 9th Bristol International Balloon Festival at Ashton Court, Bristol, Avon on 15 August 1987.

**The largest hot-air balloon ever flown** was the Thunder & Colt *Virgin Otsuka Pacific Flyer*, with an envelope volume of 2 600 000 ft³ (73 624 m³) and height of 223 ft (68 m). (See also *Firsts*.)

**The world's largest passenger-carrying hot-air balloon for regular use** is the 12-crew Thunder & Colt 300A, with a volume, diameter and height of 300 000 ft³ (8495 m³), 86 ft 8 in (26.46 m) and 89 ft 2 in (27.19 m) respectively.

*Thunder & Colt 300A, the world's largest passenger-carrying hot-air balloon in regular use. (Thunder & Colt)*

## Fastest:

**The fastest manned hot-air balloon ever flown** was the *Virgin Otsuka Pacific Flyer*, which achieved a speed of 239 mph (385 km/h) for over one hour during its 15–17 January 1991 Pacific crossing (see *First transpacific crossing*). The previous record was held by the *Virgin Atlantic Flyer*, which achieved a computed speed of 153 mph (246 km/h) during its Atlantic crossing on 2–3 July 1987, having entered a jetstream at its cruising height of 27 000 ft (8230 m). (See also *Firsts*.)

## Highest:

**The current world altitude record for manned free balloons** is held by Commander Malcolm D. Ross and Lt Commander V. A. Prather of the United States Navy Reserve, who, on 4 May 1961, ascended over the Gulf of Mexico to an altitude of 113 739.9 ft (34 668 m) in the Lee Lewis Memorial Winzen Research balloon. However, the unofficial record stands at 123 800 ft (37 735 m), achieved by Nicholas Piantanid on 1 February 1966, having taken off from Sioux Falls, South Dakota, USA. Piantanid lost his life on the flight.

**The greatest altitude attained by an unmanned balloon** is approximately 170 000 ft (51 815 m), recorded in October 1972 by the 47.8 million cu ft (1.35 million m³) Winzen gas balloon, launched from Chico, California.

**The current world altitude record for mixed gas/hot-air balloons** is 14 573 ft (4442 m), achieved by Henk Brink of the Netherlands on 26 August 1985.

**The current world altitude record for manned hot-air balloons** is 64 996 ft (19 811 m), achieved by Per Lindstrand in the Thunder & Colt *Stratoquest*, flying from Laredo, Texas on 1 June 1988.

## Longest:

**The longest duration flight in a gas balloon by a woman** is 40 h 13 min, achieved by Ms C. Wolf of the USA, from 20 November 1961.

**The current world duration record for manned, mixed gas/hot-air balloons** is 96 h 24 min, achieved by Britons Donald Cameron and C. Davey between 26 and 30 July 1978.

**The current world distance record for a manned gas balloon** was established during 9–12 November 1981 by the helium-filled Raven balloon *Double Eagle V*. Crewed by Ben L. Abruzzo, Rocky Aoki, Ron Clark and Larry M. Newman, it travelled 5208.68 miles (8382.54 km) between Nagashima, Japan, and Covello, California, USA.

**The current world distance record for manned pressurized balloons** is 1485.98 miles (2391.46 km), achieved by Briton Julian Nott in the ULD-1 during 20–22 November 1984.

**The current world distance record for manned mixed gas/hot-air balloons** is 2521.36 miles (4057.732 km), achieved by H. Brink, E. Brink and W. Hageman of the Netherlands from 2 September 1986.

**The longest distance flown by a balloon of any type** is 6761 miles (10 878 km), achieved by the Thunder & Colt *Virgin Otsuka Pacific Flyer* hot-air balloon during its transpacific flight between 15 and 17 January 1991. (See also *Firsts* and *Largest*.)

**The longest planned balloon flight** is a round-the-world attempt, expected to last between 12 and 20 days. The pilot will be Briton Julian Nott, who holds the current world altitude record for hot-air balloons. The Cameron balloon, named *Endeavour*, is expected to journey continuously in a jetstream at an altitude of about 40 000 ft (12 190 m) and will have a pressurized cabin for the pilot. The date for the attempt, which will begin in Australia, had not been reported at the time of writing. A one-third scale balloon of *Endeavour*, known as the ULD-1, established 24 international and world ballooning records and flew across Australia in a little over 33 h in November 1984. (See also *Highest and Longest*.)

## Greatest:

**The second but most famous air crossing of the North Sea** was made during 12–13 October 1907 by the hydrogen balloon *Mammoth*, manned by Frenchman Monsieur A. F. Gaudron and two others. They ascended from Crystal Palace, London, and landed at Brackan on the shore of Lake Vänern in Sweden. The straight-line distance flown was about 720 miles (1160 km).

**The greatest 'balloon buster' of the First World War** in terms of numbers was French

Sous-Lieutenant Michel Coiffard, whose 34 air 'victories' included the destruction of 28 observation balloons.

**The German pilot responsible for the destruction of the greatest number of enemy balloons during the First World War** was Leutnant Heinrich Gontermann, who destroyed 18, including three confirmed in one day.

**The greatest American 'balloon buster' fighter pilot of the First World War and presumably any war** was 2nd Lt Frank Luke of the 27th Aero (Pursuit) Squadron, American Expeditionary Force. His first victory over a balloon was on 12 September 1918, and in total he destroyed 15 balloons and 6 aircraft. He was killed in action on 28 September while on an unauthorized balloon-destroying mission, later receiving a posthumous Congressional Medal of Honor.

*The huge double-deck basket under Cameron Balloons N-850, accommodating 50 persons. (Bristol United Press/Cameron Balloons)*

**The greatest number of persons carried in a tethered balloon** is 61, achieved on 19 February 1988. The balloon, the 2.6 million ft³ (73 625 m³) *Miss Champagne*, was constructed by Tom Handcock of Portland, Maine, USA, and ascended to 50 ft (12.25 m).

**The greatest number of persons carried in an untethered balloon** is 50, achieved on 17 August 1988 by the hot-air Cameron N-850 *Nashua Number One*. The flight had a duration of 25 min after take off in the Netherlands, reaching an altitude of 328 ft (100 m). The pilot was Dutchman, Henk Brink.

# AIRSHIPS

Having become airborne in hot-air and hydrogen balloons, it was not long before the more inventive aeronauts attempted to overcome the unpredictable nature of ballooning by seeking ways and means of steering and propulsion. With these, the aeronaut would be able to travel in a direction other than that dictated by the wind. The result of propulsion was the airship, the accepted term for a powered lighter-than-air aircraft. An airship capable also of being steered and guided is correctly known as a dirigible, though 'airship' is the more commonly used name for all powered and steerable craft and both conventions are used below.

## Firsts:

**The first published design for a dirigible** was that conceived by French Lt Jean-Baptiste Marie Meusnier, Corps of Engineers, in 1784. This was submitted to the Académie des Sciences but was never constructed. The design called for inner and outer envelopes, the latter to maintain the craft's steerable cigar shape when gas was released, and three large two-blade propellers were to provide propulsion, turned by 80 crew members prior to development of a suitable engine.

**The first dirigible fitted with a ballonet,** a small inner gastight compartment within the envelope which could be inflated with air to the desired volume or deflated to regulate altitude (ballonets were subsequently employed successfully for maintaining the envelope shape during variations in lifting gas volume and to adjust trim), was constructed by the Robert brothers. Based on the Meusnier concept, the craft flew for the first time on 15 July 1784 but was not particularly successful, this first flight ending with the crew piercing the envelope to relieve the dangerously high gas pressure. The dirigible is also remembered as **the first cylindrical lighter-than-air craft** and had a volume of 28 252 ft³ (800 m³).

**The world's first powered, manned dirigible** made its first flight on 24 September 1852, when the Frenchman Henry Giffard rose in a steam-powered balloon from the Paris Hippodrome and travelled approximately 17 miles (27 km) to Trappes. His average speed for the journey was 5 mph (8 km/h). The envelope was 144 ft (43.89 m) in length and had a capacity of 88 000 ft³ (2492 m³); the steam engine developed about 3 hp and drove an 11 ft (3.35 m) diameter three-blade propeller.

**The world's first aircraft to be powered by an internal combustion engine** was that built and

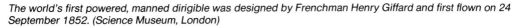

*The world's first powered, manned dirigible was designed by Frenchman Henry Giffard and first flown on 24 September 1852. (Science Museum, London)*

Santos-Dumont 15 airship in parasite experiments with the 14bis aeroplane. (Musée de l'Air)

flown by Austrian Paul Hänlein in 1872. Approximately 164 ft (50 m) in length and 29 ft 6 in (9 m) maximum diameter, the 85 000 ft³ (2407 m³) dirigible was powered by a 5 hp Lenoir-type four-cylinder gas engine which consumed gas from the envelope. This turned a 15 ft (4.57 m) diameter propeller at about 40 rpm, using 250 ft³ (7.08 m³) of gas per hour. Only tethered flights were made and lack of capital prevented further development.

**The first great German dirigible pioneer** was Dr Karl Wölfert who, in 1880, ascended in a dirigible fitted with a small engine. His flying companion was Herr Baumgarten. Load distribution problems caused the dirigible to crash, prompting Baumgarten to abandon the project. However, Wölfert was not so discouraged and on 5 March 1882 he ascended in a dirigible at Charlottenburg, when he attempted unsuccessfully to propel it using a hand-turned propeller.

**The first dirigible fitted with an electric motor** was that flown on 8 October 1883 by Frenchman Gaston Tissandier. The motor was produced by Siemens and was powered by 24 bichromate of potash batteries.

**The world's first fully controllable powered dirigible** was *La France*, an electric-powered craft which, flown by Capt Charles Renard and Lt Arthur Krebs of the French Corps of Engineers, took off on 9 August 1884 from Chalais-Meudon, France, flew a circular course of about 5 miles (8 km), returned to its point of departure and landed safely. The 9 hp Gramme electric motor drove a 23 ft (7.01 m) four-blade wooden tractor propeller. A maximum speed of 14½ mph (23.5 km/h) was achieved during the 23 min flight.

**The first successful use of a petrol engine in a dirigible** was by Dr Karl Wölfert, who designed and built a small balloon to which he fitted a 2 hp single-cylinder Daimler engine in 1888. Its first flight was carried out at Seelberg in Germany on Sunday, 12 August that year, probably flown by a young mechanic named Michaël.

**The first people to be killed in a dirigible accident** were Dr Karl Wölfert and mechanic Herr Knabe, when *Deutschland*'s engine vaporizer set fire to the envelope, resulting in a gas explosion, on 14 June 1897.

**The first all-metal dirigible**, the German Schwartz *Metallballon*, made its only ascent on 3 November 1897.

**The first floating dirigible hangar** was that constructed in 1899 to house Zeppelin LZ 1, which floated on Lake Constance.

**The first flight of a Zeppelin dirigible** was made by Count Ferdinand von Zeppelin's LZ 1 on 2 July 1900. This flight, carrying five persons and lasting about 20 min, was from the floating hangar on Lake Constance and showed that the airship lacked control. LZ 1 was 420 ft (128 m) long, had a diameter of 38 ft 6 in (11.73 m) and a volume of 400 000 ft³ (11 327 m³). Power was provided by two Daimler engines, each rated at 16 hp.

**An early demonstration of controlled flying in a dirigible** was made on 19 October 1901, when Brazilian-born Alberto Santos-Dumont flew his airship No. 6 round the Eiffel Tower in Paris, France, winning a 100 000 franc prize. With an overall length of 108 ft (33 m), maximum diameter of 19 ft 6 in (6 m) and capacity of 22 200 ft³ (630 m³), it was powered by a 20 hp Buchet/Santos-Dumont water-cooled petrol engine, driving a two-blade propeller.

**The first dirigible to be constructed and flown by an Englishman** was the work of Stanley Spencer, whose non-rigid Spencer-Moering airship *Mellin* was launched at Crystal Palace on 22 September 1902. Envelope capacity was 20 000 ft³ (566 m³), length 75 ft (22.8 m) and power was provided by a 3½ hp Simms engine.

**The first practical dirigible** was sponsored by the French Lebaudy brothers and named *Lebaudy*. It was first flown in November 1902. On 8 May 1903 it made the first cross-country flight by a powered aircraft, of 23 miles (37 km). On 24 June it flew 61 miles (98 km) and on 12 November covered 37 miles (60 km) from Moisson to the Champ-de-Mars, Paris. These were the **first fully controlled air journeys in history**.

**The first dirigible bought by a government and suited for military service** was the French Lebaudy brothers' number II enlarged. First flown in 1904, it was a semi-rigid with a capacity of 93 940 ft³ (2660 m³) and was powered by a single 40 hp Daimler engine. The Lebaudy II made a total of 12 flights.

**The first of many Zeppelin dirigibles to be destroyed in bad weather** was LZ 2, which had made its first and only ascent on 17 January 1906 and was lost in a gale while moored at Kisslegg the following day. (LZ 1 had been broken up after three flights, in 1901.)

**Zeppelin LZ 3** was first flown on 9 October 1906. This became **the first military Zeppelin** on 20 June 1909, when it was handed over to the German Army as Z1.

**The first airship used in parasite aeroplane experiments** was the non-rigid Santos-Dumont 15, which had an envelope capacity of just 6568 ft³ (186 m³) and was unpowered.

**The first British Army airship**, Dirigible No. 1 (popularly known as *Nulli Secundus*), was first flown on 10 September 1907 with three occu-

*Right   Lebaudy airship at Versailles, having first flown in 1904. (Mme Moreau)*

*Below   British Army airship* Nulli Secundus, *with Col Capper and Capt King already aboard. (Science Museum, London)*

pants: Col John Capper, RE, pilot; Capt W. A. C. King, Adj of the British Army Balloon School; Mr Samuel Cody, 'in charge of the engine'. The engine was a 50 hp Antoinette. The airship was 122 ft (37 m) long, 26 ft (8 m) in diameter and had a capacity of 55 000 ft³ (1555 m³). The second and third Army airships were *Beta* (35 hp Green engine) and *Gamma* (80 hp Green engine) respectively.

**The République** was the first dirigible to be used by the French Army on manoeuvres, in 1908.

**The first Italian Army dirigible** was the semi-rigid SCA *Ibis*, launched in 1908. Envelope capacity was 97 115 ft³ (2750 m³), length 206 ft 8¼ in (63 m) and a speed of 31 mph (50 km/h) could be attained on the power of a single 100 hp engine.

**The first Russian Army dirigible** was named *Ljebedy*, a semi-rigid purchased from France. Launched in 1908, it had a capacity of 128 015 ft³ (3625 m³), was 203 ft 5 in (62 m) in length, and was powered by a single 70 hp Panhard engine.

**The first dirigible used by the Austrian Army** was the M1, an 81 224 ft³ (2300 m³) non-rigid airship built in Austria by Motor-Luftfahrzeug to the German Parseval PL4 Type B design and first flown in 1909. 165 ft (50 m) in length and pow-

ered by a single 75 hp Austro-Daimler engine, it could attain a speed of 28 mph (45 km/h).

**The first Spanish military dirigible** was the *España*, a non-rigid airship built by Astra in France and launched in 1909. Capacity was 148 322 ft³ (4200 m³), length 213 ft 3 in (65 m), and a speed of 28 mph (45 km/h) could be attained from the power of a single 110 hp Panhard engine. *España*'s most important passenger was the King of Spain.

**The first dirigible to be used to bring attention to a political cause** was one flown over the British House of Commons by a suffragette on 21 June 1908, from which leaflets were dropped.

**The first dirigible to be used by a commercial airline** was Zeppelin LZ 6, which was first flown on 26 May 1909. (Details of the airline, Delag, can be found on p. 29.) LZ 6 was 472 ft (144 m) long, had a maximum diameter of 42 ft 6 in (13 m) and a volume of 565 035 ft³ (16 000 m³). Power was provided by a 145 hp Maybach and two 115 hp Daimler engines, giving a maximum speed of 37 mph (60 km/h).

**The first International Airship Exhibition** (ILA) was staged at Frankfurt/Main between July and October 1909. Zeppelin LZ 5 was flown to the exhibition.

**The first occasion on which four people lost their lives in an air accident** was on 25 September 1909, when the French dirigible *République* lost a propeller which pierced the gasbag; the craft fell from 400 ft (122 m) at Avrilly, near Moulins, the crew of four being killed.

**The world's first commercial airline** was formed as Delag (Die Deutsche Luftschiffahrt Aktiengesellschaft) by Count Ferdinand von Zeppelin on 16 November 1909. Between 1910 and November 1913 the airline carried more than 34 000 passengers between major German cities without injury, although, of the six original airships employed on the services, three were lost.

**The first dirigible to fly from Continental Europe to Great Britain** was the non-rigid Clément-Bayard II, which first flew in 1910. It had an envelope capacity of 22 445 ft³ (635 m³) and was powered by two 125 hp engines.

**The first non-rigid dirigible to be moored by mast** was the British Army's *Beta 1*, which first flew on 3 June 1910. This was also **the first British dirigible to have wireless telegraphy installed.**

**The first occasion on which five people lost their lives in an air accident** was on 13 July 1910 when a German non-rigid dirigible, of the Erbslön type, suffered an explosion of the gasbag and fell from 920 ft (280 m) near Opladen, Germany. The crew of five, including Oscar Erbslön, was killed.

**The first dirigible to make the journey from London to Paris, and indeed the first to fly from England to France,** was the British Willows III *City of Cardiff* on 4 November 1910, a non-rigid airship constructed by E. T. Willows.

**The first Japanese Army dirigible** was the non-rigid No. 1, built by Yamada and Heraka and launched in 1911. Capacity was 103 475 ft³ (2930 m³) and power was provided by a single 60 hp Wolseley engine. This was operated successfully as a training airship.

**The first rigid dirigible with a wooden structure** was the German Schütte-Lanz SL1, launched on 17 October 1911 and featuring laminated plywood girders. Capacity was 688 636 ft³ (19 500 m³), length about 430 ft (131 m), and a speed of 42 mph (68 km/h) could be attained on the power of two 240 hp Mercedes engines. SL1 was taken into German Army service. The more successful and larger wooden SL2, launched in February 1914, used four 180 hp Maybach engines and had such advanced features as cruciform tail surfaces with elevators and rudders, and an enclosed control car near the nose for the flight crew. The SL2 was, therefore, **the first of the modern style rigid dirigibles.**

**The first British rigid dirigible** was the Vickers R1 *Mayfly*. It was 512 ft (156 m) long and was destroyed in a handling accident at Barrow on 24 September 1911 before making a single flight.

*Zeppelin LZ 14, as L1 becoming the German Navy's first military Zeppelin and its first rigid airship to be lost. (M. B. Passingham)*

**The first German naval rigid dirigible** was Zeppelin LZ 14, military designated L1. Ordered in April 1912, the L1 was first flown on 7 October that year and during 13–14 October undertook a 900 mile (1450 km) proving flight. It was the success of this airship that led to the Navy's programme of airship construction for long-range military operations. LZ 14 had a capacity of 793 700 ft³ (22 475 m³), was 518 ft 2 in (158 m) in length and could attain a speed of 50 mph (80 km/h) on the power of three 165 hp Maybach engines. LZ 14 was lost during manoeuvres over the North Sea on 9 September 1913, with heavy loss of life.

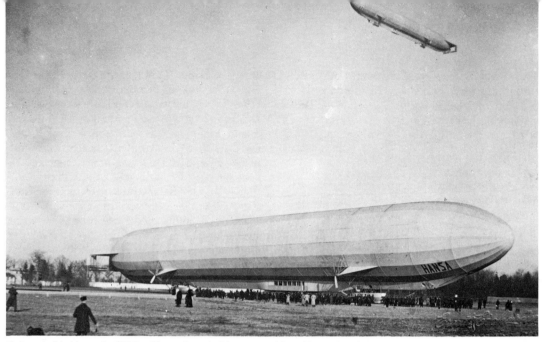

*Delag airship* Hansa *in 1912, with another airship approaching. (Deutsches Museum)*

**The first airmail carried in Germany** was flown on an experimental service between Darmstadt and Frankfurt-on-Main by the dirigibles *Schwaben* and *Gelber Hund*. This service lasted from 10 to 22 June 1912.

**The first international commercial airship service** was begun by the Delag dirigible *Hansa* on 19 September 1912, flying between Hamburg, Copenhagen (Denmark) and Malmö (Sweden).

**The first Zeppelin dirigible designed to be capable of reaching Britain in case of war** (with a bomb load) and **the largest airship completed before the outbreak of the First World War** was LZ 18, designated L2 in German naval service. Launched on 9 September 1913, L2 was 518 ft 4 in (158 m) long and had a volume of 953 500 ft³ (27 000 m³). Power was provided by four 165 hp Maybach engines. Intended to be the first of 10 large dirigibles to equip two Navy units, it was lost, however, on 17 October 1913, when it caught fire while airborne. All 28 crew were killed.

**The first Allied airship attack of the First World War** took place on 9 August 1914, by the French Army *Fleurus* operating from Verdun.

**The first successful mission by a German dirigible during the First World War** was carried out on 12 August 1914, when L3 located the Dutch battleship *de Zeven Provincien* and destroyers off Terschelling, Waddeneilanden.

**The first dirigible to be shot down by French infantry** was *Dupuy-de-Lôme* on 24 August 1914, a French airship mistakenly identified as a Zeppelin.

**The first Zeppelin dirigible with cruciform tail surfaces** was LZ 27, designated L4 by the Navy, first flown on 28 August 1914. After just under 50 flights it was destroyed during a forced landing in 1916.

**The first airship raid on Great Britain** was carried out on 19 January 1915 by three German Navy Zeppelins, L3, L4 and L6. They took off from Fuhlsbüttel and Nordholz. L6 was forced to return through engine trouble but L3 and L4 arrived over the Norfolk coast at about 20.00 h; nine bombs were dropped in the Great Yarmouth area at 20.25 h by L3, killing two persons and wounding three others. Meanwhile L4 had gone north-west towards Bacton and dropped incendiary bombs on Sheringham, Thornham and Brancaster as well as a high-explosive bomb on Hunstanton wireless station. Following that, it dropped bombs on Heacham, Snettisham and King's Lynn, where seven high-explosive bombs were dropped and an incendiary, killing two people and injuring 13. The two airships were both wrecked on the coast of Jutland on 17 February 1915, after running into a gale on their homeward journey from a mission to spot the British fleet.

**The first dirigible with a volume of more than one million cubic feet** was the German Navy's Schütte-Lanz SL3, which was completed in February 1915. Powered by four 210 hp Maybach engines, it was 502 ft 4 in (153 m) in length and had a volume of 1 144 200 ft³ (32 400 m³). This airship was lost in 1916.

**The first British anti-submarine warfare dirigible** was the non-rigid SS 1 (Sea Scout), built by Armstrong-Whitworth and launched in 1915. The first of 36 SS class airships used by the Royal Naval Air Service, it was 100 ft (30.48 m) in length and could attain a speed of 48 mph (77 km/h) on the power of a 70 hp engine in the nose of a car fabricated from the fuselage of a BE2c observation aeroplane. Sixty-six improved SS Zs followed from 1916.

**The first partially successful attack on a submarine by an airship** was performed in the early afternoon of 3 May 1915, when Zeppelin LZ 36 (L9) spotted four British submarines and managed to damage the conning tower of one, D4, by dropping five 50 kg bombs from an altitude of 3280 ft (1000 m).

**The first air raid on London** was by Zeppelin LZ 38 on 31 May 1915. The Kaiser had authorized bombing of London, east of the Tower, a few days before and on the night of the 31st 3000 lb (1360 kg) of bombs were dropped on north-east London, killing seven people and injuring 14 others.

**The first French Navy dirigibles** were the four Astra-Torres non-rigids designated AT 1 to AT 4, first flown in 1916. Each had a capacity of 229 545 ft³ (6500 m³), was powered by two 150 hp Renault engines and could attain a speed of 50 mph (80 km/h).

**The first Zeppelin to be set on fire** was LZ 47, during an attack on 21 February 1916.

**The first airship to be brought down by air attack** was Zeppelin LZ 37 on the night of 6–7 June 1915. In company with LZ 38 and LZ 39, the airship set out from Bruges to bomb London but adverse weather later forced them to alter course for their secondary targets—railways in the Calais area. LZ 37 was located and attacked by Flt Sub Lt R. A. J. Warneford of No. 1 Squadron, RNAS, flying a Morane-Saulnier Type L from Dunkirk. Warneford's only means of attack were six 20 lb

(9 kg) bombs; he followed the airship from Ostend to Ghent, being forced to keep his distance by fire from the airship's gunners. He made a single pass over the airship dropping all six bombs from about 150 ft (45 m) above it. The sixth exploded, and the airship fell in flames on a suburb of Ghent, killing two nuns. Only one member of Oberleutnant Otto van de Haegen's crew survived. Warneford returned safely to base after making a forced landing to repair a broken fuel line. He was informed the following evening that he had been awarded the Victoria Cross; he died 12 days later when the tail of a Henry Farman pusher biplane collapsed in mid-air.

*Warneford's Morane-Saulnier Type L, used in the successful attack on Zeppelin LZ 37. (Imperial War Museum)*

**The first Zeppelin to be shot down while over the British Isles** was LZ 48 (German Navy designation L15). In the company of six other Zeppelins, it had taken off on 31 March 1916 to attack London and the south of England. Two Zeppelins soon turned back but the five remaining dirigibles continued. L15 had reached a point north of London by 10.30 p.m. when it was caught by searchlights near Dartford and hit by groundfire. The dirigible dropped bombs to gain height but was attacked by 2nd Lt A. Brandon, RFC, flying a BE2c biplane, who released explosive darts. L15 slipped away in the darkness but was in very bad shape. Attempting to limp home, it flew over Purfleet, where it was struck again by groundfire from an anti-aircraft gun. Unable to continue, L15 went down into the sea just off Kentish Knock Lightship, at Fundress. Taken in tow, it eventually sank off Westgate on the morning of 1 April. Two gold medals were made for Sir

Charles Wakefield (then Lord Mayor of London) to commemorate the action, these being presented to Lance Corporal R. Rowe and a Purfleet officer, who were recognized as having shot down the L15.

**The first German airship to be brought down on British soil** was the Schütte-Lanz SL XI, which was attacked on the night of 2 September 1916 by Lt W. Leefe Robinson, RFC, using the newly-invented Pomeroy incendiary ammunition. It crashed in flames near Cuffley, Hertfordshire. Robinson was awarded the VC. This action demoralized German airship crews, particularly because it had demonstrated the effectiveness of British defences, and is said to have prevented a large-scale airship attack on London. However, on the night of 23–24 September eleven Zeppelins raided England, three with London as their target. One airship, LZ 76 (L33), was hit by anti-aircraft fire and came down at Little Wigborough and another, LZ 74 (L32), was shot down by a British aircraft (flown by 2nd Lt Sowrey) over Great Burstead.

**The first US Navy dirigible** was the DN-1 (or A-1), constructed by the Connecticut Aircraft Company and flown for the first time (of only three flights) on 20 April 1917. Capacity was 150 000 ft³ (4247.5 m³), length 175 ft (53.34 m), and a speed of 35 mph (56 km/h) could be attained on the power of a single 140 hp Sturtevant engine; it had been built originally with two engines but was modified after it proved too heavy to leave the ground.

**The US Navy's first dirigibles to be series produced** were of the B series for anti-submarine warfare and training, each of the 17 airships (3 later enlarged) carrying the crew in converted aeroplane fuselages. Launched in 1917 and built by Goodyear, the Connecticut Aircraft Company and Goodrich, each B series craft (unmodified) had a capacity of 77 000 ft³ (2180 m³), was 160 ft (48.77 m) in length, and attained a speed of 45 mph (72 km/h) on the power of a single 100 hp Curtiss OXX-2 engine. **The first successful dirigible of the US Navy** was, therefore, the Goodyear B-1 acquired under the initial 14 March 1917 contract and first flown from Chicago, Illinois, to Wingfoot Lake, near Akron, Ohio, on 30 May 1917.

**The worst losses suffered by the German Naval Airship Division on a single day of operational missions** were five Zeppelins that failed to return to base on 20 October 1917. LZ 85 (L45) and LZ 96 (L49) force-landed in France, LZ 93

*Left The wreck of German Navy Zeppelin L33 at Little Wigborough, attracting the attention of His Excellency the French Ambassador. (Imperial War Museum)*

*Right USS Los Angeles moored to USS Patoka. The airship accumulated 5368 flying hours before being retired and was undoubtedly the most successful of the US Navy's rigid airships. (US Navy)*

(L44) was shot down over France, LZ 89 (L50) was lost over the Mediterranean and LZ 101 (L55) force-landed in Germany. LZ 50 (L16) had also been wrecked the previous day. On 5 January 1918 five Navy dirigibles were destroyed in an explosion at the Ahlhorn sheds, raising the total number of airships lost to the German Navy in three months from October 1917 to twelve.

**The last German airship attack on England which resulted in death or injury** was made on 12 April 1918. Altogether, during the 51 Zeppelin airship raids on Great Britain during the war, 196 tons (199 tonnes) of bombs were dropped, killing 557 people and injuring many more.

**The first airship crossing, and first two-way crossing of the Atlantic by any type of aircraft**, were achieved by the British airship R-34 between 2 and 6 July (westward) and 9 and 13 July (eastward) 1919. Commanded by Sqn Ldr G. H. Scott, with a crew of 30, the R-34 set out from East Fortune, Scotland, and flew to New York, returning afterwards to Pulham, Norfolk, England. The total distance covered, 6330 miles (10 187 km) in 183 h 8 min, constituted a world record for airships.

**Delag,** the pre-war commercial airline flying dirigibles, reopened services on 24 August 1919 with the airship *Bodensee,* flying the route between Friedrichshafen and Berlin. However, this service was suspended on 1 December by order of the Allied Control Commission. Between these dates about 103 flights had been made, carrying 2400 passengers and 66 140 lb (30 000 kg) of cargo. Each flight carried 23 passengers.

**The first dirigible with a volume of more than 2½ million cubic feet** was the British Shorts R-38. Launched in 1921, it was **then the largest airship in the world**, with a length of 695 ft (212 m), maximum diameter of 85 ft (26 m) and volume of 2 740 000 ft³ (77 600 m³). Power was provided by six Cossack engines with a total output of 2100 hp. It was destroyed when it broke up over Hull, England, on 24 August 1921. It was to have been sold to the United States and at the time of the disaster there were 16 Americans aboard in addition to the crew of 33. All the Americans and 28 of the British lost their lives.

**The first airship to use helium gas** instead of hydrogen was Goodyear C 7, one of 16 C series non-rigid airships ordered for the US Navy as coastal patrol and convoy craft. This made its first flight on 1 December 1921. The first C series airship, the C 1 launched in September 1918, was the first non-rigid dirigible to demonstrate the 'parasite' concept, when on 12 December 1918 it lifted a Curtiss Jenny biplane to an altitude of 2500 ft (760 m) and successfully released it. Previous experiments in Germany and Britain using the rigid airships L35 and R-23 had seen the air launch of an Albatros D.III and Sopwith Camel respectively. The Albatros had been released on 26 January 1918, making this **the first demonstration of the parasite fighter concept.** The first British parasite experiment was conducted on 6 November 1918.

**The first Japanese naval dirigible** was a non-rigid Vickers SS Twin type, launched in 1922. Of 100 000 ft³ (2832 m³) capacity, it was powered

by two 100 hp Sunbeam engines and attained a speed of more than 60 mph (97 km/h). Unfortunately, No. 1 was destroyed by fire in its shed soon after, on 10 July 1922.

**The US Navy's first rigid dirigible** was the ZR-1 *Shenandoah* (see below).

**The first helium-filled American rigid airship** was the Zeppelin-type ZR-1 *Shenandoah*, which first flew on 4 September 1923 at Lakehurst, New Jersey, USA. On 3 September 1925 it was destroyed in a storm over Caldwell, Ohio, with heavy loss of life.

**The first and only dirigible received by the US Navy from Germany as war reparations** was the newly built LZ 126, known as ZR-3 *Los Angeles*. This was flown from Friedrichshafen to Lakehurst, USA, during 12–14 October 1924. A very successful airship that made 331 flights up to 1932, it was initially filled with hydrogen gas.

**The first successful 'hook on' parasite experiment between a dirigible and an aeroplane** was conducted between the US Army non-rigid and helium-filled training dirigible TC-3 and a Sperry Messenger biplane on 15 December 1924. A previous attempt, by 1st Lt Clyde V. Finter on the 13th, failed when the aeroplane's propeller was damaged after striking the dirigible's 'hook on' trapeze structure.

**The French rigid airship** *Dixmude*, in fact Zeppelin LZ 114 (L72), received as war reparations, remained airborne for 118 hours and 41 minutes in September 1925, landing on the 25th. This was by far the greatest duration flight of the period.

**The first airship flight over the North Pole** was made by the Italian-built N-class semi-rigid airship N.1, subsequently named *Norge* by Roald Amundsen, who bought the airship for Arctic exploration. During the period from 11 to 14 May 1926, the *Norge* was flown from Spitzbergen to Teller, Alaska. Among the distinguished crew were Amundsen, Umberto Nobile and Lincoln Ellsworth, who dropped Norwegian, Italian and American flags at the Pole on 12 May. On 23 May 1928 Nobile set off in another attempt to fly over the North Pole, in the Italian dirigible *Italia*. This crashed on the return journey. Nobile and most of his crew survived but Amundsen, who joined the international rescue attempt, was killed.

ZR-1 Shenandoah, *the first helium-filled American rigid dirigible. (Smithsonian Institution)*

*In 1918 both Germany and Britain carried out parasite fighter experiments using fighter biplanes released from airships. Britain began with a Sopwith Camel attached by hook to the R-23, the first airborne release taking place on 6 November. The fighter pilot on this occasion was Lieutenant R. E. Keys. (Imperial War Museum)*

The first airship flight round the world was accomplished by the German *Graf Zeppelin* between 8 and 29 August 1929. Captained by Dr Hugo Eckener, the craft set out from Lakehurst, New Jersey, and flew via Friedrichshafen, Germany, Tokyo, Japan, and Los Angeles, California, returning to Lakehurst in 21 days 5 h and 31 min. The total distance covered was more than 21 870 miles (35 200 km). Most successful of all the passenger-carrying airships, the *Graf* had flown well over a million miles and had carried a total of some 13 100 passengers before being scrapped at the beginning of the Second World War.

The last rigid commercial airships to be developed in Great Britain were the R-100 and R-101. The latter crashed on 5 October 1930 at Beauvais, France, on a flight from Cardington, Bedfordshire, England, to Egypt and India. The accident, which destroyed the airship and killed 48 of the 54 occupants (including Lord Thomson, Secretary of State for Air, and Maj Gen Sir Sefton Brancker, Director of Civil Aviation), brought to

Above   Norge, *the first airship to fly over the North Pole.*

Below   *The ill-fated* Italia *ready for the North Pole flight in 1928. (Italian Ministry of Defence)*

an end the development of large passenger-carrying airships in Britain. The R-101 was, however, the largest ever British airship, with a length of 777 ft (236.8 m) and volume of 5 508 800 ft³ (155 995 m³). The R-100 was designed by Barnes

Neville Wallis (later Sir Barnes) for the Airship Guarantee Company. It was for this craft that he originated his unique geodetic form of basic airframe structure, used later in the construction of Vickers Wellesley and Wellington bomber aircraft. In a test on 16 January 1930 the R-100 achieved a speed of 81½ mph (131 km/h), making it **the fastest airship in the world**.

During July and August 1930 the R-100 made a double Atlantic crossing, flying between Cardington and Montreal, Canada. But, following the R-101 disaster, it was scrapped.

**The first non-rigid dirigible to be fuelled with blaugas** (German gas used for both fuel and envelope, comprising ethylene, methylene, propylene, butylene, hydrogen and ethane) was the US Navy airship K-1, built by Goodyear and launched in 1931. Capacity was 319 900 ft³ (9058.5 m³), length 218 ft (66.4 m), and a speed of 65 mph (105 km/h) could be attained from the power of two 330 hp Wright J-6-9 engines. The gas for fuel was contained in a ballonet.

**The world's first fighter-carrying airship intended for operational service**, USS *Akron*, was flown for the first time on 25 September 1931. This operated successfully with four Curtiss F9C-2 Sparrowhawk fighters until 4 April 1933 when it crashed into the sea off the New Jersey coast during a storm. (See below.) On 3 November 1931 *Akron* ascended with 207 persons on board, **the greatest number ever carried by an airship**.

**The final French Navy dirigible** was the nonrigid Zodiac V12 of 1936 launch, which was designed to be towed while attached to its mooring mast to ease ground handling. Over 161 ft (49 m) in length, with an envelope capacity of 141 965 ft³ (4020 m³) and powered by two 270 hp Salmson engines, it could attain a speed of 64 mph (103 km/h).

**The last major airship disaster** involved the destruction of the German *Hindenburg*, then the world's largest airship, on 6 May 1937. It was destroyed by fire when approaching its moorings

*The fastest airship in the world was the British R-100, which made a double Atlantic crossing in 1930.*

Above   *USS Akron, the first of two operational fighter-carrying airships. Akron was lost with 74 of its 78 crew on 4 April 1933 in a violent squall off Barnegat Light, NJ. (Goodyear Tire and Rubber Company)*

Left   *The prototype Sparrowhawk fighter, the XF9C-1, being hoisted to the hangar inside the airship USS Akron. (US Navy)*

at Lakehurst, New Jersey, USA, after a flight from Frankfurt, Germany. Thirty-five of the 97 occupants were killed in the fire which engulfed the huge craft and which was attributed to the use of hydrogen—the only gas available to Germany owing to the United States' refusal to supply commercial quantities of helium. With its sister craft, the LZ 130 *Graf Zeppelin II*, it was the largest rigid airship ever built.

**The first airship built in Britain following the R-101 disaster** made its first flight at Cardington, Bedfordshire, on 19 July 1951. This was a small airship named *Bournemouth*, built by the Airship Club of Great Britain under the leadership of Lord Ventry.

**The world's first hot-air airship** was first flown on 3 January 1973 at Newbury, England. Constructed by Cameron Balloons, D-96 (G-BAMK) was 100 ft (30.5 m) in length, with a maximum diameter of 45 ft (13.72 m). It was powered by a converted Volkswagen motorcar engine and had a speed of 17 mph (27.5 km/h). The lightweight nylon fabric envelope had a gross capacity of 96 000 ft³ (2718 m³) and was inflated by hot air generated by a propane gas burner carried in the lightweight tubular-metal gondola. More highly developed hot-air airships followed from the Cameron.

**The first post-Second World War scheduled passenger service by airship** began on 23 April 1986, when Airship Industries Skyship 500-02

*The final moments of* Hindenburg, *engulfed in flames at Lakehurst on 6 May 1937. (US National Archives)*

was used to conduct four daily sightseeing flights over London, taking off from Leavesden.

**The first full-authority fly-by-light flight control system in the world** was test flown in Airship Industries Skyship 600–04 from 23 October 1988. GEC Avionics combined in the development of the system, intended to be fitted into the planned US Navy Sentinel AEW airships being developed by Westinghouse Airships in the USA.

**The first US FAA type certificate issued to a civil airship** was received by the Airship Industries (now Slingsby) Skyship 600 in May 1989.

**The first hot-air airship World Championships** were held in Luxembourg during 27 July –7 August 1989. Seventeen airships took part, with the Colt AS 56s taking first and third places, and the Cameron DP-70 managing second place. Pilot of the winning AS 56 was Oscar Lindström.

**The producer of the largest number of airships** is the Goodyear Tire & Rubber Company, which has built well over 310; of these more than 250 were constructed for the US military services. The company also operates a fleet of airships, comprising three non-rigid craft for public relations and advertising.

*Largest:*

**The largest British airship** was the R-101 (see 'The last rigid commercial airships to be developed in Great Britain').

**The largest rigid dirigibles built in the United States of America** were the Goodyear USS *Akron* and *Macon*. These identical craft had capacities of 6 500 000 ft³ (184 059 m³), were 785 ft (239.3 m) in length and were each powered by eight 560 hp German-built Maybach engines. (See also *Firsts*.)

**The largest rigid dirigible ever built** was the German passenger craft LZ 130 *Graf Zeppelin II*. First flown on 14 September 1938, it had a capacity of 7 062 270 ft³ (199 981 m³), was 803 ft 10 in (245 m) in length, and was powered by four 1200 hp Mercedes Benz diesel engines. Officially, its last flight was made on 20 August 1939; in May and August 1939 it carried out radar spying missions against British interests. It was scrapped in April 1940.

**The largest non-rigid airships ever built** were four Goodyear ZPG 3-W early warning radar craft ordered for the US Navy. The first of these was launched on 21 July 1958 but crashed in 1960. All remaining craft were deleted in 1962. Each was 403 ft 4 in (122.9 m) long and had a volume of 1 516 300 ft³ (42 937 m³).

**The world's largest fully-certificated non-rigid airship** is the German WDL 1B, of which four have been built. Length is 196 ft 6 in (59.6 m), diameter (maximum) 53 ft 9¾ in (16.4 m) and volume 254 265 ft³ (7200 m³). Powered by two 210 hp Teledyne Continental IO-360 piston engines, it has a 2600 lb (1180 kg) payload (including seven passengers). The first flew on 30 August 1988.

**The world's largest hot-air airship** is the Thunder & Colt AS 261, with a length, diameter (maximum) and volume of 156 ft 10 in (47.80 m), 61 ft 8 in (18.80 m) and 261 000 ft³ (7391 m³) respectively. The prototype first flew in 1989. The AS 261 is also the **first hot-air airship with cargo carrying capability**.

3967.137 miles (6384.5 km), established by the German airship LZ 127 *Graf Zeppelin* between 29 October and 1 November 1928. Captain was the legendary Dr Hugo Eckener. Unaccredited is the approximately 4500 mile (7250 km) return flight by the Zeppelin L 59 during 21–25 November 1917, flying between Yambol, Bulgaria and near Khartoum, Sudan.

**The longest duration flight by a non-rigid dirigible** without refuelling is 264 h 12 min, established between 4 and 15 March 1957 by a US Navy Goodyear ZPG 2 class craft. This flight, crewed by Cdr J. R. Hunt, Lt Cdr Robert S. Bowser and 12 others, began from South Weymouth NAS, Massachusetts, and ended at Key West, Florida. The distance flown was 9448 miles (15 205 km), a record for lighter-than-air craft.

**The longest duration flight (without refuelling) by a fully equipped non-rigid dirigible on a mission** is 95 h 30 min, achieved by the crew of a US Navy ZPG 2 airship between 25 and 29 March 1960. In command of the crew of 19 was Lt Lundi A. Moore.

**The longest distance and duration flight by a hot-air airship** was achieved by Oscar Lindström in a Colt AS 56 one-man craft on 20 March 1988, recording a distance of 57.8 miles (93.033 km) in 3 h 41 min 55 secs. (See also *Firsts*.)

*Greatest:*

**The greatest dirigible captain** was undoubtedly Dr Hugo Eckener (born 1868), who joined Count Zeppelin prior to the first flight of LZ 3 in 1906 and subsequently headed the company after the Count's death. Among his many achievements was the development of *Graf Zeppelin* and *Hindenburg*. He died in 1954.

**The greatest number of rigid airships operated by an armed service** was the 69 Zeppelins and Schütte-Lanz craft flown by the German Naval Airship Division during the First World War.

**The greatest number of persons carried by a dirigible** stands at 207, achieved by US Navy rigid airship *Akron*, on 3 November 1931. (See also *Firsts*.)

**The greatest number of persons carried across the Atlantic by dirigible** stands at 117, performed in 1937 by Zeppelin LZ 129 *Hindenburg*.

This photograph of Akron under construction gives a good idea of the huge size of the craft and its complex structure. (Goodyear Tire and Rubber Company)

*Highest:*

**The world altitude record for hot-air airships** stands at 10 365 ft (3159 m), achieved by Australian R. W. Taaffe in a Cameron D-38 at Cunderdin, Western Australia, on 27 August 1982.

*Longest:*

**The FAI accredited world straight-line distance record for rigid dirigibles** stands at

ZPG-3-W early warning non-rigid airship (right) between the Goodyear Airdock's massive clamshell doors. (Goodyear Tire and Rubber Company)

# Rotorcraft

*Design and backward notes by Leonardo da Vinci for a corkscrew-rotor helicopter. (Science Museum, London)*

Today, it seems difficult to imagine an aviation scene in which helicopters had no significant part, but that was basically the situation for the first 40 or so years of powered flight. Now, unless beneath the airspace of a major airport, the helicopter is the aircraft most frequently seen by the general public, the thud-thud of rotor blades announcing its approach as it moves along low-altitude sky lanes, busy on a wide variety of tasks. Their use in many civil roles is well known, banner headlines shouting the life-saving benefits of air ambulance and search and rescue helicopters across the globe. Simultaneously however, they are occupied by such daily routine tasks as pipe and power line surveillance, policing and transport, and their significant place in the development and maintenance of off-shore gas and oil fields is almost immeasurable.

Not surprisingly, the military use of helicopters mushroomed following their first major introduction during the Korean War. Such was their importance in warfare that it has led to the development of combat types intended to intercept and destroy opposing helicopters of an enemy.

This wide-scale civil and military scene that has evolved during the past half-century will make it difficult for many readers to appreciate that ideas for flight by rotorcraft stretch back more than 500 years. Leaving aside the string-pull helicopter toys illustrated in the 14th century, the first documented reference to the possibility of propelling upwards a vehicle by means of rotating surfaces is attributed to Leonardo da Vinci (1452–1519), whose design sketches for such are believed to have originated in about the year

1500. Leonardo was otherwise devoted to the concept of flapping wings (i.e. the ornithopter) to achieve forward flight, and he was not aware of the lifting characteristics of aerofoils, nor was he acquainted with the properties of the propeller. As a result his design for a helicopter was based strictly on an 'air screw'—literally a rotating helical wing which would 'screw' its path upwards through the air.

Numerous attempts to evolve model helicopters followed during the next four centuries, culminating in those of W. H. Phillips who, in 1842, succeeded in launching a steam-driven craft whose rotating *blades* were propelled by tip jets.

It is perhaps useful here to interpose simple definitions of the helicopter and autogyro. Basically a helicopter achieves vertical flight by means of aerodynamic lift from rotor blades which are rotated under power; to eliminate torque (i.e. to prevent the fuselage of the aircraft from spinning uncontrollably on the axis of the rotor), either coaxial rotors, balanced sets of rotors or small tail-mounted rotors are geared to the power plant. Forward flight is achieved by tilting the rotor 'disc' so that its resulting thrust provides a degree of propulsion as well as lift.

An autogyro, on the other hand, is rather nearer to a conventional aeroplane in that forward motion is achieved by a conventional engine (either jet or piston engine-driven propeller); as forward motion is achieved the freely rotating rotor blades provide lift as aerofoils, enabling the autogyro to perform short, steep take-offs and landings.

## Firsts:

**The first helicopters to fly** were small models powered by the string-pull method, the first of which appeared in the 14th century. One such toy was illustrated in a Flemish manuscript of 1325.

**The first person to use the name 'helicopter'** was Italian artist, philosopher and inventor, Leonardo da Vinci (1452–1519), whose knowledge of Greek translated spiral and wing into *helix* and *pteron*. Among his aircraft designs was a helicopter intended to use a form of corkscrew rotor built from starched flaxen linen. One suggested form of power for the rotor was for the pilot to wind rope around the mast and then pull it to cause rotation in the established string-pull method already used for toys.

**A clockwork-powered model helicopter**, with two contra-rotating rotors, was constructed and flown in 1754 by the Russian Mikhail Vasilyevich Lomonosov. This was probably **the first self-propelled model helicopter**. (A similar type of model helicopter was constructed by Jacob Degen in 1816.)

**The first recognized self-propelled model helicopter** appears to have been that demonstrated on 28 April 1784, in France, by Launoy and Bienvenu. It consisted of a stick with a two-blade propeller at each end. The model was powered by a bowdrill arrangement; as the string of the bowdrill unwound the propellers counter-rotated. It was on this model that Sir George Cayley based his model helicopter in 1796, using a similar bowdrill arrangement but powering two four-blade rotors made from feathers.

**The first model helicopter to use a pressure-jet system to drive the rotor** was that flown by Englishman W. H. Phillips in 1842. Steam passed through the tips of the blades to turn the rotor.

**The first attempt to produce a convertiplane** (an aircraft that can achieve vertical flight supported by a rotor/rotors and horizontal translational flight using wings for lift) is generally attributed to Englishman Sir George Cayley. His Aerial Carriage, designed in 1843, had four circular wings (in pairs), mounted on outriggers from the boat-like wheeled fuselage. When the rotating wings were needed to provide lift, they were designed to open out into eight-bladed rotors. Forward propulsion was by two rear-mounted propellers.

*Model of Sir George Cayley's Aerial Carriage of 1843. (Science Museum, London)*

**The first person to suggest the need for cyclic pitch control on helicopters** was Italian G. A. Crocco, in 1906.

**The first helicopter to lift a man from the ground** was the French Breguet-Richet helicopter of 1907. Although the craft lifted off the ground at Douai, France, on 29 September that year, it did not constitute a free flight as four men on the ground steadied the machine with long poles which, while not contributing to the aircraft's lift, constituted a form of control restriction. Power was provided by a 50 hp Antoinette engine.

**The first true free flight by a man-carrying helicopter** was performed by Paul Cornu in his 24 hp Antoinette-powered twin-rotor (each 19 ft 8 in [6.0 m] diameter) aircraft near Lisieux,

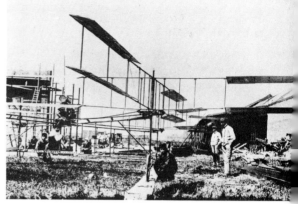

Top right   *Breguet-Richet* Gyroplane 1 *helicopter of 1907, showing the central 50 hp Antoinette engine and one of the multi-blade rotors.*

Right   *Paul Cornu astride his 1907 twin-rotor helicopter. (Musée de l'Air)*

Below   *Dane Jacob Ellehammer stands by his cyclic control helicopter during its first flight in 1912, ready to switch off the ignition. This photograph was autographed two years later. (Royal Danish Ministry for Foreign Affairs)*

France, on 13 November 1907. The flight, which lasted only 20 s, attained a height of 1 ft (0.3 m).

**The first demonstration of a helicopter with basic cyclic control** was the contra-rotating machine flown in 1912 by Dane Jacob C. H. Ellehammer. Power for the 24 ft 6 in (7.5 m) rotors was provided by a 36 hp radial engine.

**Probably the first helicopter to be tested from water** was the work of Frenchmen Papin and Rouilly. This had the unusual arrangement of the 80 hp Le Rhone engine powering a fan to produce air that was forced out of the single hollow rotor blade to cause rotation, while residual air was intended to provide directional control. Tested on Lake Cercey on 31 March 1915, the helicopter proved unstable and sank.

**The first helicopter to be flown during the First World War intended for military use** was the work of Oberstleutnant Stefan von Petroczy, Austrian Army Balloon Corps. His second full-size man-carrying helicopter was a large triple-outrigger machine with a cylindrical cockpit at its centre for an observer and gunner. One 120 hp Le Rhone engine was carried on each outrigger, all three powering a single pair of 19 ft 8 in (6 m) diameter contra-rotating rotors that turned beneath the cockpit. At all times the helicopter was intended to be tethered to the ground, being winched in and out as would an observation balloon. A parachute was carried which would be released mechanically should the rotor speed fall dangerously low. During tests, the helicopter remained in the air for approximately one hour and remained stable in 20 mph (33 km/h) winds.

**The first helicopter to fly carrying three persons** was built in Budapest by Dr Ing Theodor von Karman and Wilhelm Zurovec. The PKZ 1 was based upon the first full-size helicopter produced earlier by von Petroczy and thereby was powered by an electric motor, though the later machine featured four rotors. Completed in March 1918, it is thought that a total of four flights were made, on all but one with three persons on board.

**The first full-size British helicopter to achieve partially successful free flights** was produced by Louis Brennan and tested at Farnborough. The subject of great secrecy, the helicopter had a large two-blade rotor that was driven by tip-mounted four-blade propellers powered by a common

*The secretly tested Brennan helicopter at Farnborough, with the designer standing and pilot Robert Graham in the cockpit.*

engine. The pilot was Robert Graham and approximately 70 free flights were made between 7 December 1921 and 2 October 1925, when the machine crashed due to control failure and the programme was abandoned. The maximum altitude achieved was about 10 ft (3 m). However, it is worth mentioning the little-known earlier British experiments conducted at the Leven Shipyard, Dumbarton, of William Denny Brothers. Here, work on developing a rotor suitable as the lifting surface of an aircraft began in 1905, culminating initially in the testing of a 25 ft (7.62 m) diameter silk and bamboo rotor in October 1906. Subsequent work encompassed also engines and gearbox, airframe, controls and much else, with a conventional elevator and rudder chosen to control the flight of the intended helicopter. Finally, the Denny helicopter weighed a massive 1577 lb (715 kg), due in part to the weight of the 40 hp V4 engine that powered six elm-framed rotors mounted in tandem pairs. Several tethered flights were achieved in 1912–13, up to a height of 10 ft (3 m). Unfortunately, the helicopter was destroyed in a gale before the First World War.

**The first flight was recorded in France of the Oehmichen No. 2 multi-rotor helicopter** on 11 November 1922. On 4 May 1924 Etienne

Oehmichen established the **first helicopter 1 km distance record in a closed circuit**. However, compared to other helicopters then being tested elsewhere, the No. 2 was a huge and impractical design. Power was provided by a 180 hp Gnome engine, driving four primitive rotors carried on the cruciform structure and eight propellers intended to provide directional control.

**The first successful gyroplane** was the C.4 Autogiro, designed by Spaniard Juan de la Cierva and first flown on 9 January 1923. The secret of its success was in the adoption of flapping hinges joining the blades to the rotor head, and the C.4 was therefore **the first practical rotorcraft of any type**.

**The first demonstration of successful cyclic pitch control** was by Argentinian Marquis de Pateras Pescara in his No. 3 helicopter that used a 180 hp Hispano-Suiza engine to power coaxial contra-rotating rotors. Each rotor had a four biplane blade arrangement (eight individual blades), the pitch of the blades being adjustable by warping. The pilot could thereby choose collective pitch and cyclic pitch control. On 18 April 1924 the Pescara No. 3 flew 2414 ft (736 m) at Issy-les-Moulineaux in France, setting a world record.

**The first cross-country flight in a rotorcraft** was made by Spaniard Juan de la Cierva on 12 December 1924. Piloting a Cierva C.6, he flew 7½ miles (12 km) from Cuatro Vientos to Getafe in 8 min 12 s.

**The first two-seat autogyro**, Juan de la Cierva's C.6D, made its first flight on 29 July 1927. On the following day, de la Cierva became **the first passenger to be carried in an autogyro**.

**The first rotating-wing aircraft to fly the English Channel** was the Cierva C.8L Mark II (G-EBYY) Autogyro, flown by Juan de la Cierva with a passenger from Croydon to Le Bourget on 18 September 1928.

**The first successful autogyro of American design** was flown by Harold Pitcairn in Philadelphia on 19 December 1928.

**The first Soviet autogyro to fly successfully** (indeed the first Soviet rotary-winged aircraft of any type) was the KaSKr-1, which flew for the first time in September 1929. Designed by Nikolai Skrzhinskii and Nikolai Kamov, its fuselage was taken from a U-1 aeroplane.

**The RAF's first operational rotary-winged aircraft** were twelve Avro Rota Mk Is, licence-built Cierva C.30As, received during 1934 and 1935. Initially based at an Army co-operation training school, from 1940 they were operated by a Flight

*The successful though impractical Oehmichen No 2 helicopter in flight. (Musée de l'Air)*

from Duxford and then by No. 529 Squadron at Halton. No. 529 Squadron is remembered as **the RAF's only autogyro squadron**, surviving until October 1945. A civil British-registered C.30A was **the first autogyro with a pre-spin mechanism for the rotor**, allowing a 'jump' take-off.

**The first US Army rotary-winged aircraft** was the Kellett YG-1 autogyro, a military version of the civil KD-1 ordered in 1935 and powered by a 225 hp Jacobs R-755-1 engine. Other Kellett models followed, including the YG-1A and seven YG-1Bs.

**The first-ever aircraft to make an intentional safe landing on the roof of a building** was a Kellett KD-1B in May 1935 during an experimental airmail service, to commemorate the opening of the Philadelphia post office. (See 6 July 1939.)

**The first helicopter to fly successfully** was the French *Gyroplane Laboratoire*, designed by Louis Breguet and René Dorand. Fitted with a 350 hp Hispano-Suiza 9Q engine to drive two contrarotating two-blade coaxial rotors, it demonstrated a speed of more than 60 mph (80 km/h) on 22 December 1935, climbed to an altitude of 519 ft (158 m) in 1936 and proved an endurance of more than an hour during a 27 mile (44 km) flight. It was destroyed in an air raid in 1943.

**The first entirely successful helicopter in the world** was the Focke-Wulf Fw 61 twin-rotor

*Cierva C.8L Mark II Autogiro, the first rotorcraft to fly the English Channel.*

*Gyroplane Laboratoire, the first helicopter to fly successfully.*

helicopter designed by Professor Heinrich Focke during 1933–34. The first prototype Fw 61 V1 (D-EBVU) made its first free flight on 26 June 1936 and was powered by a 160 hp Siemens-Halske Sh 14A engine. This aircraft, flown by Ewald Rohlfs in June 1937, established a world's closed-circuit distance record for helicopters of

76.025 miles (122.35 km) and a helicopter endurance record of 1 h 20 min 49 s. On other occasions it set an altitude record of 11 243 ft (3427 m) and a speed record of 76 mph (122 km/h). It gave a flying demonstration in the Berlin Deutschland-Halle during 1938 in the hands of the famous German woman test pilot Hanna Reitsch.

**The first scheduled airmail service to be flown by a rotary-wing aircraft** was recorded in the United States on 6 July 1939, by a Kellett KD-1B autogyro in service with Eastern Air Lines.

**The first helicopter to go into limited production** was the Focke-Achgelis Fa 223. The experimental Focke-Wulf Fw 61 (q.v.) was not exploited commercially, being too heavy structurally to carry a payload. Instead, a commercially developed derivative, the Fa 266 Hornisse, appeared in 1939 as a prototype six-seat civil transport helicopter. **This was the first real transport helicopter.** The Fa 266 made a free flight in August 1940 and was redesignated Fa 223 Drache, by which time it had changed into a military helicopter. By 1942 the Fa 223 was ready for operational trials although only two examples had flown because of Allied bombing. Because of the bombing, the factory had been moved from Bremen to Laupheim and eventually finished up in Berlin. By the end of the war only a small number of helicopters had flown, three of which were used for transport duties by Luft-Transportstaffel 40.

**The first successful and practical helicopters to be designed outside Germany** were those of the Russian-born American Igor Sikorsky. His first

The first entirely successful helicopter was the German Focke-Wulf Fw 61.

Above   Kellet KD-1B, with 'First scheduled autogiro air mail route in the world' printed on its side.

Left   Third prototype Focke-Achgelis Fa 223 Drache. (Imperial War Museum)

Right   Focke-Achgelis Fa 330 Bachstelze, for towing behind submarines. This example ended up in America and was photographed in May 1946. (US Air Force)

Vought-Sikorsky VS-300, the first successful and
practical helicopter designed outside Germany.
(Sikorsky Aircraft)

successful helicopter was the Vought-Sikorsky
VS-300, which featured full cyclic pitch control
and was powered by a 75 hp engine. This made its
first recognized free flight on 13 May 1940,
although it had made a tethered flight on 14 September 1939. In May 1941 a 90 hp engine was
installed and the VS-300 set up a new endurance
record of 1 h 32 min 26 s. By 1942, after further
improvement, the VS-300 became established as
the first US successful and practical helicopter.

**The first armed autogyro** was the Soviet A-7Za,
carrying three 7.62 mm PV-1 machine-guns. Production armed and unarmed A-7s were deployed
operationally for reconnaissance and spotting and
were used at the time of the German invasion, in
1941.

**The first autogyros to be armed for ground**

and submarine attacks using bombs and depth
charges, as well as for observation, were Japanese Kayaba Ka-1s, based on the Kellett
KC-1A. First flown on 26 May 1941, examples of
the Ka-1 joined the Army initially for observation
but were later put on the deck of the *Akitsu Maru*,
a converted cruiser, for coastal anti-submarine
patrols. Power was provided by a 240 hp Argus
As 10C engine and normal attack armament was
two 60 kg bombs.

**Undoubtedly the first helicopter to be tested
from a ship's gun platform** was one of 45 prototype and pre-production German Flettner Fl 282
Kolibris, which was experimentally flown from the
cruiser *Köln* in 1942. The intended mass production of the Fl 282 was hindered by Allied bombing
raids and only 24 were delivered, three being used
by Luft-Transportstaffel 40.

**The first gyro-kite intended for military ser-
vice** was the British Rotachute, designed by
Austrian Raoul Hafner working at the Airborne
Forces Experimental Establishment in Manchester. Expected to be towed by an aircraft and
released to allow a man to be dropped accurately
behind enemy lines (replacing a parachute), the
first towed flight (behind a land jeep) of a full-size
Rotachute II was made on 29 May 1942. Trials
ended in 1943.

**The first operational gyro-kite** was the single-
seat Focke-Achgelis Fa 330 Bachstelze. Designed
in early 1942, it was intended for use as an observation platform by Germany's ocean-going Type
IX U-boats, towed behind the surfaced submarine

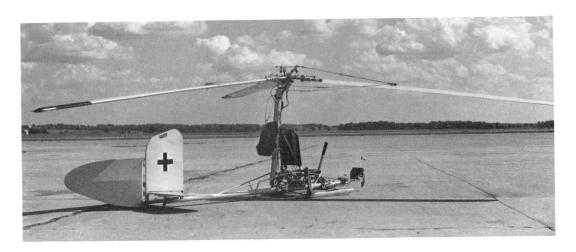

Above *World's first helicopter assembly line was set up by Sikorsky at Bridgeport to construct R-4Bs. (Sikorsky Aircraft)*

Left *Sikorsky R-4B prepares to land on a ship's deck in the Pacific, 24 May 1945. (US Air Force)*

at a height of 400 ft (122 m) to give its pilot a 25 mile (40 km) clear-weather field of view. Issued from mid-1942, it served in the South Atlantic, Indian Ocean and Gulf of Aden but was little used as U-boat crews believed it would pinpoint their position and also create crash-dive problems.

**The first helicopter designed and built for military service** was the Sikorsky XR-4, first flown on 13 January 1942. Its delivery flight from Stratford, Connecticut to Wright Field, Ohio was the **first cross-country helicopter delivery flight**, accomplished between 13 and 18 May 1942. A small development batch of R-4s, built on the first helicopter production line, saw limited service and training use during 1944–45. R-4s were the first helicopters to fly in Alaska and Burma, first to be tried on board a US ship (1943), and the first to be flown by the British Fleet Air Arm.

**The first jet-driven helicopters in the world** were the Doblhoff/WNF 342 V1 to V4, built in the suburbs of Vienna during 1942–45. Jet power was produced by mixing fuel with compressed air (from a compressor driven by a piston-engine), which was channelled via the three hollow rotor blades to combustion chambers at the rotor tips. The V1 first flew during the spring of 1943, and the modified V4 flew well before development ended in 1945.

Arguably the first entirely successful coaxial rotor helicopter was the US Hiller XH-44, which was first demonstrated in public in August 1944.

The first helicopter with intermeshing rotors to be tested in the United States of America was the Kellett XH-8, first flown on 7 August 1944.

The first helicopters to be given USAAF 'R for Rotary-wing' military designations were the Platt-Le-Page XR-1 and XR-1A, ordered by the US government for evaluation and featuring twin rotors carried on wide outriggers.

The first successful tandem twin-rotor helicopter to enter production was the Piasecki PV-3 (US Navy designation HRP-1), flown first during March 1945; powered by a 600 hp Pratt & Whitney R-1340 Wasp engine it could fly at 120 mph (193 km/h). Designed to carry six stretchers or cargo, the first production example was completed on 15 August 1947. The type served initially with USN and USMC experimental squadrons VX-3 and HMX-1.

The first helicopter to cross the English Channel was a Focke-Achgelis Fa 223 (No. 14) which

Right   *Hiller XH-44 at San Francisco in August 1944. This was the first entirely successful coaxial rotor helicopter.*

Below   *Piasecki PV-3 as the prototype US Navy XHRP-1 'Flying Banana', first flown in March 1945.*

arrived at Brockenhurst, Hampshire, in September 1945, piloted by a German crew of three. Fa 223 No. 14 had first flown in July 1943 and with No. 51 was confiscated by the Americans in May 1945. No. 14 was destroyed in October 1945 during evaluation trials.

**The first-ever Type-Approval Certificate for a commercial helicopter** was awarded for the Bell Model 47 on 8 March 1946; this aircraft made its first flight on 8 December 1945 and provided the design basis for a family of Bell helicopters that continued in production for close on 40 years.

**The first US experimental delivery of airmail by helicopter** began on 1 October 1946; the operations were carried out in the Chicago suburbs in a combined exercise by the US Post Office and the USAAF.

**The first British-designed and -built production helicopter** was the Bristol Sycamore, which first flew on 27 July 1947 and entered service with both the Army and Air Force. The Army versions were the HC10 ambulance and HC11 communications helicopters, the latter flying initially on 13 August 1950 and being delivered from 29 May 1951. The first RAF version, HR.12, was sent to St Mawgan for trials on 19 February 1952.

**The world's first scheduled helicopter service** was inaugurated on 1 October 1947 by Los Angeles Airways (LAA), using a Sikorsky S-51. The CAB had awarded LAA a temporary (three-year) certificate for mail carrying, on 22 May 1947.

**The first helicopter built in Great Britain to enter service with the RAF** was the Sikorsky-designed Westland/Sikorsky Dragonfly (the S-51 built under licence by Westland Aircraft Ltd at Yeovil, Somerset). The first Westland-built S-51 was for commercial use and flew in 1948. The RAF's first Dragonfly HC Mark 2 (WF 308) was powered by an Alvis Leonides engine and delivered in 1950; subsequent aircraft equipped No. 194 (Casualty Evacuation) Squadron, the RAF's first helicopter squadron, on 1 February 1953.

**The first helicopter mail service in Great Britain** was inaugurated on 1 June 1948 by British European Airways, with the Westland/Sikorsky S-51 (G-AKCU). Based at Peterborough, Northants, it served Norwich, Great Yarmouth and Kings Lynn.

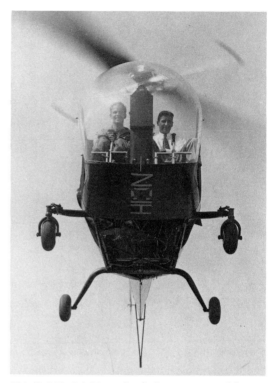

This Bell Model 47 was the first ever commercial helicopter to be awarded a Type-Approval Certificate. (Bell Helicopter Textron)

**The first experimental night helicopter service** was inaugurated on 14 February 1949 by British European Airways, flying the Westland/Sikorsky S-51 G-AKCU. The service, from Westwood, Peterborough, to Norwich, became regular from 17 October 1949 and continued until April 1950.

**The first helicopter station in New York**, which had been established at Pier 41 East River, became operational on 18 May 1949.

**The United Kingdom's first night airmail services to be operated by helicopter** began on 17 October 1949, the inaugural flight being made by BEA's Sikorsky S-51 G-AJOV, flown by Capt J. Cameron.

**The first helicopter to have the engine mounted in the nose of the fuselage** was the Sikorsky S-55, which first flew on 7 November 1949. This layout provided increased cabin area for the accommodation of passengers or cargo.

**The first ramjet-powered helicopter to receive US certification** was the Hiller HJ-1 Hornet of

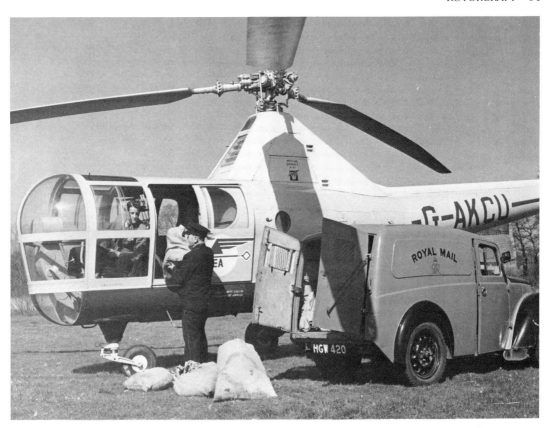

1950 appearance, a very small two-seat helicopter whose two-blade rotor was driven by tip-mounted 38 lb (17 kg) thrust Hiller 8RJ2B ramjet motors.

**The Royal Navy's first all-helicopter squadron** was No. 705, formed at Gosport, Hampshire, during 1950. Equipped with the Westland Dragonfly, this type of aircraft soon demonstrated its value for 'plane-guard' duties and ship-to-shore communications.

**The first scheduled helicopter passenger services in the UK** were those made between 9 and 19 May 1950 during the British Industries Fair. The services were flown between London and Birmingham by a Westland/Sikorsky S-51.

**The first sustained and regular scheduled helicopter passenger services in the UK,** between Liverpool and Cardiff, began on 1 June 1950. The service was operated by British European Airways with Westland/Sikorsky S-51s, but due to low demand was terminated on 31 March 1951 after carrying 819 passengers.

Above    BEA Westland/Sikorsky S-51 G-AKCU which flew the first helicopter mail service in Great Britain.

Below    Hiller HJ-1 Hornet, the first ramjet-powered helicopter to receive US certification.

**The first tandem-rotor helicopter to gain CAA Type Approval** was the McCulloch MC-4, which had first flown on 20 March 1951.

**The US Navy's first ASW helicopter squadron,** Squadron HS-1, was commissioned at Key West, Florida Keys, on 3 October 1951.

**The first helicopter to use turboshaft engine power** was a US Navy Kaman K-225 re-engined with a 175 shp Boeing YT50 and flown as such on 10 December 1951.

**The first helicopter to use twin turboshaft engines** was the re-engined Kaman HTK-1 128657, one of 29 piston-engined three-seat helicopters of this type received by the US Navy for training purposes from a September 1950 order.

**The first twin-rotor twin-engined helicopter to be designed and flown in Britain,** the Bristol Type 173 prototype (G-ALBN), was flown for the first time at Filton, Bristol, on 3 January 1952.

**The first tandem-rotor helicopter received by the USAF** was the Piasecki H-21 Workhorse, first flown on 11 April 1952. Versions of the H-21 served in Arctic rescue, assault and cargo transport, and other roles from 1953. The main user of

the H-21 was, however, the US Army, with whom it was better known as the Shawnee.

**The first east–west crossing of the North Atlantic by helicopters** was made in stages by two Sikorsky S-55s, between 13 and 31 July 1952.

**The first French convertiplane** was the Sud-Ouest SO 1310 Farfadet, seating a crew of two plus eight passengers, first flown as a helicopter on 8 May 1953. It combined aeroplane and helicopter by cruising on the power of a Turboméca Artouste II turboprop engine in the nose with 'lift' from short wings and an autorotating rotor. For transitional, vertical and hover modes, a Turboméca Arius II turbo-compressor supplied compressed air to the jet-driven rotor.

The Belgian airline Sabena operated **the first international helicopter flight into central London** on 7 July 1953. The flight was made by a Sikorsky S-55, between the Allee Verte Heliport

*Below   The Korean War of the early 1950s established the helicopter as an indispensable workhorse. The little Bell Model 47 became known as the Korean Angel for its stretcher carrying of wounded from the front line to field hospitals. During three years of war some 23000 United Nations wounded were carried by helicopter, about 18000 by Model 47s alone.*

Above  *Sud-Ouest SO 1310 Farfadet, the first French convertiplane.*

in Brussels and London's South Bank Heliport near Waterloo.

**The world's first international helicopter service** was inaugurated on 1 September 1953 by the Belgian airline Sabena, flying Sikorsky S-55s. Services included flights from Brussels to Lille, Maastricht and Rotterdam.

**Claimed to be the first rocket-powered rotary-wing aircraft to fly**, on 13 May 1954, the American Kellett KH-15 research helicopter had a small liquid propellant rocket motor mounted at the tip of each of its main rotor blades.

**The first tilt-rotor convertiplane to be flown** was the Bell XV-3; the first of two made its initial vertical flight on 23 August 1955. Powered by a 450 hp Pratt & Whitney R-985 engine, the XV-3 had a large fuselage (seating four) and fixed wings of 31 ft 3½ in (9.54 m) span. The rotor/propellers, at each wingtip, were positioned by electric motors: upward (for vertical) or forward (for horizontal) flight. The first transition from vertical to horizontal flight was made on 18 December 1958; by 1966 more than 250 flights had been logged.

**The US Navy's first helicopter assault carrier,** the USS *Thetis Bay*, was commissioned on 20 January 1956.

**The first rotating-wing aircraft to be literally a 'flying boat',** was the Bensen Model B-8B Gyro-

*US Army Vertol (Piasecki) H-21C is flight refuelled by an Otter tanker during the first non-stop US transcontinental helicopter flight. (de Havilland Canada)*

Boat. A variant of the Gyro-Glider, it was basically a small dinghy with a free-turning two-blade rotor and, in later models, stabilizing floats. The Gyro-Boat would become airborne when towed by motorboat to a speed of 23 mph (37 km/h). The prototype first flew on 25 April 1956 and large numbers of these aircraft were built.

**The first non-stop transcontinental flight across the USA by a rotary-winged aircraft** was made during 23–24 August 1957. The flight from San Diego, California to Washington DC was accomplished in an overall time of 31 h 40 min by

a specially-prepared Vertol H-21C twin-rotor hel-icopter. En route the H-21C was flight-refuelled four times by a U-1A Otter tanker, and twice from the ground while hovering.

**The first successful British convertiplane and first large VTOL transport** was the Fairey Rotodyne, the prototype flown first on 6 November 1957. Seating 40 passengers and a crew of two, the prototype Rotodyne Y had two Napier Eland turboprop engines mounted below the fixed wings to drive tractor propellers. The large rotor above the fuselage was driven by pressure-jets at the blade tips when power was required, usually for take-off and landing, but autorotated in normal flight, forward propulsion and much of the lift then coming from the turboprop engines and wings respectively. The first transition from verti-cal take-off to horizontal flight was made on 10 April 1958, but although potential operators were enthusiastic, in 1962 the project was cancelled by government cutbacks.

**The first post-war German helicopter** was the three-seat Borgward Kolibri I, designed by Heinrich Focke and flown for the first time on 8 July 1958 with Ewald Rohlfs at the controls. Power for this helicopter was provided by a 260 hp Lycoming VO-435-A1B piston engine.

**The first specially designed anti-submarine helicopter ordered for the Royal Navy** was the Westland Wessex, developed from the Sikorsky

Above   *The first successful British convertiplane and first large VTOL transport was the Fairey Rotodyne.*

S-58. Equipped with an automatic pilot, the Wessex could be operated by day or night in all weathers. Earliest first-line squadron to be equipped was No. 815, commissioned at Culdrose on 4 July 1961.

**The first US helicopter unit to operate in Viet-nam to assist South Vietnamese forces** was the 57th Transportation Light Helicopter Company which, equipped with Vertol H-21s, arrived at Tan Son Nhut in December 1961.

**The first support mission by US helicopters in Vietnam** occurred on 23 December 1961, when H-21s of the US 57th Transportation Light Heli-copter Company embarked 360 South Vietnam-ese troops on a search and destroy mission.

**The first pilotless anti-submarine helicopter to enter service with the US Navy** was the Gyrodyne QH-50A, in 1963; the Navy's drone helicopters each carried two homing torpedoes.

**The first true attack helicopter demonstrator,** the Bell Model 207 Sioux Scout, was first flown during July 1963. Based on the airframe of the Bell H-13 Sioux, it introduced tandem stepped cock-pits, stub wings, and a chin turret incorporating a Minigun. Flown and demonstrated to the US serv-ices in this form, it was developed as the produc-tion AH-1 HueyCobra.

**The first Fleet Air Arm helicopter used extensively from platforms on frigates, and smaller vessels,** was the Westland Wasp. The first Small Ship Flight was formed on 11 November 1963. Though small, the Wasp could pack a hefty punch, carrying two homing torpedoes, or depth charges or air-to-surface missiles.

**The first non-stop coast-to-coast helicopter flight across the North American continent** was accomplished on 6 March 1965 by a Sikorsky SH-3A Sea King. The 2116 mile (3405 km) flight was made from the deck of the carrier USS *Hornet* at San Francisco, California, to the carrier USS *Franklin D. Roosevelt* at Jacksonville, Florida.

**The first specially designed combat helicopter to go into large-scale service** was the Bell Model 209 HueyCobra. First flown on 7 September 1965, the two-seat 'Huey' was designed for ground attack and escort duties, carrying guns, a grenade launcher, rockets and missiles. Its 3 ft 2 in (0.965 m) wide fuselage makes it a difficult target for ground fire, and aids concealment beneath trees or small camouflage nets. The first of 1078 AH-1Gs for US Army service were delivered from June 1967, and use and development of the type continues.

**The first non-stop transatlantic flights by helicopters** were made during 31 May to 1 June 1967 by two Sikorsky HH-3Es *en route* to the Paris Air Show. Air-refuelled nine times during their 4270 mile (6872 km) flight from New York to Paris, the journey was accomplished in 30 h 46 min.

**The first helicopter automatic terrain clearance flight** was made on 26 April 1968 by a Sikorsky CH-53A during development of the Integrated Helicopter Avionics System specified for this aircraft.

**The US Navy's first helicopter mine countermeasures (MCM) squadron,** HM-12, was established in late 1970. A special version of the twin-turbine Sikorsky S-65 was developed to stream and retrieve a tow, and the first of these RH-53D helicopters was delivered to HM-12 in September 1973. The special equipment deployed by the tow was designed to destroy acoustic, magnetic or mechanical mines. In 1982 Sikorsky received a contract to develop a more advanced version, given the designation MH-53E Sea Dragon, and the first of 32 was delivered to the US Navy on 26 June 1986. Operational deployment with Squadron HM-14 began on 1 April 1987, and by early 1990 a total of 25 MH-53Es had been delivered. Some were allocated to HM-15 for Pacific Fleet use, and the first carrier deployment by HM-15, on 9 December 1989, was made on board the USS *Tripoli*.

**The first non-stop transpacific flight by rotary-wing aircraft** was that completed on 22 August

Bell Model 207 Sioux Scout
attack helicopter demonstrator.
(Bell Helicopter Textron)

1970 by two Sikorsky HH-3C helicopters. These two aircraft covered a distance of 9000 miles (14 484 km), flight-refuelled *en route* by Lockheed Hercules tankers.

**The first Russian purpose-designed attack helicopter** was the Mil Mi-24 Hind which became operational in the early 1970s, the first true gunship version being the 'Hind-D'. This had an extensively revised forward fuselage introducing two heavily armoured individual cockpits in tandem, and other changes saw the installation of more powerful TV3-117 engines and a 12.7 mm four-barrel Gatling gun for use against ground or air targets. The following Mi-24W 'Hind-E' was equipped to carry either AT-6 'Spiral' anti-tank missiles or AA-8 'Aphid' air-to-air missiles, and the Mi-24P 'Hind-F' replaced the Gatling gun with a twin-barrel 30 mm gun. Combined production was estimated to exceed 2300 by 1990, and in addition to the use of the Mi-24 by the Russian Air Force, export versions are known to serve with no fewer than 18 foreign air forces.

**The first occasion US Army HueyCobra attack helicopters fired TOW anti-armour missiles in action** was during the spring of 1972. In April 1972 a number of the eight HueyCobras that had been modified to fire TOW missiles for trials under the Improved Cobra Armament Program (ICAP) were sent to Kontum in Vietnam to help meet an expected Viet-Cong offensive. By 27 June, they had flown 77 missions and had destroyed 39 armoured vehicles, trucks and guns without loss. Prior to this action each HueyCobra crew had launched only one TOW in training.

**The largest production helicopter in the world, and the first to operate successfully with an eight-blade main rotor** is the Mil Mi-26 'Halo', a twin-turbine heavy transport helicopter first flown in prototype form on 14 December 1977. Already built to a total of more than 70 (10 for India and the remainder for the Russian armed forces), it continues in production in 1991. Its cargo hold and payload (maximum 44 090 lb/ 22 000 kg) are similar to those of the Lockheed C-130 Hercules, and its overall length (rotors turning) of 131 ft 3¾ in (40.03 m) is almost identical to the wing span of the Hercules. During three days in February 1982, the Mi-26 set five payload-to-height records. These included on 2 February (pilot G. P. Karapetyan) a 10 000 kg payload to 20 997 ft (6400 m), and on 3 February (pilot G. V. Alfeurov) a payload of 25 000 kg to

*Sikorsky MH-53E Sea Dragon towing a magnetic-influence hydrofoil vehicle. (Sikorsky Aircraft)*

13 451 ft (4100 m), and a total mass of 125 153.8 lb (56 768.8 kg) to a height of 2000 m.

**The first single-main rotor helicopter to fly without an anti-torque tail rotor** was the experimental Hughes NOTAR (No-Tail-Rotor), a modified Hughes OH-6, which flew for the first time on 17 December 1981. The advantages of eliminating the tail rotor promised improvements in aerodynamic efficiency, better on-ground safety, less noise and reduced maintenance costs. The concept utilizes low-pressure air discharged via controllable louvres to offset the torque of the

Left *Mil Mi-24* Hind-A, *identified by its cabin-style flight deck.*

Below *Ross Perot Jr and Jay W. Coburn with LongRanger II The Spirit of Texas. (Bell Helicopter Textron)*

main rotor. The pioneering research by Hughes has been continued by McDonnell Douglas Helicopters which, at the time of writing, is marketing and producing the MD 520N and MD 530N NOTAR helicopters.

**The first round-the-world flight in a helicopter** (in 29 stages) was achieved by Americans H. Ross Perot Jr and Jay W. Coburn flying Bell 206L LongRanger II *The Spirit of Texas*, between 1 and 30 September 1982. (See also *Fastest*.)

**The first round-the-world solo flight in a helicopter** (in stages) took place between 5 August 1982 and 22 July 1983. Australian pilot, Dick Smith, covered 35 258 miles (56 742 km) in his Bell JetRanger III, *Australian Explorer*.

**The first Soviet attack helicopter designed from the start to have a tandem two-seat crew arrangement** is the Mil Mi-28 'Havoc'. Of what is now accepted as conventional gunship configuration, it has a five-blade main rotor and 'scissors' type anti-torque rotor, is powered by two TV3-117 turboshafts, and its crew accommodation is protected by titanium and composite armour. A wide range of armament can be carried for its multi-role use, which is expected to include air-to-air missions, amphibious assault support and night attack. The first prototype made its maiden flight on 10 November 1982, and the type is scheduled to enter operational service during 1991–92.

**The first operational purpose-built armed attack helicopter of European design** is the tandem two-seat Italian Aeritalia A 129 Mangusta, which first flew as a prototype on 15 September 1983 and joined Italian Army Aviation squadrons from 1988. Powered by two Rolls-Royce Gem 2 turboshafts, it has a maximum dash speed of 196 mph (315 km/h) and can carry eight TOW anti-armour missiles or other weapons.

What was almost certainly **the first dual-helicopter synchronized night aerial display, flown under spotlights inside the confines of a football stadium,** occurred each night during the Durban Military Tattoo held from 10 to 18 July 1987. The aircraft involved were Aérospatiale Alouette IIIs, from No. 15 Squadron South African Air Force, under the leadership of Major Chris Milbank, with Captain Terry Pike flying the second Alouette III on the first night. The result was a spectacular 6-minute aerial 'ballet' of synchronized vertical and horizontal hovering manoeuvres.

The current version of the **first composites-built human-powered helicopter,** the *Da Vinci III*, designed and constructed by students of the California Polytechnic University in an attempt to win the American Helicopter Society's Igor I. Sikorsky Human-Powered Helicopter Prize of $20,000, made three flights during November and December 1989. The first two, on 12 and 27 November, were very brief, but that on the 12th marked the **first known lift-off by a human-powered helicopter.** Then, on 10 December 1989, powered by cyclist Greg McNeil, a representative of the National Aeronautic Association witnessed a flight which lasted 7.1 s and reached a height of 8 in (0.20 m), long enough and high enough to be regarded as **the first official human-powered helicopter flight.** To win the prize a man-powered helicopter must hover for 60 s within a 10 m square and attain an altitude of 3 m, and the CPU students hope to achieve this with a new helicopter of improved design.

**The first flight of the EH 101 Heliliner PP8 prototype** was completed successfully at Yeovil, Somerset on 24 April 1990. Designed and developed by EH Industries Limited, an international company formed by Agusta of Italy and Westland Helicopters in the UK, the Heliliner is a civil development of the EH 101 three-turbine multi-role helicopter intended for military use. The first civil prototype (PP3) was flown initially on 30 September 1988 and this will be responsible for the main certification programme, PP8 serving as the demonstrator for interested customers. There is accommodation for a flight crew of two and a cabin attendant, plus airline-style seating for 30 passengers, with adequate stowage for their luggage.

**The first Soviet NOTAR (No-Tail Rotor) helicopter** was believed to be still in the research stage in 1991, with a Kamov Ka-26 which has twin rotors (coaxial contra-rotating) being used as a testbed for an anti-torque jet-thruster control system. The developed system is to be incorporated in the turbine-powered Kamov Ka-118 light multi-role single rotor helicopter.

**The first flight of the Eurocopter Tiger anti-tank helicopter PT1 prototype** took place on 27

Left  *Hughes XH-17, which had a 130 ft rotor.*

Below  *The largest helicopter ever flown was the Russian Mil Mi-12. (Air Portraits)*

April 1991, this being the first of three aerodynamic prototypes required in the programme. Two further prototypes are to follow, PT4 to be configured as the French HAP Tigre (Hélicoptère d'Appui Protection), and PT5 for the combined Franco/German anti-tank role, with the respective designations HAC (Hélicoptère Anti-Char) and PAH-2 (Panzerabwehr-Hubschrauber-2nd generation).

### Largest:

**The largest rotor fitted to an engine-powered helicopter** was 130 ft (37.62 m), used on the experimental American Hughes XH-17 flying-crane that first flew on 23 October 1952.

**The largest helicopter flown anywhere in the world** was the Russian Mil Mi-12, which took to the air for the first time on 12 February 1969. A twin-rotor aircraft with an overall span over the rotor tips of 219 ft 10 in (67 m) and fuselage length of 121 ft 4½ in (37 m), it was powered by four 6500 shp Soloviev D-25VF turboshaft engines. First indication of the existence of this enormous helicopter to reach the West was in 1969, when the Soviet Union submitted to the FAI a number of payload-to-height records. Later, on 6 August 1969, the Mi-12 set a world record by lifting a payload of 88 636 lb (40 204.5 kg) to a height of 7398 ft (2255 m). No production followed.

**The largest helicopter built outside of Russia** is the US Sikorsky CH-53E Super Stallion. This has a seven-blade main rotor of 79 ft (24.08 m) diameter that is powered by three 4380 shp General Electric T64-GE-416 turbo-shafts, a fuselage length of 73 ft 4 in (22.35 m) that can accommodate a crew of three and 55 troops or up to 30 000 lb (13 076 kg) of internal cargo, and weighs 73 500 lb (33 340 kg) when carrying an external payload. The prototype YCH-53E first flew on 1 March 1974.

**The largest helicopter assault in aviation history** was that mounted for Operation *Desert Sabre* (the land battle to remove Iraqi troops from Kuwait) which began on 24 February 1991. Preparatory work involved using helicopters to airlift troops to a desolate area of the Iraqi desert (known as *Cobra*), which was used as a refuelling and logistics base. Home to a combined force of helicopters numbering more than 300, and comprising McDonnell Douglas Helicopters AH-64 Apaches and Bell AH-1G HueyCobras, in the ensuing days these were to wreak havoc on Iraqi armour.

**The largest attack in aviation history to be made by helicopter-borne troops** occurred on 24 February 1991, at the beginning of the ground war phase of the Gulf War. As coalition forces with powerful air and artillery support, thrust deep into Kuwait and southern Iraq, over 2000 men of the US Army's 101st Airborne Division were airlifted to strategic points. This was accomplished by a fleet of Boeing Vertol CH-47 Chinooks and Sikorsky UH-60 Black Hawks, escorted by Bell AH-1 HueyCobra, Bell AH-58 Warrior and McDonnell Douglas AH-64 Apache helicopters with a total of some 550 aircraft involved.

*Fastest:*

**The current FAI world distance in a straight line record for autogyros** is held by Briton Wg Cdr K. H. Wallis. Flying his WA-116/F from Lydd Airport, Kent, he flew 543.274 mile (874.315 km) to Wick, Scotland, on 28 September 1975.

**The current FAI world speed record for convertiplanes:** see *Highest*, 7 October 1961.

**The current FAI world helicopter speed record for a round-the-world flight** is held by Americans H. Ross Perot Jr and Jay W. Coburn a 35.4 mph (56.97 km/h). Flown from and back t

Left  *World speed record-holding Westland Lynx. (Westland Helicopters)*

Right  *Wing Cdr Ken Wallis in his record-breaking WA-121/Mc at Boscombe Down on 20 July 1982, having bettered his previous altitude record.*

Dallas, Texas, their Bell 206L LongRanger II *The Spirit of Texas* took between 1 and 30 September 1982 to establish the record.

The fastest speed achieved in an autogyro, and the current ratified world speed record for autogyros is that set by Wg Cdr K. H. Wallis in his WA-116, powered by a 72-hp McCulloch engine. On 18 September 1986, over a straight course of 1.86 miles (3 km), he flew the WA-116 at a speed of 120.5 mph (193.9 km/h).

The current FAI world speed record for helicopters is held by Briton Trevor Egginton in a Westland Lynx fitted with BERP III main rotor blades. Set on 11 August 1986, the Lynx attained 249.09 mph (400.87 km/h).

*Highest:*

The current FAI world records for altitude and speed in a straight line for convertiplanes are held by the Russian Kamov Ka-22 Vintokryl. The former, established on 24 November 1961 at Bykovo, stands at 8491 ft (2588 m), while the speed record was set on 7 October 1961 at Joukovski-Petrovskoe over a 15/25 km course and stands at 221.4 mph (356.3 km/h). The pilot for the speed record was E. Efremov.

On 20 July 1982, Wg Cdr K. H. Wallis, flying from Boscombe Down, Wiltshire, attained an altitude of 18 516 ft (5643.7 m) in his Wallis WA-121/Mc which was powered by a Wallis-McCulloch

Above  *The Russian Kamov Ka-22 Vintokryl set the current FAI world altitude and speed in a straight line records for convertiplanes in 1961.*

engine of about 100 hp. This is the **current world altitude record for autogyros.**

The current world altitude record for helicopters of 40 820 ft (12 442 m) was established on 21 June 1972 by Jean Boulet of France, flying an Aérospatiale SA 315B Lama general-purpose helicopter. A Lama carrying out demonstration flights in the Himalayas during 1969 **also made the**

**highest landings and take-offs that have been recorded**, at an altitude of 24 600 ft (7500 m).

*Longest:*

**The first helicopter to set an FAI accredited world record of over 1 km** was an Italian machine designed by d'Ascanio (actually 0.67 mile; 1.078 km), in October 1930. The two two-blade contra-rotating rotors, plus the three variable-pitch propellers for longitudinal and lateral control, were driven by a 90 hp Fiat A-50 engine.

**The current FAI world speed record for convertiplanes in a 100 km closed circuit** is held by New Zealand, when on 5 January 1959 Sqn Ldr W. R. Gellatly and J. G. Morton flew at 190.9 mph (307.22 km/h) in the British-designed Fairey Rotodyne.

**The current FAI world distance in a straight line record for helicopters** is held by American R. G. Ferry, who flew a Hughes OH-6A 2213 miles (3561.55 km) during 6–7 April 1966.

**The longest period of hovering flight recorded in a helicopter** totals 50 h 50 s between 13 and 15 December 1989. This was achieved in the USA by Rod Anderson, Doug Daigle, Dave Meyer and Brian Watts flying a 1947 Bell Model B.

*Worst:*

**The worst accident involving a helicopter** took place on 10 May 1977 when 54 people were killed in an Israeli Sikorsky CH-53D Stallion at the West Bank.

*Most:*

**The autogyro that has been produced in greater numbers than any other non-military rotorcraft** is the Bensen B-8 Gyro-Copter, the prototype of which first flew on 6 December 1955. More than 5000 examples of the B-8M were built

over the next three decades and the final version was usually powered by the 72 hp McCulloch Model 4318AX engine which gave it a maximum speed of 85 mph (137 km/h).

**The only modern purpose-designed attack helicopter having coaxial contra-rotating rotors** originates from the Soviet Kamov bureau; in the absence of confirmed Kamov or service designations it is known only by the NATO-allocated codename of 'Hokum'. It is believed that production aircraft will have a conventional two-seat tandem arrangement, although it has been stated that one prototype has been seen with side-by-side seating for two. First reported during the summer of 1984, those prototypes which have been seen in flight appear to carry armament only for air-to-air use and if on service entry (expected to begin during 1991) this proves to be true, this Kamov helicopter will also rate as **the world's first purpose-designed air-to-air combat helicopter.**

**The world's only tilt-rotor aircraft currently in the flight test and development stage** is the Bell/Boeing multi-mission V-22 Osprey. Originating from the Bell/NASA XV-15, the first V-22 prototype made the type's maiden flight on 19 March 1989, achieving its first conversion from vertical to horizontal flight on 14 September 1989. Due to economic cutbacks by the US armed services, the development programme is considerably in arrears, but more than ten per cent of the planned 4000 hours of flight trials have been completed. The results have been impressive, including a demonstrated level speed of 402 mph (647 km/h), a 1392-mile (2240-km) cross-country flight in 5.3 hours on 7 May 1990, and effective sea trials aboard USS *Wasp* during December 1990; so impressive, indeed, that the V-22 gained the National Aeronautic Association's Collier Trophy for 'the greatest achievement in aeronautics during the past year'. Subject to continuing funding, the V-22 could enter service first with the US Marine Corps during 1994.

# Parachutes, Kites and Gliders

It is undeniable that parachutes, kites and gliders were the very building blocks of aviation, and all three of them still play a part in today's world, though now in a very different form from when they first served as tools for the pioneers and researchers who sought to 'fly like the birds'. Significantly, they antedate what many may consider the more direct route to modern aviation, via the balloon, airship and pioneering aircraft. Observation suggested that gliding or soaring was the simplest form of bird flight, wings outstretched and unmoving, so it is logical that the earliest known aviation artifact is a carved wooden model from Egypt, which many believe could have been intended as a model glider, or the design for a larger version, especially as it almost certainly had cruciform tail surfaces. Indeed, many of the early pioneers strapped slavishly copied birds' wings to their arms or shoulders, and thus the 'tower jumpers' were among the earliest to attempt gliding flight.

Clearly, the first parachutes gave promise of a form of flight, for then there were no aircraft to escape from, and perhaps it was not until 22 October 1797, when the Frenchman Garnerin made a successful parachute descent from a balloon at a height of 2230 ft (680 m), that their potential for aerial escape became apparent. Had they but known that modern controllable parachutes have proved capable of a cross-Channel flight, they might have felt that their ideas were vindicated. Instead, parachutes were used to provide spectacle, and of course, they still are, in addition, a means of escape.

The practicality of the kite as a flying machine was first recorded by Marco Polo, who saw man-lifting kites being used in China during the 14th century. But even more important was the work of the Australian Lawrence Hargrave in the late 19th century, whose development of box kites and the design of strong and lightweight structures for them led directly to aircraft such as the pioneering designs of Alberto Santos-Dumont and the Voisin brothers in France. Before that, on 2 August 1899, Wilbur Wright had flown a kite of box form which could be controlled in flight by wing warping. This led to Orville and Wilbur Wright's gliders No. 1 and No. 2 of 1900 and 1901 respectively, both flown as a kite before being tested as a glider. But it was their highly successful No. 3 glider of 1902 that led directly to the powered *Flyer* of 1903.

Next time you see even the most unsophisti-

Engraving of Robert Cocking's parachute suspended below the Great Nassau Balloon. *(The Science Museum, London)*

cated home-made kite airborne on the wind, its restraining string in the hand of some bright-eyed boy or girl, remember that it represents a stepping stone to the whispering Airbus cruising overhead.

## Firsts:

**The first known model that could have represented a flying machine** was a carved wooden bird, thought to be some 2300 years old. Originally discovered at Saqqara, Egypt, in 1898, and rediscovered in a storage box at the Cairo museum by Dr Khalil Messiha in 1972, it has a high-mounted wing with a finely carved aerofoil section, a body with the rear portion of narrow elliptical shape, and a deep vertical tail-fin with a groove for a horizontal surface.

**Almost certainly the first recorded case of structural failure in flight,** one that caused the death of Saracen of Constantinople, occurred in the 11th century. For his attempt at gliding flight he wore a cloak incorporating stiffening ribs, but unfortunately one of these ribs snapped and he plunged to the ground.

**The first 'tower jumper' to achieve some measure of gliding flight** was probably the English Benedictine monk Oliver of Malmesbury, in about AD 1020. Known as 'the Flying Monk', he jumped from Malmesbury Abbey with wings. A measure of gliding flight must have been achieved, as his only injuries were two broken legs. To Oliver can also be attributed **the first practical lesson in heavier-than-air gliding flight,** as his injuries convinced him of the necessity for tail surfaces attached to the feet.

**The first recorded successful quasi-parachute jumps** were made in China in 1306, as part of the celebrations during the coronation of Fo-Kin.

**The first witnessed and properly recorded manned flights** took place in Cathay (China) in the 14th century. These were recorded by the Venetian merchant traveller Marco Polo, while in Cathay with his father and uncle. He witnessed the use of man-carrying tethered kites and a translation of his report appears in *The Description of the World,* edited by A. C. Moule and P. Pelliott and published in London in 1938. In brief, he found that kites, in the form of a hurdle made of withies and attached to a long rope, were launched into the air with a man bound to the hurdle. Used to

predict good or bad prospects for a voyage by ship, if the kite flew high the ship set sail; if it did not take to the air the voyage was postponed.

**The first known design for a parachute proper** was that by the Italian Leonardo da Vinci, dated about 1485. This square-section parachute was drawn to be hand held.

**The first design for a parachute to appear in published form** was to be found in *Machinae novae,* a Venetian work of 1595 by Fausto Veranzio. This was a square cloth attached to a frame, the corners of which were roped to a body harness.

**Perhaps the first sustained flight by a man-carrying glider** was performed in the 17th century by Hezarfen Celebi of Turkey. Leaping from a tower at Galata, he is said to have covered some distance before meeting the ground.

**The first documented parachute jump to be made successfully outside of China** was that accomplished by an athlete in Siam during 1687. Detailed by M. de la Loubères, following a journey to Siam, the athlete is said to have jumped from height with two umbrellas, the handles of which were attached to his girdle.

**The first demonstration in Europe of a quasi-parachute** was given by the Frenchman Sebastien le Normand, who, in 1783, jumped from an observation tower at Montpellier (at a height equivalent to a first floor) under a braced conical canopy of 2 ft 6 in (0.76 m) diameter.

**The first man to identify and correctly record the parameters of heavier-than-air flight** was the Englishman, Sir George Cayley (1773–1857). The following is a list of notable achievements by this remarkable scientist who was first to:
☐ set down the mathematical principles of heavier-than-air flight (ie lift, thrust and drag)
☐ make use of models for flying research, among them a simple glider – the first monoplane with fixed wing amidships, and fuselage terminating in horizontal and vertical tail surfaces (constructed in 1804)
☐ draw attention to the importance of streamlining (in his definition of 'drag')
☐ suggest the benefits of biplanes and triplanes to provide increased lift with minimum weight
☐ construct and fly a man-carrying glider
☐ demonstrate the means by which a curved

'aerofoil' provided 'lift' by creating reduced pressure over the upper surface when moved through the air

☐ suggest the use of an internal-combustion engine for aeroplanes and construct a model gunpowder engine in the absence of low-flashpoint fuel oil.

**The first living creatures to descend by parachute from a balloon** were animals released on 2 August 1791 over Vienna by the famous aeronaut Jean-Pierre Blanchard. (Following this and the release of a dog over Strasbourg, Blanchard made a parachute descent at Basle but broke a leg, in 1793.)

**The first parachute descent ever performed successfully by man from a vehicle** was accomplished by the Frenchman André Jacques Garnerin, who jumped from a balloon at 2230 ft (680 m), having ascended from the Parc Monçeau near Paris on 22 October 1797.

**The first parachute descent in England** was made by André Jacques Garnerin on 21 September 1802. However, he was injured in the descent, when one strap supporting the basket snapped.

**The first man to bale out of a damaged aircraft with a parachute and survive** was R. Jordarki Kuparanto who, on 24 July 1808, escaped from his Montgolfier hot-air balloon when it caught fire over Warsaw, Poland.

**The first parachute descent from a balloon in America** was that made by Charles Guille who, on 2 August 1819, jumped from a hydrogen balloon at a height of about 8000 ft (2440 m) and landed at New Bushwick, Long Island, New York.

**The first public demonstration** of a new form of parachute with an upside-down canopy to prevent oscillations, designed by Briton Robert Cocking and released from about 6600 ft (2000 m) on 24 July 1837, ended in tragedy. Lifted to height under the *Great Nassau Balloon*, the parachute, with Cocking underneath in a basket, descended well after release until the upper rim collapsed and he plunged to his death.

**The first person to be carried aloft in a heavier-than-air craft** in sustained (gliding) flight was a 10-year-old boy who became airborne in a glider constructed by Sir George Cayley at Brompton Hall, near Scarborough, Yorkshire, in 1849. The glider became airborne after being towed by manpower down a hill against a light breeze.

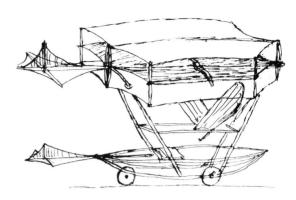

*Sketch of the boy-carrying glider by Cayley himself. Note the triplane wings, combined elevator/rudder and the flapping power system. (The Science Museum, London)*

**The first man to be carried aloft in a heavier-than-air craft**, but not in control of its flight, was Sir George Cayley's coachman at Brompton Hall, reputedly in June 1853. A witness of the event stated that after he had landed, the coachman struggled clear and shouted, 'Please, Sir George, I wish to give notice! I was hired to drive, not to fly.'

**A first short free flight in a bird-form glider of his own design** was made during 1857 by French sea-captain Jean Marie le Bris. This was made at Tréfeuntec, near Douarnenez, le Bris mounting his glider on a cart which was drawn along at speed to allow him to release the glider and make a short flight. His second attempt was less successful, the aircraft crashing and breaking his leg.

**The first aircraft designed to save life** was the man-carrying sea rescue kite developed by Irishman Cordner and first flown in 1859.

**The first scientist correctly to deduce the main properties (i.e. lift distribution) of a cambered aerofoil** was F. H. Wenham (1824–1908), who built various gliders during the mid-19th century to test his theories. In collaboration with John Browning, Wenham built **the world's first wind tunnel** in 1871 for the Aeronautical Society of Great Britain.

**First exponent of the box-kite** was Australian Lawrence Hargrave (1850–1915), who invented this mode of kite construction in 1893. This

Samuel Cody on horseback, directing trials of one of his man-lifting kites.

simple structure provided good lift and stability and formed the basis of early aeroplanes such as the French Voisin.

**The first heavier-than-air aircraft to be built in quantity** (and available for sale) was the No. 11 glider designed and built by Germany's Otto Lilienthal. Records survive of two which were sold to customers in the United Kingdom during 1895, at a cost of £25 each.

**American-born Samuel Franklin Cody (1861–1913) made his first experiments relating to the construction and use of man-lifting kites** at Farnborough (Hampshire) during 1899. This work led directly to development of the military observation kite, as used during the First World War.

**The first test of their theories on the control of flight by wing warping** was made by the Wright brothers (Wilbur and Orville) in August 1899, using a 5 ft (1.5 m) span biplane kite as the test vehicle.

**The Wright brothers constructed and flew their first glider during 1900.** This No. 1 glider, of biplane configuration, was flown also as a kite but had insufficient span. Using wing warping for

lateral control, it was their first man-carrying aircraft and the first to be tested at the later famous Kill Devil Hills, North Carolina. Wing span was 17 ft (5.18 m). The Wrights' No. 2 glider was built in 1901. Of increased span, it was not as successful as hoped and resulted in the decision to undertake further research on aerofoils, using models. The No. 3 glider, built during August and September 1902, reflected this research and flew a great many times. This formed the basis of the powered *Flyer*.

**The first glider flight from a balloon** was performed by American Daniel Maloney on 29 April 1905. In a similar flight on 18 July Maloney lost his life.

**The first manned flight of a glider in Australia** was made on 5 December 1909, by the Australian artist-inventor-journalist-poet George Augustus Taylor at Narrabeen Beach, New South Wales.

**The first woman glider pilot in the world** was Florence Taylor (wife of the above), who flew her husband's glider at some time during December 1909, after his first flight.

**The first parachute descent from an aeroplane in America** was performed by Capt Albert Berry who, on 1 March 1912, jumped from a Benoist aircraft flown by Anthony Jannus at 1500 ft (460 m) over Jefferson Barracks, St Louis, Missouri.

**The first parachute descent by a woman from an aeroplane** was made by the 18-year-old American girl, Georgia ('Tiny') Broadwick who, using an 11 lb (5 kg) silk parachute, jumped from an aircraft flown by Glenn Martin at about 1000 ft (305 m) over Griffith Field, Los Angeles, California, on 21 June 1913.

**The first parachute descent from an aeroplane over Great Britain** was made by W. Newell at Hendon on 9 May 1914 from a Grahame-White Charabanc flown by R. H. Carr. From a height of 2000 ft (610 m) Newell's drop in his 40 lb (18 kg) and 26 ft (7.9 m) diameter parachute took 2 min 22 s.

**The first recorded free-fall jump from an aeroplane**, before deployment of the parachute, was made by Leslie Leroy Irvin on 19 April 1919.

**The first glider competition** was held during 1920 at Rhon, Germany, organized by the Aero Technical Association of Dresden.

**The first glider flight of more than one hour duration** was made in Germany on 18 August 1922, by pilot Martens in a *Vampyr*.

**The first American to escape from a disabled aeroplane by parachute** was Lt Harold R. Harris, US Army, who on 20 October 1922 jumped from a Loening monoplane at 2000 ft (610 m) over North Dayton, Ohio.

**The first cross-Channel flight in a sailplane** was made on 22 April 1939 by Geoffrey Stephenson in a Slingsby Gull.

**The first glider to be towed across the North Atlantic** was an RAF Hadrian (American Waco CG-4) transport glider piloted by Sqn Ldr Reginald G. Seys with a French-Canadian co-pilot, Sqn Ldr Fowler Gobeil. Its tug was an RAF Dakota, and during June 1943 it was flown in stages from Montreal to the UK in 28 h.

**The first UK National Hang-Gliding Championships** were held on the South Downs at Steyning Hill (Sussex) on 13 July 1974. Highlighting the growth of hang-gliding as an aviation sport, more than 100 pilots attended this inaugural competition with some 80 gliders involved.

*The Guardian Angel parachute was issued to crews of British observation balloons during the First World War. Here, a Guardian Angel is demonstrated with a jump off Tower Bridge, London.*

**The first crossing of the English Channel by parachute** (involving a lateral fall) was made on 31 August 1980 by a team of six parachutists comprising Sergeant Bob Walters (British Army) plus three soldiers and two Royal Marines. Jumping from a height of 25 000 ft (7620 m) over Dover, Kent their landing was made 22 miles (35.4 km) distant at Sangatte, France.

*Largest:*

**The largest star formation of parachutists in free-fall** to be approved under US Parachuting Association rules involved a team of 72 men. This was achieved at De Land (Florida) on 3 April 1983, the formation in free-fall being held for the required time of 3.4 s.

**The world's largest free-fall formation of parachutists** was achieved at Quincy, Illinois on 11 July 1988. Jumping from a height of 16 000 ft (4877 m), a total of 144 parachutists linked up in a formation that was held for 8.8 s.

Above  Massive glider operations were conducted during the Second World War by both Allied and Axis powers as a method of transporting huge numbers of troops and their equipment by air. Among the biggest operations was the June 1944 D-Day Normandy landings, with hundreds of Allied gliders taking part. Here Halifax towing bombers prepare to haul some of the 250 or so Airspeed Horsa and 70 General Aircraft Hamilcar gliders used during the D-Day operations. (Imperial War Museum)

Robin Robinson of the 782nd Maintenance Battalion, 82nd Airborne Division, leaves the Sicily Drop Zone after the first ever all female parachute jump was conducted at Fort Bragg in 1991. (US Army/Arnold Fisher)

### Highest, Longest and Greatest:

**The longest recorded parachute descent** was that by Lt Col William H. Rankin of the US Marine Corps who, on 26 July 1959, ejected from his LTV F8U Crusader naval jet fighter at 47 000 ft (14 326 m). Falling through a violent thunderstorm over North Carolina, his descent took 40 min instead of an expected time of 11 min, as he was repeatedly carried upwards by the storm's vertical air currents.

**The longest straight distance flight in a single-seat glider** is that of 908 miles (1460.8 km) set by Hans-Werner Grosse, between Lübeck, Germany and Biarritz, France on 24 April 1972. Flown in a Schleicher ASW-12, it is but one of 12 international records held currently by this highly experienced pilot, all of them achieved in Schleicher gliders of different models. **The longest straight distance in a two-seat glider, and also distance to a declared goal**, was established in Australia by Hans-Werner Grosse and Karin Grosse. This flight was made on 14 January 1990 in a Schleicher ASH-25, and covered a distance of 678 miles (1092.8 km).

The first ejection-seat escape from a moving aeroplane while still on the ground was accomplished by Sqn Ldr J. S. Fifield on 3 September 1955, when he ejected from a modified Gloster Meteor 7 that was travelling at 120 mph (194 km/h). This shows Sqn Ldr Fifield moments before the Martin-Baker seat released a parachute.

The longest distance travelled to make a con-nected series of 50 parachute jumps, one in each of the US States, was recorded by Kevin Sea-man during the period 26 July to 15 October 1972. Travelling in, and with the jumps being made from, a Cessna Skylane piloted by Charles E. Merritt, the total distance covered was 12 186 miles (19 611 km).

Below   The largest glider of the Second World War was the huge German Messerschmitt Me 321 Gigant, with a wing span of 181 ft 3 in (55.24 m) and weighing 77 160 lb (35 000 kg) at take-off (loaded). The immense towing power required to get it airborne eventually led to an armed six-engined version of the same aircraft, designated Me 323 (as shown). Production totals for the Me 321 and 323 were 200 and 150 respectively. (MBB)

The longest distance to a declared goal in single-seat gliders, from Te Anau to Te Araroa, New Zealand, was flown on 14 January 1978 by New Zealanders Bruce Drake, S. H. 'Dick' Georgeson and David Speight. Each piloting their own Schempp-Hirth Nimbus 2, their record dis-tance was 779 miles (1254.26 km).

The longest straight distance flight made by a woman pilot in a single-seat glider stands at 590 miles (949.7 km). This was achieved in Australia, on 20 January 1980, by Karla E. Karel of Great Britain flying a Rolladen-Schneider LS-3. The women's two-seat glider record is of much longer standing, having been set in the Soviet Union on 3 June 1967. This was achieved in a Blanik sailplane flown by Tatiana Pavlova and L.

Filomechkina over a distance of 537.4 miles (864.85 km).

**The longest straight line distance flown in a hang-glider (and also a declared goal distance)**, of 303.36 miles (488.2 km), was achieved by American Larry Tudor in a Wills Wing. This was flown from Hobbs Airpark, New Mexico to Elkhart, Kansas on 3 July 1990.

**The greatest altitude from which a successful emergency escape from an aeroplane has been reported** is 56 000 ft (17 070 m). At this altitude, on 9 April 1958, an English Electric Canberra bomber exploded over Monyash, Derbyshire, and the crew, Flt Lt John de Salis and Flying Officer Patrick Lowe, fell free in a temperature of −70°F (−56.7°C) down to an altitude of 10 000 ft (3050 m), at which height their parachutes were deployed automatically by barometric control.

**The greatest altitude from which a man has fallen and the longest delayed drop ever achieved by man** was that of Capt Joseph W. Kittinger, USAF, over Tularosa, New Mexico, on 16 August 1960. He stepped out of a balloon gondola at 102 200 ft (31 150 m) for a free fall of 84 700 ft (25 816 m) lasting 4 min 38 s, during which he reached a speed of 614 mph* (988 km/h) despite a stabilizing drogue and experienced a minimum temperature of −94°F (−70°C). His 28 ft (8.5 m) parachute deployed at 17 500 ft (5334 m) and he landed after a total time of 13 min 45 s. The step by the gondola was inscribed 'This is the highest step in the world.'

---

*The speed of 614 mph (988 km/h) reached by Kittinger during his fall represents a Mach No. of 0.93 in the Stratosphere and would have been reached at an altitude of about 60 000 ft (18 300 m); thereafter his fall would have been retarded fairly rapidly to less than 200 mph (322 km/h) as he passed through the Tropopause at about 36 000 ft (11 000 m). The speed of 614 mph (988 km/h) almost certainly represents the greatest speed ever survived by a human body not contained within a powered vehicle beneath the interface (i.e. within the earth's atmosphere).

**The greatest height gain made in a single-seat glider** stands at 42 303 ft (12 894 m) and was achieved by Paul F. Bikle at Mojave, California. This was set in a Schweizer SGS 1-23E on 25 February 1961, and it is intriguing that this record, established more than 30 years ago, has not yet fallen to any of the new generation of gliders.

**The greatest free-fall parachute record by a man to be ratified by the FAI** is that achieved by the Russian parachutist E. Andreev, near Volks, on 1 November 1962 with a free-fall distance of 80 380 ft (24 500 m).

**The greatest height from which a group of British parachutists has made a delayed drop** stands at 39 183 ft (11 942 m), achieved by five Royal Air Force parachute jumping instructors over Boscombe Down, Wiltshire, on 16 June 1967. They were Sqn Ldr J. Thirtle, Flt Sgt A. K. Kidd, and Sgts L. Hicks, P. P. Keane and K. J. Teesdale. Their jumping altitude was 41 383 ft (12 613 m).

**The greatest known landing altitude for a parachute jump** was 23 045 ft (7134 m), the height of the summit of Lenina Peak on the border of Tadzhikistan and Kirgiziya in Kazakhstan, CIS. It was reported in May 1969 that 10 Russians had parachuted on to this mountain summit but that four had been killed.

**The greatest FAI-ratified heights attained by women in single- and two-seat gliders** have now stood for a number of years. Both set in the USA, the oldest is the height of 35 463 ft (10 809 m) which Mary Nurr and Hanna Duncan reached in their Schweizer SGS 2-32 two-seater on 5 March 1975. Almost four years later, on 14 February 1979, Sabrina Jackintell's solo record was attained in her Grob Astir CS, flown to an altitude of 41 460 ft (12 637 m).

**The greatest height to which a single-seat glider has been flown** and the current absolute altitude record for a glider in this category, was achieved on 17 February 1986 by Robert R. Harris in California, who flew his Grob G102 to a height of 49 010 ft (14 938 m).

**The greatest height gain made in a single-seat glider by a female pilot** was achieved at Omarama, New Zealand by Yvonne Loader on 12 January 1988. This was flown in a Schempp-Hirth Nimbus 2, with the height gain being ratified at 33 504 ft (10 212 m).

**The greatest number of parachute jumps to be recorded within a period of 24 hours** (and made in accordance with United States Parachute Association rules) was a total of 301. This was achieved by US citizen Dale Nelson at Pennsylvania during 26–27 May 1988.

The record for **the greatest height gain in a hang-glider** is held by the USA's Larry Tudor, the figure of 14 250 ft (4343.4 m) being set at Owens Valley, California on 26 June 1988.

*Most:*

**The most effective demonstration of the capability of his man-lifting kites** was staged by English schoolteacher George Pocock. In 1827 he attached one of his kites to a road carriage and was pulled at speed between Bristol (Avon) and Marlborough (Wiltshire), a distance of some 31 miles (50 km).

**The most northerly parachute jump** was that made by American Dr Jack Wheeler on 15 April 1981, who landed on the polar ice cap at latitude 90° 00′ N.

**The oldest man and woman to make voluntary parachute jumps** both recorded their achievements in 1986. First to jump was Edwin C. Townsend (USA), aged 89, over Vermillion Bay, Louisiana on 5 February. Just over six months later, on 23 August, he was followed by Mrs Sylvia Brett (UK) who was then aged 80 years 166 days, and made her jump over Cranfield, Bedfordshire.

**One of the most amazing parachute rescues** was that made by Gregory Robertson at Coolidge (Arizona) on 18 April 1987. In a multiple free-fall Debbie William collided with another parachutist at about 9000 ft (2745 m) and was knocked unconscious. Seeing the situation, Robertson manoeuvred alongside her and at a height of only 3500 ft (1065 m) managed to pull the ripcord of William's parachute, thus saving her life by a margin of about 10 s.

**The three most outstanding pioneers of gliding flight, prior to successful powered flight,** were the German Otto Lilienthal (1848–96), the Englishman Percy Sinclair Pilcher (1866–99) and the American Dr Octave Chanute (1832–1910). Their achievements may be summarized as follows:

**Otto Lilienthal,** German civil engineer, published a classic aeronautical textbook *Der Vogelflug als Grundlage der Fliegekunst* (The Flight of Birds as the Basis of Aviation) in 1899. Although he remained convinced that powered flight would ultimately be achieved by wing-flapping (i.e. in the ornithopter), Lilienthal constructed five fixed-wing monoplane gliders and two biplane gliders between 1891 and 1896. Tested near Berlin and at the Rhinower Hills near

*At the height of his success, Otto Lilienthal pilots one of his gliders in 1894. (Deutsches Museum, Munich)*

Percy Pilcher flying his tailed Hawk glider. (The Science Museum)

A Chanute biplane glider in classic biplane configuration.

Octave Chanute. (Smithsonian Institution)

Stöllen, these gliders managed sustained gliding flight; the pilot, usually Lilienthal himself, supported himself by his arms, holding the centre section of the glider. Thus, he could run forward and launch himself off the hills. During this period he achieved gliding distances ranging from 330 ft (100 m) to more than 820 ft (250 m). Although he had been experimenting with a small carbonic acid gas engine, he died on 10 August 1896 after one of his gliders crashed on the Rhinower Hills on 9 August before he could progress further with powered flight.

**Percy S. Pilcher**, British marine engineer, built his first glider, the *Bat*, in 1895 and flew that year on the banks of the River Clyde. Following advice by Lilienthal, as well as early practical experiments, Pilcher added a tailplane to the *Bat* and achieved numerous successful flights. This aircraft was followed by others (christened the *Beetle*, *Gull* and *Hawk*), the last of which was constructed in 1896 and included a fixed fin, a tailplane and a wheel undercarriage. It had a cambered wing with a span of 23 ft 4 in and an area of 180 ft² (7 m and 16.72 m² respectively). Pilcher had always set his sights upon powered flight and was engaged in developing a light 4 hp oil engine (probably for installation in his *Hawk*) when, having been towed off the ground by a team of horses, he crashed in the *Hawk* at Stanford Park, Market Harborough, on 30 September 1899, and died two days later.

**Octave Chanute**, American railroad engineer, was born in Paris, France, on 18 February 1832. His book *Progress in Flying Machines*, published in 1894, was the first comprehensive history of heavier-than-air flight and is still regarded as a classic of aviation literature. As well as providing a valuable information service for pioneers on both sides of the Atlantic, he began designing and building improved Lilienthal-type hang-gliders in 1896. After experimenting with multiplanes fitted with up to eight pairs of pivoting wings and a top fixed surface, he evolved the classic and successful biplane configuration. Flight-testing of his gliders was performed mainly by Augustus M. Herring (1867–1926), as Chanute was too old to fly himself. The Wright brothers gained early inspiration from *Progress in Flying Machines*, became close friends of Chanute, and learned from him the advantages offered by a Pratt-trussed biplane structure and, later, a catapult launching system for their wheel-less aircraft.

# Civil Aviation and Route Proving

The dream of the aviation pioneers was civil aviation: aeroplanes for competition, sport and, most importantly, improved wide-ranging travel. In the days when international communications were slow, and beset by difficulties that included even the vagaries of the weather, there were many who believed that any form of transport able to bring the peoples of the world more closely together could do nothing but good. Their growing awareness and understanding of each other's hopes and aspirations would, hopefully, help to strengthen the often fragile foundations of world peace. They should have done their homework more diligently! Those who spent time in dusty libraries could have turned the pages of Thomas Gray's *Luna Habitabilis* (1737) to find this then innocuous verse:

> *The time will come, when thou shalt lift thine eyes*
> *To watch a long-drawn battle in the skies,*
> *While aged peasants, too amazed for words*
> *Stare at the flying fleets of wond'rous birds.*

What a frighteningly accurate vision of the skies above southern England just over two centuries later, when RAF and Luftwaffe fighters were drawing their vapour trails of conflict during the Battle of Britain. On the fields beneath them, English farmers, busy with the harvest, leaned on their pitchforks to 'watch the long-drawn battle'. But, of course, in reality it had taken far less than two centuries to shatter the 'dream'.

Within a little less than eight years from the memorable day of 17 December 1903, when Orville and Wilbur Wright achieved the first man-carrying powered and sustained flight in their *Flyer No 1*, the aeroplane had already gone to war – on 22 October 1911 – and the development and progress of Air Warfare and Military Aviation is chronicled in the following section of this book.

Here we have the story to tell of the part of the 'dream' that has become reality, for on the credit side of aviation there are remarkable achievements by civil aircraft. It stretches from the first tentative 'hop' flights by the pioneers to the remarkable story of 1087 refugees carried in a single civil transport aircraft; it embraces the world's largest aeroplane, the Antonov An-225 Mryia and the diminutive CFM Shadow microlight which carried Eve Jackson from England to Australia. In fact, it tells the story of the aeroplane in the service of mankind that was the dream, however naïve, of aviation's pioneers.

Karl Jatho's semi-biplane, which flew 195 ft (60 m) just prior to the Wright brothers' first flights. (Historischen Museums am Hohen Ufer)

## Firsts:

**The first powered model aeroplane to have flown** is thought to have been that constructed in 1647 by the Italian Titus Livio Burattini, then residing at the court of King Wladyslaw IV of Poland. It is recorded to have had four sets of wings in tandem and a tail unit, the two centre pairs fixed and the forward and rear pairs for propulsion as an ornithopter. Drive was via springs. (Eight years later, Englishman Robert Hooke also flew a model ornithopter.)

**The first 'rational design' for a flying machine,** in the opinion of the Royal Aeronautical Society, is attributed to the Swedish national Emanuel Swedenborg (1688–1772). Details of his design were first published in that country during 1717.

**The first man in the world to identify and correctly record the parameters of heavier-than-air flight** was the Englishman, Sir George Cayley. (See also *Parachutes, kites and gliders*.)

**The first modern aeroplane design,** incorporating wire-braced constant chord wings (constructed using spars and cambered ribs, with double skinning), an enclosed fuselage for the crew and passengers and housing the power plant, propellers, a fixed tricycle landing gear, and a vertical tail and large-area tailplane, was the *Aerial Steam Carriage* (also known as the *Ariel*). Designed by Englishman William Samuel Henson (1812–88) from 1842, the design received a patent in 1843 and was expected to be built for service with the proposed Aerial Transit Company, **the first ever projected commercial air-**line. The full-size *Aerial Steam Carriage* was to have had a span of 150 ft (45.72 m), a wing chord of 30 ft (9.14 m), and a length of about 84 ft 9 in (25.83 m), and the single 25–30 hp Henson steam engine was expected to drive two 10 ft (3.05 m) diameter six-blade pusher propellers. Although the subject of many engravings, it was never built. This is partly because of the failure of a scale model of the *Aerial Steam Carriage* to make a sustained flight. This model, with a span of 20 ft (6.10 m) and also steam powered, was tested between 1844 and 1847. Although launched using a ramp, it proved incapable of sustaining flight. Having seen the failure of his dreams, Henson emigrated to America in 1848. However, this model was **the first to be powered by a steam engine.**

**The first powered model aeroplane to fly successfully** is the subject of some controversy. The first claim is made for John Stringfellow, an associate of Henson who was to have been the co-founder of the Aerial Transit Company (had the founding of this public company for world-wide air travel been accepted more favourably). Continuing Henson's work, but using a 10 ft 6 in (3.20 m) span steam-driven model with curved wings, Stringfellow launched his model from a high cable at Chard, Somerset, England in 1848 but this is thought not to have sustained flight. However, Stringfellow is also remembered for a model triplane exhibited at the first aeronautical exhibition at Crystal Palace in 1868, which, although unsuccessful in flight, introduced the concept of superimposed straight wings on a model. (It should be remembered that the triplane concept in itself was not new, Cayley having produced a triplane glider with superimposed wings in 1849—see *Gliders*.)

The person credited with producing **the first powered model aeroplane to fly successfully** was Frenchman Félix du Temple de la Croix, who in 1857–8 flew a model powered successively by clockwork and steam.

**The first design for a jet-propelled aeroplane** in the modern sense (remembering the rocket-powered model bird designed by the Italian Joanes Fontana in about 1420, and before this the wooden model bird propelled by steam or compressed air jet demonstrated in about 400–350 BC by Greek-born Archytas of Tarentum, Italy) was produced by Frenchman Charles de Louvrie in 1865. Known as the *Aéronave*, it had a canopy-type wing supported on a strut above a wheeled cart which carried twin jetpipes through which vaporized oil or similar fuel was to have been burned and ejected. This was not constructed.

**The Aeronautical Society of Great Britain** was founded on 12 January 1866. In 1868 it staged the **first ever aeronautical exhibition**, held at Crystal Palace. The exhibits included model engines driven by steam, oil gas and guncotton.

**The first design for a powered delta-winged aeroplane** was that by Englishmen J. W. Butler and E. Edwards and patented in 1867. This was also the **first British design for a jet-propelled aeroplane**.

Undoubtedly the **first ornithopter to fly successfully** was completed in 1870 by Gustave Trouvé. This bird-like model was powered by revolver cartridges which, when fired, forced down the wings, which returned by springs. It was reported that flights of 195 ft (60 m) were possible.

**The first powered man-carrying aeroplane to achieve a brief 'hop', after gaining speed down a ramp,** was a monoplane with swept-forward wings built by Félix du Temple and piloted by an unidentified young sailor, at Brest in about 1874.

*Aeronautical Society's first exhibition at the Crystal Palace, 1868. Depicted among the exhibits is a Stringfellow triplane hanging from the roof. (The Science Museum, London)*

The power plant was a hot-air or steam engine, driving a tractor propeller.

**The first unmanned aeroplane to fly from level ground** was the *Aerial Steamer*, designed and built by Englishman Thomas Moy. A tandem wing craft with two six-blade pusher paddle-like propellers positioned between the wings and powered by a 3 hp steam engine, it lifted a few inches from the ground in 1875 in tethered flight from a circular track.

**The four-stroke cycle gas engine** was patented by Nikolaus Otto in Germany in 1876, and in 1877 he invented the four-stroke petrol internal combustion engine.

**Among the first manned and powered aeroplanes to achieve a 'hop' flight after gaining speed down a slope** was the huge monoplane built by Russian Alexander Fedorovich Mozhaiski and hopped in 1884. With a wing 74 ft 10 in (22.80 m) in span and 46 ft 7 in (14.20 m) in chord, and powered by a 20 hp steam engine driving a four-blade tractor propeller forward of the wings and a 10 hp steam engine driving two smaller pusher propellers inset in the wings, it was piloted by I. N. Golubev at Krasnoye Selo.

**The first man-carrying aeroplane to achieve a powered 'hop' after rising from supposedly level ground** was the bat-winged *Éole* monoplane built and flown by Clément Ader (1841–1925), at Armainvilliers, France, on 9 October 1890. Powered by an 18–20 hp steam engine, the *Éole* covered about 165 ft (50 m), but never achieved sustained or controlled flight. Ader's second aeroplane, the *Avion III* military model, was tested twice on 12–14 October 1897 but did not fly.

**The first British powered aeroplane to fly tethered from a circular track, with a load equivalent to that of a pilot,** was probably an early example of the *Multiplane*, a steam-powered multi-winged aeroplane designed by Horatio Phillips and flown at Harrow, England, with a 72 lb (33 kg) load in May 1893. This had 41 wings, each 19 ft (5.8 m) in span and with a chord of only 1½ in (3.8 cm). This type of wing set the pattern for his later successful aircraft.

**The Aéro Club de France** was founded in 1898.

**The first man to achieve sustained powered flight with an unmanned heavier-than-air craft** was the American Samuel Pierpont Langley (born 22 August 1834 at Roxbury, Massachusetts; died 27 February 1906, at Aiken, South Carolina). Mathematician and solar radiation physicist, Langley commenced building powered model aeroplanes during the 1890s, launching them from the top of a houseboat on the Potomac River near Quantico. His 14 ft (4.25 m) span models achieved sustained flights of up to 4200 ft (1280 m) from 6 May 1896 and incorporated a single steam engine mounted amidships, driving a pair of propellers. In 1898 Langley was requested to continue his experiments with a $50 000 State subsidy and set about the design and construction of a full-scale version. As an intermediate step he built a quarter-scale model which, in June 1903, became **the world's first aeroplane powered by a petrol engine to achieve sustained flight.** His full-size *Aerodrome*, with a span of 48 ft (14.6 m) and powered by a 52 hp Manly-Balzer five-cylinder radial petrol engine, was completed in 1903, and attempts to fly this over the Potomac River with Charles M. Manly at the controls were made on 7 October and 8 December 1903. On both occasions the aeroplane fouled the launcher and dropped into the river. In view of the Wright brothers' success immediately thereafter, the American Government withdrew its support from Langley and his project was abandoned.

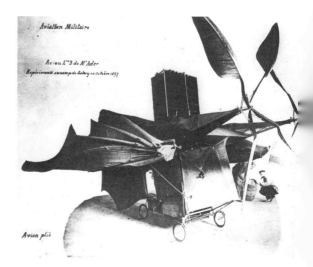

Ader's *Avion III* built to a French Ministry of War contract of 3 February 1882, requiring two crew and a 75 kg bomb load. Tested on a circular track at Satorg in 1897, it partially lifted from the ground but could not fly successfully. (*Musée de l'Air*)

Perhaps now considered the most controversial aviation figure of 1901–2 was Bavarian born Gustav Whitehead, whose claimed aviation feats are not officially recognized and often divide opinion. On 14 August 1901 at Bridgeport, Connecticut (having emigrated to America), he is said to have piloted in sustained flight an aeroplane of his own design, covering a distance of about 880 ft (270 m) at an altitude of 50 ft (15 m). The single engine powered both the propellers and the landing gear wheels. On 17 January 1902 Whitehead is reported to have flown a controllable twin-engined flying-boat over a circular distance of about 7 miles (11 km), finally alighting on water. Other flights and achievements are said to have followed these. Photographs of Whitehead and his aircraft on the ground appeared in the press and he was the subject of many contemporary write-ups. Others stated thereafter that they saw him fly.

**The first 'hop' from water by a seaplane** was probably performed by Austrian Wilhelm Kress in a tandem-winged machine, powered by a 30 hp Daimler petrol engine, in October 1901. There is some doubt, as a few sources claim that he capsized the seaplane before leaving the water during the taxying phase. The trials were conducted on the Tullnerbach reservoir. This seaplane preceded Langley's full-size *Aerodrome* as **the first manned aeroplane fitted with a petrol engine**.

**In Britain** the Aero Club was founded on 29 October 1901, becoming the Royal Aero Club on 15 February 1910.

**The first 'hop' flight in New Zealand was made by Richard William Pearse** on or about 31 March 1903 in a monoplane of his own design. He had constructed the airframe largely from bamboo with aluminium fittings, and built a horizontally-opposed two-cylinder engine to power it. There have been claims that this flight was made a year earlier, but there appears to be no recorded evidence for either date; the majority of witnesses of the flight have stated March 1903 and no substantial evidence has been found to suggest or confirm a flight in 1902. Pearse coaxed his aircraft into the air from level ground and flew about 160 ft (50 m) before crashing into a hedge. There are enthusiastic claims from supporters that his flight ante-dated that of the Wright brothers. However, if the same parameters of manned, powered, sustained and controlled flight from level ground, and a landing at the same level or higher, are applied to the Pearse flight, then it fails to meet the last two parameters. Research in New Zealand has so far resulted in the discovery of only two written accounts of his work by Pearse, both being letters to newspapers (in 1919 and 1928), and from these he, apparently, did not consider that his achievement warranted the description of 'flight'.

**The first aeroplane to achieve man-carrying powered, sustained flight** in the world was the *Flyer*, designed and constructed by the brothers Wilbur and Orville Wright, which first achieved such flight at 10.35 h on Thursday, 17 December 1903, at Kill Devil Hills, Kitty Hawk, North Carolina, with an undulating flight of 120 ft (36.5 m) in about 12 s. Three further flights were made on the same day, the longest of which covered a ground distance of 852 ft (260 m) and lasted 59 s. It should be emphasized that these flights were the natural culmination of some four years' experimenting by the Wrights with a number of gliders, during 1899–1903. Powered by a 12 bhp four-cylinder engine, *Flyer* took off under its own power from a dolly which ran on two bicycle hubs along a 60ft (18 m) wooden rail.

*Langley full-size* Aerodrome *plunges towards the water. (Smithsonian Institution)*

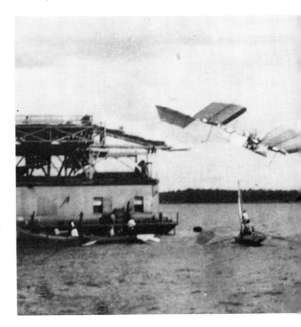

**The first full-size aeroplane to feature ailerons** was a biplane flown by Frenchman Robert Esnault-Pelterie in October 1904.

**The first aeroplane flight with a duration of more than five minutes** was that by Wilbur Wright in the *Flyer II*, which covered 2¾ miles (4.4 km) on 9 November 1904.

**The Aero Club of America** was founded on 30 November 1905.

**The world's first full-time air correspondent** was Englishman Harry Harper, who worked for the *Daily Mail* from September 1906.

**The first tethered sustained flight in Europe** was made by the Danish engineer Jacob C. H. Ellehammer on 12 September 1906. Piloting a curious and primitive biplane fitted with a 20 hp radial engine, he covered about 140 ft (43 m) in circular flight, as the biplane was tethered to a post. For this the rudder had been fixed, making the flight uncontrollable by the pilot.

*Ellehammer lifting off to a height of about 18 in (50 cm) on the 985 ft (300 m) circular track at Lindholm in 1906. (Royal Danish Ministry of Foreign Affairs)*

**The first accredited sustained flight (i.e. other than a 'hop') achieved by a manned, powered aeroplane in Europe** was made on 12 November 1906 by the Brazilian constructor-pilot Alberto Santos-Dumont (1873–1932), a resident of Paris, France, who flew his '14-bis' 722 ft (220 m) in 21.2 s. His aeroplane was in effect a tail-first box-kite powered by a 50 hp Antoinette engine, and this flight won for him the Aéro-Club de France's prize of 1500 francs for the first officially observed flight of more than 100 m. A previous flight,

carried out on 23 October, covered 197 ft (60 m) and had won Santos-Dumont the Archdeacon Prize of 3000 francs for the first sustained flight of more than 25 m. Santos-Dumont's flight on 12 November was the first ever FAI recognized world record for distance flown. (See 26 October 1907.)

**The first powered aeroplane flight in Great Britain**, though not officially recognized, was almost certainly made by Horatio Phillips (1845–1924) in a 22 hp *Multiplane* in 1907. The aircraft had four of Phillips's unique narrow 'Venetian blind' wing-frames in tandem. It covered a distance of about 500 ft (152 m).

**The first of many Daily Mail prizes offered for aeroplane achievements** was one for a model aeroplane exhibition and competition held at the Agricultural Hall, London, on 6 April 1907. In a fly-off finish at Alexandra Palace, Alliott Verdon Roe was awarded £75 for the flight of one of his model biplanes. This was half the first prize, as the judges considered no model had deserved the full amount. With this, Roe went on to construct a full-size aeroplane.

**The first aeroplane to be flown with cantilever wings** was Louis Blériot's Type VI *Libellule*, which also featured wingtip ailerons. The Type VI made its first flight on 11 July 1907.

**The second official distance record** was set by Frenchman Henry Farman in the Voisin-Farman I at 2530 ft (771 m), on 26 October 1907. This aeroplane had first flown on 30 September. To be official as a world record, the achievement had to be recognized by the FAI, which had been established in France on 14 October 1905.

**The first monoplane with tractor engine, enclosed fuselage, rear-mounted tail-unit and two-wheel main undercarriage with tailwheel** was the Blériot VII powered by a 50 hp Antoinette engine. This was Louis Blériot's third full-size monoplane and was built during the autumn of 1907 and first flown by him at Issy-les-Moulineaux, France, on 10 November 1907. Before crashing this aeroplane on 18 December that year Blériot had achieved six flights, the longest of which was more than 1640 ft (500 m). This success confirmed to the designer that his basic configuration was sound—so much so that despite a 30-year deviation into biplane design, Blériot's basic configuration is still regarded as fun-

*Wilbur Wright looks on as Orville guides the* Flyer *on the first recognized powered, sustained and controlled flight by an aeroplane.*

damentally conventional among propeller-driven aeroplanes of today.

**The first US aeroplane company** was formed on 30 November 1907 by Glenn Curtiss as the Curtiss Aeroplane Company.

**The first circuit aeroplane flight made in Europe** was undertaken by Henry Farman on 13 January 1908 in his modified Voisin biplane at Issy-les-Moulineaux when he took off, circumnavigated a pylon 1625 ft (500 m) away and returned to his point of departure. By so doing, Farman won the Grand Prix d'Aviation, a prize of 50 000 francs offered by Henry Deutsch de la Meurthe and

Ernest Archdeacon to the first pilot to cover a kilometre. The flight took 1 min 28 s and, owing to the distance taken in turning, probably covered 4875 ft (1500 m).

**The first aeroplane flight in Italy** was made by the French sculptor-turned-aviator Léon Delagrange in a Voisin in May 1908. At this time, aircraft built by the French brothers Gabriel and Charles Voisin were flown by two pilots, Henry Farman and Léon Delagrange. Henry Farman was born in England in 1874 and retained his English citizenship until 1937 when he became a naturalized Frenchman. Having turned from painting to

*Santos-Dumont* 14-bis *tail-first biplane, the first European aeroplane to make a sustained flight.*

cycling before the turn of the century, he progressed to racing Panhard motor cars and at one time owned the largest garage in Paris. Gabriel Voisin later remarked that Farman possessed considerable mechanical and manipulative skill, whereas Delagrange 'was not the sporting type' and knew nothing about running an engine. Delagrange was killed flying a Blériot monoplane on 4 January 1910.

*Henry Farman pilots his Voisin-Farman I on a circular flight of over one kilometre, 13 January 1908. (Musée de l'Air)*

**The first aeroplane flight in Belgium** was made by Henry Farman, at Ghent, in May 1908.

**The first passenger ever to fly in an aeroplane** was Charles W. Furnas who was taken aloft by Wilbur Wright on 14 May 1908 for a flight covering 1968 ft (600 m) of 28.6 s duration. Later the same morning Orville Wright flew Furnas for a distance of about 2½ miles (4 km), which was covered in 3 min 40 s. Interestingly, it was only on 6 May that the Wrights had begun flying again after a three-year self-imposed absence.

**The first passenger to be carried in an aeroplane in Europe** has long been regarded as Ernest Archdeacon, the Frenchman whose substantial prizes contributed such stimulus to European aviation, and who was flown by Henry Farman on 29 May 1908. However, there is written evidence that Henry Farman carried Léon Delagrange in a Voisin on 21 March 1908.

**The first American to fly after the Wright brothers** was Glenn H. Curtiss, who flew his *June*

*Bug* for the first time on 20 June 1908. During this flight Curtiss covered a distance of 1266 ft (386 m) and exactly a fortnight later, on 4 July, he made a flight of 5090 ft (1550 m) in 102.2 s to win the *Scientific American* trophy for the first official public flight in the USA of more than 1 km.

**The first aeroplane flight in Germany** was made by the Dane J. C. H. Ellehammer, in his No IV machine at Kiel on 28 June 1908. However, this flight had a duration of only 11 s. A development of this aeroplane was flown by **the first German pilot**, Hans Grade, at Magdeburg in October 1908.

**The world's first woman passenger to fly in an aeroplane** was Madame Thérèse Peltier who, on 8 July 1908, accompanied Léon Delagrange at Turin, Italy, in his Voisin for a flight of 500 ft (150 m). She soon afterwards became the **first woman to fly solo**, but never was a qualified pilot.

**The world's first full-size triplane to fly** was the French Goupy I, which first took to the air on 5 September 1908. Built by Ambroise Goupy, it was powered by a 50 hp Renault engine. The later Goupy II, actually built by Blériot and first flown in March 1909, is recognized as the first of the classic tractor-engined biplanes.

**The first flight in Europe of about 30 min duration** was performed on 6 September 1908 by Léon Delagrange at Issy-les-Moulineaux, when he covered a distance of 15¼ miles (24.4 km) in 29 min 53 s.

**The most important endurance flight to date** was made by Wilbur Wright on 21 September 1908, when he covered 41⅓ miles (66.5 km) in France.

**The first resident Englishmen to fly in an aeroplane** (albeit as passengers) were Griffith Brewer (the first), the Hon C. S. Rolls, Frank Hedges Butler and Maj B. F. S. Baden-Powell, who were taken aloft in turn by Wilbur Wright in his biplane at Camp d'Auvours on 8 October 1908. Butler had founded the Aero Club of Great Britain, while Baden-Powell was Secretary of the Aeronautical Society. The 'resident' qualification is necessary here as of course the English-born, French-resident Henry Farman had been flying for more than a year by the time the four Englishmen were taken aloft by Wright.

*Goupy I, the world's first full-size triplane to fly.*

The first European cross-country flight was made by Henry Farman on 30 October 1908, when he flew from Châlons to Reims, a distance of about 16 miles (26 km).

The first successful Russian aeroplane was the Gakkel-3 of 1909, designed by Yakov M. Gakkel.

The first German aviator to fly a German aeroplane was Hans Grade who, on 12 January 1909, flew a triplane of his own design at Magdeburg.

Probably the most successful monoplane designed and built before the First World War was the French Blériot XI, the work of Louis Blériot and first flown on 23 January 1909 while powered by a 30 hp REP engine.

The first aerodrome to be prepared as such in England was the flying-ground between Leysdown and Shellness, Isle of Sheppey (known as 'Shellbeach'), where limited established facilities were provided. It was opened in February 1909 by the joint effort of the Aero Club of Great Britain and Short Bros Ltd.

The first aeroplanes to be manufactured in series were six Wright biplanes produced by the British Short Brothers under an agreement concluded between Wilbur Wright and Eustace Short in February 1909. Therefore, Short Brothers was the first aeroplane manufacturing company proper in aviation history.

The first sustained, powered flight by an aeroplane in the British Empire was made on 23 February 1909 by J. A. D. McCurdy, a Canadian, over Baddeck Bay, Nova Scotia, in the Aerial Experimental Association's biplane *Silver Dart*, which he had designed. He had made his own first flight at Hammondsport, New York, USA, the previous December.

The first aeroplane flight in Austria was made by the Frenchman G. Legagneux, at Vienna in April 1909 in his Voisin. The first Austrian to fly was Igo Etrich, in his *Taube* at Wiener-Neustadt in November of that year. This aircraft gave its name to the type in fairly widespread use by Germany at the beginning of the First World War.

The first cinematographer to be taken up in an aeroplane was at Centocelle, near Rome, on 24 April 1909, in a Wright biplane flown by Wilbur Wright.

The first resident Englishman to make an officially recognized aeroplane flight in England was J. T. C. Moore-Brabazon (later Lord Brabazon of Tara) who made three sustained flights of 450, 600 and 1500 ft (137, 180 and 450 m) between 30 April and 2 May 1909 at Leysdown, Isle of Sheppey, in his Voisin biplane. He had learned to fly in France during the previous year and on 30 October 1909 won the £1000 *Daily Mail* prize for the first Briton to cover a mile (closed circuit) in a British aeroplane—the Short No. 2 biplane. He was awarded the Royal Aero Club of Great Britain's Aviator Certificate No. 1 on 8 March 1910. Lord Brabazon died in 1969.

**The first aeroplane flight in France of one hour endurance** was performed by Frenchman Paul Tissandier in a Wright biplane on 20 May 1909. He also set the first official FAI world speed record for aeroplanes.

**The first aeroplane to carry a pilot and two passengers** was the Blériot XII, piloted on 12 June 1909 by Louis Blériot and with passengers Santos-Dumont and Fournier.

**The first apprentice to an aeroplane manufacturing company** was Howard (Dinger) Bell, who joined Short Brothers on 10 July 1909. His father, nicknamed 'Father Bell' by the employees, was the company's first foreman.

**The first Briton to fly an all-British aeroplane** was Alliott Verdon Roe (1877–1958), in his Roe 1 triplane on 13 July 1909 at Lea Marshes, Essex. Lack of funds to build the triplane had forced Roe to construct it from wood instead of light-gauge

steel tubing, to cover the wings with paper and to use the same 9 hp JAP engine that had powered his unsuccessful biplane. The 100 ft (30 m) flight that was achieved on the 13th was much improved upon on the 23rd, when he flew 900 ft (274 m) at an average height of 10 ft (3 m).

**Conquest of the English Channel.** In response to an offer by the *Daily Mail* of a prize of £1000 for the first pilot (of any nationality) to fly an aeroplane across the Channel, **the first attempt** was made by an Englishman, Hubert Latham, flying an Antoinette IV. He took off from Sangatte, near Calais, at 06.42 h on Monday, 19 July 1909, but alighted in the sea after only 6–8 miles (10–13 km) following engine failure which could not be rectified in the air. He was picked up by the French naval vessel *Harpon*. The occasion of this attempt was also the **first instance of wireless telegraphy being used to obtain weather reports**, the first report being transmitted from

Right *The Short Brothers' Leysdown factory, in which the first aeroplane production line was established in 1909 to build six Wright Model As. (Short Brothers)*

Below *The third Short-Wright Model A went to Frank McClean in October 1909. Having been returned to Shorts for modification, it reappeared in May 1910 with a new engine, wheels and a tailplane aft of the rudders. (Short Brothers)*

Sangatte, near Calais, to the Lord Warden Hotel, Dover, at 04.30 h on that morning.

Despite working furiously to get a replacement Antoinette, Latham was beaten by Louis Blériot. The Frenchman took off in his Blériot XI monoplane at 04.41 h, from Les Baraques, on Sunday, 25 July 1909, and landed at 05.17.5 h in the Northfall Meadow by Dover Castle to become **the first man to cross the English Channel in an aeroplane**.

Latham made a second attempt to fly the Channel two days later (on 27 July), taking off at 05.50 h from Cap Blanc Nez. When only 1 mile (1.6 km) from the Dover cliffs, his engine failed and once again he had to alight in the sea.

**The first woman passenger to fly in an aeroplane in England** was Mrs Cody, wife of Samuel, who was taken up by her husband during the last week of July 1909 over Laffan's Plain, Hants, in the *British Army Aeroplane No 1*.

**The first aeroplane flight in Sweden** was made by the Frenchman Legagneux at Stockholm in his Voisin biplane on 29 July 1909.

**The first passenger to be carried by an aeroplane in Canada** was F. W. 'Casey' Baldwin who was taken aloft on 2 August 1909 at Petawawa, Ontario, in an aeroplane flown by J. A. D. McCurdy.

**The first International Aviation Meeting in the world** opened on 22 August 1909 at Reims, and lasted until 29 August 1909. Thirty-eight aeroplanes were entered to participate, although only 23 managed to leave the ground; the meeting also attracted aviators and aeroplane designers from all over Europe and did much to arouse widespread public interest in flying. The types of aeroplanes which flew were: Antoinette, Blériot XI, Blériot XII, Blériot XIII, Breguet, Curtiss, Henry Farman, REP, Voisin and Wright.

**The first aeroplane flight in Denmark** was made by Léon Delagrange in September 1909.

Above  *Returning Hubert Latham's wrecked Antoinette to Calais after his unsuccessful attempt to be the first to fly the English Channel.*

Left  *Alliott Verdon Roe made history in his paper-covered triplane by becoming the first Briton to fly an all-British aeroplane.*

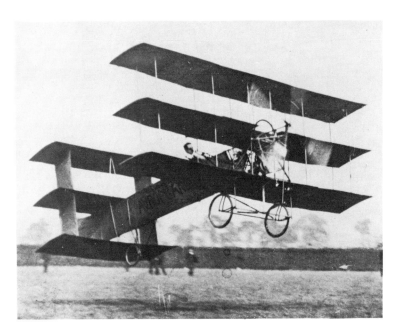

*Louis Blériot's moment of triumph, having landed in Northfall Meadow after making the first aeroplane flight across the English Channel. (Air France)*

**The first pilot to be killed flying a powered aeroplane** was Eugène Lefebvre, on 7 September 1909; he crashed while flying a new Wright Type A at Port Aviation Juvisy. Soon afterwards, on 22 September, Captain Ferber was killed when his Voisin hit a ditch while preparing for take-off.

**The first Aviation Meeting held in Great Britain** was that organized by the Doncaster Aviation Committee on the Doncaster Racecourse between 15 and 23 October 1909. This meeting was not governed by rules laid down by the FAI, nor was it officially recognized by the Aero Club of Great Britain. Twelve aeroplanes constituted the field, of which five managed to fly. **The first officially recognized meeting** was held at Squires Gate, Blackpool, between 18 and 23 October 1909, being organized by the Blackpool Corporation and the Lancashire Aero Club; seven of the dozen participants were coaxed into the air.

**The first American woman passenger in an aeroplane** was Mrs Ralph van Deman, who flew with Wilbur Wright on 27 October 1909.

**The first major prize in Great Britain for all-British aviation activity** was the £1000 offered by the *Daily Mail* to the first British pilot to complete a circular flight of 1 mile (1.6 km) in an all-British aeroplane. This prize was won by J. T. C. Moore-Brabazon on 30 October 1909 at Shellbeach when, flying the Short Biplane No 2, he achieved the one mile flight in a time of 2 min

36 s. Similar in configuration to the Short-built Wright biplanes, the Short No 2 differed considerably in detail and was powered by a 50–60 hp Green four-cylinder inline engine.

**The first piglet to fly in a powered aeroplane in Britain** took to the air as J. T. C. Moore-Brabazon's passenger on 4 November 1909. Intended to debunk the old adage that 'pigs can't fly', pig and pilot did admirably with a 3.5 mile (5.6 km) cross-country flight.

**The first successful still photographs taken from an aeroplane** were by M Meurisse, in December 1909, and showed the flying-fields at Mourmelon and Châlons. The aeroplane was an Antoinette piloted by Latham.

**The first American monoplane to fly** was the Walden III, designed by Dr Henry W. Walden and flown on 9 December 1909 at Mineola, Long Island, New York. It was powered by a 22 hp Anzani engine.

**The first aeroplane flight in Australia** was made by Colin Defries on 9 December 1909. Defries, a well-known racing driver, flew an imported Wright biplane over a distance of 1 mile (1.6 km) at a height of 35 ft (11 m) at Victoria Park Racecourse, Sydney, New South Wales.

**The first passenger to be carried by aeroplane in Australia** was Mr C. S. Magennis, who flew with Colin Defries on 10 December 1909.

The first aeroplane flight in Ireland was made by Harry G. Ferguson of Belfast on 31 December 1909. The aeroplane was of his own design and manufacture; it resembled a Blériot, and was powered by an eight-cylinder 35 hp air-cooled JAP engine.

Aeroplanes and sheds at the October 1909 Doncaster Aviation Week. (Topical Press)

J. T. C. Moore-Brabazon won a £1,000 Daily Mail prize for being the first Briton to make a circular one-mile flight in a British aeroplane, the Short No 2.

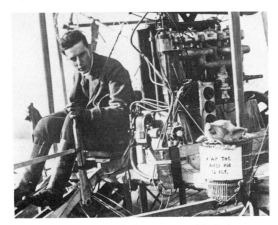

Winning a bet, Moore-Brabazon proved that pigs can fly.

The first British woman to fly solo in an aeroplane was almost certainly Miss Edith Maud Cook, who performed various aerial acts under the name of Miss 'Spencer Kavanagh'. She achieved several solo flights on Blériot monoplanes with the Grahame-White Flying School at Pau in the Pyrenees in early 1910. She was also a professional parachute-jumper, known as 'Viola Spencer', and was killed after making a jump from a balloon near Coventry, England, in July 1910.

The first aeroplane meeting to be held in the USA was organized by the Aero Club of California at the Dominguez Field, Los Angeles on 10 January 1910.

The first Aviation Certificate awarded by the Royal Aero Club was received by Moore-Brabazon on 8 March 1910. The Aero Club had become the Royal Aero Club on 15 February 1910.

The first certificated woman pilot in the world was Mme la Baronne de Laroche, a French woman who received Pilot's Certificate No. 36 on 8 March 1910, having qualified on a Voisin biplane. She was killed in 1919 in an aeroplane accident.

The first night flights were made by Emil Aubrun, a Frenchman, on 10 March 1910 flying a Blériot monoplane. Each of the two flights began and ended at Villalugano, Buenos Aires, Argentina, and was about 12.4 miles (20 km) long.

The first aeroplane flight in Switzerland was made by Capt Engelhardt on 13 March 1910.

The first take-off from water by an aeroplane was made by Henri Fabre, a Frenchman, in his Gnome-powered seaplane *Hydravion* at La Mède harbour, Martigues, France, on 28 March 1910.

The first aeroplane flights in Spain were made by Gaudart, Poillot, Le Blond, Mamet and Olieslaegers between March and April 1910.

The first aeroplane to be 'forced down' by the action of another was the Henry Farman biplane of Mr A. Rawlinson during the Aviation Meeting at Nice, France, in mid-April 1910. Mr Rawlinson was flying his new Farman over the sea when the Russian Effimov passed so close above him (also in a Farman) that his downdraught forced the Englishman into the water. The Russian was fined 100 francs for dangerous flying.

**The first recorded night flight in Great Britain** was made by Claude Grahame-White from 27 to 28 April 1910, in an attempt to overhaul Louis Paulhan competing in the *Daily Mail* £10 000 London to Manchester race (which had to be started from a point within 5 miles of the newspaper's London offices and finish at a point within 5 miles of its Manchester offices). This was the first aeroplane event in Britain to offer a £10 000 prize. Paulhan, who eventually won despite Grahame-White's night flight, thus made the first London to Manchester aeroplane flight and the first straight line aeroplane flight in Britain of more than 100 km.

**The first England to France and two-way crossing of the English Channel** was accomplished by the Hon C. S. Rolls (the 'Rolls' of 'Rolls-Royce') flying a French-built Wright biplane on 2 June 1910. He took off from Broadlees, Dover, at 18.30.5 h, dropped a letter addressed to the Aéro Club de France near Sangatte at 19.15 h, then flew back to England and made a perfect landing near his starting-rail at 20.06 h. He was thus the **first man to fly from England to France in an aeroplane, the first man to make a non-stop two-way crossing, and the first cross-Channel pilot to land at a pre-arranged spot without damage to his aeroplane**.

**The first Romanian aeroplane to fly** was the *Vlaicu I* parasol-winged monoplane, designed by Aurel Vlaicu and flown on 17 June 1910. This date is marked as the National Aviation Day in that country.

**The first British pilot to lose his life while flying an aeroplane** was the Hon Charles Stewart Rolls (born in London, 27 August 1877, the third son of the first Baron Llangattock), who was killed at the Bournemouth Aviation Week on 12 July 1910 when his French-built Wright biplane suffered a structural failure in flight.

**The first flight in Australia by an Australian in an indigenous aeroplane** was made by John R. Duigan of Mia Mia, Victoria, on 16 July 1910 in an aeroplane constructed from photographs of the Wright *Flyer*. On that day Duigan flew only 28 ft (8.5 m), but on 7 October he covered 588 ft (179 m) at a height of about 12 ft (3.65 m).

**The first mail carried unofficially in an aeroplane in Great Britain** was flown by Claude Grahame-White on 10 August 1910 in a Blériot monoplane from Squires Gate, Blackpool; he did not reach his destination at Southport, having been forced to land by bad weather.

**The first Channel crossing with a passenger** was by Franco-American John B. Moisant and his mechanic in a Blériot two-seater aeroplane, from Calais to Dover, on 17 August 1910.

**The first use of radio between an aeroplane and the ground** was on 27 August 1910 when

James McCurdy, flying a Curtiss, sent and received messages via an HM Horton wireless set at Sheepshead Bay, NY State.

**The first American woman to fly solo in an aeroplane** was Blanche Scott on 2 September 1910.

**The first air collision in the world** occurred on 8 September 1910 between two aeroplanes piloted by brothers named Warchalovski at Wiener-Neustadt, Austria. One of the pilots suffered a broken leg. A passenger in one of the aircraft was the Archduke Léopold Salvator of Austria.

**The first crossing of the Irish Sea** was made by Robert Loraine who, flying a Farman biplane on 11 September 1910, set off from Holyhead, Anglesey. Although engine failure forced him down in the sea 180 ft (55 m) offshore from the Irish coast near Baily Lighthouse, Howth, he was generally considered to have been the first to accomplish the crossing.

**The first flight over the Alps** was made by the Peruvian Georges Chavez in a Blériot on 23 September 1910. His flight from Brig, Switzerland, to Domodossola, Italy, via the Simplon Pass, ended in disaster when he crashed on landing and was killed.

**The first successful use in Britain of a radio in an aircraft** was recorded on 29 September 1910. The transmitter, designed by Mr Thorne Baker in conjunction with the Marconi Company, and installed in a Bristol Boxkite, was used by Robert Loraine while the aircraft was in flight near Stonehenge, Wilts, to transmit a signal to the ground at Larkhill, almost one mile (1.6 km) distant.

**The first ever carriage of freight by air** was undertaken on 7 November 1910. On this occasion it had been arranged between the Wright Company and the Morehouse-Martens Company of Columbus, Ohio, which operated an emporium named The Home Dry Goods Store, for two packages of silk to be transported by air between Dayton and Columbus to bring attention to a sale. A Wright Model B, at the last minute piloted by Philip O. Parmalee (see below), was used to carry nearly 542 yds of silk, at a cost to the company of $5000. Despite this carriage fee, the store made a profit of more than $1000, partly by cutting up some of the material and selling it in small pieces as souvenirs mounted on postcards.

**The world's first 'hop' flight by a jet-powered aircraft** was recorded on 10 December 1910. This was achieved by the Romanian Henri Coanda in a conventional aeroplane, but with its 50 hp Clerget piston engine being used to drive a centrifugal air compressor to create thrust.

**The first British pilot to survive a spin (probably first in the world)** was Fred Raynham who, flying an Avro biplane during 1911, stalled while climbing through fog. The stall occurred after he

Left   *Henri Fabre takes off from La Mède harbour in his* Hydravion *seaplane, 28 March 1910. (Musée de l'Air)*

Right   *M Christiaen in a Henry Farman biplane during the July 1910 Bournemouth Aviation Week. (The Science Museum, London)*

Left *Max Morehouse alongside the pilot for the first freight flight, Philip O. Parmalee (right).*

Right *Postmaster-General Hitchcock hands Earl L. Ovington the first official US air mail.*

had stooped to adjust his compass as he thought that it was malfunctioning; the next he knew was that he was standing upright on the rudder pedals with his aeroplane whirling round. Quite how he recovered from the spin will never be known, for his recollection was that he *pulled the stick back*; notwithstanding this he caught sight of the ground and was able to perform a controlled landing.

**The first flight in New Zealand by a practical aeroplane** was made in a Howard Wright type biplane piloted by Vivian C. Walsh at Auckland on 5 February 1911. With his brother Leo, Vivian Walsh imported materials from England with which to build the aircraft and installed a 60 hp ENV engine. Vivian Walsh also made **the first seaplane flight in New Zealand** on 1 January 1914.

**The first government (official) air-mail flight in the world** was undertaken on 18 February 1911 when the French pilot Henri Pequet flew a Humber biplane from Allahabad to Naini Junction, a distance of about 5 miles (8 km) across the Jumna River, with some 6500 letters. The regular service was established four days later as part of the Universal Postal Exhibition, Allahabad, India, the flights being shared by Capt W. G. Windham and Pequet. The envelopes of this first air-mail service were franked 'First Aerial Post, UP Exhibition, Allahabad, 1911' and are highly prized among collectors.

**The first non-stop flight from London to Paris** was made on 12 April 1911 by Pierre Prier in 3 h 56 min, flying a Blériot monoplane powered by a 50 hp Gnôme engine. Prier, who was Chief Flying Instructor at the Blériot Flying School, Hendon, took off from Hendon and landed at Issy-les-Moulineaux.

**The first American woman pilot** was Harriet Quimby who, on 2 August 1911, gained her licence. On 16 April 1912 she became **the first woman to fly an aeroplane across the English Channel.**

**The first recorded carriage of freight by air in Britain** was a box of Osram lamps carried on 4 July 1911 by a Valkyrie monoplane flown by Horatio Barber from Shoreham to Hove in Sussex, England, on behalf of the General Electric Company who paid £100 for the flight.

**The first British woman pilot** was Mrs Hilda B. Hewlett, who gained Pilot's Certificate No. 122 on 29 August 1911.

**The first official mail to be carried by air in Great Britain** was entrusted to the staff pilots of the Grahame-White and Blériot flying schools, who commenced carrying the mail between Hendon and Windsor on Saturday, 9 September 1911. The first flight was undertaken on that day by Gustav Hamel in a Blériot monoplane, covering the route in 10 min at a ground speed of over

105 mph (169 km/h) with a strong tailwind. The service lasted until 26 September, having been instituted to commemorate the coronation of HM King George V. The total weight of mail carried between the Hendon flying-field and Royal Farm, Windsor was 1015 lb (460.4 kg).

**The first coast-to-coast flight across America** was made by Calbraith P. Rodgers between 17 September and 5 November 1911. Rodgers, trying to win a $50 000 prize offered by William Randolph Hearst, flew from New York to Pasadena in a Burgess-Wright biplane. Making a series of short flights, he arrived at the destination 19 days outside the specified 30-day limit and so failed to qualify for the prize.

**The first Italian air-mail service** started on 19 September 1911 and covered Bologna, Venice and Rimini.

**The first official carriage of mail by air in the USA** was by Earl L. Ovington on 23 September 1911 in a Blériot-type monoplane known as the Queen monoplane. The journey of 6 miles (9.6 km) began from Nassau Boulevard, New York. Ovington became *Air Mail Pilot No 1*, a title given to him by Postmaster-General Hitchcock.

**The first all-metal aeroplane to fly** was the *Tubavion* monoplane, constructed by the Frenchmen Ponche and Primard and exhibited at the 3rd Paris Salon on 16 December 1911. Two were built.

**The first seaplane competition** was held at Monaco in March 1912. Seven pilots attended (Fischer, Renaux, Paulhan, Robinson, Caudron, Benoit, Rugère), the winner being Fischer on a Henry Farman biplane.

**The first of the great flying days at Hendon** was held on 20 April 1912, when approximately 15 000 spectators paid to gain admission to the 6d, 1s and 2s 6d enclosures.

**The first completed crossing from Great Britain to Ireland by aeroplane** was achieved by Englishman Denys Corbett Wilson on 22 April 1912, flying across the St Georges Channel.

**The first recognized flight in an aeroplane with a fully enclosed cabin for the pilot** was made by A. V. Roe on 1 May 1912, in his Avro Type F.

**The first American woman to be killed in an aeroplane accident** was Julie Clark of Denver, Colorado, whose Curtiss biplane struck a tree on 17 June 1912 at Springfield, Illinois, and turned turtle. She had qualified for her Pilot's Certificate on 19 May 1912.

**The first crossing of the English Channel by an aeroplane with a pilot and two passengers** was made on 4 August 1912 by W. B. Rhodes Moorhouse (later, as a Lt in the Royal Flying Corps, the first British airman to be awarded the Victoria Cross, on 26 April 1915) who, accompanied by his wife and a friend, flew a Breguet tractor biplane from Douai, France, via Boulogne and Dungeness, to Bethersden, near Ashford, Kent, where they crashed in bad weather. Nobody was hurt.

**The first man to fly underneath all the Thames bridges in London** between Tower Bridge and Westminster was F. K. McClean who, flying the Short S.33 pusher biplane from Harty Ferry, Isle of Sheppey, on 10 August 1912, passed between the upper and lower spans of Tower Bridge, and then underflew all the remaining bridges to Westminster where he landed on the river. No regulations forbade this escapade, but the police instructed McClean to taxi all the way back to Shadwell Basin before mooring! On the return trip the aeroplane side-slipped soon after take-off and damaged one of the floats after hitting a barge. The machine was then towed into Shadwell Dock and dismantled for the return by road to Eastchurch.

Left  *Frank McClean passes between the spans of Tower Bridge.*

Right  Le Grand, *the first four-engined aeroplane to fly. (Sikorsky Aircraft)*

**The number of Pilots' Certificates which had been awarded in the world by the end of 1912** was 2490, though the number of actual pilots was slightly smaller as some had been awarded certificates in more than one country. One or two others had received certificates in countries which were not members of the Fédération Aéronautique Internationale. The massive superiority of France at this time is evident:

| | | | | | |
|---|---|---:|---|---|---:|
| 1 | France | 966 | 10 | Holland | 26 |
| 2 | Great Britain | 382 | 11 | Argentine | |
| 3 | Germany | 345 | | Republic | 15 |
| 4 | United States | | 12 | Spain | 15 |
| | of America | 193 | 13 | Sweden | 10 |
| 5 | Italy | 186 | 14 | Denmark | 8 |
| 6 | Russia | 162 | 15 | Hungary | 7 |
| 7 | Austria | 84 | 16 | Norway | 5 |
| 8 | Belgium | 58 | 17 | Egypt | 1 |
| 9 | Switzerland | 27 | | | |
| | | | | Total | 2490 |

**The first Schneider Trophy Contest** (more correctly titled 'La Coupe d'Aviation Maritime Jacques Schneider'), was included as one item of the second international Hydro-aeroplane Meeting held at Monaco during the two weeks beginning 3 April 1913. It created initially little interest, with only seven entries for the first contest, reduced to four starters after the eliminating trials. The course consisted of twenty-eight 10 km laps and this 1913 contest, flown on 16 April, was won by Maurice Prévost flying a 160 hp Gnome-powered Deperdussin. Second was late-starter Roland Garros, flying a Morane-Saulnier monoplane powered by an 80 hp Gnome engine.

**The first non-stop aeroplane flight between England and Germany** was made by Gustav Hamel on 17 April 1913, flying a military-type Blériot XI monoplane between Dover and Cologne in a time of 4 h 18 min.

**The first four-engined aeroplane to fly** was the *Le Grand* ('The Great One', known also as *Russky Vityaz* or Russian Knight) biplane designed, and first flown on 13 May 1913 at St Petersburg, by Igor Sikorsky, then Head of the Aeronautical Department of the Russian Baltic Railway Car Factory at Petrograd. It had a wing span of over 92 ft (28 m) and was powered by four 100 hp Argus engines, originally mounted in tandem pairs but later in all-tractor configuration (from June). The first flight lasted under ten minutes. From *Le Grand* was evolved the Ilya Mourometz, which became the **first four-engined bomber to see active service.**

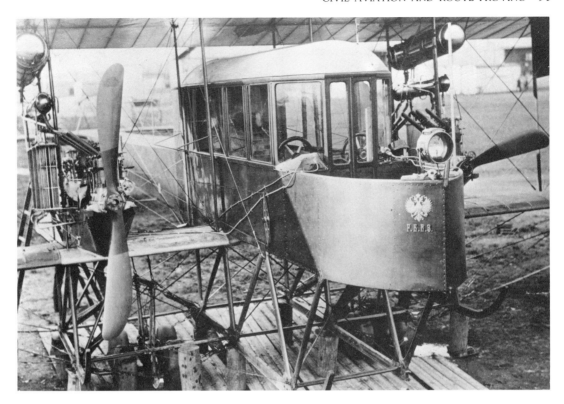

**The first major British competition for seaplanes** was the *Daily Mail* Hydro-Aeroplane Trial, started on 16 August 1913. The regulations stated a specified course round Britain, involving a distance to be flown of 1540 miles (2478 km) by an all-British aircraft before 30 August. Four aircraft were entered, but Samuel Cody was killed in a crash at Laffan's Plain on 7 August. F. K. McClean withdrew his Short S.68 due to engine trouble, and the Radley-England Waterplane was scratched for the same reason. This left Harry Hawker, accompanied by his mechanic, H. A. Kauper, as the only contender. He left the water at Southampton at 11.47 h, in a Sopwith three-seater tractor biplane which was powered by a 100 hp Green six-cylinder inline engine. The route was from Southampton via Ramsgate, Yarmouth, Scarborough, Aberdeen, Cromarty, Oban, Dublin, Falmouth and back to Southampton. After an abortive attempt, which ended at Yarmouth owing to a cracked engine cylinder, Hawker took off again from Southampton on 25 August. He managed to fly round the course as far as Dublin when, just before alighting on the water, his foot slipped off the rudder-bar and the aircraft struck the water and broke up. The *Daily Mail* prize of £5000 was not awarded, but Hawker received £1000 as consolation.

**The first pilot in the world to perform a loop** was Lt Nesterov of the Imperial Russian Army who, flying a Nieuport Type IV monoplane, performed the stunt at Kiev on 27 August 1913.

**The first pilot to fly inverted in sustained flight** (as distinct from becoming inverted during the course of the looping manoeuvre) was Adolphe Pégoud who, on 21 September 1913, flew a Blériot monoplane inverted at Buc, France. Notwithstanding the above definition, Pégoud's manoeuvre involved two 'halves' of a loop, in that he assumed the inverted position by means of a half-loop, and after sustained inverted flight recovered by means of a 'pull-through'. He thus did not resort to a roll or half-roll, which manoeuvre had not apparently been achieved at this time. As a means of acclimatizing himself for the ordeal of inverted flight, Pégoud had had his Blériot mounted inverted upon trestles and had remained strapped in the cockpit for periods of up to 20 min at a time!

**The first air crossing of the Mediterranean** was achieved on 23 September 1913 by a Morane-Saulnier monoplane piloted by Roland Garros, who flew 453 miles (730 km) from Saint-Raphaël, France, to Bizerte, Tunisia, in 7 h 53 min.

**The first British aeroplane to beat all comers in a major international competitive event** was the Sopwith Tabloid. Designed as a small, fast biplane scout aircraft, it first flew in the autumn of 1913. Official tests at Farnborough on 29 November 1913 showed it had exceptional performance, with a maximum rate of climb of 1200 ft (366 m)/min and a maximum speed of 92 mph (148 km/h). Its outstanding competitive success was its victory in the second contest for the Schneider Trophy held at Monaco on 20 April 1914 when, equipped as a floatplane, the aircraft was flown by Howard Pixton over the 280 km course at an average speed of 86.78 mph (139.66 km/h). After completing the race, Pixton continued for two extra laps to establish a new world speed record for seaplanes at 86.6 mph (139.37 km/h) over a measured 300 km course.

**The first flight from France to Egypt** was accomplished by Jules Védrines in a Blériot powered by an 80 hp Gnôme engine, between 20 November and 29 December 1913. Setting out from Nancy, France, his route was via Würzburg, Prague, Vienna, Belgrade, Sofia, Constantinople, Tripoli (Syria), Jaffa and Cairo.

**The first scheduled airline using aeroplanes** was the St Petersburg–Tampa Airboat Line, which started its operations on 1 January 1914, flying between St Petersburg and Tampa, Florida. The aircraft was a Benoist flying-boat piloted by Anthony Jannus. The operation lasted four months.

**The first flight across the North Sea by an aeroplane** was achieved by the Norwegian pilot Tryggve Gran flying a Blériot monoplane on 30 July 1914.

**The last aviation sporting events to be held in Britain before the outbreak of the First World War** took place at Hendon on 3 August 1914. They consisted of a cross-country and a speed handicap race, the former being won by R. J. Lillywhite, the latter by the American W. L. Brock.

The first flight from Paris to Berlin was made by Daucourt and Roux. In an attempt to also be the first to fly from France to Egypt, they left Issy on 20 October 1913 in a Borel monoplane. The journey ended with Daucourt alone crashing in the Taurus mountains on 26 November, by which time Jules Védrines had begun his successful bid.

**NACA**, the National Advisory Committee for Aeronautics, was founded in America on 3 March 1915.

**The first American forest fire to be observed by aeroplane** is thought to have been one blazing in Wisconsin, on 22 June 1915.

**The first British airline company to be registered** was Aircraft Transport and Travel Ltd, in London on 5 October 1916 by George Holt Thomas.

**Official carriage of mail by aeroplane in Italy** began on 22 May 1917, when military flights started between the cities of Turin and Rome.

**The first French mail to be carried by aeroplane** was flown between Paris, Le Mans and St Nazaire on 17 August 1917. A regular service was established thereafter.

**The first variable-incidence variable-geometry aeroplane in the world** was the Swedish Pålson Type 1 single-seat sporting aircraft of 1918–19. It is said that the aircraft featured a system of cranks to alter the position of the biplane's top wing as well as its angle of incidence as a means of achieving optimum lift/drag in cruising flight. It is not known what success attended flight trials (if any).

**The first scheduled regular international airmail service in the world** was inaugurated between Vienna and Kiev, via Kraków, Lvóv and Proskurov on 11 March 1918. The service was principally for military mail and was operated with Hansa-Brandenburg CI biplanes, continuing until November 1918.

**The first air crossing of the Andes** was achieved by the Argentine army pilot Teniente Luis C. Candelaria, flying a Morane-Saulnier parasol monoplane on 13 April 1918 from Zapala, Argentina, to Cunço, Chile, a distance of approximately 124 miles (200 km). The maximum altitude was about 13 000 ft (4000 m). Candelaria had attended the fifth military flying course at El Palomar which commenced in September 1916.

*First US experimental airmail service, begun on 15 May 1918 by the US Army Signal Corps. (US National Archives)*

**The first experimental airmail service in the USA** was flown by US Army Signal Corps Curtiss JN-4 and Standard J aircraft on 15 May 1918, between Washington, DC, and New York City. Lt Torrey H. Webb was the first pilot.

**The first official airmail flight in Canada** was flown on 24 June 1918 in a Curtiss JN-4 from Montreal to Toronto by Capt Brian A. Peck, RAF, accompanied by Corp Mathers.

**The first flight from England to Egypt** was accomplished by Maj A. S. MacLaren and Brig Gen A. E. Borton, flying a Handley Page O/400 bomber, between 28 July and 8 August 1918.

**The first flight from Egypt to India** was accomplished by Capt Ross M. Smith, Brig Gen A. E. Borton, Maj Gen W. Salmond and crew of a Handley Page O/400, between 29 November and 12 December 1918. Their journey took them from Heliopolis to Karachi.

**The first US Army coast-to-coast flight across the USA** was made by four Curtiss JN-4 Jennies between 4 and 22 December 1918. The points spanned were San Diego and Jacksonville.

**The first passenger and mail services between London and Paris** were initiated on 10 January 1919 by No. 2 (Communications) Squadron, RAF. Aircraft used were Airco (de Havilland) DH4As, which were DH4s modified to provide enclosed accommodation for two passengers. This service, intended for communications to and from the Peace Conference at Versailles, was terminated in September 1919.

**The first sustained commercial daily passenger service** was by Deutsche Luft-Reederei, which operated between Berlin and Weimar, Germany, from 5 February 1919. Aircraft used on the service were five-seat AEG biplanes and two-seat DFWs. The 120 mile (193 km) flight took 2 h 18 min.

**The first airline passenger flight between Paris and London** was made on 8 February 1919 by a Farman F60 Goliath, owned by the Farman brothers and piloted by Lucien Bossoutrot. As civil flying was not then permitted in the UK, the token payload consisted of military passengers, who flew from Toussus le Noble to Kenley. The flight is not recognized as a genuine scheduled operation.

*Farman F60 Goliath on the historic first Paris–London airline passenger flight. (Air France)*

**The first purely commercial aircraft to be built for passenger carrying in Britain after the First World War**, one of the first new civil types in the world, was the de Havilland DH16, the prototype of which flew for the first time in March 1919. The type entered service with Aircraft Transport and Travel Ltd in May. Altogether, nine DH16s were

*Deutsche Luft-Reederei five-seat AEG JII biplane airliner. (Lufthansa Archiv)*

built by June 1920; the first six were powered by the 320 hp Rolls-Royce Eagle VIII engine; the others had a 450 hp Napier Lion engine. Accommodation was for four passengers. The last DH16 was withdrawn from use in August 1923.

**The first American international airmail** was inaugurated between Seattle, Washington, and Victoria, British Columbia, Canada, by the Hubbard Air Service on 3 March 1919, using a Boeing Model CL-4S aircraft. The service was regularized by contract on 14 October 1920.

**The first sustained regular (not daily) international service for commercial passengers** was opened between Paris and Brussels by the Farman brothers on 22 March 1919. The fare for the 2 h 50 min flight was 365 francs. The pilot was again Lucien Bossoutrot. **The first Customs examination of passengers** took place at Brussels after the third of the weekly flights, on 6 April.

**Civil flying in Britain restarted**, after the First World War, on 1 May 1919, following publication of the Air Navigation Regulations.

**The first British aeroplane to carry civil markings** (K-100) was a de Havilland DH6 in 1919. It was sold to the Marconi Wireless Telegraph Co. Ltd, and used for radio trials; it became the second aircraft entered on the British Civil Register (as G-EAAB; see below).

**The first British civil aeroplane** (i.e. the first on the British Civil Register proper) was a de Havilland DH9 (G-EAAA, previously C6054), operated as a mailplane by Aircraft Transport and Travel Ltd in mid-1919, between London and Paris.

**The first occasion on which newspapers were distributed by an aircraft on a daily basis** was in May 1919. A Fairey IIIC seaplane was used on a week-long experimental freighting service to distribute the *Evening News* from the Thames, near Westminster Bridge, to coastal towns in Kent. This service saved about two hours' distribution time.

**The first British Certificate of Airworthiness** was issued on 1 May 1919 to the Handley Page O/400 (F5414) which thereafter became registered as G-EAAF, owned by Handley Page Air Transport Ltd.

**The first transatlantic crossing by air** was achieved by the American Navy/Curtiss NC-4 flying-boat commanded by Lt Cdr A. C. Read between 8 May and 31 May 1919. Three flying-boats, the NC-1, NC-3 and NC-4, under the command of Cdr John H. Towers, had set out from Rockaway, New York, on 8 May. Only NC-4 completed the crossing, arriving at Plymouth, England, on 31 May. The total distance flown was 3925 miles (6315 km) in 57 h 16 min flying time, at a speed of 68 mph (110 km/h). Both NC-1 and

NC-3 were forced down on the sea short of the Azores, and NC-1 sank, its crew being rescued. NC-3, with Cdr Towers aboard, taxied the remaining 200 miles (320 km) to the Azores.

**The first practical light aeroplane to be produced in Britain after the First World War** was the Avro 534 Baby. The prototype crashed after its first take-off on 10 May 1919, but its 35 hp Green water-cooled engine was salvaged and installed in the second aircraft, which won the handicap section of the Aerial Derby on 21 June 1919.

**The first regular civil air service in England** was started by A. V. Roe and Co. on 10 May 1919 and discontinued on 30 September 1919. Using three-seat Avro aircraft, services were flown from Alexander Park, Manchester, to Southport, and also to Blackpool. One hundred and ninety-four scheduled flights were made during this period; the cost of a one-way flight was four guineas.

**The first stage of a planned US transcontinental airmail service** was inaugurated on 15 May 1919, between Chicago and Cleveland. Realizing that only a really long air route would show any advantage over surface transportation in terms of journey time, the US Post Office had purchased more than 125 ex-military aircraft, mostly de Havilland DH4Ms, with which it hoped to carry airmail between New York and San Francisco at the standard first class surface rate of 2 cents per ounce. The final link from Omaha to Sacramento, over the Rockies, was proved practicable on 8 September 1920. After months of careful planning, **the first coast-to-coast airmail service in the USA** left San Francisco at 04.30 h on 22 February 1921 and arrived at Mineola, Long Island, New York, at 16.50 h the following day. It was carried from San Francisco to North Platte, Nebraska, by a succession of pilots. At North Platte it was taken over by a pilot named Jack Knight, flying one of the open-cockpit DH4Ms. When he reached Omaha, weather conditions along the route were so bad that the pilot scheduled to fly the next stage to Chicago had not put in an appearance. So Knight carried on through the darkness to Chicago, over unfamiliar country, becoming a national hero for 'saving the mail service'. A system of lighting for safer flying by night was installed along part of the route in 1923. Regular transcontinental night mail flights were inaugurated on 1 July 1924.

Navy-Curtiss NC-4 flying boat, the first aircraft to make a transatlantic crossing (US Navy)

**The first post-war aviation event to be held in Britain** took place at Hendon on 7 June 1919, when Lt G. R. Hicks won a cross-country handicap race flying an Avro 504K.

Capt John Alcock and Lt Arthur Whitten Brown. (Aer Lingus)

**The first non-stop air crossing of the Atlantic** was accomplished on 14–15 June 1919 by Capt John Alcock and Lt Arthur Whitten Brown who flew in a Vickers Vimy bomber from St John's, Newfoundland, to Clifden, County Galway, Ireland. Powered by two Rolls-Royce engines, the Vimy was equipped with long-range fuel tanks and achieved a coast-to-coast time of 15 h 57 min. Total flying time was 16 h 27 min. Both Alcock and Brown were knighted in recognition of this achievement; Sir John Alcock, as Chief Test Pilot of Vickers, was killed on 18 December 1919 in a flying accident caused by bad weather near Rouen, France.

**The world's first purpose-built all-metal commercial transport aircraft** was flown in Germany. This was the F13 designed by Hugo Junkers, the prototype of which took to the air on 25 June

*Alcock and Brown's Vimy leaves Newfoundland on the historic first ever non-stop air crossing of the Atlantic. (Aer Lingus)*

1919. Eventually, 322 were built up to 1932. Among the first to order the aircraft were SCADTA of Colombia and the US Post Office. Wing span was 58 ft 2¾ in (17.75 m), length with a 185 hp BMW engine 31 ft 6 in (9.60 m), and cruising speed was 87 mph (140 km/h).

**The first London airport at which customs clearance could be obtained for outward bound flights** was at Hounslow, Middlesex, in operation from July 1919.

**The first non-stop flight between Rome and Paris** was made on 14 July 1919 by an Italian Fiat BR light bomber.

**The first flight across the Canadian Rocky Mountains**, and also **the first airmail flight across the Rockies**, was made on 7 August 1919 in a Curtiss Jenny flown by Capt Ernest C. Hoy. He flew from Vancouver to Calgary via Lethbridge in 16 h 42 min.

**The first two women passengers to fly on an airline service between England and France**, on 26 August 1919, were carried in an aircraft of Handley Page Transport.

**The first scheduled daily international commercial airline flight anywhere in the world** was from London to Paris on 25 August 1919. It was made in a de Havilland DH16 flown by Cyril Patteson of Aircraft Transport and Travel Ltd, which took off from Hounslow with four passengers and landed at Le Bourget, Paris, 2 h 30 min later. The fare was £21 for the one-way crossing.

**The first Schneider Trophy Contest to take place off the British coast** was that flown at Bournemouth, Hampshire, on 10 September 1919. Fog turned the event into chaos and it was eventually abandoned. Guido Janello of Italy completed 11 laps, but as there was doubt concerning one of his turning points it was not allowed to count as a victory. As a gesture, Italy was asked to organize the next event. The 1919 contest at Bournemouth was the first in which an aircraft was involved that had been especially prepared by R. J. Mitchell, a 24-year-old recruit of the Supermarine Company.

**The first Dutch national airline**, KLM (Royal Dutch Airlines), was founded on 7 October 1919. It is the oldest airline in the world still operating under its original name.

**The first airline to provide food on its services** was Handley Page Transport, on 11 October 1919, when it introduced lunch baskets at a cost of 3 shillings each.

**The first American international scheduled passenger air service** was inaugurated on 1 November 1919 by Aeromarine West Indies Airways between Key West, Florida, and Havana, Cuba. On 1 November 1920 the airline was awarded the first US foreign airmail contract.

**The first flight from Britain to Australia** was completed between 12 November and 10 December 1919 by two Australian brothers, Capt Ross

Smith and Lt Keith Smith, with two other crew members. They set out from Hounslow, Middlesex, in a Vickers Vimy bomber powered by two Rolls-Royce Eagle engines, and flew to Darwin, a distance of 11 294 miles (18 175 km) in under 28 days with a Hounslow-Darwin flying time of 135 h 55 min. Their feat earned them the Australian government's prize of £10 000 ($40 000) and knighthoods. Sir Ross Smith was killed in a flying accident near Brooklands Aerodrome, England, on 13 April 1922. By tragic coincidence, both Sir Ross and Sir John Alcock (famous for his Atlantic crossing, see above) were killed in Vickers Viking amphibians.

**The first men to fly across Australia** were Capt H. N. Wrigley and Lt A. W. Murphy, from Melbourne to Darwin in a BE2e between 16 November and 12 December 1919 in 46 h flying time.

**The first Boeing commercial aircraft**, the B-1 flying-boat of its own design, made its maiden flight on 27 December 1919.

**The first aircraft with a practical form of retractable landing gear** was the Dayton-Wright RB Racer, designed and built to compete in the 1920 Gordon Bennett Aviation Cup Race.

**The first automatic pilot to be installed in a British commercial aircraft**, the Aveline Stabilizer, was fitted in a Handley Page O/10 during 1920.

**The Soviet Union's first internal airline service**, between Sarapul and Yekaterinburg, was flown during January 1920 by demilitarized *Ilya Mourometz* bombers.

Above   *Pilot Henri Biard aboard the Supermarine Sea Lion, the Schneider Trophy seaplane prepared by R. J. Mitchell for the 1919 contest off Bournemouth.*

**The first flight from Britain to South Africa** was made between 4 February and 20 March 1920 by Lt Col Pierre van Ryneveld and Sqn Ldr Christopher Quintin Brand. They set out from Brooklands in a Vickers Vimy bomber but crashed at Wadi Halfa, Sudan, while attempting an emergency landing. The South African government provided the pilots with another Vimy aircraft and after 11 days they set off again, only to crash at Bulawayo, Southern Rhodesia, on 6 March. Once again the government provided an aircraft, a war-surplus DH9, and on 17 March they set off again. Finally, on 20 March, they reached Wynberg Aerodrome, Cape Town. They received subsequently £5000 prize-money and were knighted by HM King George V.

**The first regular use of Croydon as London's air terminal** began on 29 March 1920. On that date the main airport facilities were transferred

Below   *Junkers F13, the first purpose-built all-metal airliner. (Lufthansa Archiv)*

from Hounslow, Middlesex, to Croydon—or Waddon, as the airport was known originally. It was opened officially on 31 March 1921.

**The first Australian commercial airline,** QANTAS (Queensland and Northern Territory Aerial Service) was registered on 16 November 1920 for air taxi and regular air services in Australia. The company's first chairman was Sir Fergus McMaster (1879–1950), and its first scheduled services began on 2 November 1922 with flights between Charlesville and Cloncurry, Queensland.

**The first Pulitzer Trophy Race** was flown on 25 November 1920 from Mitchell Field, Long Island, New York. It was won by Capt Corliss C. Moseley flying a Verville-Packard 600.

**The first fatal accident on a scheduled British commercial flight** occurred on 14 December 1920 when a Handley Page O/400 crashed soon after take-off in fog at Cricklewood, London. Pilot R. Bager, his engineer and two passengers were killed, but four other passengers escaped.

**The first solo coast-to-coast flight across the United States** was recorded between 21 and 24 February 1921 by Lt William D. Coney of the US Army Air Service. His route, from Rockwell Field, San Diego, to Jacksonville, Florida, was completed in a flying time of 22 h 27 min.

**The first and only Oxford versus Cambridge University Air Race ever staged** was flown on 16 July 1921 and resulted in a flyaway victory for Cambridge. Each team flew three SE5as and the 129 mile (208 km) course of three laps lay along the route from Hendon via Epping and Hertford, returning to Hendon. Cambridge gained maximum points by achieving the first three places, the fastest lap being flown at an average speed of 118.55 mph (190.79 km/h). One of the Oxford aircraft failed to complete the course.

**The first Air League Challenge Cup Race** was flown at Croydon on 17 September 1921. Because there were then so few civil aircraft available for competitive events, it was decided to award the cup initially to RAF teams. The first winners were a team from No. 24 Squadron, then based at RAF Kenley, Surrey.

**The first regular scheduled air services in Australia** were inaugurated by West Australian Airways on 5 December 1921.

**The first aircraft designed by the Soviet Union's Andrei N. Tupolev,** the ANT-1 light sporting monoplane, was flown for the first time during 1922.

**A South Atlantic flight attempt** was started on 13 March 1922 by Portuguese pilots Capt Gago Coutinho and Capt Sacadura Cabral. Taking off from Lisbon in a Fairey IIIC, they arrived in Brazil on 16 June in the Fairey IIID *Santa Cruz*, the original aircraft having been wrecked *en route*.

The four-man crew of the US Army Air Service Martin MB-1 bomber that circumnavigated the United States of America, November 1919. This is remembered as the 'Round the Rim' flight. (US Air Force)

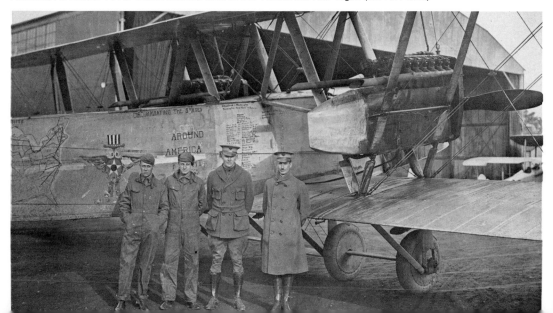

**The first air collision between airliners on scheduled flights** occurred on 7 April 1922, between a Daimler Airways de Havilland DH18 (G-EAWO) flown by Robin Duke from Croydon, and a Farman Goliath of Grands Express Aériens flown by M. Mier from Le Bourget. The two aircraft, which were following a road on a reciprocal course, collided over Thieuloy-Saint-Antoine 18 miles (29 km) north of Beauvais. All seven occupants were killed.

**The first civil airline night flight between France and England** was flown on the night of 9 June 1922 by a Farman Goliath of the French airline Grands Express Aériens.

**The first coast-to-coast crossing of the United States in a single day** was made by Lt James H. Doolittle who flew a modified DH4B from Pablo Beach, Florida, to Rockwell Field, San Diego, California, on 4 September 1922. Actual flying time to cover the 2163 miles (3480 km) was 21 h 19 min; elapsed time with a refuelling stop at Kelly Field, Texas, was 22 h 35 min.

**The first King's Cup Air Race**, over a course from Croydon, England, to Glasgow, Scotland, and return, was won during 8–9 September 1922 by Capt F. F. Barnard piloting a de Havilland DH4A.

**The first German aeroplane to land in the UK post-war** was a Dornier Komet four-passenger airliner (D-223) of Deutsche Luft-Reederei, which landed at Lympne Aerodrome, Kent, on 1 January 1923.

**The first variable-pitch aeroplane propeller**, designed by Turnbull in America, was demonstrated during 1923.

**The former Soviet Union's first state airline**, Dobrolet, was established during March 1923, its initial operations carried out with assistance from the Air Force.

**The first Czechoslovakian national airline**, Ceskoslovenske Statni Aerolinie (CSA), began its first operations on 1 March 1923.

**The first scheduled air service between London and Berlin** was inaugurated by Daimler Airways, in conjunction with interested German organizations, on 1 May 1923, with intermediate landings at Bremen and Hamburg.

**The first non-stop air crossing of the United States by an aeroplane** was achieved on 2–3 May 1923 by Lts O. G. Kelly and J. A. Macready, USAAS, in a Fokker T-2 aircraft. Taking off from Roosevelt Field, Long Island, at 12.36 h (Eastern Time) on 2 May, they arrived at Rockwell Field, San Diego, California, at 12.26 h (Pacific Time) on 3 May. They overflew Dayton, Ohio; Indianapolis, Indiana; St Louis, Missouri; Kansas City, Missouri; Tucumcari, New Mexico; and Wickenburg, Arizona. The distance flown, 2516 miles (4050 km), was covered in 26 h 50 min. Kelly and Macready had also established a new world endurance record for aeroplanes, on 16–17 April 1923, flying the Fokker T-2 a distance of 2518 miles (4052 km) over a measured course in 36 h 5 min.

**The first Grosvenor Challenge Cup contest**, for British aircraft with engines of under 150 hp, was won on 23 June 1923 by Flt Lt W. H. Longton, RAF, flying a Sopwith Gnu.

**The first use of electric beacons mounted on the ground**, to provide flight directions for night flying operations, were introduced in the USA on 21 August 1923.

**The first light-plane competition held in Great Britain** was at Lympne, Kent, in October 1923, organized by the Royal Aero Club. The competition was for single-seat aircraft, and the prizes included £1000 offered by the *Daily Mail* and £500 by the Duke of Sutherland for the longest flight on one Imperial gallon of petrol made by an aircraft with an engine not exceeding 750 cc capacity. The prize money for the one-gallon flight was shared between Flt Lt Walter Longton, who flew an English Electric Wren, and Jimmy H. James in an ANEC monoplane, both flying 87.5 miles (140.8 km). Another prize of £500, offered by the Abdulla Company for the highest speed over two laps, was won in a Parnall Pixie by Capt Norman Macmillan, who attained an average speed of 76.1 mph (122.5 km/h).

**The world's first aerial crop-dusting company**, Huff Daland Dusters, was formed at Macon, Georgia, in 1924. It became named Delta Air Service, subsequently Delta Air Lines, when passenger services were initiated during 1929.

**The first British national airline**, Imperial Airways, was formed on 1 April 1924. This was

Above  *A winner at the Lympne 'Motor Glider' competition of 1923 was the English Electric Wren. Many of the aircraft, though remarkable and economical, were nevertheless impractical.*

Right  *Douglas DWC* Chicago, *one of two Air Service aircraft to complete the 1924 round-the-world flight.*

the manifestation of the British government's determination to develop air transport, and the company was to receive preferential air subsidies, having acquired the businesses of British Marine Air Navigation Co., Daimler Airways, Handley Page Transport and Instone Air Lines. Its fleet consisted of seven DH34s, two Sea Eagles, three Handley Page W8bs and one Vickers Vimy.

**The first round-Australia flight** was made by Wing Cdr S. J. Goble and Flying Off I. E. McIntyre in a Fairey III-D during 6 April–19 May 1924. Distance covered was 8568 miles (13 790 km).

**The first successful round-the-world flight** was accomplished by two Douglas DWCs (Douglas World Cruisers) between 4 April and 28 Septem-

ber 1924. Four DWCs set out from Seattle, Washington, and two of them circumnavigated the world. These were No. 2, named *Chicago*, crewed by Lt Lowell H. Smith and Lt Leslie P. Arnold, and No. 4, *New Orleans*, with Lt Erik Nelson and Lt John Harding Jr.

The total mileage by each of the two aircraft which completed the historic flight was 27 553 miles (44 340 km) and the elapsed time 175 days. The flying time was given as 371 h 11 min. It should be noted that this flight included the first staged crossing of the Pacific Ocean as well as the first staged east–west crossing of the North Atlantic. (Two of these aircraft are preserved to this day, one at the Smithsonian Institution in Washington, the other in the Air Force Museum at Wright–Patterson Air Force Base.)

**The first all-metal aircraft to be built in the former Soviet Union**, the ANT-2, made its maiden flight on 26 May 1924. Designed by Andrei N. Tupolev, its method of construction was based on that of the German Junkers types.

**The first Light Aeroplane Competition for two-seat aircraft**, organized by the Royal Aero Club, was held at Lympne, Kent, between 27 September and 4 October 1924. Lightest aircraft in the competition was the Hawker Cygnet, which had an empty weight of 373 lb (169 kg). Two examples were built, G-EBMB and G-EBJH, the former powered originally by a 34 hp British Anzani two-cylinder engine, the latter with a 34 hp ABC Scorpion, also of two cylinder configuration. The Cygnet was also Sydney Camm's first design for the H. G. Hawker Engineering Company. Winner of the competition, and the Air Ministry's £3000 prize, was Mr Piercy with the Beardmore Wee Bee monoplane, powered by a 32 hp Bristol Cherub engine.

The prototype of the de Havilland DH60 Moth, a small **two-seat biplane that revolutionized private flying** and was the true starting point of the flying club movement, was flown for the first time on 22 February 1925.

Henry Ford initiated **the first regular US air freight service**, linking Detroit, Michigan and Chicago, on 13 April 1925.

**The first three-engined all-metal monoplane transport in the world to enter commercial airline service** was the Junkers G 23, four of which served with Swedish Air Lines (AB Aerotransport) on the Malmo–Hamburg–Amsterdam route from 15 May 1925. This aircraft, built in Germany and Sweden, provided the basis for the later and famous Junkers Ju 52/3m.

**The first aeroplane flight between London and Cape Town** was made by Alan Cobham, with his mechanic A. B. Elliott and cine photographer B. W. G. Emmott, in the second de Havilland DH50 that was built (G-EBFO). They left Croydon on 16 November 1925 and reached Cape Town on 17 February 1926. Cobham landed back at Croydon after the 16,000 mile (25 750 km) round trip on 13 March 1926. Three months later, on 30 June, Cobham and Elliott took off from the River Medway in the same aircraft, converted into a seaplane for the largely overwater flight to Australia and back. G-EBFO returned to a triumphant welcome on the Thames, at Westminster, on 1 October. The success was marred by the death of Elliott, who had been killed by a stray bullet fired by a bedouin while flying over the desert between Baghdad and Bazra on the outward leg. Cobham was knighted for these flights, which pioneered future Empire air routes.

Flying a Dornier Wal flying-boat, Commandante Franco achieved **the first staged east–west air crossing of the South Atlantic** between 22 January and 10 February 1926.

Left   *Sir Alan Cobham's de Havilland DH50, returning for a triumphant welcome.*

Fokker F.VIIA-3m *Josephine Ford* on exhibition.

**The first commercial airmail flights in the USA** were started on 6 April 1926 by Varney Speed Lines. These were flown between Pasco and Elko using Swallow biplanes.

**The first aeroplane flight over the North Pole** was accomplished by Lt Cdr Richard E. Byrd (USN) and Floyd Bennett, in the Fokker F.VIIA-3m *Josephine Ford* on 9 May 1926. The total distance flown was 1600 miles (2575 km).

**The first successful passenger aircraft built in America** was the Ford 4-AT Trimotor, which first flew on 11 June 1926. Powered by three 220 hp engines, it could accommodate 10 passengers and had a cruising speed of 105 mph (169 km/h). From 1926 to 1933, Ford built around 200 Trimotors, designated from 3-AT to 7-AT, and this aircraft was operated by many airlines.

**The first known use of aircraft for violence in civil crime** occurred on 12 November 1926, when three small bombs (which failed to explode) were dropped from an aeroplane on to a farmhouse in Williamson County, Illinois. The raid was carried out by a member of the Shelton gang, against members of the rival Birger gang, in a Prohibition feud involving illicit supplies of beer and rum.

**The first light aeroplane flight from London to Karachi**, India, was flown by T. Neville Stack in the de Havilland DH60 Moth G-EBMO (Cirrus II engine), accompanied by B. S. Leete in a similar aircraft, G-EBKU, between 15 November 1926 and 8 January 1927.

**The first non-stop solo air crossing of the North Atlantic** was made by Capt Charles Lindbergh during 20–21 May 1927 in the Ryan NYP high-wing monoplane *Spirit of St Louis*. Taking off from Long Island, New York, on 20 May 1927, his epic flight to Paris of 3610 miles (5810 km) was accomplished in 33 h 39 min at an average speed of 107.5 mph (173 km/h).

**The first demonstration of an outside loop manoeuvre** was by American James Doolittle, on 25 May 1927, flying an Army Curtiss.

**The first flight from New York to Germany** was made by Americans Clarence Chamberlin and Charles Levine, leaving on 4 June 1927 in the Wright-Bellanca *Columbia*. They covered 3911 miles (6294 km).

Richard E. Byrd as a Lt Cdr in 1925, a few months before his first epic polar flight. (US Navy)

**The world's first charter flight,** flown in both directions between Amsterdam and Jakarta, was completed between 15 June and 23 July 1927. The Fokker F.VIIA (H-NADP) was chartered by an American, W. van Lear Black, and flown a total out and return distance of 18 710 miles (30 111 km) under the command of Capt G. J. Geysendorffer.

**The first non-stop flight between the United States and Hawaii** was achieved by Lts Albert F. Hegenberger and Lester J. Maitland during 28–29 June 1927. Flying the US Army Fokker C-2 monoplane *Bird of Paradise*, they covered the 2407 miles (3874 km) from Oakland, California, to Honolulu, Hawaii, in 25 h 30 min.

Above   *Charles Lindbergh.*
Below   Spirit of St Louis.

**The first flight by a light aircraft from London to Cape Town,** South Africa, was accomplished by Lt R. R. Bentley, SAAF, flying the de Havilland DH60X Moth *Dorys*. Taking off on 1 September 1927, the flight was completed on the 28th of the month.

**The first non-stop air crossing of the South Atlantic by an aeroplane** was made on 14–15 October 1927. Capt Dieudonne Costes and Lt Cdr Le Brix flew the Breguet XIX *Nungesser-Coli* from Saint-Louis, Senegal, to Port Natal, Brazil, a distance of 2125 miles (3420 km) in 19 h 50 min.

**The first air service by Pan American Airways** was inaugurated on 19 October 1927 on the 90 mile (145 km) route between Key West, Florida, and Havana, Cuba.

**The first solo flight from England to Australia** was made by Sqn Ldr H. J. L. ('Bert') Hinkler in the Avro 581 Avian light aircraft prototype G-EBOV. Flying from Croydon to Darwin, between 7 and 22 February 1928, his 11 005 mile (17 711 km) route was via Rome, Malta, Tobruk, Ramleh, Basra, Jask, Karachi, Cawnpore, Calcutta, Rangoon, Victoria Point, Singapore, Bandoeng and Bima. His aircraft was placed on permanent exhibition in the Brisbane Museum.

**The first flight by a woman from South Africa to England** was achieved by Lady Heath in an Avro Avian III, flying from Cape Town to Croydon between 12 February and 17 May 1928. This was also **the first solo flight from South Africa to Britain** and, en route, **the first solo flight from the Cape to Cairo.**

*Passengers prepare to board a Fokker F.VIIA-3m before Pan Am's first scheduled passenger flight on 16 January 1928, between Key West and Havana. Non-scheduled services had begun in October 1927. (Pan American World Airways)*

**The first solo return flight by a woman between London and South Africa** was achieved by Lady Bailey who, in a de Havilland Moth (G-EBSF), left London on 9 March 1928. This aircraft was damaged beyond repair at Tabora a month later, but the pilot completed her flight to the Cape in a replacement Moth, G-EBTG. She subsequently toured round Africa before returning to London on 16 January 1929.

**The first east–west air crossing of the North Atlantic**, between Baldonnel, Ireland, and Greenly Island, Labrador, was recorded during 12–13 April 1928. This was achieved by Hermann Köhl, the Irish Capt J. Fitzmaurice and Baron von Hunefeld, flying the Junkers W33 *Bremen*.

**The first complete crossing of the Arctic polar basin by air** was achieved by Capt G. H. Wilkins and Lt Carl B. Eielson flying a Lockheed Vega monoplane. Taking off from Point Barrow, Alaska, on 15 April 1928, they were within half an hour's flying time of their destination when they were forced by poor weather to land on Dead Man's Island. There they sheltered in the cabin of

their aircraft for five days before taking off and landing at Spitzbergen on 21 April.

**The Australian Flying Doctor Service** was inaugurated on 15 May 1928, using the joint services of the Australian Inland Mission and QANTAS at Cloncurry. The first aircraft was the de Havilland DH50 *Victory*, modified to accommodate two stretchers; its first pilot was Dr K. H. Vincent Welsh. The founder of the service was the Rev. J. Flynn, OBE.

**The first true transpacific flight**, discounting that of the Douglas World Cruisers, was that accomplished by the Fokker F.VIIB-3m *Southern Cross*, flown by Capt Charles Kingsford Smith and C. T. P. Ulm (pilots), accompanied by Harry Lyon (navigator) and James Warner (radio operator). Taking off from Oakland Field, California, on 31 May 1928, their route was via Honolulu, Hawaii, and Suva, Fiji, landing at Eagle Farm, Brisbane, on 9 June 1928. The flight covered 7389 miles (11 890 km), with a flying time of 83 h 38 min. The *Southern Cross* has been preserved and is displayed at Eagle Farm Airport. It was **the first aircraft ever to land in Fiji**.

**The first woman to fly over the Atlantic** was American Amelia Earhart, on 18–19 June 1928. She was a passenger in the Lockheed Vega *Friend-*

*ship*, crewed by Wilmer Stultz and Slim Gordon, taking 20 hours 49 min to fly from Harbour Grace, Newfoundland, to Burry Port, Wales, Great Britain.

**The first air crossing of the Tasman Sea** was made by the *Southern Cross* during 10–11 September 1928. Again piloted by Charles Kingsford Smith and C. T. P. Ulm, the aircraft flew from Richmond Aerodrome, Sydney, to Wigram, Christchurch, New Zealand.

**The first commercial air route between London and India** was inaugurated by Imperial Airways on 30 March 1929. The route was from London to Basle, Switzerland, by air (Armstrong Whitworth Argosy aircraft); Basle to Genoa, Italy, by train; Genoa to Alexandria, Egypt, by air (Short Calcutta flying-boats); and Alexandria to Karachi, India, by air (de Havilland DH66 Hercules aircraft). The total journey from Croydon to Karachi occupied seven days, for which the single fare was £130. The stage travelled by train was necessary as Italy forbade the air entry of British aircraft, an embargo which lasted several years and substantially frustrated Imperial Airways' efforts to develop the Far East route.

**The first non-stop flight from Great Britain to India** was accomplished by Sqn Ldr A. G. Jones Williams and Flt Lt N. H. Jenkins (pilot and navigator respectively) between 24 and 26 April 1929. Flying from Cranwell, Lincolnshire, to Karachi, India, in the Fairey Long Range Monoplane J9479, they covered the 4130 miles (6647 km) in 50 h 37 min. It had been intended to fly to Bangalore to establish a world distance record but the attempt was abandoned owing to headwinds. Another Fairey Long Range Monoplane, K1991, crewed by Sqn Ldr O. R. Gayford and Flt Lt G. E. Nicholetts, made **the first non-stop flight from England to South Africa**, between 6 and 8 Feb-

ruary 1933. The total distance covered from Cranwell to Walvis Bay, South-West Africa, was 5309 miles (8544 km), which was completed in 57 h 25 min and set a new world distance record.

**The first flight over the South Pole** was made during 28–29 November 1929 by the Ford 4-AT Trimotor *Floyd Bennett*. Its crew was Cdr R. E. Byrd, US Navy, with Bernt Balchen (pilot), Harold June (radio operator) and Ashley McKinley (survey).

**The first solo flight by a woman from Great Britain to Australia** was achieved by Amy Johnson, between 5 and 24 May 1930, flying the de Havilland DH60G Gipsy Moth *Jason* (G-AAAH) from Croydon to Darwin. This record remained unbeaten until 1934 when New Zealand airwoman Jean Batten, flying a de Havilland DH60M Moth (G-AARB) during the period 8–23 May 1934, took 14 d 22 h 30 min for the flight from Lympne, Kent, to Darwin, Australia, thus beating Amy Johnson's England–Australia record by more than four days.

**The Boeing Company's first commercial monoplane**, the Model 200 *Monomail*, made its first flight on 6 May 1930. This significant aeroplane, used as a mail/cargo carrier, introduced a cantilever low-set monoplane wing, retractable landing gear and other advanced features.

**The first airline stewardess** was Ellen Church, a nurse who, with Boeing Air Transport (later absorbed into United Air Lines), made her first flight, between San Francisco, California, and Cheyenne, Wyoming, on 15 May 1930.

*Fairey Long-Range Monoplane K1991, which made the first non-stop flight between England and South Africa in 1933.*

Right *Boeing Model 200 Monomail. (The Boeing Company)*

Below *The first air stewardesses, with Ellen Church third from left.*

The first east–west staged crossing of the North Atlantic in a flying-boat was achieved by a Dornier Wal piloted by Capt Wolfgang von Gronau. Taking off from the island of Sylt, on 18 August 1930, with co-pilot Edward Zimmer, Fritz Albrecht (radio) and Franz Hack (mechanic), a landing in New York harbour was made on 26 August.

The first lightplane flight around the world was achieved by Briton, Hon Mrs Victor Bruce, between 25 September 1930 and 20 February 1931. Flying the Blackburn Bluebird IV *Bluebird*, she made many stopovers, including Istanbul, Baghdad, Karachi, Rangoon, Hanoi, Hong Kong, Shanghai, Tokyo, Seattle, Vancouver, New York, Plymouth, Le Bourget and Croydon.

The first coast-to-coast all-air passenger service in the United States was inaugurated by Transcontinental and Western Air, between New York and Los Angeles, California, on 25 October 1930.

The first commercial air route between London and Central Africa was inaugurated on 28 February 1931 by Imperial Airways. The route lay from Croydon to Alexandria (using Argosy aircraft from Croydon to Athens, and Calcutta flying-boats from Athens to Alexandria via Crete), and from Cairo to Mwanza, on Lake Victoria (using Argosy aircraft). Passengers were taken only as far as Khartoum, mail being carried over the remainder of the route.

The first woman to fly solo from Brisbane, Australia, to London, England, was Australian Lores Bonney, flying a de Havilland DH60 Moth between 12 April and 21 June 1931.

A record round-the-world flight of 8 d 15 h 51 min was recorded between 23 June and 1 July 1931 by the Lockheed Vega *Winnie Mae*. Piloted by Wiley Post, with Harold Gatty as navigator, the flight from and to New York covered a distance of nearly 15 500 miles (24 945 km) in about 106 flying hours, following a route via Chester (UK), Berlin, Irkutsk (Soviet Union) and Alaska.

Flying her Puss Moth G-AAZV *Jason II*, Amy Johnson achieved a **flight from England to Japan in less than nine days**. Taking off from Lympne, Kent, on 28 July 1931, she arrived at Tokyo on 6 August in a total flying time of 79 h.

**The first non-stop flight from Japan to the United States (and as a corollary the first non-stop transpacific flight)** was achieved by Hugh Herndon Jr and Clyde E. Pangborn flying a Bellanca monoplane. Taking off from Samushiro Beach, some 300 miles (483 km) north of Tokyo, on 4 October 1931, they landed at Wenatchee, Washington, on 5 October after 41 h 13 min.

Landing at Stag Lane aerodrome on 16 January 1932 in the DH80A Puss Moth G-ABJO, Wg Cdr R. H. McIntosh and the Hon Mrs R. Westenra completed a journey to Africa, around the continent and back to London. During the course of this trip they recorded **the first British flight across the Sahara, and the first by a lightplane**.

**The first solo crossing of the North Atlantic by a woman** was achieved by the American pilot Miss Amelia Earhart (Mrs Putnam). Taking off from Harbor Grace, Newfoundland, in a Lockheed Vega monoplane on 20 May 1932, she landed at Londonderry, Northern Ireland, on the following day.

**The first east–west solo flight across the North Atlantic**, from Portmanock Strand north of Dublin to Pennfield Ridge, New Brunswick, was achieved by J. A. Mollison. Flying the DH80A Puss Moth *The Hearts Content* (G-ABXY), he took off on 18 August 1932, recording a flight time of 31 h 20 min.

**The first non-stop transcontinental flight by a woman across the United States**, from Los Angeles, California, to Newark, New Jersey, was achieved by Amelia Earhart in a Lockheed Vega on 25 August 1932.

**A Travel Air biplane with a steam engine power plant** was flown successfully in the United States during 1933. Its Besler two-cylinder double-acting vee engine developed 150 hp at a boiler pressure of 1200 lb/in² (84.37 kg/cm²).

**The true ancestor of modern airliners**, with all-metal structure, cantilever low wings and retractable landing gear, was the Boeing Model 247, the prototype of which was flown on 8 February 1933. A total of 75 was built. The major production version was the Model 247D, powered by two 550 hp Pratt & Whitney Wasp engines driving controllable-pitch propellers. Cruising speed with ten passengers and 400 lb (181 kg) of mail was 180 mph (304 km/h).

Landing at Port Natal, Brazil, on 9 February 1933, after a flight from Lympne, Kent, in the Puss Moth

Above   *Amelia Earhart with Mr McCallion, the first person to greet her after her solo Atlantic crossing. (Aer Lingus)*

Left   *Amelia Earhart's Lockheed Vega where it stopped after her transatlantic crossing, just feet from a hedge in Springfield, Londonderry. (Aer Lingus)*

Above *Mollison leaves Dublin on his solo east–west crossing of the North Atlantic in* The Hearts Content *(Syndication International)*

Right *Boeing Model 247, the first modern airliner.*

Below *The Marquess of Clydesdale's Westland PV-3 approaches Everest.*

*The Hearts Content*, J. A. Mollison had attained a remarkable series of achievements. He was the first pilot to make a solo flight between England and South America, the first to fly the South Atlantic solo from east to west, and the first to have made solo flights across both the North and South Atlantic.

**The first flights over Mount Everest** were made on 3 April 1933 by the Marquess of Clydesdale in a Westland PV-3, and by Flt Lt D. F. McIntyre piloting a Westland Wallace, each with one passenger.

**The Douglas DC-1 first flew** on 1 July 1933 at Clover Field, Santa Monica, California. Only one was built, flying mainly in TWA insignia. After service during the Spanish Civil War, it was written-off following a take-off accident near Malaga, Spain, in December 1940. From it were developed the famous DC-2 and DC-3, which established the reputation of Douglas as an airliner manufacturer.

**The first solo flight around the world** was achieved by Wiley Post between 15 and 22 July

Left  *In an attempt to fly non-stop from England to India, Sir Alan Cobham's Airspeed Courier used experimental in-flight refuelling techniques from a modified Handley Page W.10 tanker. Having taken off from Portsmouth on 24 September 1934, mechanical problems with the aircraft meant that the flight had to be abandoned at Malta. (Flight Refuelling Ltd)*

Below  *Wiley Post with his Vega* Winnie Mae.

1933, when he flew his Lockheed Vega monoplane, *Winnie Mae*, from Floyd Bennett Field, New York, for a distance of 15 596 miles (25 099 km) in 7 d 18 h 49 min. His route was via Berlin, Moscow, Irkutsk and Alaska, back to New York. Post later pioneered the development of an early pressure suit during high altitude flights in *Winnie Mae*. He was killed in a crash in 1935, together with the famous comedian/philosopher Will Rogers.

Indian National Airways began **the first daily air service in India** on 1 December 1933, with inauguration of a passenger, freight and mail service between Calcutta and Dacca.

**The first European airline to introduce air-hostesses to provide cabin service** was Swiss Air Transport. This occurred in 1934 when the 16-passenger Curtiss Condor was introduced into service, with Nelly Diener being the first hostess to don a uniform.

**The first regular internal airmail service in Great Britain** was started by Highland Airways on 29 May 1934. The de Havilland Dragon G-ACCE, flown by E. E. Fresson, carried 6000 letters on this first flight from Inverness to Kirkwall, and the service operated thereafter on every weekday.

**The first non-stop flight from Canada to England** was made during 8–9 August 1934 by L. G. Reid and J. R. Ayling, flying the de Havilland Dragon (G-ACJM) *Trail of the Caribou*. Their flight, from Wasaga Beach, Ontario, to Heston, Middlesex, took 30 h 50 min.

**The first 'trans-World' air race** was the MacRobertson Race from England to Australia which started on 20 October 1934. In March 1933 the Governing Director of MacRobertson Confectionery Manufacturers of Melbourne, Sir MacPherson Robertson, offered £15 000 in prize money for an air race to commemorate the centenary of the foundation of the State of Victoria. The race was won by one of three specially built de Havilland DH88 Comets. Charles W. A. Scott and Tom Campbell Black were first to cross the finishing line at Flemington Racecourse, Melbourne in the DH88 *Grosvenor House* (G-ACSS), having completed the 11 333 miles (18 239 km) from Mildenhall, Suffolk, in 70 h 54 min 18 s at an average speed of 158.9 mph (255.7 km/h). Second home in the Handicap Race was, surprisingly, the Douglas DC-2 *Uiver* (PH-AJU) passenger transport aircraft of the Dutch airline KLM, flown by K. D. Parmentier and J. J. Moll.

The first flight by an aeroplane from Australia to the United States was made in the Lockheed Altair *Lady Southern Cross* by Sir Charles Kingsford Smith accompanied by Capt P. G. Taylor. Taking off from Brisbane on 22 October 1934, their flight ended successfully at Oakland, California, on 4 November after staging via Fiji and Hawaii.

The first regular weekly airmail service between Britain and Australia, from London to Brisbane via Karachi and Singapore, began on 8 December 1934. The participating airlines were Imperial Airways, Indian Trans-Continental Airways and Qantas Empire Airways. Mail which left London on 8 December reached Brisbane on 21 December.

The first woman in the United States to pilot an airmail transport aircraft on regular scheduled operations was Helen Richey. Her first scheduled flight, in a Ford Trimotor from Washington, DC, to Detroit, Michigan, was flown on 31 December 1934.

The first solo flight by a woman from Honolulu, Hawaii, to the United States was made by Amelia Earhart during 11–12 January 1935. Flying a Lockheed Vega, she landed at Oakland, California, after a flight lasting 18 h 16 min.

A privately sponsored civil aircraft that led to one of Britain's main bomber types of the early war years was the Bristol 142. Ordered by Lord Rothermere of the *Daily Mail* as a six-passenger high-speed transport aircraft, at a cost of around £18 500, the 142 was first flown on 12 April 1935. Powered by two 650 hp Bristol Mercury engines, it proved to have a maximum speed of 307 mph (494 km/h). This was some 80 mph

*Grosvenor House, the first aircraft to cross the finishing line in the MacRobertson trans-World air race.*

(128 km/h) faster than the RAF's latest fighter, the Gloster Gauntlet. On seeing that the Air Ministry was suitably impressed with his aircraft, Lord Rothermere gave the 142 to the nation and named it *Britain First*. A bomber derivative was soon on the production line as the Bristol Blenheim.

The first through passenger air service between London and Brisbane, Australia, was inaugurated on 13 April 1935 by Imperial Airways and Qantas Empire Airways. The single fare for the 12 754 mile (20 525 km) route was £195. However, owing to heavy stage bookings, no through passengers were carried on the inaugural flight. The journey took 12½ days.

The first airline flight from the American mainland to Hawaii was made by a *Clipper* flying-boat of Pan American Airways during 16–17 April 1935. Taking off from Alameda, California, this was the airline's proving flight over this route, representing the first stage in a trans-Pacific route from the US to the Philippines.

The first solo air crossing of the South Atlantic by a woman was accomplished by New Zealand's Jean Batten, flying a Percival Gull from Lympne, Kent, to Port Natal, Brazil, via Thies, Senegal, during the period 11–13 November 1935.

On 22 November 1935 and 21 October 1936, Pan American Airways inaugurated its first trans-Pacific mail service and passenger service respectively. The route was between San Francisco and Manila in the Philippines, via Honolulu, Midway Island, Wake Island and Guam, and took about six days. The aircraft used was the

Martin 130 *China Clipper*, which was a high-wing monoplane flying-boat, powered by four 830 hp Pratt & Whitney Twin Wasp engines. Maximum cruising speed was 163 mph (262 km/h); range was 3200 miles (5150 km), and accommodation was for up to 43 passengers by day or 18 in a night sleeper layout.

**The first flight of the Douglas DC-3 prototype** was made on 17 December 1935, by Carl A. Cover from Clover Field, Santa Monica. A development of the DC-1 (Douglas Commercial No. 1) and DC-2, the DC-3 first entered service with American Airlines. Its inaugural passenger-carrying service was from Chicago, Illinois, to Glendale, California, on 4 July 1936. Certainly the most famous airliner in aviation history, some remain in civil and military service in 1991, 56 years after the prototype's first flight.

**The first case in Britain involving the prosecution and punishment of an airline passenger for smoking on board an aircraft in flight** was heard at Croydon, Surrey, on 17 March 1936. The passenger, who had travelled on an Imperial Airways Paris–London flight aboard the HP45 *Heracles*, was fined the sum of £10.

**The original British Airways airline** began using Gatwick Airport, Surrey, as its operating base on 17 May 1936.

**The first Short C-class Empire flying-boat** *Canopus* (G-ADHL) made its first flight on 3 July 1936 with John Lankester Parker, Short's Chief

*Pan American Martin 130 Clipper flying-boats were instrumental in inaugurating commercial services over the Pacific.*

Test Pilot, at the controls. Its first flight with Imperial Airways was made on 30 October 1936. The Empire 'boats represented the last word in luxury air travel before the Second World War and, as their name implied, were flown on the Empire routes to Africa and the Far East. When 28 of these aircraft were ordered by Imperial Airways before the first aircraft was built, it **then represented one of the biggest gambles in commercial aviation history**.

**The first Imperial Airways all-air trans-Mediterranean service** was flown on 12 January 1937 by the C-class flying-boat *Centaurus* as the final leg on an India–UK service.

**The first woman to fly solo from Brisbane, Australia, to Cape Town** was Australian Lores Bonney in April 1937, flying a de Havilland DH60 Moth.

**The inaugural flight of Britain's Empire Air Mail Programme** was made on 29 June 1937, when the Imperial Airways C-class flying-boat *Centurion* (G-ADVE) left Southampton with 3500 lb (1588 kg) of unsurcharged mail.

**The first North Atlantic trials involving the use of depot ships** were started by Deutsche Lufthansa on 15 August 1937. These vessels were equipped to retrieve, refuel and catapult-launch four-engined Blohm und Voss Ha 139 seaplanes which had been developed specially for this purpose.

**The first fully automatic landing by an aeroplane** was made on 23 August 1937 at Wright Field, Ohio. This was accomplished by on-board

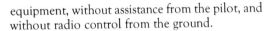

Pan Am Flying Clipper *leaves Marine Terminal, New York Municipal Airport, on a transatlantic flight, 31 March 1940. (Pan Am)*

*Luxuries were few in the early days of London's Heathrow Airport, and included tented passenger terminals. (British Airways)*

equipment, without assistance from the pilot, and without radio control from the ground.

**The first airmail and freight service between the United States and New Zealand** was inaugurated on 23 December 1937 by the Pan American flying-boat *Samoa Clipper.*

**The first flight refuelling test with a C-class Empire flying-boat** of Imperial Airways was carried out under the supervision of Sir Alan Cobham, the founder of Flight Refuelling Ltd. The tanker used in these tests, started on 20 January 1938, was the Armstrong Whitworth AW 23 bomber/transport prototype which had been loaned to Flight Refuelling by the Air Ministry.

**The first commercial use of composite aeroplanes in the world** occurred during 21–22 July 1938, when the Short S21 *Maia* flying-boat and the Short S20 *Mercury* seaplane took off from Foynes, Ireland. The S20 upper component then separated and flew the North Atlantic non-stop to Montreal, Canada, with a load of mail and newspapers. It covered 2930 miles (4715 km) in 20 h 20 min, at an average speed of 140 mph (225 km/h). Numerous composite flights and separations were carried out and the pair of aircraft continued to operate on the Southampton to Alexandria air route until the outbreak of the Second World War. When launched from its 'mother-plane' *Maia*, the seaplane *Mercury* carried sufficient fuel to fly 5995.5 miles (9652 km) from Dundee, Scotland, to the Orange River, South Africa. In doing so, on 6–8 October 1938, it established a record that has never been beaten.

**The first flight of a Danish airliner to the United Kingdom** was made on 28 July 1938, the inaugural service made by the Focke-Wulf Fw 200 Condor *Dania* (OY-DAM) flying between Copenhagen and Croydon.

**The first airliner with a pressurized cabin to enter service** was the Boeing Model 307 Stratoliner, the prototype of which was flown for the first time on 31 December 1938. Derived from the B-17 Flying Fortress bomber, it was advertised as the first airliner to fly above most bad weather conditions because of its pressurized cabin. The first version to enter service, with Trans-Continental and Western Air in April 1940, was the Model 307B, accommodating 33 passengers.

**The first regular airmail service over the North Atlantic** began on 20 May 1939 with the departure of the Pan American Airways' Boeing 314 *Yankee Clipper* (NC18603) from New York.

**The first transatlantic flight by a British prime minister** was made by the Rt Hon Winston Churchill on 16–17 January 1942. The flight, between Bermuda and Plymouth, was made in the Boeing 314 flying-boat *Berwick* operated by British Overseas Airways Corporation (BOAC).

**The first flight of an aircraft powered completely by turboprop engines** was made by the 18th production Gloster Meteor F.1. Re-engined by Rolls-Royce with two RB.50 Trent turboprops, driving 7 ft 11 in (2.41 m) diameter five-blade propellers, it was flown for the first time on 20 September 1945.

**The first post-war British survey flight to South America** was made on 9 October 1945, when Capt O. P. Jones took off from Hurn, Hampshire, in the Avro Lancastrian G-AGMG.

**The first regular British air service to South America** was inaugurated on 15 March 1946, the service flown initially by Lancastrians.

**The first transatlantic arrivals at London's Heathrow Airport**, opened officially on 31 May 1946, were Lockheed Constellations of Pan American Airways and American Overseas Airlines.

**The first US airmail to be carried by turbojet-powered aircraft** was that flown on 22 June 1946, by two USAAF Lockheed P-80 Shooting Star fighters, from Shenectady to Washington D.C. and Chicago, Illinois.

**The first non-stop flight between Hawaii and Egypt**, over the North Pole, was made in a USAAF Boeing B-29 Superfortress on 6 October 1946, covering a distance of 10 873 miles (17 498 km).

**The first aircraft to land on and take off from Mount Washington**, New Hampshire, on 12 March 1947, was a ski-equipped Piper Cub flown by Carmen Onofrio.

**The first car ferry flight operated by Silver City Airways** was made on 14 July 1948, the Bristol Freighter G-AGVC making the initial flight carrying two cars.

**The world's first turboprop-powered civil transport** (when it entered airline service) was the prototype Vickers Viscount (G-AHRF), first flown on 16 July 1948.

Cathay Pacific Airways, incorporated on 24 September 1946, was a charter company carrying passengers, mail and cargo. Just less than two years from its formation, on 16 July 1948, Cathay was to be involved in **the world's first act of air-piracy.** This occurred on 16 July 1948 when the airline's Consolidated Catalina amphibian *Miss Macao* was on its return flight from Maco to Hong Kong; three armed men ordered the pilot, Dale Cramer, to surrender the flying controls. When he refused he was shot, the weight of his body on the controls throwing the aircraft into a dive that ended in the ocean. There was only one survivor from the 27 people on board, ironically one of the attackers, otherwise the loss of the aircraft might have remained an unexplained accident.

A Vickers Viking carrying urgent medical supplies, and prevented by thick fog from taking off from Blackbushe, Surrey, on 30 November 1948, **became the first commercial aircraft to make use of the British wartime FIDO fog dispersal system** to become airborne.

The de Havilland DH106 Comet I, which was to become the **world's first turbojet-powered airliner** when it entered airline service in 1952, was first flown in prototype (G-ALVG) form on 27 July 1949.

**The first turbine-powered airliner in the world to receive an Airworthiness Certificate** was the Vickers V630 Viscount prototype (G-AHRF), with Rolls-Royce Dart turboprop engines, which was awarded Certificate No. A907 on 28 July 1950. The following day British European Airways operated this aircraft to record **the world's first scheduled passenger service to be flown by a gas-turbine powered airliner**. How-

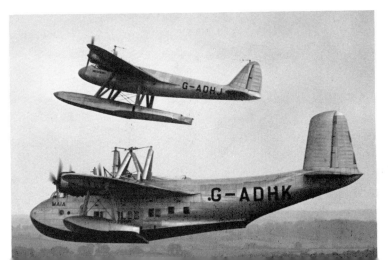

Left *The Short-Mayo Composite, a method of extending the seaplane's range patented by Major R. H. Mayo and used successfully by Short Brothers/Imperial Airways. (Short Brothers)*

Above  *Prototype Vickers Viscount in BEA livery, 1950.*

Right  *First flight of the prototype de Havilland Comet turbojet-powered airliner. (British Aerospace)*

ever, this service was not sustained for a long period. Piloted by Capt Richard Rymer, the Viscount took off from London (Northolt) and flew to Paris (Le Bourget), carrying 14 fare-paying passengers and 12 guests of the airline. Capt Rymer was also **the world's first holder of a pilot's licence for a turbine-powered civil transport aircraft.**

**The first solo trans-Polar flight** was made on 29 May 1951 in a North American P-51 Mustang by American C. Blair from Bardufoss, Norway, to Fairbanks, Alaska.

**The first freight service operated by turbo-prop-powered aircraft,** between Northolt and Hanover, was flown by Rolls-Royce Dart-engined Douglas DC-3s of BEA. The first flight was made on 15 August 1951 by G-ALXN *Sir Henry Royce.* This aircraft and a second DC-3, G-AMBD *Claude Johnson,* had been used for development flying of the Dart power plants introduced on the Vickers Viscount.

**The world's first Certificate of Airworthiness for a turbojet-powered civil airliner** was awarded to the de Havilland Comet I on 22 January 1952.

**The world's first turbojet airliner to enter commercial service** was the de Havilland DH106 Comet I, powered by four de Havilland Ghost 50 turbojet engines. **The world's first regular passenger service to be flown by turbojet aircraft** was inaugurated by British Overseas Airways Corporation on 2 May 1952, using the de Havilland Comet I G-ALYP between London and Johannesburg, South Africa. Its route was via Rome, Beirut, Khartoum, Entebbe and Livingstone, and the aircraft was captained in turn by Capts A. M. Majendie, J. T. A. Marsden and R. C. Alabaster. It carried 36 passengers and the total elapsed time for the 6724 miles (10 821 km) flight was 23 h 34 min. On 2 May 1953, a BOAC Comet I (G-ALYV) crashed near Calcutta after structural failure, with the loss of 43 lives. This was **the first**

fatal accident involving a turbojet airliner on scheduled service. Subsequent accidents caused the grounding of Comets, on 8 April 1954. By the time of Comet 4 services, the aircraft's technology lead had been lost to the US Boeing 707.

**The first commercial flights over the Polar regions** between Europe and North America began on 19 November 1952. Flown by SAS (Scandinavian Airlines System) Douglas DC-6Bs, these first flights were unscheduled, but scheduled operations over this route were initiated during 1954.

**The world's first fatal accident involving a turbojet airliner** occurred on 3 March 1953 when *Empress of Hawaii*, the de Havilland Comet I CF-CUN of Canadian Pacific Airlines, crashed on take-off at Karachi, Pakistan. This occurred during the aircraft's delivery flight from London to Sydney, its intended operating base, and all eleven occupants were killed. It was stated that the accident was caused by the pilot lifting the aircraft's nose too high during take-off, thereby causing it to stall.

**The first scheduled flight on BEA's London–Nicosia route**, made by the Vickers Viscount V.701 *Sir Ernest Shackleton* (G-AMNY) on 18 April 1953, marked the beginning of **the world's first sustained passenger service to be operated by turboprop-powered airliners.**

**The first woman in the world to fly faster than the speed of sound** was Miss Jacqueline Cochran, pilot extraordinary and American cosmetics tycoon who, flying a Canadian-built version of the North American F-86 Sabre, exceeded the speed of sound on 18 May 1953, and on the same day established a world's speed record for women of 652 mph (1049 km/h).

**The first US turbojet-powered transport aircraft**, the Boeing Model 367-80 ('Dash-Eighty'), made its first flight as the prototype of a flight refuelling tanker/transport for the USAF on 15 July 1954. Built extensively for the USAF in this form, it was to be developed simultaneously as the Boeing Model 707 civil transport, the founder member of a remarkable family of commercial transports now in worldwide use.

**The first post-war landing in the UK by a German civil-registered aircraft** was made on 15 April 1955. The aircraft was the Deutsche Lufthansa Convair CV-340 D-ACAD on a route proving flight. Lufthansa's first regular post-war air services to the UK began on 16 May 1955.

**The first multi-engined airliner with its turbojet powerplant installed in pods, one on each side of the rear fuselage**, was the French Sud-Est Aviation SE.210 Caravelle. The first of two prototypes made its maiden flight on 27 May 1955, powered by two 10 000 lb (4536 kg) thrust Rolls-Royce Avon RA.26 turbojets. This adoption of a rear-mounted engine installation was intended to ensure that the wing remained aerodynamically 'clean', free from the interference to airflow caused by wing-mounted engines and nacelles. The Caravelle was also **the first French turbojet-powered airliner**.

**The first turbojet-powered airliner to enter service with Aeroflot** was the Tupolev Tu-104, the prototype (SSSR-L5400) making its first flight on 15 June 1955. Its use on domestic routes was inaugurated by Aeroflot on 15 September 1956, thus the Soviet Union became the second nation in the world to introduce turbojet-powered civil transport aircraft. The use of the Tu-104 revolutionized Aeroflot's operations, these aircraft on long-range domestic routes providing a reduction of some 60 per cent in flight times by comparison with the piston-engined aircraft that they replaced.

**The first non-stop flight by an airliner from London to Vancouver**, on the Pacific Coast of Canada—a distance of 5100 miles (8208 km)—was completed by the turboprop-powered Bristol Britannia 310 G-AOVA on 29 June 1957.

**The first transatlantic passenger service to be flown by turbine-powered airliners** was inaugurated by BOAC on 19 December 1957, using Bristol Britannia 312 turboprop aircraft. The first flight from London to New York was by G-AOVC captained by Capt A. Meagher.

**The first aircraft to be designed and built in the Chinese People's Republic**, a twin-engined light transport designated Beijing (Peking) No. 1, made its first flight on 24 September 1958.

The termination of the Southampton–Madeira service of Aquila Airways, on 30 September 1958, represented **the end of UK commercial flying-boat operations**.

Canadair CL-44D-4, with hinged tail swung open. (Canadair)

BOAC inaugurated the first transatlantic passenger services to be flown by a turbojet-powered airliner, the de Havilland Comet 4, on 4 October 1958. Simultaneous London–New York (Capt R. E. Millichap with G-APDC) and New York–London (Capt T. B. Stoney with G-APDB) services were flown.

The first turbojet-powered airliner service linking South America and the UK was inaugurated by Aerolineas Argentinas on 19 May 1959, the service between Buenos Aires and London flown by a de Havilland Comet 4.

Australia's Qantas Empire Airways inaugurated its first trans-Pacific service with turbojet-powered airliners on 29 July 1959, when the Boeing 707-138 *City of Canberra* was flown from Sydney to San Francisco.

More than 30 years after being established as the hub of British civil aviation, London's Croydon Airport was finally closed down on 30 September 1959.

The first round-the-world passenger service by jet airliners was established by Pan American World Airways during October 1959. The inaugural service was flown by the Boeing 707-321 *Clipper Windward*.

The first nonstop flight between London and Bombay was recorded by a Boeing 707 during 20–21 February 1960, made during the course of the aircraft's delivery flight to Air India from the Boeing Company at Seattle, via London.

H ('Jerry') Shaw who had piloted KLM's first Amsterdam–London service on 17 May 1920, was carried as a passenger on KLM's 40th Anniversary flight on 17 May 1960.

The last scheduled service operated by a piston-engined aircraft from London Heathrow was that flown by a Douglas DC-3 on 31 October 1960. Operating on a flight from London to Birmingham, it was also the last scheduled service by a DC-3 to be flown by BEA.

The world's first aircraft to incorporate a hinged tail for rear loading, the Canadair CL-44D-4, was flown for the first time on 16 November 1960. Powered by four Rolls-Royce Tyne 515/10 two-shaft two-spool turboprops, each rated at 5730 ehp, it had a range of 5660 miles (9110 km) with a 37 300 lb (16 920 kg) payload. Its maximum payload was 66 048 lb (29 960 kg).

The first civil airliner to be powered by turbofan engines was the Convair 990 Coronado. First flown in prototype form on 24 January 1961, its powerplant comprised four General Electric CJ-805-23B aft-fan turbofans.

The first outsize transport conversion of a Boeing Stratocruiser, designed by Aero Spacelines and then designated B-377PG (later named Pregnant Guppy), made its first flight on 19 September 1962. Derived Super Guppies are used currently by Airbus Industrie to transport internationally built major assemblies of the Airbus to Toulouse for final assembly.

The first transpacific solo flight by a woman was achieved between 30 April and 12 May 1963 by American Betty Miller. She flew from Oakland, California, to Brisbane, Australia, in four stages.

US airwoman Jerrie Mock became **the first woman to complete a solo flight around the world** when she landed at Columbus, Ohio, on 17 April 1964. This achievement had been completed in 29 days in her Cessna 180 lightplane, *Spirit of Columbus*.

Silver City Airways, which in mid-1948 had established the first UK cross-Channel car ferry, announced on 6 June 1964 that in its operations from that date a total of **one million cars had been carried between the UK and Europe.**

The McDonnell Douglas DC-9 twin-turbofan short/medium-range airliner, first flown on 25 February 1965, subsequently became **the second of the world's commercial turbine-powered airliners to exceed a sales total of 1000.**

**The first British woman pilot to complete a solo round-the-world flight** was Sheila Scott, who landed her Piper Comanche 260B *Myth Too* at London Heathrow on 20 June 1966. She also established a new round-the-world speed record in Class 3 and the longest solo round-the-world flight at that time of 33 d 3 min.

The delivery of a Model 707-120B to American Airlines on 5 June 1967 marked a significant milestone for The Boeing Company, this being the **1000th jet airliner produced by the company.**

**The first completely automatic approach and landing by a four-engined turbojet airliner** with passengers on board was recorded by a Boeing Model 707-321B (N419PA) of Pan American Airways on 7 July 1967.

**The first non-stop transatlantic flight by a turbine-powered executive jet** was made on 5 May 1968. The flight from Teterboro, New Jersey, to London Gatwick, of 3500 miles (5633 km) was achieved by a Grumman Gulfstream II, powered by two Rolls-Royce Spey Mk 511-8 turbofan engines, each of 11 400 lb (5171 kg) thrust.

**The world's first supersonic transport aircraft to fly** was the Soviet Union's Tupolev Tu-144, the prototype of which (SSSR-68001) flew for the first time on 31 December 1968. On 26 May 1970 this prototype became the **world's first commercial transport to exceed a speed of Mach 2**, by flying at 1335 mph (2150 km/h) at a height of 53 475 ft (16 300 m). The maiden flight of the prototype was also **the first time that its Kuznetsov NK-144 turbofan engines had been tested in the air**. Then rated at 28 660 lb (13 000 kg) thrust without afterburning and 38 580 lb (17 500 kg) thrust with afterburning, the four turbofan engines of production aircraft were each rated at 44 090 lb (20 000 kg) thrust with afterburning. **Regular supersonic flights, the first in the world** by an aircraft of this category, were started by Aeroflot on 26 December 1975, but were confined to the carriage of freight and mail. The first scheduled passenger flights began on 1 November 1977 and a total of 102 flights had been made by 1 June 1978 when the service was terminated.

**The world's first wide-body commercial transport aircraft** was the Boeing Model 747 'jumbo-jet', the first of which flew on 9 February 1969 from Paine Field, near Seattle, Washington. The

*French prototype Concorde supersonic airliner. In 1992 Concorde remains the only aircraft (military or civil) to fly daily, and for most of its time, while airborne, at supersonic speed.*

first commercial service with the 747 was inaugurated by Pan American Airways on its New York–London route on 22 January 1970. In addition to standard passenger versions, combi or convertible variants are available for various and easily-changed permutations of cargo/passengers, as well as a purpose-designed freighter with a nose-loading door and a special cargo handling system. Other versions include the 747SP low-weight long-range passenger transport, and during 23–24 March 1976 one of these aircraft on delivery to South African Airways set a world record for non-stop distance flown by a commercial transport. Carrying 50 passengers, the aircraft was flown from Paine Field, Washington, to Cape Town, a distance of 10 290 miles (16 560 km). From 1 to 3 May 1976 a Pan American 747SP, commanded by Capt Walter H. Mullikin, completed a round-the-world flight in 1 d 22 h 0 m 50 s to set a round-the-world record speed of 502.84 mph (809.24 km/h). A 747SR short-range version was also made available, but the only version being marketed in 1991 was the Model 747-400. Orders for this totalled 406 by 18 March 1991.

**The world's first supersonic commercial transport to operate regular scheduled passenger services** is the British Aircraft Corporation/Aérospatiale Concorde. The Aérospatiale 001 prototype made its first flight on 2 March 1969, and the BAC 002 flew for the first time on 9 April 1969. The Concorde test programme was the most comprehensive ever undertaken for a civil airliner, involving eight flight test aircraft plus two airframes for structural ground testing. Just prior to the type's entry into service, test aircraft had flown more than 5500 hours, of which more than 2000 hours were at supersonic speed. In route proving, test and demonstration flights, Concordes had then landed at 83 airports in 49 countries and had flown more than 5 million miles (8 million km). **The first passenger services were operated** on 21 January 1976, when simultaneous take-offs were made by Air France's 205 from Paris to Rio de Janeiro, via Dakar, and British Airways' 206 from London to Bahrain. Prior to that, on 1 September 1975, the fourth production Concorde became **the first aircraft in the world to record two return transatlantic flights (London–Gander–London), or four transatlantic crossings in a single day.** Due to different forms of opposition, primarily from environmentalists, it

was not until 22 November 1977 that Air France and British Airways were able to inaugurate services to New York.

**The world's first scheduled jet service within the Arctic circle** was inaugurated by Nordair on 19 March 1969, providing a weekly return service between Montreal, Canada, and Resolution Bay, Cornwallis Island.

**The Daily Mail Transatlantic Air Race,** held between 4 and 11 May 1969 to celebrate the 50th anniversary of the first non-stop crossing of the North Atlantic by Alcock and Brown, required the winner to record the shortest time to travel from the top of the Post Office Tower, London, to the top of the Empire State Building, New York. It was won by Lt Cdr Brian Davis, RN, flying in the reverse direction in a McDonnell Douglas Phantom II. His time of 4 h 46 min 57 s for the Atlantic crossing was then a record, and his point to point winning time was a remarkable 5 h 11 min.

**The first airline in the world to introduce an inertial navigation system (INS)** on scheduled passenger services was Finnair, on 20 October 1969, so dispensing with a navigator in the flight crew. In simple terms, an INS combines gyroscopes and accelerometers that provide data to a computer, and this in turn integrates the linear displacement from the start of the flight. Since the starting point is known, the INS can provide the exact position of the aircraft at all times, without any reference to an outside source.

**An England–Australia Commemorative Air Race** began on 18 December 1969, sponsored to mark the 50th anniversary of the first England–Australia flight by the brothers Ross and Keith Smith, as well as the bi-centenary of the discovery of Australia. It was won by Capts W. J. Bright and F. L. Buxton, flying the Britten-Norman BN-2A Islander G-AXUD.

**The world's first all-paper man-carrying aircraft,** assembled from paper, glue and masking tape as an aeronautical teaching aid at Ohio State University, flew on three occasions in August 1970. Towed into the air by a motor car, the all-paper glider had no wheels, but slid over the grass field on a fuselage undersurface of waxed corrugated paper. Maximum airspeed recorded was approximately 60 mph (96 km/h).

The first round-the-world cargo service was inaugurated by Trans-Mediterranean Airways on 14 April 1971.

In the course of its development programme, the French-built **Concorde 001 prototype made its first completely automatic approach and landing** at Toulouse on 13 May 1971.

During the period 11 June to 4 August 1971, the British airwoman Sheila Scott, flying a Piper Aztec D, achieved the **first flight to be made by a lightplane from Equator to Equator via the North Pole.**

**The first circum-polar flight around the world** was achieved by Captain Elgen M. Long flying a twin-engined Piper Navajo. The total distance of 38 896 miles (62 597 km), involving 215 flying hours, was flown during the period 5 November to 3 December 1971. While flying over Antarctica the cabin temperature fell as low as −40°F (−40°C).

In early May 1972, the Cessna Aircraft Company became **the first aircraft manufacturer in the world** to deliver its 100 000th production aircraft. Ten years later the figure had risen to the remarkable total of almost 172 000 aircraft, but this rate of acceleration has since fallen as a result of a recession in general aviation activities and US liability laws. By the end of 1990 the total had risen to only 177 553 aircraft.

The Boeing Company announced on 22 September 1972 that with the receipt of its most recent order for the Model 727, placed by Delta Air Lines, this aircraft had become **the first jet-pow-**ered airliner in the world to reach a sales total of 1000.

**The first wide-body commercial transport aircraft produced by the aircraft industry of Europe** was the Airbus Industrie A300 Airbus, the first example of which (F-WUAB) made its maiden flight on 28 October 1972. Bought initially by Air France, it entered service with this airline on its Paris–London route on 23 May 1974. A truly international project, the A300 and ensuing versions are built primarily by Aérospatiale of France, Deutsche Airbus of Germany, Fokker in the Netherlands, CASA in Spain and British Aerospace in the United Kingdom; other European countries are also involved in some sub-contract work. A variant of the A300 flown on 6 October 1981 was **the first wide-body transport aircraft in the world to be specially equipped for operation by a two-man flight crew,** and certification in this configuration was gained on 8 January 1982. At the end of 1990, by which time additional versions designated A310, A320, A321, A330 and A340 were being marketed, combined orders for all versions had exceeded 1600.

During its development programme, an Airbus Industrie A300B Airbus prototype recorded **the first fully automatic approach and landing to be made by the type,** on 8 May 1973.

*The first European company to produce a wide-body jet airliner, Airbus Industrie is now studying concepts for a super wide-body aircraft capable of accommodating 600 or more passengers (see Most). (Airbus Industrie)*

The first no-booking guaranteed-seat air shuttle service in Europe was inaugurated on 12 January 1975 by British Airways. Operated by Hawker Siddeley Trident I airliners, it linked London Heathrow and Glasgow Airport, Scotland.

The first solo Australia–England flight in an aircraft of amateur construction was completed on 1 July 1976. This was achieved by Clive Canning, flying his home-built Thorp T-18 Tiger, a two-seat all-metal sporting aircraft for which more than 1300 sets of plans were sold. Just one month later, on 1 August 1976, Don Taylor set out to make a round-the-world flight in his Thorp T-18. This was completed successfully on 30 September 1976, the distance of 24 627 miles (39 633 km) completed in 171.5 flying hours, his T-18 becoming the first home-built aircraft to circumnavigate the world.

The prototype of the Il-86, the Soviet Union's first wide-body jet transport aircraft, made its first flight from the old Moscow Central Airport of Khodinka on 22 December 1976. The Il-86, which has the NATO reporting-name *Camber*, is powered by four pylon-mounted Kuznetsov NK-86 turbofan engines, each of 28 660 lb (13 000 kg) thrust. With accommodation for up to 350 passengers, the aircraft is unusual in having three low-level airstair-type doors, through which passengers can enter at ground level to leave their coats and hand baggage on the lower deck, before climbing one of the three fixed staircases to the main cabin. Aeroflot, which flew its first scheduled and first international services with the Il-86 on 26 December 1980 and on 3 July 1981 respectively, has a requirement for more than 100 by 1995; of this total at least 60 had been delivered in early 1991.

On 18 April 1978 the Vickers Viscount became the first turbine-powered airliner to complete a quarter-century of regular commercial airline service.

The first crossing of the English Channel by a powered hang-glider was recorded on 9 May 1978 by David Cook flying a Volmer VJ-23 Swingwing. Its McCulloch MC-101B piston engine had been installed by David Cook, enabling him to complete the crossing from Walmer Castle, Deal, to Blériot Plage, France, in a flying time of 1 hr 15 min.

The first circumnavigation of the world by two lightplanes was achieved during 1–19 July 1978. The aircraft concerned were two Beech Bonanzas, piloted by Frank Haile Jr and William H. Wisner, with co-pilots Walter G. Hedren and Bryce C. Wisner respectively. The US National Aeronautic Association certificate was awarded for the achievement, covering the flight of 20 710 nautical miles (38 380 km), each aircraft having flown 159.91 flight hours.

The de Havilland Comet 4C G-BDIW made the last revenue flight of the type from London Gatwick Airport on 9 November 1980. Just over 31 years earlier, on 27 July 1949, the Comet I prototype had made its first flight. Early development flying and initial in-service use suggested that Britain had a world-beating aircraft that would be built in large numbers. Unfortunately for de Havilland this failed to materialize, and it was the Boeing Model 707 and its successors that captured the lion's share of the commercial market for jet airliners.

A woman's solo flight record between England and Australia was set by British pilot Judith Chisholm between 18 and 21 November 1980, flying a Cessna Turbo Centurion cabin monoplane. Although her 3 d 13 h record reflected the very considerable improvement in aircraft and facilities from the time that Jean Batten set the previous record, this in no way detracted from her achievement. She then set out from Australia to complete a solo round-the-world flight, landing back at London Heathrow on 3 December 1980. Judith Chisholm thus established a woman's solo round-the-world flight record of 15 d 22 min 30 s, halving the time set by Sheila Scott in 1966.

After operating the Boeing 707 for just over 22 years, Pan American Airways flew its last revenue service with this type of aircraft on 26 January 1981.

Offering large potential savings in fuel costs, an Avco Lycoming engine was modified to operate with liquefied petroleum gas (LPG). Installed in a SOCATA TB 10 Tobago lightplane, this engine became airborne for the first time on 15 May 1982.

The first flight across the Mediterranean by a microlight took place on 22 May 1983, by a French Aviasud Sirocco.

The first round-the-world flight by a microlight was completed in stages between September 1984 and March 1987 by Frenchman Patrice Franceschi in an Aviasud Sirocco. The 27 960 miles (45 000 km) took about 700 actual flying hours.

The first circum-polar flight around the world in a single-engined aircraft was accomplished by Captain Richard Norton and Calin Rosetti in a Piper PA-46-310P Malibu. Flown from and to Le Bourget airport, Paris, France during the period 21 January to 15 June 1987, the total distance of 34 342 miles (55 268 km) was completed in a flying time of 185 h 41 min.

The first England–Australia flight by a woman pilot in a microlight aircraft was achieved by Eve Jackson (UK). With only 70 hours of flight experience she set off from Biggin Hill, Kent, on 26 April 1986 in her CFM Shadow microlight, with a wing span of 32 ft 11 in (10.03 m), length of 21 ft (6.40 m), and relying on a 38 hp Rotax 447 engine to keep them airborne. Her journey, not without considerable trials and tribulations, finally ended in Sydney, New South Wales, on 1 August 1987, after accumulating a total of 279 h 55 min flying time. A good example of the kind of guts and determination that carried Amy Johnson to the same destination 57 years earlier, Eve Jackson has since been awarded the prestigious Seagrave Trophy for her achievement.

The first airliner to fly with a propfan engine was a Boeing Model 727-100 testbed aircraft, which carried a General Electric UDF (unducted fan) engine with two eight-blade fans of about 11 ft (3.35 m) diameter on its starboard side. This first flight took place on 20 August 1986.

The first aeroplane to fly around the world non-stop and unrefuelled was the Voyager Aircraft Inc *Voyager*, between 14 and 23 December 1986, a trimaran monoplane with high aspect ratio

Left   *This Boeing Model 727-100 was the world's first airliner flown with a propfan engine.*

Below   *Voyager, the first aircraft ever to fly non-stop around the world without refuelling. (Doug Shane)*

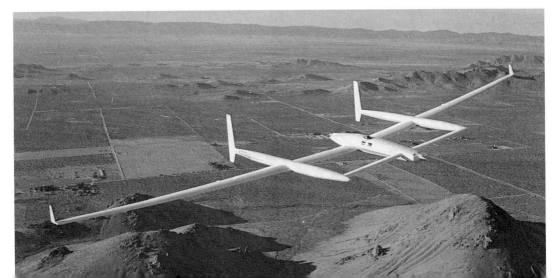

wings and constructed of composite materials that included Magnamite graphite and Hexcel honeycomb. Crewed on its 9 d 3 min 44 s westbound flight from and back to Edwards Air Force Base by Dick Rutan and Jeana Yeager, *Voyager* established world absolute distance in a straight line and closed circuit records by an aeroplane, of 24 986.664 miles (40 212.139 km).

**The first flight of a large transport aircraft with one of its three engines fuelled by liquid hydrogen** occurred on 15 August 1988. The aircraft concerned was a Tupolev Tu-155, basically a Tu-154 which had been converted especially for trials with liquid hydrogen and methane fuels. More interestingly, under an agreement between Deutsche Airbus and the Tupolev design bureau, it is possible that an A300 Airbus may be tested with liquid hydrogen and/or liquid methane fuel. The first step is to experiment with a Tu-154 converted to Tu-156 configuration, in which all three engines will run on liquefied gas fuel.

Design and development of **the world's first supersonic business jet** has been initiated by an international partnership that unites the P.O. Sukhoi OKB in Russia and Gulfstream Aerospace Corporation in the USA. The first version which is planned would accommodate a crew of two or three and eight to 19 passengers according to internal layout, and is to be powered by three augmented turbofan engines to be developed by Lyulka (Russia) and Rolls-Royce (UK), to provide a maximum cruising speed in excess of Mach 2. It is planned that the first of two or three prototypes will make its maiden flight during 1994.

*Largest and Smallest:*

**The largest aeroplane to lift itself off the ground briefly in the 19th century** was designed and built by Sir Hiram Maxim (1840–1916). Basically a biplane test rig with 4000 ft² (372 m²) of lifting area, it was powered by two 180 hp steam engines and ran along a railway track 1800 ft (550 m) long which was fitted with wooden restraining guard-rails to prevent the machine from rising too high.

On 31 July 1894, during a test run, the machine lifted about 2 ft (60 cm) before fouling the guardrails and coming to rest.

Above  *Sir Hiram Maxim's epic steam-powered aeroplane of the 1890s, at Baldwyn's Park.*

**The largest flying-boat built between the wars** was the Dornier Do X, the prototype of which made its maiden flight on 25 July 1929, at which time it was also **the largest aeroplane of any kind in the world.** Powered by 12 engines

Below  *Dornier Do X at New York in 1931.*

Above    *Probably the best remembered racing aeroplanes of all time were the two Gee Bee Super Sportsters of the 1930s, designed around the concept of the smallest airframe around the largest engine. On 3 September 1932, Major James H. Doolittle flew the Super Sportster R-1 to a record 294.418 mph (473.820 km/h) during the US National Air Races in Cleveland. Both the R-1 and R-2 (shown) eventually crashed, killing their pilots. Power was provided by a 730 hp Pratt & Whitney T3D1 radial piston engine.*

(initially 525 hp Siemens Jupiters, later 600 hp Curtiss Conquerors), mounted in tandem pairs on the 157 ft 5¾ in (48.00 m) monoplane wing, the Do X once carried (on 21 October 1929) a crew of ten and 159 passengers (nine of whom were stowaways). Altogether three Do Xs were built. The most famous flight was that made by the prototype from Germany to New York, which took from 2 November 1930 to 27 August 1931 because of damage to the wing and hull and lengthy stops at various places including Amsterdam, Calshot, Lisbon, the Canary Islands, Portuguese Guinea and Rio de Janeiro. In commercial terms the Do X was quite impracticable, and the two examples delivered to an Italian airline were never put into service. Although it had a respectable maximum speed of 134 mph (216 km/h), the Do X weighed 123 460 lb (56 000 kg) with full load and had a service ceiling of 1640 ft (500 m).

**The largest aeroplane ever flown, the largest flying-boat in the world, and the aircraft with the greatest wing span ever built** was the Hughes H4 Hercules. The 180 ton (183 tonne) flying-boat was powered by eight 3000 hp Pratt & Whitney R4360 piston engines, had a wing span of 320 ft (97.54 m), an overall length of 219 ft (66.75 m) and reportedly cost its sponsor, the American millionaire Howard Hughes, $22 million to complete. Big enough to accommodate up to 700 passengers, it was intended primarily as a freighter and therefore had no cabin windows. It flew on only one occasion, on 2 November 1947 when, piloted by Howard Hughes, it covered a distance of about a mile (1.6 km) at a height of approximately 80 ft (24 m), over Los Angeles Harbor, California.

**The world's second largest aircraft** is the Antonov An-124 'Condor', first flown in prototype form on 26 December 1982, which has a wing span of 240 ft 5¾ in (73.30 m) and overall length of 226 ft 8½ in (69.10 m). On 26 July 1985, the An-124 lifted a payload of 377 473 lb (171 219 kg) to a height of 35 269 ft (10 750 m), exceeding by some 53 per cent the record then held by the Lockheed C-5A Galaxy for payload lifted to a height of 6562 ft (2000 m). The An-124, which has since established many more records, entered service with Aeroflot in January 1986 and with the Military Transport Aviation Force (VTA) of the Soviet Air Force during 1987. The type remains in production in 1991.

**The largest airline maintenance hangar in the world** is Hangar V of Lufthansa, situated at Frankfurt, which is known as the *Jumbohalle* by the airline's personnel. With an area of more than 301 390 ft² (28 000 m²) it is used for the maintenance of Lufthansa's fleet, those of its charter subsidiary Condor, and also the aircraft of other customers who have maintenance contracts with Lufthansa. To provide the technical competence for such a task, Lufthansa has more than 3200 engineers, technicians and mechanics employed at Frankfurt.

**The world's largest airport** is King Khalid International, outside Riyadh, Saudi Arabia, which covers an area of 86 square miles (221 km²). Opened on 14 November 1983, it also has **the world's largest control tower** which is 243 ft (74 m) in height.

**The world's largest airline** is Russia's Aeroflot, so named since 1932 after it was founded on 9 February 1923. In 1989 it employed 500 000 people to operate some 1650 aircraft over 621 400 miles (1 000 000 km) of routes, carrying 132 million passengers and 2 952 610 tons (3 000 000 tonnes) of freight. Seventy per cent of the airline's routes are international, with regular flights being made to 99 countries; its domestic network links some 3600 towns.

**The world's largest aerospace company** is Boeing of Seattle, Washington, which – in 1990 – had sales totalling $27.6 billion and a worldwide workforce of some 160 000 people. In terms of production, the Cessna Aircraft Company of Wichita, Kansas had, by the end of 1990, built more than 177 000 since Clyde Cessna built his first aircraft in 1911.

**The world's smallest aeroplane of monoplane configuration** is the *Baby Bird*, designed and built by Mr Don Stits. Flown in 1987 by retired US Navy pilot, Commander Harold Nemer, it is an unbraced high-wing monoplane with a wood and welded steel tube structure, fabric covered. Wing span is 6 ft 3 in (1.91 m), length 11 ft (3.35 m) and empty weight 252 lb (114 kg).

**The world's smallest aeroplane of biplane configuration to fly** was the *Bumble Bee Two*, designed and built by Robert H. Starr of Arizona, USA. With a wing span of 5 ft 6 in (1.68 m), overall length of 8 ft 10 in (2.64 m) and empty weight of 396 lb (179.62 kg), it had been flown to a speed of 190 mph (305.8 km/h). On 8 May 1988, it was totally destroyed in a crash from a height of 400 ft (122 m).

**The world's largest aircraft** is the Antonov An-225 Mryia 'Cossack', which is also **the first aircraft designed and built to fly at a gross weight exceeding one million pounds** (maximum take-off weight 1 322 750 lb (600 000 kg). Based closely on the Antonov An-124 'Condor' and first flown on 21 December 1988, it has, by comparison, greater wing span and fuselage length, six

instead of four turbofan engines, and a tail unit comprising twin fins and rudders mounted on a dihedral tailplane; this serves to eliminate airflow problems when large 'piggy-back' loads (such as space orbiters) are being carried. Just over 15 months after its first flight, on 22 March 1989 in one 3½-hour flight, the An-224 established no fewer than 106 new world records in related altitude, distance, payload and speed parameters.

Believed to be **the smallest aircraft to have flown between England and Australia** is an Andreasson BA-4B biplane; this has a wingspan of 17 ft 7 in (5.34 m) and length of 15 ft 0 in (4.60 m). Owned by John M. Vening of Lyminster, West Sussex, his 'excuse' for the flight was an urge to take part in Australia's bi-centennial celebrations. Taking off from Goodwood, West Sussex on 26 June 1989, he arrived at Sydney, New South Wales on 21 July 1989.

**The largest homebuilt aircraft in the Soviet Union** is the VK-8 Aushza, a two-seat agricultural, training and transport aircraft designed and built by Vladas Kensgaila. Its vital statistics include a wing span of 49 ft 3 in (15.00 m), overall length of 31 ft 4¾ in (9.57 m) and empty weight of 2513 lb (1140 kg).

**The world's largest new amphibian aircraft** is the Beriev A-40 Albatross, which has a wing span of 137 ft 1½ in (41.80 m) and length of 141 ft (43.0 m). Powered by two turbofan engines, it was originally designed and built for multi-role military use, but with improved East–West relations it is being proposed as a 105-passenger airliner and, as such, could have considerable appeal to some inter-island operators.

**The smallest nation with an airline capable of intercontinental operations** is the Republic of Seychelles (pop 69 719). To foster tourism, Air Seychelles currently operates a Boeing 767-200ER to link the islands with Frankfurt, Kuala Lumpur, London, Mauritius, Paris, Rome and Singapore. The aircraft's cost of US $65 million represents about $930 for every man, woman and child of the population.

## *Fastest:*

**The world's first speed record over 100 km** was established by the Englishman, Hubert Latham, during the Reims International Meeting between 22 and 29 August 1909. Flying an Antoinette (powered by a 50 hp eight-cylinder Antoinette engine) he covered the distance in 1 h 28 min 17 s, at an average speed of 42 mph (67 km/h). In so doing he won the second largest prize of the meeting amounting to 42 000 francs. Latham also won the altitude competition by reaching 508 ft (155 m). First prize went to Henry Farman who, flying a Gnôme-powered Farman, set up new world records for duration and distance in a closed circuit, covering 111.847 miles (180 km) in 3 h 4 min 56.4 s, winning 63 000 francs.

**The first 'over 200 km/h' world speed record** was set by Frenchman Maurice Prévost in the Deperdussin 'monocoque' of 1913 at Reims on 29 September 1913, at 126.666 mph (203.850 km/h). This was **officially the fastest aircraft prior to the First World War**, as no further records were set until 1920.

*Macchi MC72 which, after more than half a century, still holds the world speed record for seaplanes.*

One of the most enduring speed records was that set on 23 October 1934 by Italian Francesco Agello flying a Macchi MC72 seaplane. Still unbeaten in 1988, this world speed record of 440.683 mph (709.209 km/h) in FAI sub-class C-2 was achieved in the Macchi seaplane which had been intended to compete in the Schneider Trophy Contest of 1931.

**The fastest round-the-world flight** by a commercial airliner (under FAI rules which permit for inclusion as circumnavigation flights those exceeding the length of the Tropic of Cancer or

Capricorn – 22 858.754 miles (36 787.599 km)) was recorded between 28–30 January 1988. This was achieved by Captain Clay Lacy, carrying 141 passengers in the United Airlines Boeing 747SP *Friendship One*, flown from and to Seattle, Washington and refuelling only in Athens, Greece and T'ai-pei, Taiwan. The eastabout flight of 23 125 miles (37 216 km) was completed in a time of 36 h 54 min 15 s.

*Highest and Lowest:*

**The first flight at an altitude of 1000 m (3280 ft)** was achieved by Hubert Latham on 7 January 1910 at Châlons, France, flying an Antoinette VII monoplane.

**The first pilot to fly at a height of over 1 mile** was American Walter Brookins on 10 July 1910, when he piloted a Wright biplane at Indianapolis to about 6230 ft (1900 m).

**The current world altitude record for piston-engined aeroplanes** stands at 56 046 ft (17 083 m), established on 22 October 1938 by an Italian Caproni Ca 161*bis*.

The current world altitude record in a microlight aircraft ratified by the FAI was achieved by Australia's Eric S. Winton, flying from Tyagarah Aerodrome, New South Wales on 11 April 1989, when he climbed to a remarkable 29 999 ft (9144 m).

**The world's highest landing field,** 14 315 ft (4363 m) above sea level, is La Sa (Lhasa) airport in the People's Republic of China.

**The lowest landing field** is at El Lisan, on the east shore of the Dead Sea, which is 1180 ft (360 m) below sea level. However, during the Second World War, BOAC Short C-class flying-boats operated from the surface of the Dead Sea, which is 1292 ft (394 m) below sea level.

*Longest and Shortest:*

**The longest flight by the end of 1908** was by Wilbur Wright on 31 December 1908, at Camp d'Auvours, where he achieved a stupendous 77 miles (124 km) in 2 h 20 min. This won for him the Michelin prize of 20 000 francs—apart from breaking all his own records. Details of the longest flights made by Wilbur Wright in 1908 follow, together with a list of the more significant flights made by other aviators that year.

**Wilbur Wright**

| | | | | |
|---|---|---|---|---|
| 14 May 1908 | Kill Devil Hills | 5 miles | (8 km) | In 7 min 29 s. |
| 8 August 1908 | Hunaudières, France | — | — | Demonstration flight 1 min 45 s. |
| 16 September 1908 | Auvours, France | — | — | Flight taking 39 min 18 s. |
| 21 September 1908 | Auvours, France | 41⅓ miles | (66.5 km) | First major endurance flight. Flew more than 100 times at this location. |
| 3 October 1908 | Auvours, France | 34¾ miles | (56 km) | In 55 min 37 s. |
| 10 October 1908 | Auvours, France | 46 miles | (74 km) | In 1 h 9 min 45 s, with M. Painleve as passenger. |
| 18 December 1908 | Auvours, France | 62 miles | (99.8 km) | In 1 h 54 min 53 s. Climbed to 330 ft (100 m) to establish new altitude record. |
| 31 December 1908 | Auvours, France | 77 miles | (124 km) | In 2 hr 20 min 23 s, to win Michelin prize and set up new world record. |

**Léon Delagrange**

| | |
|---|---|
| 11 April 1908 | Covered over 2½ miles (3.9 km) at Issy-les-Moulineaux. |
| 23 June 1908 | Covered 8¾ miles (14.08 km) in 18 min 30 s at Milan, Italy. |
| 6 September 1908 | Covered 15¼ miles (24.4 km) in 29 min 53 s at Issy-les-Moulineaux. |
| 17 September 1908 | Flight lasting 30 min 27 s at Issy-les-Moulineaux. |

**Henry Farman**

| | |
|---|---|
| 13 January 1908 | Covered a 1 km circuit in 1 min 28 s at Issy-les-Molineaux. |
| 6 July 1908 | Covered 12½ miles (20 km) in 20 min 20 s. |
| 30 October 1908 | Covered 17 miles (27.3 km) in 20 min on cross-country flight from Châlons to Reims. |

**Glenn H. Curtiss**

| | |
|---|---|
| 4 July 1908 | Covered 5090 ft (1550 m) in 1 min 42 s to win *Scientific American* trophy. |

**The airline with the longest continuous record of scheduled services**, Aerovias Nacionales de Colombia SA (Avianca), was founded on 5 December 1919.

**The longest period between solo flights in the same aircraft** is a most unusual category, but British Airways pilot Captain Arthur Whitlock makes this claim in relation to a de Havilland DH82 Tiger Moth with the constructors number 86069. On 26 March 1947, Arthur Whitlock made his first solo flight in this aircraft (then registered VT-ARQ) at the Madras Flying Club. Despite a busy life as a civil airline pilot he always retained an interest in the old 'Tiger', eventually tracing her (now registered N6353) to Dallas, Texas. There, thanks to the kindness of its present owner, Henry 'Bud' Malloy, he flew his first love again on 15 April 1991, just over 44 years after the original 5-minute solo.

**The longest association of a navigator and pilot** must be that recorded by William G. Crooks, who retired from regular communication flights for Hawker Siddeley Aviation on 30 June 1974. After service in the RAF from March 1942, he first crewed with pilot R. J. Chandler in April 1948. From then, until his retirement, William Crooks recorded 6554 h as navigator/radio operator on flights with R. J. Chandler.

**The current world distance in a straight line record for seaplanes** was established by Capt D. C. T. Bennett and 1st Officer I. Harvey in the Short-Mayo *Mercury* during 6–8 October 1938, at 5997.5 miles (9652 km). The flight, which began in Dundee, Scotland, ended at the Orange River, South Africa.

**Farthest travelling amateur-constructed aircraft** is almost certainly the original Volmer VJ-22 Sportsman two-seat amphibian designed by Volmer Jensen in the United States. First flown on 22 December 1958, it has since logged more than 1840 flying hours, covering a total distance equal to six times round the world.

Believed to be **the longest consecutive period of daily flying** is the 1315 days recorded by Robert Armstrong. Owner of a small air service at Hutchinson, Kansas he flew at least once every day between 1 June 1965 and 15 January 1969 – a grand total of 3 years, 7 months and 15 days.

**The longest aircraft runway in the world** is at Edwards Air Force Base, on the bed of Rogers Dry Lake at Muroc, California. The total length available is 7 miles (11.3 km), but of this total only 15 000 ft (4572 m) is concreted.

**The longest duration flight established in a lightplane** is a total of 64 days 22 h 19 min 5 s, flown by Robert Timm and John Cook in the Cessna 172 *Hacienda*. Taking off from McCarren Airfield, Las Vegas, Nevada at 3.53 pm local time on 4 December 1958, they landed at the same airfield just before 2.12 pm on 7 February 1959, having covered a distance equivalent to six times round the world. No interim landing was made and food and fuel, when needed, were picked up by hook and line from a truck speeding down the airport runway.

**The current world distance in a closed circuit record for jet-powered aeroplanes** was set during 6–7 May 1987 by a Soviet Antonov An-124 piloted by Vladimir Terski, at 12 521.201 miles (20 150.921 km).

**The current world distance record in a microlight aircraft** ratified by the FAI is that which was set by Austrian Wilhelm Lischak on 8 June 1988, flying from Volsau, Austria to Brest, France, a distance of 1011.48 miles (1627.78 km).

**The longest delivery flight by a four-turbine commercial airliner,** and also **the first non-stop flight by an airliner between London and Sydney,** was made during 16–17 August 1989. This was accomplished by a Qantas Boeing Model 747-400, using 176.6 tons (179 500 kg) of specially-formulated high-density fuel, with the 11 250 mile (18 105 km) flight taking 20 h 9 min.

**The longest delivery flight by a twin-turbine commercial airliner** in the FAI Class C–1Q was made by a Boeing Model 767-200ER for Royal Brunei Airlines, flown between Seattle, Washington and Nairobi, Kenya during 8–9 June 1990. Consuming 74.2 tons (75 390 kg) of fuel, the great-circle distance of 9252 miles (14 890 km) was flown in 18 h 29 min.

**The longest civil airport runway** is that at Pierre Ryneveld Airport, Upington, South Africa, which measures 16 076 ft or 3.04 miles (4.9 km).

**The longest scheduled non-stop flights,** operated both by Qantas and United Airlines, are those flown between Los Angeles, California and Sydney, Australia. Carried by Boeing Model 747SPs over a route of approximately 7487 miles (12 050 km), passengers must be prepared for a scheduled flight time of 15 h 50 min.

**The shortest scheduled flight by a piston-engined aircraft** is that between the Orkney Islands of Westray and Papa Westray. This service, flown by the Scottish airline Loganair, has been operated by Britten-Norman BN-2A Islanders since September 1967, and has a scheduled flight time of just 2 mins. On at least one occasion, with favourable wind conditions, the journey has been made in less than a minute.

**The shortest scheduled flight by a turbine-engined aircraft** is that between San Francisco and Oakland, California, flown by Boeing Model 727 aircraft of United Airlines. The 12 miles (19.3 km) separating the two airports occupies an average flight time of 5 minutes.

*Greatest:*

**The world's greatest air tragedy** occurred on 27 March 1977 when, in conditions of bad visibility, two Boeing 747's collided on the runway at Santa Cruz Tenerife, killing 583 people.

**The greatest number of passengers handled and aircraft movements recorded in each year** are those reported by Chicago O'Hare, Illinois. For the year of 1989 this totalled 59 130 007 passengers, and the 780 658 aircraft movements represented a take-off or landing every 40.4 seconds around the clock.

**The commercial transport aircraft with the world's greatest sales total** is the Boeing 737 twin-turbofan short-range airliner, which had received 2773 orders by 31 March 1990; at that date 1883 had been delivered.

**The current world record for payload lifted to 2000 m** stands at 377 473 lb (171 219 kg), set by a Soviet Antonov An-124 on 26 July 1985. The pilot was Vladimir Terski. (See also *Largest*.)

**The greatest number of flying hours accrued by a turbofan engine in commercial service, without removal from the airframe since installation,** is the proud record attained by a

Rolls-Royce RB.211. One of the three engines which powers a Lockheed L.1011 TriStar of Delta Airlines, it was installed during April 1987; by August 1991 it had exceeded 20 900 hours in service, beating the record of 20 534 hours held previously by a General Electric CF.6. Assuming the TriStar concerned (which flies daily between Atlanta, Georgia and London's Gatwick Airport) operates at an average cruising speed of 500 mph (805 km/h), it will have flown some 10.45 million miles (16.82 million km) in that period, and since which time it has been accruing approximately 16 more hours in operation per day.

**The greatest passenger load yet carried by any single commercial airliner** totals 1087; this occurred during *Operation Solomon*, which began on 24 May 1991. Just prior to this date, when the former Ethopian regime appeared to be crumbling rapidly, the Jewish nation mounted the operation to accelerate its long-term evacuation of the Falasha people to Israel. One of 33 aircraft involved, the specially prepared El Al airliner which created this record was a combined passenger/cargo Boeing 747 which had all its galleys and all but four toilets removed. Seven hundred and sixty seats were installed, with armrests in the folded position so that six people could be accommodated in four seats. During the flight to Israel three babies were born, the births attended by on-board doctors with assistance from El Al cabin crew.

## Most and Oldest:

**Eleven passengers were first carried in an aeroplane** on 23 March 1911 by Louis Breguet over a distance of 3.1 miles (5 km) at Douai, France, in a huge aircraft of his own design. **Twelve passengers were first carried in an aeroplane** on 24 March 1911 by Roger Sommer over a distance of 2625 ft (800 m) in a Sommer biplane powered by a 70 hp engine.

**The oldest airline route still operated by the original airline company** is the London–Amsterdam service which was first flown by KLM (Royal Dutch Airlines) on 17 May 1920. The aircraft used for the pioneer flight was an Eagle-engined DH16 (G-EALU) of Aircraft Transport and Travel, piloted by H. 'Jerry' Shaw. After that date, all early KLM services were operated by this British airline under charter.

The pilot with **the most flying hours** is John Edward Long (b. 10/11/1915) of Alabama, USA, who, between 1 May 1933 and 7 September 1989, had recorded a total of 53 290 h 5 min in his log book and, at that time, beat Max Conrad's long-held 'most' by 361 hours.

**The only mass hijacking of civil airliners** occurred on 6 September 1970, when four aircraft fell victim to Palestinian activists. Of these, the first, a Boeing 707 of El Al, made an emergency landing at London (Heathrow) after one of the attackers had been killed and the other (Leila Khaled) overpowered. The second was a Pan American Boeing 747 which was forced to land at Cairo; after evacuation of the passengers it was blown up. The third and fourth, a Swissair Douglas DC-8 and a TWA Boeing 707, were flown to a desert airstrip in Jordan known as Dawson's Field. On 9 September, in an attempt to force the release of Leila Khaled, a BOAC Vickers VC10 en route to Heathrow was hijacked and flown to Dawson's field where, on 12 September 1970, after all passengers and crew had been evacuated, the three airliners were destroyed.

**The most flights across the North Atlantic**, totalling 2880, were recorded by Charles M. Schimpf (a Flight Service Manager). These were logged during the period between March 1948 and his retirement on 1 September 1984.

**The most recent of the new wide-body airliners in the Soviet Union** is the Ilyushin Il-96-300, the first of five prototypes making **the type's maiden flight** on 28 September 1988. To offer performance improvements by comparison with the similar Il-86, it introduces supercritical wings incorporating winglets, and replaces the four Kuznetsov NK-86 engines of the Il-86 by advanced and more powerful Soloviev PS-90A turbofans. Seating 300 passengers in its basic all-tourist configuration, the new airliner is scheduled to enter service in 1992. A projected Il-96M with a lengthened fuselage to accommodate 375 tourist-class passengers could fly in prototype form by 1993, subject to United States approval for planned use of American powerplant comprising four Pratt & Whitney PW2037 turbofans.

**The airport handling the most international passengers each year** is London, Heathrow, which for 1989 totalled 31 525 476; the second

Above   *The largest hot-air balloon ever flown, the 2.6 million cu ft* Virgin Otsuka Pacific Flyer, *rises from Miyakonojo, Japan, in January 1991, to begin its historic transpacific crossing. (Thunder & Colt)*

Left   *Richard Branson and Per Lindstrand, crew of* Virgin Otsuka Pacific Flyer. *(Thunder & Colt)*

**Left** *The aircraft with the largest wing span, and the largest flying-boat ever flown, was the Hughes H4, which flew once in 1947. This single example is now preserved alongside the ocean liner* Queen Mary *in California.*

**Right** *Replica of the original Roe 1 that had made a 'hop' flight at Brooklands on 8 June 1908. This replica appeared at the Brooklands Museum 80 years later, on 5 June 1988. A.V. Roe had built the original using in part the £75* Daily Mail *prize won on 6 April 1907 by his model aeroplane. (Brooklands Museum)*

**Below** *The largest hot-air airship flown is the Thunder & Colt AS 261. Capable of carrying a crew of five plus a ¾-ton suspended payload, this airship was used to lift an inflatable platform (seen on left) to tree tops in the Brazilian rain forest for botanical investigations. (Thunder & Colt)*

*Gulfstream IV Pursuit of Perfection that established a round the world speed record (eastbound) of 637.71 mph (1026.29 km/h) on 26–27 February 1988, covering 23 048.6 miles (37 093.1 km) in 36 h 8 min 34 s. Bettering the 747SP flight of the previous month (see Civil Aviation, 28–30 January 1988), the Gulfstream carried an 8000 lb (3629 kg) long-range internal fuel tank. (Gulfstream Aerospace)*

Above   The largest flying-boat/amphibian in the world is the Russian Beriev A-40 Albatross, and the only current type to use turbofan engines. (Brian M. Service)

Above left   Undoubtedly the world's most famous aerobatic display team is the RAF Red Arrows, seen here with their current BAe Hawk T.Mk 1As. (British Aerospace)

Above   The RAF's first over-400 mph fighter was the Hawker Typhoon. Disappointing as an interceptor to counter the Focke-Wulf Fw 190, it carved a name for itself as a hard-hitting fighter-bomber with the 2nd Tactical Air Force, using guns, bombs and rockets to attack sea and ground targets from late 1942 and clear German armoured divisions during the Allied push into occupied Europe during 1944. This Typhoon Mk IB, built by Gloster, is being armed with two large bombs. (Imperial War Museum)

Left   The world's largest aircraft, the Russian Antonov An-225 Mriya, carrying Buran, the first Russian Space Shuttle Orbiter. (Brian M. Service)

Left   *The oldest aircraft carrier in US Navy service until retirement in November 1991 was the AVT 16 USS* Lexington, *laid down on 15 July 1941 and commissioned on 17 February 1943. Lexington was taken out of active service in 1962, to begin a long career as a training carrier. (US Navy)*

Right   *Produced in greater number than any other Western transport aircraft, and with an unrivalled longevity of service, the Douglas DC-3 (military C-47) was still to be found in military and commercial service in 1991. Here, two of five Papua New Guinea Defence Force C-47s are being refuelled at Port Morseby. (PNGDF)*

Below   *Lockheed F-117A stealth fighters, their incredible multi-faceted pyramidal airframes making them unique among the world's operational combat aircraft. (Lockheed)*

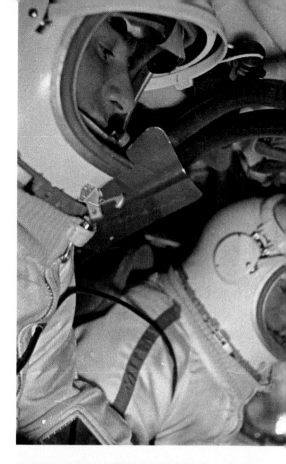

Right  *Cosmonauts Pavel Belyayev and Alexei Leonov, crew of Voskhod 2, launched on 18 March 1965. During the mission, Leonov undertook the first spacewalk.*

Below  *Spectacular lift-off of the Apollo 17 Lunar Module* Challenger *ascent stage from the Taurus-Littrow landing site on 14 December 1972, during the final manned moon mission. (NASA)*

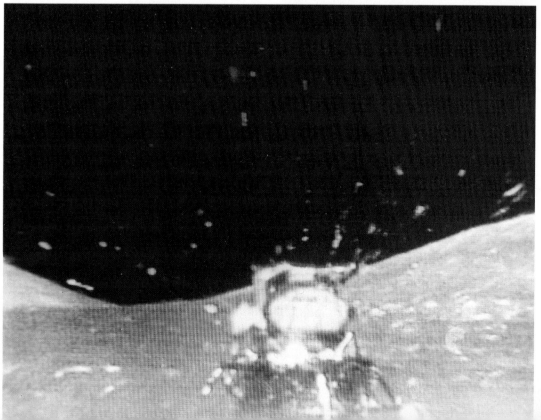

busiest is London, Gatwick, which for the same year handled 19 870 000 international passengers.

The Boeing Company recorded a **major production milestone** on 10 March 1990, when Britannia Airways took delivery in Seattle of a 767-200 which was the 6000th jet airliner produced by the company. This remarkable record was achieved in 32 years, the first 707-120 being handed over to Pan American during August 1958.

**The most experienced aircraft passenger** is believed to be Edwin A. Shackleton of Bristol, Avon, who, in 47 years, has flown in 392 different types of aircraft. He first became airborne in a de Havilland Dominie (R9548) during March 1943, and has since been flown in a wide variety of fixed-wing aircraft, helicopters, gliders, microlights, and even gas and hot-air balloons.

**The most extensively-produced post-war (WWII) biplane** is the Antonov An-2 'Colt', of which the prototype was flown for the first time on 31 August 1947. Built initially in the Soviet Union to a total in excess of 5000, its production was transferred to Poland in 1960 where it is continued in 1991, when about 12 000 had been completed. If the estimated figure of over 1000 licence-built in China (as the Yunshuji-5 or Y-5) is added, more than 18 000 of these invaluable general-purpose biplanes have been built.

**The most flights as a passenger in a supersonic aircraft** is the claim of Fred Finn, who completed his 687th crossing of the North Atlantic in Concorde during February 1991. Commuting regularly between New Jersey and London, by April 1991 he is believed to be the first passenger to exceed 10 million miles (16.09 million km) of air travel in Concorde.

**The most powerful commercial turbofan engines being offered in 1991** as an option for installation in developed versions of the Boeing Model 777, are the Pratt & Whitney PW4084 rated at 84 600 lb static thrust and the General Electric GE90-B4 rated at 84 700 lb st. General Electric have quoted that further developed versions of this latter engine may attain 95 000 lb st. The basic 777-200 version of this new Boeing long-range high-capacity twin-turbofan airliner is scheduled to fly for the first time in July 1994.

That it possesses **the world's oldest essentially original aeroplane and engine combination in flyable condition,** and **the oldest British aeroplane in flyable condition,** is the proud claim of the Shuttleworth Collection based at Biggleswade, Bedfordshire. The first is the Blériot XI monoplane, first flown on 23 January 1909, which was the type used by the pioneering Louis Blériot to make the first successful flight across the English Channel. The latter, the Blackburn Monopolane of 1912, was one of the earliest designs by Robert Blackburn, founder of the Blackburn Aeroplane Company, who had flown his first aircraft in 1910.

It is possible that the long reign of the Boeing Model 747 as the **largest capacity civil transport aircraft** may be ended in the next few years, for there are proposals in 1991 for at least two **even larger capacity airliners** The first of these is the Airbus Industrie A350 project for a 650/800-seat civil transport which, subject to an early go-ahead decision, could be in service by the end of the 1990s. Available details are few, but its large fuselage would probably be very wide to gain some lifting-body effect, and it would have an estimated range of some 8080 miles (13 000 km). More ambitious is a Soviet/Japanese proposal to develop three versions of the Antonov An-225. The first of these is a de luxe 328-passenger aircraft with seating on an upper deck, private cabins and some sleeping berths on a centre deck, and with more sleeping berths, bar, casino, restaurant and duty-free shops on the lower deck. The largest capacity version is for a total of 830 passengers in three classes, and the third is a combi variant for 400–500 passengers and 75–100 LD-3 containers. We will have to wait and see, but remember that if you had read of the 'Jumbo Jet' in 1959, ten years before the first one flew, you might never have believed it.

**The world's only supersonic commercial airliner in service in 1991** is the Aérospatiale/British Aircraft Corporation Concorde. The type entered revenue service simultaneously with Air France and British Airways on 21 January 1976, and from that date until the end of July 1991, the combined fleets of these two airlines have accumulated a total in excess of 99 500 hours of supersonic flight, considerably more than the combined total of the world's air forces.

# Air Warfare and Military Aviation

The start of 1991 witnessed a war in which air power proved so decisive that the fighting capability of one of the world's major military powers was overwhelmed by an international coalition within six weeks. Such demonstration of air superiority, and the advantages that having almost total control of the skies can provide, is an historical 'first' and may well lead to a more peaceable future for mankind under the banner of the United Nations.

Operation *Desert Storm* also highlighted the immense advantages of possessing the very latest technologies, including stealth aircraft capable of flying 'unseen' and undetected, and 'smart' weapons of super accuracy. So will such success lead to security or the hurried pursuit of ever more 'clever' weapons? Two pointers suggest the former. Firstly, only seven per cent of the air weapons used were 'smart', the bulk remaining were of more conventional types. More importantly, the late 1980s and early 1990s have witnessed a far greater awareness that nations must work together to prosper and that the wishes of the people can alter governments.

*Desert Storm* was very much a television war, watched by tens of millions around the world who were kept abreast of events as they happened by 'on site' reporters. Perhaps the time is right to recall the sombre words of Orville Wright in 1917: 'When my brother and I built and flew the first man-carrying flying machine, we thought that we were introducing into the world an invention which would make further wars practically impossible. What a dream it was; what a nightmare it has become.'

*The wrecked Wright in which Lt Thomas Etholen Selfridge was killed, 17 September 1908.*

In retrospect this seems somewhat naïve, for since time immemorial man has adapted for war-like purposes any invention which could speed his legs, extend the reach of his arms, or enhance his vision to ascertain the movements of his enemies. Though Orville's sentiment was genuine, the Wrights had earlier profited from the sale of the first military aeroplane (bought by the US Army), but would not have expected the 'armed' encounters then raging over several fronts.

Perhaps the earliest recorded adaptation of a flying machine for military use was some 200 years before the birth of Christ, when the Chinese General Han Hsin is reported to have used kites to measure the distance between his troops and an enemy position. There are many references to European use of kites during the 14th and 15th centuries to drop bombs on enemy strongholds. Only about a decade after the first manned flight (tethered) of a hot-air balloon, this new aircraft had also been adopted for war use (observation, June 1794) and 55 years later bomb dropping (unmanned hot-air, 22 August 1849).

Almost certainly the concentrated thought which the Wright brothers put into the realization of powered flight left little time for them to learn about the military use of balloons, and it is interesting to record the amazing speed of development of *The Flyer*. The real effort can be dated from 30 May 1899 when Wilbur wrote to the Smithsonian Institute asking for papers on aviation and details of books on the subject. 'I wish', he wrote, 'to avail myself of all that is already known and then if possible add my mite to help on the future worker who will attain final success.' Wilbur and Orville were to be the workers.

This section details the major events of the years that separate the Wright *Flyer* from the supersonic fighters of the 1990s. Milestones of the first half of this period must be the development of reliable powerplants during the First World War, the Schneider Trophy Contests of 1913 to 1931 which inspired new structures and engines for high-speed flight, the development of ground and airborne radar, the introduction of gas turbines during the 1940s, and the development of new weapons, climaxed by the awesome power of the nuclear bombs dropped over the Japanese cities of Hiroshima and Nagasaki on 6 and 9 August 1945 respectively. Tragically some 120 000 people were killed in these two attacks, a figure which greatly increased as others died from the effects of exposure to radiation. If there is any justification for such a scale of human sacrifice, perhaps it can be found in recently declassified American planning documents for Operation 'Downfall', the invasion of Japan which had been scheduled to begin on 1 November 1945 (X-Day) with preliminary small-scale landings four days earlier. With Japan's home defence troops augmented by some 28 million members of the Japanese National Volunteer Combat Force, US planners anticipated the possible loss of 1 million of their troops, and with perhaps a minimum 2 million Japanese lives being lost before the nation would be forced to surrender.

Since the late 1940s the threat of mutual destruction in an all-out nuclear war has been sufficient to ensure an uneasy peace between East and West. But matters have been altering for the common good. During the 1980s military transports and helicopters of East and West joined in efforts to save millions of Africans caught in famine, and in the 1990s changes in Eastern Europe spelled the end of the need for 'peace through fear'. Weapons of mass destruction have been going to the 'breakers yard', the huge rocket launchers destroyed under controlled and witnessed conditions. Such reductions in strategic forces may serve to put even greater emphasis on conventional air power in the future.

*Firsts:*

**The first aerial bombers** were bomb-carrying pennon kites, first illustrated in Europe in 1326.

**The first contract for a military aeroplane** was awarded to Clément Ader on 3 February 1892, to construct a two-seater capable of lifting a bomb-load of 165 lb (75 km). This contract was not fulfilled, as the aeroplane failed to fly at Satorg, France, on 14 October 1897.

**The first specification for a military aeroplane ever issued for commercial tender** was drawn up by Brig-Gen James Allen, Chief Signal Officer of the US Army, on 23 December 1907. The specification (main points) was as follows:

☐ Drawings to scale showing general dimensions, shape, designed speed, total surface area of supporting planes, weight, description of the engine and materials.
☐ The flying machine should be quick and easy

to assemble and should be able to be taken apart and packed for transportation.

- Must be designed to carry two persons having a combined weight of about 350 lb and sufficient fuel for a flight of 125 miles.
- Should be designed to have a speed of at least 40 mph in still air.
- The speed accomplished during the trial flight will be determined by taking an average of the time over a measured course of more than 5 miles, against and with the wind.
- Before acceptance a trial endurance flight will be required of at least 1 h.
- Three trials will be allowed for speed. The place for delivery to the Government and trial flights will be Fort Myer, Virginia.
- It should be designed to ascend in any country which may be encountered in field service. The starting device must be simple and transportable. It should also land in a field without requiring a specially prepared spot, and without damaging its structure.
- It should be provided with some device to permit of a safe descent in case of an accident to the propelling machine.
- It should be sufficiently simple in its construction and operation to permit an intelligent man to become proficient in its use within a reasonable length of time.

**The first tenders accepted by the US Army for military aeroplanes** were received on 6 February 1908. These came from A. Herring, the Wright brothers and J. Scott. Contracts for these aircraft were signed four days later but only the Wright brothers eventually delivered an aeroplane for testing. Interestingly, on 15 February Captain Thomas Baldwin's tender for the US Army's first dirigible was delivered.

**The first fatality to the occupant of a powered aeroplane** occurred on 17 September 1908 at Fort Myer, Virginia, when a Wright biplane flown by Orville Wright crashed killing the passenger, Lt Thomas Etholen Selfridge, US Army Signal Corps. Wright was seriously injured. The accident happened during US Army acceptance trials of the Wright biplane and was caused by a failure in one of the propeller blades. This imbalanced the good blade, which tore loose one of the wires bracing the rudder-outriggers to the wings, and so sending the aircraft crashing to the ground from about 75 ft (925 m).

**The first officially recognized aeroplane flight in Great Britain** was made by the American (later naturalized British citizen) Samuel Franklin Cody in his *British Army Aeroplane No. 1*, powered by a 50 hp Antoinette engine. The flight of 1390 ft (424 m) was made at Farnborough, Hampshire, on 16 October 1908 and ended with a crash-landing, but without physical injury to Cody.

**The first aeroplane flight of more than one mile in Britain** was achieved on 14 May 1909 by Samuel Cody, who flew the *British Army Aeroplane No. 1* from Laffan's Plain to Danger Hill, Hampshire—a distance of just over 1 mile—and landed without incident. The Prince of Wales requested a repeat performance during the same afternoon, but Cody, turning to avoid some troops, crashed into an embankment and demolished the tail of his aeroplane.

Following the fatal accident of 17 September 1908, it was not until 27 July 1909 that Orville Wright (with Lieutenant Frank P. Lahm as passenger) was able to record at Fort Myer **the first official test of the US Army's first aeroplane**. During this flight a new two-man endurance record was established of 1 h 12 m 40 s. The second test was carried out on 30 July, the Army's Wright completing successfully the required 10 mile (16 km) cross-country flight.

**The first aeroplane procured for service with the US Army** was the Wright Model A biplane which, following satisfactory completion of the acceptance tests mentioned above, was accepted officially on 2 August 1909. Its basic price was $25 000, but as the cross-country flight had been completed at an average speed of 42.58 mph the Wright brothers were awarded a stipulated bonus of 10 per cent for each mile-per-hour in excess of 40, making the purchase price $30 000.

**The first man to drop missiles from an aeroplane** was Lt Paul Beck on 19 January 1910, when he released sandbags (representing bombs) over Los Angeles from an aeroplane piloted by Louis Paulhan. On 30 June, the same year, Glenn Hammond Curtiss dropped dummy bombs from a height of 50 ft (15 m) on the shape of a battleship marked by buoys on Lake Keuka.

**The first military pilot to get the Brevet of the Aéro-Club de France** was Lt Camerman on 7 March 1910, receiving Brevet No. 33.

The first Scottish aeroplane pilot and the first British serving officer to qualify as a pilot (in France) was Capt Bertram Dickson of the Royal Horse Artillery. Born in Edinburgh on 21 December 1873, he was issued with Aero Club de France certificate no. 71 on 12 May 1910, having qualified at Mourmelon on 19 April. His subsequent achievements included winning first prize at the Tours meeting in the General Classification, on 3 May 1910, the first major prize won by a British pilot at an international meeting. On 11 August 1910, at Lanark, he carried **the first aeroplane passenger in Scotland,** but on 28 September he collided with an Antoinette at Milan, suffering bad injuries.

**The first French reconnaissance flight** was undertaken by Lt Féquant in a Henry Farman biplane on 9 June 1910. The following day a Wright biplane was accepted into French Army service.

**The first naval officer in the world to learn to fly** was Lt G. C. Colmore, Royal Navy, who took flying lessons on the Short S.26 biplane at Eastchurch, England, at his own expense and was awarded British Pilot's Certificate No. 15 on 21 June 1910.

**The first German active duty officer to receive a Pilot's Licence** was Lt Richard von Tiedemann, a Hussar officer. He first flew solo on 23 July 1910.

**The first patent for a device to allow a fixed machine-gun to be fired from an aeroplane** was granted to German August Euler on 24 July 1910. Euler, who had also been **the first man in Germany to gain a pilot's licence,** later demonstrated his machine-gun mount on his biplane *Gelber Hund.*

**The first serving officer of the British Army to be awarded a Pilot's Certificate in England** was Capt George William Patrick Dawes, who was awarded Certificate No. 17 for qualification on a Humber monoplane at Wolverhampton on 26 July 1910.

**The first military firearm to be fired from an aeroplane** was a rifle used by Lt Jacob Earl Fickel, US Army, from a two-seater Curtiss biplane at a target at Sheepshead Bay, New York City, on 20 August 1910.

**The first aeroplane reconnaissance for the British Army** was performed on 21 September 1910 by Bertram Dickson flying a Bristol Boxkite, during the Grand Autumn Manoeuvres near Salisbury. Having taken off from the School of Artillery grounds at Larkhill, he climbed to 2000 ft (610 m) for the first of four sorties supporting General Morland's Red Forces.

**The first aeroplane to take off from a ship** was a Curtiss biplane flown by Eugene B. Ely from an 83 ft (25 m) platform built over the bows of the American light cruiser USS *Birmingham*, 3750 tons (3810 tonnes), on 14 November 1910. It has often been averred that the vessel was anchored at the time of take-off; this is not correct as it had been proposed to take off as the ship steamed at 20 knots into the wind. In the event, the *Birmingham* had weighed anchor in Hampton Roads, Virginia, but, impatient to take off, Ely gave the signal to release his aircraft at 15.16 h before the ship was under way. With only 57 ft (17 m) of platform ahead of the Curtiss, the aircraft flew off but touched the water and damaged its propeller; the pilot managed to maintain control and landed at Willoughby Spit, 2½ miles (4 km) distant. As Ely became airborne from the cruiser, the *Birmingham* sent an historic radio message 'Ely's just gone.'

*Eugene Ely at the controls of a Curtiss pusher talking to Glenn Curtiss. (US Navy)*

*Ely leaves the deck of USS* Birmingham *on 14 November 1910 and the aircraft carrier for aeroplanes is born, but all hold their breath as he dives seaward while gaining flying speed. (US Navy)*

**The first torpedo drop from an aeroplane** was achieved in 1911 by the Italian Capitano Guidoni, flying a Farman biplane. The torpedo weighed 352 lb (160 kg).

**The first explosive bombs deployed from the air by American pilots** were those dropped by Lt Myron Sidney Crissy and Philip O. Parmalee, from a Wright biplane, during trials on 7 January 1911 at San Francisco, California.

**The first aeroplane to land on a ship** was also a Curtiss biplane flown by Ely, on 18 January 1911, when he landed on a 119 ft 4 in (36 m) long platform constructed over the stern of the American armoured cruiser, USS *Pennsylvania*, 13 680 tons (13 900 tonnes), anchored in San Francisco Bay. It had been intended that the vessel would be under way during the landing, but the Captain considered that there was insufficient sea space to manoeuvre and the *Pennsylvania* remained at anchor. Despite landing downwind the Curtiss rolled to a stop at 11.01 h after a run of only 30 ft (9 m). Capt C. F. Pond is reputed to have remarked that 'this is the most important landing of a bird since the dove flew back to the Ark'. After lunch Ely successfully took off again from the *Pennsylvania* at 11.58 h and returned to his airfield near San Francisco.

**The first aeroplane to perform a premeditated landing on water, taxi and then take off** was a Curtiss 'hydroaeroplane' flown by Glenn Curtiss on 26 January 1911. He took off and then landed

in San Diego Harbor, turned round and took off again, flying about 1 mile (1.6 km) before coming down near his starting point. A Curtiss A-1 'hydroaeroplane' was the US Navy's first aeroplane, first flown on 1 July 1911.

**The first time an aeroplane was used in war** was on 22 October 1911 when an Italian Blériot, piloted by Capitano Piazza, Italian Air Flotilla, made a reconnaissance flight from Tripoli to Azizia to view the Turkish positions.

**The first bombs dropped from an aeroplane in war** were small Cipelli grenades, hand-released from an Italian Air Flotilla aircraft (piloted by 2nd Lt Giulio Gavotti) over Turkish positions at Taguira Oasis and Ain Zara, on 1 November 1911.

**The first single-seat scout aeroplane** was the Farnborough BS1 of 1912, which was designed mainly by Geoffrey de Havilland. Powered by a 100 hp Gnome rotary engine, this very advanced aeroplane demonstrated a speed of over 91 mph (147 km/h) over a mile course.

Another Farnborough aeroplane, the BE1, made **the first successful artillery-spotting flight** over Salisbury Plain in 1912.

**The first officer of the Royal Navy to take off from a ship in an aeroplane** was Lt Charles Rumney Samson who is said to have made a secret flight in a Short biplane from a platform on the bows of the British battleship, HMS *Africa*, 17 500 tons (17 780 tonnes), moored in Sheerness Harbour during December 1911. His first officially recorded take-off was from HMS *Africa* at 14.20 h on 10 January 1912, flying a Short S.38 biplane. Cdr Samson was appointed Officer Commanding the Naval Wing of the Royal Flying Corps in October 1912.

**The first instance of a government ordering the grounding of a specific type of aircraft** occurred in March 1912 when the French government ordered all Blériot monoplanes of the French Army to be prohibited from flying until they had been rebuilt so that their wings were braced to withstand a degree of negative-G. Five distinguished French pilots had been killed following the collapse of the Blériot's wings, but the ban was short-lived and the aircraft were flying again within a fortnight. The weakness was spotlighted by Louis Blériot himself who, despite the likely loss of prestige, published a short report explaining the weakness in his own aeroplanes. There is no doubt that his frankness increased—rather than detracted from—his very high standing in aviation circles.

**The first pilot in the world to take off in an aeroplane from a ship under way** was Cdr Samson, who took off in a Short pusher biplane amphibian from the forecastle of the battleship HMS *Hibernia* while it steamed at 10.5 knots off Portland during the Naval Review on 9 May 1912. At the conclusion of the Review, Cdr Samson was one of the officers commanded to dine with HM King George V on board the *Victoria and Albert*.

**The first American aeroplane armed with a machine-gun** was a Wright Model B biplane flown by Lt Thomas de Witt Milling at College Park, Maryland, on 2 June 1912. The gunner, who was armed with a Lewis gun, was Capt Charles de Forest Chandler of the US Army Signal Corps.

**The first French aircraft to take off from a French ship** was a Navy Voisin piloted by Lt Cayla, which left the deck of the cruiser *La Foudre* anchored in the St Raphael Roads, on 27 June 1912. Cayla flew on to Cannes, returned and was hoisted back on board.

**The first military aeroplane trials to be held in Great Britain** took place at Larkhill, Salisbury Plain, in August 1912. The most important section, the speed competition, was won by Samuel Franklin Cody flying his primitive *Cathedral* biplane. Of about 30 British and French aircraft that took part, the most advanced was the Farnborough BE2, a development of the BE1.

**The first use of US Army Signals Corps aeroplanes during army manoeuvres** was recorded on 10 August 1912.

**The first pilot to perform, recover from and demonstrate recovery from a spin** was Lt Wilfred Parke, Royal Navy, on 25 August 1912 while flying the Avro cabin tractor biplane during the Military Trials of that year. On this occasion Parke and his observer, Lt Le Breton, RFC, were flying at about 600 ft (183 m) and commenced a spiral glide prior to landing; finding that the glide was too steep, Park pulled the stick back, promptly stalled and entered a spin. With no established procedure in mind for recovery he attempted to extricate himself from danger by pulling the stick further back and applying rudder *into* the direction of spin, and found that the spin merely tightened. After carefully noting this phenomenon he decided, *when only 50 ft (15 m) from the ground—*and from disaster—to reverse the rudder, and the machine recovered instantly. Parke was able to give a carefully reasoned résumé of his corrective actions, thereby contributing immeasurably to the progress of aviation.

**The first officer of the Royal Flying Corps Reserves to be killed** while engaged on military flying duties was 2nd Lt E. Hotchkiss (the Bristol Company's Chief Flying Instructor at Brooklands) who, with Lt C. A. Bettington, was killed on 10 September 1912 when their Bristol monoplane crashed on a flight from Salisbury Plain. The aircraft suffered a structural failure, after which the wing fabric started to tear away and the aircraft crashed near Oxford.

**Germany formed its first Military Aviation Service** on 1 October 1912. This lasted until just after the end of the First World War.

*Historic first, as Capitano Piazza stands in front of the Blériot that became the very first aeroplane used in war. (Italian Air Force)*

**The first trials in America to determine the suitability of aeroplanes for anti-submarine warfare** began on 26 October 1912, under the command of Lt John H. Towers.

**The first British aeroplane designed and built as an armed fighting machine** was the Vickers Destroyer EFB 1, ordered by the British Admiralty in November 1912 and displayed at the Olympia Aero Show in February 1913.

**The first aeroplane to be successfully catapult-launched from a boat** was a Curtiss A-1 Triad hydroaeroplane, piloted by Lt T. Ellyson, on 12 November 1912. The operation was performed from an anchored barge, at the Washington Navy Yard, using a compressed-air launcher invented by Capt W. I. Chambers.

**The first Russian aeroplane with a machine-gun fitted** was the Dux-1, a pusher-engined biplane intended for ground attack. This appeared in 1913.

**The first aeroplane unit of the US Army,** the 1st Aero Squadron, was formed on 5 March 1913.

**The US Army's first aerial map** (of the route from San Antonio to Texas City) was made by Lt T. C. Sherman who was riding as passenger in the aircraft flown by Lt T. D. Milling on 31 March 1913.

**The first bombs to be dropped by aeroplane on an enemy warship** were those released by Didier Masson, a supporter of General Alvarado Obregon, on Mexican gunships in the Guaymas Bay, on 10 May 1913.

The Sopwith Tabloid was **the world's first single-seat scout to enter production for military service.** Designed before the war and first flown during November 1913, a Tabloid won the 1914 Schneider Trophy contest and later became standard equipment of the early RNAS. Examples serving with the Eastchurch Squadron were armed with a wing-mounted machine-gun from February 1915.

**The first ever aerial combat between aircraft** took place in November 1913, when, over Mexico, an aeroplane piloted by Phillip Rader in support of General Huerta exchanged pistol shots with one flown by Dean Ivan Lamb operating with the forces of Venustiano Carranza.

Lt T. C. Ellyson (right), the first designated naval pilot, instructs Lt John H. Towers. (US Navy)

Curtiss AB and Triad seaplanes at Pensacola Naval Aeronautic Station in March 1914, just prior to leaving for the Vera Cruz incident. (US Navy)

**The first French airmen to be killed on active service** were Capt Hervé and his observer, named Roëland. During the colonial campaign in Morocco, early in 1914, they made a forced landing in the desert and were killed by local Arabs.

The first military operations involving the use of American aeroplanes were those during the Vera Cruz incident (Mexico) in April 1914, when five Curtiss AB flying-boats were carried to the port on board the battleship USS *Mississippi* and the cruiser USS *Birmingham*. The first such military flight was undertaken by Lt (Jg) P. N. L. Bellinger, who took off in the Curtiss AB-3 flying-boat on 25 April in order to search for mines in the harbour. The AB flying-boats flew on 43 consecutive days, and some damage was sustained from rifle fire. Bellinger's aircraft sustained the first damage by ground fire, on 6 May while on a reconnaissance flight, **the first US military aeroplane to be hit by enemy fire while on active service**.

**The first air service of the US Army** was established on 18 July 1914, when the Aviation Section was formed as part of the Signal Corps with a 'paper' strength of 60 officers and 260 men, plus six aeroplanes. This superseded the Aeronautical Division of the Signal Corps.

**The first standard naval torpedo dropped by a naval airman in a naval aircraft** was a 14 in (35.6 cm) torpedo weighing 810 lb (367 kg), dropped by a Short seaplane flown by Sqn Cdr Arthur Longmore, RN (Royal Aero Club Pilot's Certificate No. 72), on 28 July 1914. This followed a similar demonstration by Short's test pilot, Gordon Bell, the previous day.

**The first air operations undertaken by airmen of the Royal Navy during the First World War** were reconnaissance flights by Eastchurch Squadron commanded by Wg Cdr Charles Samson in support of a Brigade of Royal Marines on the Belgian coast in August 1914.

**The first British airmen killed on active service** were 2nd Lt R. B. Skene and a mechanic R. K. Barlow, of No. 3 Squadron, RFC, on 12 August 1914. Flying from Netheravon to Dover to form up for the Channel crossing, their aircraft, a Blériot two-seater of 'C' Flight, landed because of engine trouble. Shortly after taking off again, the aircraft crashed into trees and both occupants were killed.

**The first German Air Service pilot to be killed on active service** was Oberleutnant Reinhold Jahnow. He was fatally injured in a crash at Malmédy, Belgium, on 12 August 1914. He was holder of German Pilot's Licence No. 80, and a veteran of several reconnaissance flights for the Turks during the Balkan campaign of 1912.

**The first British squadrons to fly over the English Channel to France after the outbreak of war** were numbers 2, 3, 4 and 5, equipped with BE2s, Blériots and Farman biplanes; BE2s and Farmans; and Be8s and Avro 504s respectively, starting on 13 August 1914. The first of these aircraft to land was BE2a No. 347, flown by Lt H. D. Harvey-Kelly. Farmans of No. 4 Squadron were later **the first British armed aircraft to be flown in action**.

**The first bombing attack of the First World War** was made by an aeroplane flown by Lt Césari and Corp Prudhommeau, French Aviation Militaire, against the Zeppelin sheds at Metz-Frescaty, on 14 August 1914.

**The first British reconnaissance flight over German territory** was carried out by Lt G. Mappleback and Capt P. Joubert de la Ferté of No. 4 Squadron, RFC, flying a BE2a and a Blériot monoplane respectively. The flight took place on 19 August 1914.

**The first RFC aeroplane to be brought down in action** was an Avro 504 of No. 5 Squadron, piloted by Lt V. Waterfall, on 22 August 1914. The aircraft was shot down by rifle fire from troops in Belgium.

**The first RFC 'air victory'** was achieved on 25 August 1914, when Lt Harvey-Kelly flying an unarmed reconnaissance machine, in company with two other unarmed planes from No. 2 Squadron, forced a German two-seater to land.

**The first aeroplane to be destroyed by ramming** was an Austrian two-seater flown by Leutnant Baron von Rosenthal, rammed over the air base at Sholkiv on 26 August 1914 by Staff Capt Petr Nikolaevich Nesterov of the Imperial Russian XI Corps Air Squadron, who was flying an unarmed Morane Type M monoplane scout. Both pilots were killed. Nesterov (remembered also as the **first pilot to loop the loop**) was the Imperial Air Service's **first battle casualty**.

**The first RNAS Squadron to fly to France after the start of the war** was the Eastchurch Squadron, led by Wg Cdr C. R. Samson (the first British pilot to take off in an aeroplane from a ship). Arriving at Ostend on 27 August 1914, its equip-

*Voisin 'Chicken Coops' served throughout the First World War, despite its outdated design and poor performance. The Voisin X of 1918 used a 300 hp Renault engine to increase speed, carried a big 37 mm Hotchkiss cannon and up to 300 kg of bombs. Nine hundred were produced.*

ment included two Sopwith Tabloids, three BEs, two Blériots, one Short seaplane, one Bristol biplane and one Farman biplane. The only armed aircraft attached to the Squadron was the Astra-Torres airship No. 3.

**The first bombs to be dropped upon a capital city from an aircraft** fell on Paris, on 30 August 1914. The pilot of the Taube monoplane is thought to have been Leutnant Ferdinand von Hiddessen, who dropped five bombs and a message on the Quai de Valmy, killing one woman and injuring two other people.

**The first great land battle in which victory was generally attributed to aerial reconnaissance** was the battle of Tannenberg, where 120 000 Russian soldiers and 500 guns were captured by German forces in late August 1914.

**The first Japanese naval vessel converted to support seaplanes** was the 7600-ton (7722 tonnes) *Wakamiya Maru*, converted in 1913. It began operations against German forces at Kiaochow Bay, China, on 1 September 1914, using Farman seaplanes. Dropping improvised bombs made from naval shells, two Farmans of the Second Naval Squadron succeeded in sinking a German torpedo boat on 16 September. The boat was **the first warship sunk from the air.**

**The first British air raid on Germany** was by four aircraft of the Eastchurch RNAS Squadron. On 22 September 1914 two aircraft took off from Antwerp to attack the airship sheds at Düsseldorf,

two to attack the airship sheds at Cologne. Only the aircraft flown by Flt Lt Collet found the target—the sheds at Düsseldorf—and his three 20 lb (9 kg) Hales bombs, while probably on target, failed to explode. All aircraft returned safely.

**The first French bomber Groupe** was formed on 27 September 1914, equipped with Voisin pusher biplanes nicknamed 'Chicken Coops'.

**The first aeroplane in the world to be shot down and destroyed by another** was a German two-seater, possibly an Aviatik, shot down at Jonchery, near Reims on 5 October 1914 by Sergent Joseph Frantz and Caporal Quénault in a Voisin pusher of Escadrille VB24. The weapon used is believed to have been a Hotchkiss machine-gun.

**The first successful British air raid on Germany** took place on 8 October 1914. Sqn Cdr D. A. Spenser-Grey and Flt Lt R. L. G. Marix of the Eastchurch RNAS Squadron flew from Antwerp in Sopwith Tabloids (Nos. 167 and 168) to attack airship sheds at Düsseldorf and Cologne with 20 lb (9 kg) Hales bombs. Grey failed to find the target, bombed Cologne Railway Station and returned to Antwerp. Marix reached his target at Düsseldorf, bombed the shed from 600 ft (183 m) and destroyed it and Zeppelin LZ25/Z.IX inside. His aircraft was damaged by gunfire, and he eventually crash-landed 20 miles (30 km) from Antwerp, returning to the city on a bicycle borrowed from a peasant.

The first use of fléchettes as an aerial weapon occurred during autumn 1914 when deployed by aeroplanes of No. 3 Squadron RFC. Fléchettes were steel darts about 5 in (12.7 cm) in length and were dropped on enemy ground concentrations from containers each holding some 250. Casualties or damage were rare in such attacks.

The first British military aircraft insignia consisted of Union Jacks painted in rectangular and shield-shape forms on RFC aircraft. This was necessitated by the fact that RFC aircraft had been fired on by British and French groundtroops who (despite the adoption of Iron Cross insignia for German aircraft in September 1914) insisted they had mistaken them for German types. RNAS aircraft were instructed to bear the Union Jack on 26 October 1914. The roundel was adopted by the RFC from 11 December 1914, following the French example. On 11 December 1914 the RNAS adopted a roundel for the wings only – initially of a red outer circle with a white centre.

The first ever strategic bombing raid by a formation of aircraft was launched on 21 November 1914 against the Zeppelin sheds at Friedrichshafen. Sqn Cdr E. F. Briggs, leading the attack, was accompanied by Flt Cdr J. T. Babington and Flt Lt S. V. Sippé, all on Avro 504s of the Royal Naval Air Service. The aircraft flew from Belfort in France, each carrying four 20 lb bombs, with which Zeppelin LZ32 (L7) was damaged in its shed and the gasworks destroyed. Briggs was wounded in the head by heavy defending machine-gun fire and taken prisoner.

*Sikorsky* Ilya Mourometz *heavy bomber. (Sikorsky Aircraft)*

The first operational seaplane unit of the Imperial German Navy was formed on 4 December 1914, moving to its base at Zeebrugge two days later.

The first operational four-engined bombers and reconnaissance aircraft were *Ilya Mourometz* biplanes, which equipped the Flotilla of Flying Ships (EVK), Russian Army, from 10 December 1914 (formation date of the EVK). This force eventually operated at a strength of between 40 and 50 of these giants. The total number of these bombers built was 73 and those not used for training made about 400 bombing raids, the first against a Polish target on 15 February 1915. Powered by 125–220 hp engines, the *Ilya Mourometz* could fly at 60–80 mph (97–129 km/h) and could carry up to 1500 lb (680 kg) of bombs. It carried up to 16 crew members.

The first aeroplane raid on Great Britain, by one aircraft, took place on 21 December 1914. Two bombs fell in the sea near Admiralty Pier at Dover.

The first bomb dropped by an enemy aircraft on British soil, and the second aeroplane raid on Great Britain, took place on 24 December 1914. One Friedrichshafen FF 29 took part in the raid, dropping a single bomb in a garden near Dover Castle. Damage was slight.

The first Russian aircraft designed for air fighting was the two-seat Sikorsky S-16 biplane, which appeared in January 1915. Fitted with a type of synchronized machine-gun arrangement, S-16s were initially delivered in March to the EVK, as experimental escorts for the *Ilya Mourometz* bombers.

**The first aeroplane to be designed and built for aerial fighting** was the Vickers FB5 (Fighting Biplane No. 5) Gunbus. Armed with one forward-firing machine-gun, which was operated by a second crew member, the first examples of the FB5 were received by a unit in France on 5 February 1914, and the first FB5 fighter squadron (No. 11 Squadron RFC) joined the BEF on 25 July 1915.

**The first naval vessel fully converted for aircraft duties, while still under construction,** was HMS *Ark Royal*, and as such was the first ship in the world to be completed as an aircraft (seaplane) carrier. Launched in 1914, *Ark Royal* became the first aircraft carrier to operate aeroplanes against the enemy in Europe when, arriving at the entrance to the Dardanelles on 17 February 1915, one of her seaplanes was sent on reconnaissance against the Turks.

**The first British bombing raid in direct tactical support of a ground operation** occurred on 10 March 1915. It comprised attacks on railways bringing up German reinforcements in the Menin and Courtrai areas (Second Wing) and the railway stations at Lille, Douai and Don (bombed by the Third Wing), during the Neuve Chapelle offensive. The Divisional Headquarters at Fournes was also bombed by three aircraft of No. 3 Squadron piloted by Capt E. L. Conran, Lt W. C. Birch and Lt D. R. Hanlon.

**The first single-seat fighter to destroy an enemy aircraft using a machine-gun that fired through the propeller disc** was a French Morane-Saulnier, piloted by Roland Garros. Having first fitted deflector plates to the propeller to prevent the bullets from hitting the rotating blades, Garros claimed his first victory using this method on 1 April 1915. On 19 April Garros had to make an emergency landing behind German lines and his aircraft, along with its secret, was captured.

**The first intentional air attack by an armed German aircraft on an armed enemy aircraft** was made on 26 May 1915, when an armed Halberstadt C, crewed by Oberleutnant Kästner and Leutnant Langhoff, attacked and shot down a French Voisin biplane that was making a reconnaissance over the airfield at Douai.

**The first single-seat fighter to enter service with the RFC** was the Airco (de Havilland) DH2,

the prototype of which made its first flight on 1 June 1915. Powered by a 100 hp Gnôme rotary engine, mounted in a 'pusher' configuration, the DH2 had a maximum speed of 93 mph (150 km/h) and was armed with one forward-firing Lewis machine-gun. It entered service with the RFC in early 1916, and was one of the fighters which ended the supremacy of the Fokker Eindecker. DH2s served until mid-1917, latterly in Palestine. About 400 were built.

**The first fighter to be fitted with a successful synchronized machine-gun,** firing forward between the propeller blades, was the German Fokker E series Eindecker. The first E.Is arrived at the Douai airfield on the Western Front for operational trials in July 1915. Eventually, about 425 'E' series monoplanes were built. None flew faster than 87 mph (140 km/h), but they caused such havoc in attacks on Allied aircraft that their activities for ten months in 1915–16 are remembered as the 'Fokker Scourge'. The inherently stable BE2cs of the RFC suffered particularly heavy casualties. First Eindecker victory was achieved on 1 August 1915 by Leutnant Max Immelmann, who had prepared for its use by flying a Fokker M8 on 30 July 1915. Previously, on 1 July, a Fokker M5K (considered the prototype to the E.I) had been flown by Leutnant Kurt Wintgens when he shot down a French Morane-Saulnier, probably **the first air victory using a synchronized machine-gun.**

**The first Victoria Cross gained by the victor of air combat between aeroplanes** went to Capt Lanoe G. Hawker. Piloting a Bristol Scout C on 25 July 1915, he shot down two Aviatik C types and an Albatros, for which he received the VC.

**The first air attack using a torpedo dropped by an aeroplane** was carried out by Flt Cdr C. H. Edmonds, flying a Short 184 seaplane from HMS *Ben-My-Chree* on 12 August 1915, against a 5000 ton (5080 tonne) Turkish supply ship in the Sea of Marmara. Although the enemy ship was hit and sunk, the captain of a British submarine claimed to have fired a torpedo simultaneously and sunk the ship. It was further stated that the British submarine *E14* had attacked and immobilized the ship four days earlier. However on 17 August 1915 another Turkish ship was sunk by a torpedo of whose origin there can be no doubt. On this occasion Flt Cdr C. H. Edmonds, flying a Short

Right *Morane-Saulnier Type N appeared in 1914. Fitted with a machine-gun and deflector plates on the propeller blades, it equipped French and British squadrons and allowed Roland Garros and Gilbert to become early 'aces'. (Imperial War Museum)*

Below *Fokker Eindecker, the first fighter with a synchronized machine-gun. This is an E.III. (Imperial War Museum)*

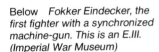

184, torpedoed a Turkish steamer a few miles north of the Dardanelles. His formation colleague, Flt Lt G. B. Dacre, was forced to land on the water owing to engine trouble but, seeing an enemy tug close by, taxied up to it and released his torpedo. The tug blew up and sank. Thereafter Dacre was able to take off and return to the *Ben-My-Chree*.

**The first sustained strategic bombing offensive** was opened by Italy on 20 August 1915, following its declaration of war against Austria–Hungary on 24 May. The first target was the Asiovizza airfield. Major aircraft type used in the early raids was the Caproni Ca 32 three-engined biplane (100 hp Fiat A10s), of which 31 were delivered in 1915 and 133 in 1916. The Ca 32 was used in the first Italian night bombing raids. It carried a crew of four.

**The first launching of an aeroplane by catapult on board ship** (excluding anchored barge), took place on 5 November 1915 when an AB-2 flying-boat was catapulted from the stern of the American battleship USS *North Carolina*, anchored in Pensacola Bay, Florida. On the following day AB-2, piloted by Lt Cdr Henry Mustin, was catapulted from USS *North Carolina* while the ship was moving.

**The first product of the German Junkers company** and **the world's second type of all-metal monoplane to fly** was the Junkers J1, which took to the air for the first time on 12 December 1915. Intended as a reconnaissance and close-support aircraft, it had cantilever wings and the complete airframe was skinned in sheet iron. Power was provided by a 120 hp Mercedes DII engine. Only the single prototype was built.

The first major battle to see the use of large formations of fighter aircraft was Verdun, which began on 21 February 1916.

The first ever sustained military resupply by air took place between 15 and 26 April 1916. Then, BE2cs and other aircraft of No 30 Squadron, RFC, and the RNAS flew 19 000 lb (8618 kg) of food, mail, currency, gold, silver, wireless parts and more into the besieged town of Kut el Amara, Mesopotamia, surrounded by Turkish forces. Supply bags were slung over the fuselages and secured to the undercarriages.

The first aeroplane involved in parasite fighter experiments (intended to be carried to within striking distance of a Zeppelin by a larger and longer-ranged aircraft) was the Bristol Scout, mounted on the upper wing of a Porte Baby flying-boat. On 17 May 1916 the Scout C (No. 3028) of this composite completed the first (and only) mid-air separation of this combination, climbing away from its carrier over Harwich and completing a successful flight and landing.

The first pilot of the Escadrille Américaine to gain an 'air victory' was Lt Kiffin Rockwell, while escorting bombers near Mulhouse on 18 May 1916; Rockwell himself was killed on 23 September. This famous French squadron manned by American pilots had formed only a month earlier, on 16 April; it was later to become known as the Lafayette Escadrille.

The first triplane fighter to enter service was the British Sopwith Triplane, a single-seater nicknamed 'Tripehound'. The prototype flew for the first time on 28 May 1916.

The first major fleet battle in which an aeroplane was used was the Battle of Jutland on 31 May 1916, when Flt Lt F. J. Rutland (accompanied by his observer, Assistant Paymaster G. S. Trewin) spotted and shadowed a force of German light cruisers and destroyers. Taking off from alongside HM seaplane carrier Engadine at about 15.10 h, Rutland sighted the enemy ships and continued to radio position reports to the Engadine.

The first American pilot to be killed in the First World War was Victor Emmanuel Chapman of the Lafayette Escadrille, who was shot down near Verdun on 23 June 1916.

The first German airship to be brought down on British soil was the Schutte-Lanz SL XI, which was attacked on the night of 2 September 1916 by a BE2c flown by Lt W. Leefe Robinson, RFC: see Lighter than air—dirigibles.

The first radio-guided flying-bomb was tested on 12 September 1916. It was called the 'Hewitt-Sperry biplane' and was built by Curtiss. Powered by a 40 hp engine, it was capable of covering 50 miles (80 km) carrying a 308 lb (140 kg) bomb-load.

The first submarine to be sunk by an aeroplane was the French submarine Foucault, on 15 September 1916, by an Austrian Löhner flying-boat.

The first Albatros D.I single-seat fighters were used operationally for the first time on 17 September 1916, under the command of Oswald Boelcke.

The first bombs to fall on London from an aeroplane were six small bombs dropped from a German LVG C11 on 28 November 1916, falling near Victoria Station. The pilot of the attacking aircraft was Deck Offizier P. Brandt.

Left  *AB-2 flying-boat in flight after the first catapult launch from USS* North Carolina *in Pensacola Bay. (US Navy)*

Right  *Curtiss-built Hewitt-Sperry radio-guided flying-bom, (US National Archives)*

Below  *Sopwith Cuckoo torpedo seaplane.*

**The first flush-deck aircraft carrier in the world** was HMS *Argus*, 15 775 tons (16 027 tonnes). Originally laid down in 1914 as the Italian liner *Conte Rosso*, she was purchased by Great Britain and launched in 1917, and completed in 1918. She featured an unrestricted flight deck of 565 ft (172 m) length and could accommodate 20 aircraft. She was ultimately scrapped in 1947. She was **the first carrier in the world to embark a full squadron of torpedo-carrying landplanes**, when in October 1918 a squadron of Sopwith Cuckoos was activated. They did not, however, see action.

**The first intentional air victory achieved at night** was gained on the night of 11 to 12 February 1917, by Leutnant Peter and Leutnant Frohwein flying a DFW CV. On this occasion they destroyed two bombers landing at Malzeville.

**The first vessel in the world to be defined as an aircraft carrier** (in the modern sense, i.e. equipped with a flying deck for operation of landplanes) was the light battle-cruiser HMS *Furious*. Construction of this ship began shortly after the outbreak of the First World War, it being intended to arm her with a pair of 18 in (457 mm) guns. In March 1917 authority to alter her design was issued, and at the expense of one of these huge guns she was completed with a hangar and flight deck on her forecastle. With a speed of 31.5 knots, she carried six Sopwith Pups in addition to four seaplanes. Her first Senior Flying Officer was Sqn Cdr E. H. Dunning. HMS *Furious* became the **longest-lived active carrier in the world.** Between 1921 and 1925 the midships superstructure was eliminated and she emerged as a flushdeck carrier displacing 22 450 tons (22 809 tonnes), with two aircraft lifts and an aircraft capacity of 33. Her overall length was 786 ft (239 m). After an extraordinarily active and exciting career in the Second World War (and a near head-on collision at night in the Atlantic with a troopship which passed so close as to carry away some of the carrier's radio masts), she was finally scrapped in 1949.

**The first British unit to be established specifically for night bombing operations** was No. 100 Squadron, RFC, which formed at Hingham (Norfolk) on 23 February 1917 and crossed to France on 21 March. It was based initially at St-André-aux-Bois where a week later the unit received its first aircraft, 12 FE2bs, and then moving to Le Hameau on 1 April 1917. Its first operations were two raids on the night of 5/6 April on Douai airfield, home base of the 'Richthofen Circus'. One FE2b failed to return, but four hangars were badly damaged by bombs.

**The first German submarine to be sunk by an aeroplane** was the U-36, attacked in the North Sea on 20 May 1917 by a Large America flying-boat piloted by Flt Sub-Lt C. R. Morrish.

**The first mass bombing raid on England** by Gotha heavy bombers was made on 25 May 1917, when 21 aircraft attacked several towns, including Folkestone and Shorncliffe. Some 95 people were killed and 195 more were injured. RFC and RNAS aircraft flew 77 defence sorties without making contact.

**The first mass bombing raid on London** was by German Gotha heavy bombers on 13 June 1917. Fourteen bombers attacked an area around Liverpool Street Station, dropping 72 bombs and causing 162 deaths, with 432 people injured. **This was the worst bombing raid of the war** in terms of dead and injured. **The last major bombing raid on England in daylight** was on 12 August 1917.

**The first German armoured aeroplane,** designed for ground attack and low-level reconnaissance missions, was the Junkers J1 biplane, of which 227 were built. Fitted with 5 mm steel plating, the type entered service in the latter half of 1917 and was armed with three machine-guns.

**The first landing in the world by an aeroplane upon a ship under-way** was carried out by Sqn Cdr E. H. Dunning who flew a Sopwith Pup on to the deck of HMS *Furious* on 2 August 1917. Steaming at 26 knots into a wind of 21 knots, *Furious* thus provided a 47 knot headwind for Dunning who flew his Pup for'ard along the starboard side of the ship before side-slipping towards the deck located on the forecastle. Men then grabbed straps on the aircraft and brought it to a

Above   *A German Gotha long-range heavy bomber being armed with 50 kg bombs. (US National Archives)*

Below   *Junkers JI armoured biplane. (Imperial War Museum)*

Left   *Crew rush forward to grab Dunning's Pup fighter as it sideslips and lands onto HMS Furious.*

Below   *Fokker Dr.I triplane fighters. (Imperial War Museum)*

standstill. On 7 August Dunning attempted to repeat the operation in an even greater headwind but stalled as he attempted to overshoot and was killed when his aircraft was blown over the side of the ship.

**The first enemy night bomber to be destroyed over Germany** was shot down on the night of 8 to 9 August 1917 near Frankfurt-on-Main.

**The first of Germany's new Fokker FI (Dr I) triplane fighters** arrived at Courtrai on 21 August 1917. Lt Werner Voss was the first to fly one into action, destroying an RFC aircraft on 30 August.

**The first mass bombing raid at night by Gotha aeroplanes on Britain** was made on the night of 2 to 3 September 1917. The target was Dover.

**The first raid on Britain by German 'R' type bombers** was made on 17 September 1917. German Staaken R VI giant bombers were capable of dropping 1000 kg bombs, which were the largest bombs of the war.

**The first RFC unit to be formed to carry out strategic bombing of targets inside Germany** was the 41st Wing, which came into being on 11 October 1917.

**The first Gotha bomber to be shot down at night** during a bombing raid was destroyed in January 1918 by two Sopwith Camels of No. 44 Squadron, RFC, at Wickford, Essex. This proved

that even at night the Gotha could be intercepted, and stopped, and night raids on England ceased in May 1918.

**The first US pilot to gain a victory while serving with an American squadron** was Lt Stephen W. Thompson, in February 1918. His squadron, the 103rd Pursuit Squadron, had been formed from the Lafayette Escadrille on 18 February but was then still operating with French forces.

**The first combat aeroplane to enter production in the United States** was the British de Havilland DH4. The first machine was completed in February 1918.

**The first US fighter squadron to arrive in France from America** was the 95th Aero (Pursuit) Squadron, on 18 February 1918.

**The first mission carried out by the newly-formed RAF** (by combining the RFC and RNAS on 1 April 1918) was made on the same day by Bristol F2B Fighters of No. 22 Squadron.

**The first American observation aircraft to fly over enemy lines** were from I Corps Observation Squadron, on 11 April 1918.

**The first American-trained pilots to shoot down enemy aircraft** were 1st Lt Douglas Campbell and 2nd Lt Alan Winslow of the 94th Aero (Pursuit) Squadron, on 14 April 1918. Having taken off at 08.50 h, they intercepted an Albatros D V (flown by Corp Simon) and a Pfalz D IIIa (flown by Sgt Maj Wronieki) of Jagdstaffel 64 in the area of Toul, and shot both down. Both pilots survived. The first to fall was the Albatros, to the guns of Winslow. The American pilots flew Nieuport 28s. Campbell was **the first US pilot serving under American colours to become an ace**, gaining his fifth victory on 31 May 1918.

**The first US bomber squadron** of the AEF was formed in France on 18 May 1918, as the 96th Aero Squadron. The squadron's first raid was against the railway at Dommany-Baroncourt, on 12 June.

**The first pilot to take off successfully from a towed barge in an aeroplane** was the American-born Flt Sub-Lt Stuart Culley, RN, who on 1 August 1918 rose from a barge towed by HMS *Redoubt* at 35 knots. At 08.41 h on 11 August 1918 Culley took off from the barge while being towed off the Dutch coast and climbed to 18 000 ft (5500 m) to shoot down the German Zeppelin L53 using incendiary ammunition. He was thus **the first (and probably the only) pilot to shoot down an enemy aircraft after taking off from a towed vessel**. Landing in the sea alongside his towing destroyer, HMS *Redoubt*, he was rescued—and later awarded the DSO for his feat—and his Camel was salvaged by a derrick (invented by Col Samson). The only survivor of the Zeppelin baled out from 19 000 ft (5800 m)—almost certainly a record at that time.

**The first US fighter patrol at night** was undertaken by the 185th Aero (Pursuit) Squadron on 12 October 1918.

**The First World War** came to an end on the 11th hour of the 11th day of the 11th month, 1918.

**The first US-designed fighter to enter large-scale production** was the Thomas Morse MB-3, the prototype of which made its maiden flight on 21 February 1919.

**The first military aircraft designed and built in Czechoslovakia**, the Letov S1 reconnaissance and light bombing biplane, was introduced in 1919–20. Power was provided by a 260 hp Maybach Mb IVa engine and a total of 90 S1 and S2 versions was built. The SH-1 variant had a maximum speed of 120 mph (193 km/h).

**The first American aircraft carrier to carry heavier-then-air craft** was the USS *Jupiter*, an ex-collier of 11 050 tons (11 227 tonnes), which was converted during 1920 to provide a stem-to-stern flight deck. Later named USS *Langley*, it became the US Navy's first aircraft carrier when it was commissioned on 20 March 1922.

**The first post-war world speed record** was set in France on 7 February 1920 by Sadi Lecointe at a speed of 171.01 mph (275.22 km/h), flying a Nieuport-Delage 29.

**The first Japanese fighter built for operation from an aircraft carrier** was the Mitsubishi 1MF1, designed by the Englishman Herbert Smith. First flown in 1921, the 1MF1 proved very successful during flight trials.

**The US Army's first production armoured aeroplane**, the GA-1, was flown for the first time during May 1921. In addition to about a ton of ¼-in (6 mm) protective armour plating, it carried eight 0.3 in machine-guns, a 37 mm Baldwin cannon, and ten 25 lb fragmentation bombs. Designed by the Army's Engineering Division and built by Boeing, it was not very successful.

Right  *Vickers Vernon, the first aircraft designed as a troop transport.*

Left  *A 100 lb phosphorus bomb dropped from a Martin MB-2 hits the crow's nest of USS* Alabama. *(US Army)*

Below  *USS* Langley *with its funnels lowered for aeroplane operations. (US Navy)*

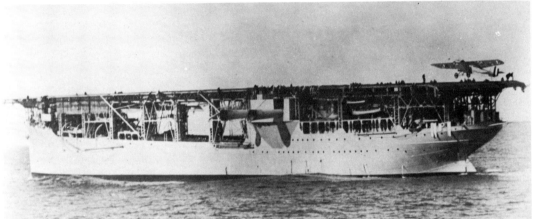

The greatest early demonstration of air power against naval vessels occurred in July 1921. Under the command of Brig-Gen 'Billy' Mitchell, US Martin MB-2 biplane bombers sank the ex-German battleship *Ostfriesland* and other surplus vessels which were at anchor on 21 July. Two days later, MB-2s sank the old battleship USS *Alabama* and two other vessels.

The first troop transport to be designed as such from the outset was the Vickers Vernon biplane. Production totalled 55, built in three versions with 360 hp Rolls-Royce Eagle VIII, 450 hp Napier Lion II and Lion III engines respectively, the first of them entering RAF service in August 1921.

The first purpose built aircraft carrier for the Imperial Japanese Navy was the *Hosho*, launched during November 1921 and commissioned on 27 December 1922. It survived the Second World War and was decommissioned after the Japanese surrender.

The first flight of the prototype Breguet 19 bomber/reconnaissance aircraft was made during May 1922. The Breguet 19 was one of the most extensively used military types of the 'between-wars' years.

The first over 200 mph world speed record was set by Sadi Lecointe on 20 September 1922, flying a Nieuport-Delage 29.

The first demonstration of radar signatures was made by technicians at Anacostia Naval Aircraft Radio Laboratory, USA, on 27 September 1922.

The first air control operation, in which an air force became entirely responsible for the internal security of a nation, began in October 1922. The RAF assumed responsibility for maintaining peace in Iraq, replacing the former large army garrison with two squadrons of Vernon transports, four of DH9As, one of Bristol Fighters and one of Snipe fighters.

**The first take-off from an American aircraft carrier**, the USS *Langley*, was made on 17 October 1922 by Lt V. C. Griffin flying a Vought VE-7SF fighter.

**The first examples of the Czechoslovakian Aero A 11 were flown in 1923.** This highly successful general purpose biplane, of which some 440 examples were built, established several duration records and, in 1926, one completed a 9320 mile (15 000 km) intercontinental flight.

**The first take-off and landing on Japan's new aircraft carrier**, the *Hosho*, were made in February 1923 by a Mitsubishi 1MF1 flown by a British pilot, Capt Jordan.

**The first successful in-flight refuelling of an aeroplane** was accomplished by Capt L. H. Smith and Lt J. P. Richter in a de Havilland DH4B on 27 June 1923 at San Diego, California. Smith and Richter established a new world endurance record by remaining airborne for 37 h 15 min 43.8 s from 27 to 28 August 1923, covering a distance of 3293.26 miles (5299.9 km) over a measured 50 km course at San Diego. Their DH4B was flight-refuelled 15 times.

**The first six-engined American aircraft**, the Barling XNBL-1 triplane bomber, was flown for the first time on 22 August 1923. Then the largest aeroplane in the world, it proved to be underpowered and no further examples were built.

**The former Soviet Union's first fighter aircraft to be built in series**, the Polikarpov I-1 (Il-400) was flown for the first time in prototype form on 23 August 1923. A cantilever low-wing monoplane, it was then powered by an American Liberty engine.

**The RAF's first new fighter after the end of the First World War**, the Gloster Grebe biplane, entered service during October 1923.

**First new Italian-designed fighter aircraft to be adopted by the Regia Aeronautica**, the Fiat C.R.1 single-seat biplane fighter was demonstrated during this air force's annual review on 4 November 1924.

**The first flight of the Gloster Gamecock prototype (J7497)** was made during February 1925. In production form this aircraft was the **last biplane fighter of wooden basic structure to serve with the RAF.**

**The first landing by night on an aircraft carrier** was accomplished by Flt Lt Boyce, RAF, on 1 July 1926, piloting the Blackburn Dart N9804 to the deck of HMS *Furious*.

**The first French aircraft carrier**, named *Béarn*, was completed on 27 May 1927 after almost seven years of construction.

**The first world speed record in excess of 500 km/h and 300 mph** was established by Maj Mario di Bernardi of the Italian Air Force. Flying a Macchi M.52*bis* floatplane, he attained a ratified speed of 318.57 mph (512.69 km/h) on 30 March 1928.

*Left  Smith and Richter undertaking flight refuelling over Rockwell Field during their 37 hour endurance flight. (US Air Force)*

*Right  The Handley Page Heyford was the RAF's last biplane bomber.*

**The world's first large-scale airlift evacuation of civilians** was undertaken by transport aircraft of the Royal Air Force between 23 December 1928 and 25 February 1929. Five hundred and eighty-six people and 24 193 lb (10 975 kg) of luggage were airlifted from the town of Kabul, Afghanistan, during inter-tribal disturbances. They were carried over treacherous country using eight Vickers Victoria transports of No. 70 Squadron RAF, and a Handley Page Hinadai.

**The first flight of the Gloster Gauntlet prototype** was made during January 1929, and this interesting fighter proved to be the **last open cockpit biplane to serve with the RAF**. In November 1937 three Gauntlets of No. 32 Squadron were directed by experimental ground radar to intercept a civil airliner flying above the River Thames, this being **the world's first successful radar-controlled interception**.

Above   *PZL P.7a gull-wing fighters of Poland's 111 Squadron, 1st Air Regiment.*

**The first electro-mechanical flight simulator** was the Link Trainer which was patented on 14 April 1929. It comprised a replica of an aeroplane, with full controls and instruments, which did not leave the ground; instead it was 'attached' to a mechanical crab that traced a path over a large scale map in such a way as to represent heading, speed and time of the replica aircraft 'flown' by its occupant. Invented by Edward Albert Link, who sold his first model in 1919, it was adopted by the US Navy in 1931 and by the US Army in 1934. By 1939 there was scarcely an air force in the world that was not using Link Trainers. They can be regarded as the forerunners of today's complex flight simulators.

**The first blind-flight take-off, level flight and landing** was accomplished by Lt James H. Doolittle on 24 September 1929, at Mitchell Field, Long Island, New York.

**The first flight of the Handley Page HP38 (J9130) prototype** was made on 12 June 1930. Later named Heyford, it was **the last heavy bomber of biplane configuration to serve with the RAF**.

**First flown in prototype form during October 1930**, the Polish PZL P.7 fighter was to confer a unique reputation on the Polish Air Force when it equipped all of its fighter squadrons in 1933, thus making it **the first air force in the world to have only all-metal monoplane fighters in first-line service**.

The first monoplane heavy bomber to enter operational service with the RAF was the Fairey Hendon. First flown in prototype (K1695) form on 25 November 1930, it was not until 1936 that the first production examples were delivered to the RAF.

The first four-engined monoplane heavy bomber to enter service with the Soviet Air Force was the Tupolev TB-3 which, under the Tupolev bureau's designation ANT-6, had first flown as a prototype on 22 December 1930.

The first formation flight across the South Atlantic, from Portuguese Guinea to Natal, Brazil, was made on 6 January 1931 by ten Savoia-Marchetti S55 flying-boats, commanded by Italian Air Minister General Italo Balbo. In 1933, from 1 to 15 July, General Balbo led the first formation flight across the North Atlantic. Taking off from Orbetello, Italy, the 24 S55s flew to the Century of Progress Exposition in Chicago, their route being via Holland, Iceland, Labrador and New Brunswick, Canada.

The RAF's first fighter aircraft able to exceed 200 mph (322 km/h) in level flight, the Hawker Fury I biplane first entered service with No. 43 Squadron at Tangmere, Sussex, in May 1931. Powered by a 525 hp Rolls-Royce Kestrel IIS liquid-cooled engine and armed with two synchronized machine-guns, the Fury, designed by the late Sir Sydney Camm, had a top speed of 207 mph (333 km/h) at 14 000 ft (4270 m).

The first blind solo flight entirely on instruments (with no check pilot on board the aircraft) was accomplished by Capt A. F. Hegenberger when flying a Consolidated NY–2 trainer at Dayton (Ohio) on 9 May 1931.

The first over 400 mph speed record was set by Flt Lt G. H. Stainforth on 29 September 1931, his six runs over the set course averaging 407.5 mph (655.81 km/h). This was achieved in the Supermarine S.6B S1595 which, just over two weeks earlier on 13 September, had been flown by Flt Lt J. N. Boothman to win the Schneider Trophy Contest outright for Britain at an average speed of 340.08 mph (547.31 km/h).

The first twin-engined bomber to be designed for the clandestine German Luftwaffe was the Dornier Do 11. Designated originally Dornier Do F, the prototype first flew on 7 May 1932, disguised as the last of a batch of mail/cargo transport aircraft. Powered by two 650 hp Siemens-Jupiter engines, some 77 Do 11s were produced.

Above   Tupolev TB-3 heavy bomber used here for parachuting.

Below   The USAAC's first all-metal monoplane fighter was the Boeing P-26. Here the XP-936 first prototype (first flown on 20 March 1932) flies with the Boeing Y1B-9A, the USAAC's first all-metal monoplane bomber with a retractable undercarriage (prototype first flown 13 April 1931 but limited production for trials only).

The first cantilever low-wing monoplane fighter to serve with the French Armée de l'Air was the Dewoitine D500. First flown in prototype form on 18 June 1932, the production aircraft did not begin to enter service until 1935 due to wing structural weakness. Variants included the D501 and D510 and many examples of the series were exported, China being the largest foreign operator with 34 D510s.

Designed and first flown as the Curtiss XF12C-1 parasol monoplane in 1933, this aircraft was almost immediately redesigned as a biplane and, as the SBC Helldiver, was the last operational US biplane. Remaining in production until 1941, at the time of the Japanese attack on Pearl Harbor in December 1941 the US Navy still had 186 Helldivers on strength.

Germany's first new post-war fighters, built to equip the secret Luftwaffe in the early 1930s, were the Heinkel He 51 and the Arado Ar 68. Many He 51s were built, in several versions, and 135 were operated by the Spanish and German air forces during the Spanish Civil War. Their useful life in this role was curtailed when the Republican forces started flying the Russian Polikarpov I-15. The He 51B-1, powered by a 740 hp BMW VI engine, had a maximum speed of 205 mph (220 km/h). The first prototype Ar 68 flew initially in 1933; the major production version was the Ar 68E which entered service from 1937, although small numbers of Ar 68Fs had entered service in 1935. Powered by a 690 hp Junkers Jumo 210D engine, the Ar 68E had a maximum speed of 208 mph (335 km/h).

*Prototype Dewoitine D500, first flown in mid-1932.*

The first aeroplane with retractable landing gear to be flown by the US Navy was the Grumman XFF-1 biplane fighter which, as the FF-1, began to enter service on 21 June 1933.

The first monoplane fighter with a fully enclosed cockpit and fully retractable landing gear to enter squadron service anywhere in the world was the Polikarpov I-16 Ishak ('Little Donkey'). The prototype was flown first on 31 December 1933, and deliveries of the Type I production fighter to Soviet squadrons began during the summer of 1934. The I-16 Type I was powered by a 450 hp M22 engine, and a top speed of 224 mph (360 km/h) at sea level, and was armed with two 7.62 mm ShKAS machine-guns.

The first RAF bomber incorporating a power-operated enclosed gun turret was the Boulton Paul Overstrand, 24 of which were built and entered service in 1934. Power was provided by

*Grumman FF-1 featuring a retractable undercarriage.*

Polikarpov I-16s with M-25 engines. (Imperial War Museum)

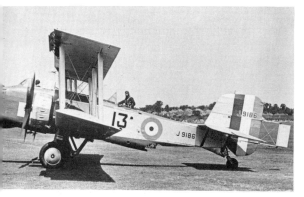

Boulton-Paul Overstrand bomber with power-operated turret. (Flight International)

Douglas TBD-1 Devastator carrier-based torpedo bomber.

two 580 hp Bristol Pegasus II M3 engines; a bomb load of 1600 lb (725 kg) could be carried.

**The first German Army rocket**, the A-1, was developed at Kummersdorf in 1933 but this never flew. Two A-2 rockets were fired from Borkum in December 1934 and achieved an altitude of about 8200 ft (2500 m). In April 1937 the Kummersdorf site was abandoned and von Braun took his team to Peenemünde on the Baltic coast. Here the A-3 and A-5 rockets were developed in preparation for the A-4. It was better known as the V-2, the initial V standing for *Vergeltungswaffe* ('reprisal weapon'). The first so-called 'reprisal weapon' was the V-1 flying bomb, better known to the British as the 'Doodlebug'.

**The first American naval aircraft to feature hydraulically operated folding wings**, and also the US Navy's first carrier-based monoplane torpedo-bomber to enter production, was the Douglas TBD Devastator. First flown in prototype form on 15 April 1935, the first production TBD-1s were delivered to US Navy Squadron VT-3 on 5 October 1937. Of 75 Devastators on strength with the US Navy on 3 June 1942, 37 were lost during the Battle of Midway (see below), Squadron VT-8 was entirely destroyed and another squadron decimated in combat with Japanese Zero fighters. Following this action the type was withdrawn from operational use.

**The first German monoplane fighter into squadron service with a fully enclosed cockpit and fully retractable landing gear** was the Messerschmitt Bf 109B-1. The prototype Bf 109V-1 (D-IABI) was first flown on 28 May 1935, powered by a 695 hp British Rolls-Royce Kestrel V engine. The first production Bf 109B-1s were delivered to Jagdgeschwader 2 'Richthofen' in the spring of 1937, and this version was the first of the series to become operational in Spain with the Legion Condor during the Civil War. The B-1 model was powered by a 635 hp Junkers Jumo 210D engine, had a top speed of 292 mph (470 km/h) at 13 100 ft (4000 m), and was armed with three 7.92 mm MG 17 machine-guns.

**The first American monoplane fighter into squadron service with a fully enclosed cockpit and fully retractable landing gear** (into fairings) was the Seversky P-35, the prototype of which was evaluated at Wright Field during August 1935. The production model, of which deliveries began

Right  *Luftwaffe Messerschmitt Bf 109B-1 fighters in 1936. (MBB)*

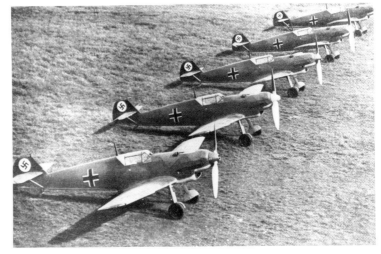

Below  *Hawker Hurricane fighters of No 56 Squadron at the height of the Battle of Britain, July 1940. In this most famous air battle of all time, Hurricanes claimed more victories than any other British fighter. (Imperial War Museum)*

in July 1937, was powered by a 950 hp Pratt & Whitney R-1830-9 engine. It had a top speed of 281 mph (452 km/h) at 10 000 ft (3050 m), and was armed with one 0.5 in and one 0.3 in machine-gun.

The first French monoplane fighter into squadron service with a fully enclosed cockpit and fully retractable landing gear was the Moraine-Saulnier M-S 406. The M-S 405, from which the series was derived, first flew on 8 August 1935, and was the first French fighter aircraft able to exceed a speed of 250 mph (402 km/h) in level flight. The first production M-S 406 (N2-66) flew for the first time on 29 January 1939, and by 1 April 1939 a total of 27 had been delivered to the French Air Force.

The first British monoplane fighter into squadron service with a fully enclosed cockpit and fully retractable landing gear was the Hawker Hurricane. It was also the RAF's first fighter able to exceed a speed of 300 mph (483 km/h), and the first of its eight-gun monoplane fighters. The prototype was flown for the first time on 6 November 1935, and initial deliveries of production aircraft were made to No. 111 Squadron at Northolt, Middlesex, during December 1937.

First moves to institute Shadow Factories in Britain were made in April 1936, initially to establish aircraft engine production by motor car engine manufacturers. The scheme was later adopted for the production of aircraft.

The first indication of the beginning of the Spanish Civil War came on 18 July 1936 with simultaneous revolt of 12 military garrisons in Spain and of 5 in Spanish Morocco.

The first large-scale military airlift began on 21 July 1936, when Junkers Ju 52/3m bomber/transports were used over a period of about six weeks to ferry some 7350 Nationalist troops, with their artillery and other equipment, from Morocco to Spain at the beginning of the Spanish Civil War.

The first multi-engined bombers of the clandestine German Luftwaffe to be used in combat were specially converted Junkers Ju 52/3m transports, each of which could carry a maximum bombload of 3,307 lb (1500 kg). Operating with the Legion Cóndor pending the delivery of Dornier Do 17 and Heinkel He 111 bombers, the first action by these aircraft occurred on 14 August 1936 when bombs were dropped on a Republican column advancing to the south of Madrid.

The first Japanese Army Air Force low-wing monoplane fighter, and first with an enclosed cockpit, was the Nakajima Ki-27. The first prototype made its initial flight on 15 October 1936, and production aircraft entered combat in Manchuria during 1938.

The first intensive air bombardment of a city during the Spanish Civil War occurred on 6 November 1936, when Nationalist attacks were made on Madrid in attempts to dislodge Republican troops.

First seeing combat in 1937 during the Sino-Japanese war while operating from the carrier Hosho, the Nakajima A4N1 fighter had entered service with the Imperial Japanese Navy during 1935. Considered obsolete by the outbreak of the Pacific War in late 1941, the A4N1 was the Japanese Navy's last carrier-based biplane fighter.

The first monoplane to enter service with the Fleet Air Arm was the Blackburn Skua dive-bomber, of which the prototype was first flown on 9 February 1937. Deliveries of production aircraft began in November 1938; a total of 165 was built, these remaining in service until 1941.

The first two-seater fighter with a power-operated four-gun turret to serve with the RAF, the Boulton Paul Defiant, was first flown in prototype form on 11 August 1937.

The first Italian monoplane fighter into service with a fully enclosed cockpit and fully retractable landing gear was the Macchi C200 Saetta ('Lightning'). First single-seat fighter designed by Dr Mario Castoldi, the prototype was flown first on 24 December 1937. Deliveries of production aircraft began in October 1939, and these were powered by the 870 hp Fiat A74RC38 radial engine, giving the C200 a maximum speed of 313 mph (505 km/h) at 15 750 ft (4800 m).

The first monoplane fighter to equip a US Navy squadron was the Brewster F2A Buffalo, flown for the first time in XF2A-1 prototype form during December 1937.

First flown in prototype (K8854) form on 23 September 1938, the Supermarine Sea Otter was the company's last production biplane flying-boat. It remained in production until July 1946 and, built to a total of 292, was the last biplane to serve with the Fleet Air Arm, which retained it in use until the early 1950s.

Flown for the first time on 1 June 1939, entering service with the Luftwaffe in August 1941 and first engaged in combat with RAF Spitfires on 27 September 1941, the Focke-Wulf Fw 190 is regarded as one of the classic fighter aircraft of the Second World War. Their first major deployment was to provide an air umbrella for the German battleships Gneisenau and Scharnhorst and the cruiser Prinz Eugen during their 'Channel-dash' on 12–13 February 1942.

The first successful use of air-to-air rockets against aeroplanes is believed to have taken place on the afternoon of 20 August 1939 when five Polikarpov I-16 Type-10 fighters, each fitted with underwing rails for eight 82 mm RS 82 rockets, went into action against Japanese fighters over the Khalkin Gol area of Mongolia. The unit, commanded by Capt Zvonariev, claimed the destruction of two Mitsubishi A5M fighters on this occasion.

The first American-built aircraft to be used operationally by the RAF during the Second World War was the Lockheed Hudson, which entered service with No. 224 Squadron at Gosport in the Summer of 1939. A Hudson operated by this squadron scored the first British victory over a German aircraft in the Second World War, directed Naval forces to the prison ship Altmark, and took part in the hunting of the battleship *Bismarck*. On 27 August 1941 a Hudson of No. 269 Squadron caused submarine U-570 to surrender to it: the first U-boat captured in a solely RAF operation.

**The first combat operation of the Second World War** began at 04.26 hours on 1 September 1939, when three Luftwaffe Junkers Ju 87B-1s of 3/Stukageschwader 1 left Elbing. At 04.34 hours they attacked the Dirschau Bridge over the Vistula in Poland, a few minutes before Germany officially declared war on Poland.

**The first occasion that a British aircraft crossed the German frontier during the Second World War** was on 3 September 1939 when

Blenheim IV (N6215) of No. 139 Squadron, flown by Flying Officer A. McPherson, and carrying Cdr Thompson, RN, and Corp V. Arrowsmith, photographed German naval units leaving Wilhelmshaven.

**The first leaflet raid over Germany in the Second World War** was carried out by three Whitley IIIs of No. 51 Squadron and seven Whitley IIIs of No. 58 Squadron on the first night of the war, 3 to 4 September 1939. Approximately six million propaganda leaflets were dropped on targets in the Ruhr and over Bremen and Hamburg.

**The first British aircraft to drop bombs on enemy targets during the Second World War** was a Blenheim IV (N6204), flown by Flt Lt K. C.

Above   *Junkers Ju 52/3mg3e bombers of 1/KG 152 'Hindenburg', in 1936.*

Right   *Prototype Macchi C200 Saetta fighter.*

Doran, leading a formation of five aircraft from No. 110 (Hyderabad) Squadron in a raid on the German Fleet in the Schillig Roads, off Wilhelmshaven, on 4 September 1939. A formation of five Blenheims from No. 107 Squadron also took part in the attack.

**The first British aircraft to attack a German U-boat during the Second World War** was an Avro Anson I of the RAF's No. 500 (County of Kent) Squadron then based at Detling. On 5 September 1939, this aircraft made a bombing attack on the enemy submarine.

On 18th and then 20th November 1939, the Luftwaffe air-dropped the first anti-shipping magnetic mines in British coastal waters. An early remedy became the Vickers Wellington DW. I, a hastily prepared conversion of the bomber to carry a 48 ft (14.6 m) diameter dural degaussing ring to explode the mines. Such operations, started in January 1940, were the first maritime operations for the Wellington. (Vickers)

**The first German aircraft to be shot down by British aircraft during the Second World War** was a Messerschmitt Bf 109E, destroyed by Sgt F. Letchford, air gunner of a Fairey Battle (K9243) of No. 88 Squadron, Advanced Air Striking Force of the RAF, over France, on 20 September 1939. **The first Fleet Air Arm victory** followed when three Dornier Do 18s of *Küstenfliegergruppe* 506 were sighted by a patrol of Swordfish aircraft flying from HMS *Ark Royal* over the North Sea on 26 September 1939. Nine Skuas were launched immediately from the carrier and these succeeded in forcing one of the Dorniers (Werke Nr 731, of 2 *Staffel*, Kü F1 Gr 506) down on to the sea in German Grid Square 3440. The German four-man crew was later rescued and made prisoner on board a British destroyer.

**The first British bombers to fly over Berlin in the Second World War** were Armstrong Whitworth Whitleys of No. 10 Squadron, which dropped propaganda leaflets during the night of 1–2 October 1939.

**The first German aircraft shot down by an RAF aircraft operating from the United Kingdom during the Second World War** was a Dornier Do 18 flying-boat destroyed by a Lockheed Hudson of No. 224 Squadron. This occurred on 8 October 1939 during a patrol by the RAF aircraft over Jutland.

**The first German aircraft shot down over British soil during the Second World War** was a Junkers Ju 88A-1 of I/KG30, piloted by Hauptmann Pohle, and destroyed over the Firth of Forth by a Spitfire of No. 603 (City of Edinburgh) squadron on 16 October 1939.

**The first enemy aircraft shot down by RAF fighters on the Western Front during the Second World War** was a Dornier Do 17 destroyed over Toul on 30 October 1939. The victorious pilot was Pilot Officer P. W. Mould, flying a Hurricane of No. 1 Squadron.

**The first long-range anti-shipping squadron of the German Luftwaffe** was formed in November 1939. In the absence of a more suitable aircraft, the unit was equipped with the Focke-Wulf Fw 200 Condor long-range civil transport. One of these aircraft, *Immelmann III* (D-2600), was Adolf Hitler's personal transport. Though not ideal for military service, the Fw 200 was responsible for the destruction of an immense number of Allied merchant ships. The Condor unit I/KG40, controlled by the German Navy, claimed more than 363 000 tons (368 800 tonnes) of shipping destroyed during one six-month period.

**The first loss suffered by the Finnish Air Force during the 'Winter War' with the Soviet Union** in 1939–40 was Sergeant Kukkonen who, flying a Fokker D XXI of Fighter Squadron HLeLv24 near Viipuri, was shot down by his own anti-aircraft guns on 1 December 1939.

**The first aerial victory claimed during the 'Winter War' between Finland and Russia** was that of Lt Eino Luukkanen on 1 December 1939; flying a Fokker D XXI (FR-104) of Fighter Squadron HLeLv24, he destroyed a Russian SB-2 bomber.

**The first British naval fighter to be armed with a power-driven gun turret** was the Blackburn Roc. Aircraft of this type entered service with the Fleet Air Arm in February 1940, but did not serve on board aircraft carriers. Proving unsatisfactory, they were retired in 1943.

**The first British air combat victory of the Second World War to be recorded by a gun-camera** was that showing the attack on and destruction of a Heinkel He 111 on 22 February 1940. This was achieved by Sqn Ldr Douglas Farquhar of No. 602 (City of Glasgow) Squadron flying a Spitfire over Coldingham, Berwickshire.

**The first Royal Air Force aircraft to drop bombs deliberately on German soil during the Second World War** is believed to have been an Armstrong Whitworth Whitley (N1380, DY-R) of No. 102 Squadron based at Driffield, Yorkshire. This squadron, in company with Whitleys of Nos 10, 51 and 77 Squadrons, and Handley Page Hampdens of No. 5 Group, attacked the German mine-laying seaplane base at Hornum on the night of 19–20 March 1940.

**The first British bombs to fall on the German mainland in the Second World War** were dropped by eight or nine Whitleys of Nos 77 and 102 Squadrons, which attacked enemy lines of communication leading to Southern Holland on the night of 10–11 May 1940.

**The first eight-gun fighter to enter service with the Fleet Air Arm** was the Fairey Fulmar, which began to equip No. 808 Squadron at Worthy Down in June 1940. Fulmars played a conspicuous part in the defence of convoys to Malta and Northern Russia.

**First Allied aircraft to bomb Berlin during the Second World War** was a Centre NC 223.4 civil transport (F-ARIN *Jules Verne*) which had been developed for transatlantic operations with Air France. Converted for operation as a bomber, on the night of 7–8 June 1940 this aircraft followed a circuitous route carrying a 4409 lb (2000 kg) bombload which it dropped on Berlin before returning over Germany and north-east France to land at Orly after a 13 h 30 min flight.

**The first British air attack on Italy in the Second World War** was mounted by Fairey Swordfish of No 767 Training Squadron, FAA, on 14 June 1940, striking at Genoa with bombs.

**The first successful torpedo attack by aeroplanes against a capital ship** was recorded on 6 July 1940, when Fairey Swordfish of Nos 810 and 820 Squadrons, FAA, flew from HMS *Ark Royal* and heavily damaged the cruiser *Dunkerque*.

**The first regular-serving American pilot to die in action during the Second World War** was Pilot Officer William M. L. Fiske, RAF, who on 17 August 1940 died of wounds suffered in action the previous day at Tangmere, Sussex, during the Battle of Britain.

**The first Japanese monoplane fighter with a fully enclosed cockpit and fully retractable landing gear** to enter squadron service was the Mitsubishi A6M2, known popularly as the Zero-Sen. The A6M1 prototype was flown first on 1 April 1939, and the '12-Shi fighter project', as it had been known, was adopted officially by the Imperial Japanese Navy on 31 July 1940, under the designation A6M2 Type 0 Carrier Fighter Model 11. The Zero was first used operationally on 19 August 1940, when a formation of 12 aircraft, led by Lt Tamotsu Yokoyama, escorted a force of bombers attacking Chungking.

**The first Second World War bombing attack on London** was made by the Luftwaffe on the night of 24–25 August 1940.

**The first Italian jet aircraft** was the Caproni-Campini CC.2, first flown on 28 August 1940 by pilot Mario di Bernardi. Although termed a 'jet', it used a piston engine driving a three-stage variable pitch fan, propelling air out of a variable-area nozzle at the rear of a jet-pipe, where fuel was burned to raise the thrust. Heavy weight and low power meant that the CC.2 was not successful and remained a prototype.

**The first air victory scored in the Greek–Italian campaign of 1940–41** was achieved by a Greek pilot of No. 21 Squadron of the Royal Hellenic Air Force. Flying a Polish PZL P24, he destroyed an Italian aircraft north of Yannina on 1 November 1940.

**The first organized transatlantic ferry flights of aircraft built in the United States,** for service with the Allied nations involved in the Second World War, began on 10 November 1940.

**The first occasion air power alone crippled a naval fleet** was during the night of 11/12 Novem-

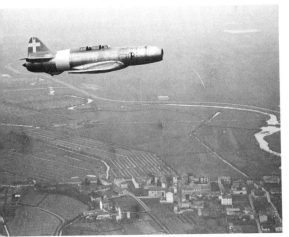

*Caproni-Campini CC.2, the first Italian jet aircraft.*

ber 1940, when Fairey Swordfish of Nos 813, 815, 819 and 824 Squadrons from HMS *Illustrious* badly damaged or sank three battleships, two destroyers, a cruiser and two auxiliary ships of the Italian Navy at Taranto harbour, and caused damage to on-shore facilities.

**The first British single-seat monoplane fighter to serve on board aircraft carriers of the Royal Navy** was the Hawker Sea Hurricane. The type equipped No. 880 Squadron in January 1941 and was embarked in HMS *Furious* in July of the same year. They were used also aboard merchant ships and a number of small naval catapult ships under the 'Catafighter' scheme. Their first success in this role came on 3 August 1941 when the Sea Hurricane of HMS *Maplin*, flown by Lt R. W. H. Everett, RNVR, shot down a German Fw 200 Condor.

**The first airborne operation carried out by British paratroops in the Second World War** had the codename 'Operation Colossus'. On 10 February 1941 the paratroops were dropped by Whitley Vs of Nos 51 and 78 Squadrons in an unsuccessful attack against the viaduct at Tragino, Campagna, Italy.

**The first RAF squadron to fly four-engined bombers operationally during the Second World War** was No. 7, which used three of its new Short Stirlings (led by Sqn Ldr Griffith-Jones) to bomb oil storage tanks at Rotterdam on the night of 10–11 February 1941.

**The first 4000 lb 'block buster' bomb to be used operationally by the RAF** was dropped by a Wellington of No. 149 Squadron, during an attack on Emden on 1 April 1941.

**The first aircraft designed as a jet fighter, and also the first twin-engined jet aircraft,** was the German Heinkel He 280. The first prototype, the 280V-1, was first flown on 2 April 1941 powered by two Heinkel HeS 8 turbojets, each developing approximately 1102 lb (500 kg) static thrust. Maximum level speed of the He 280V-5, with HeS 8A engines of 1650 lb (750 kg) static thrust, was demonstrated to be 510 mph (820 km/h) at 19 680 ft (6000 m). It did not achieve production status, being abandoned in favour of the Messerschmitt Me 262.

**The first combat mission flown by the Boeing B-17 Flying Fortress** was a daylight raid at 30 000 ft (9150 m) against Wilhelmshaven by three aircraft of No. 90 (Bomber) Squadron, RAF, on 8 July 1941. Twenty B-17Cs had been supplied to the RAF, and were used by that service under the name Fortress I. From 1942 onwards about 200 B-17F and B-17G aircraft were delivered to the RAF, which designated the 'Fs' as Fortress II and IIA, the 'Gs' as Fortress III. All of the II and IIA aircraft served with Coastal Command's Very Long Range force for mid-Atlantic patrol.

**The first single-engined American aircraft equipped with a power-operated gun turret,** and also the first to carry a 22 in (55.9 cm) torpedo, was the Grumman TBF Avenger. First flight of an XTBF-1 prototype was made during August 1941. The first operational use of production aircraft was at the Battle of Midway, on 4 June 1942, when five out of six aircraft deployed were lost. Despite this inauspicious start, the Avenger became one of the most outstanding naval aircraft of the Second World War. Almost 10 000 were built, of which nearly 1000 served in 15 first-line squadrons of the British FAA.

**The first RAF fighter capable of exceeding a speed of 400 mph (644 km/h)** was the Hawker Typhoon, which entered squadron service with No. 56 at Duxford in September 1941. Armed with four 20 mm cannon, and able to carry two 1000 lb bombs or eight 60 lb rocket-projectiles beneath its wings, the Typhoon became famous for 'train-busting' activities and devastated German *Panzer* divisions at Caen and the Falaise gap after the Allied invasion of Europe.

The first RAF Coastal Command aircraft to be equipped with ASV Mk II long-range radar were the Whitleys of No. 502 Squadron. On 30 November 1941 one of the Squadron's aircraft, a Whitley VII (Z9190), made the Command's first ASV 'kill', sinking U-206 in the Bay of Biscay.

The first Japanese attack on the US Pacific Fleet and shore installations at Pearl Harbor, Hawaii, was made on 7 December 1941. The attack, made without any previous declaration of war, brought immediate reaction from the United States, which declared war on Japan on 8 December. This marked the beginning of the Pacific War and American participation in the Second World War.

Flying Tigers' Curtiss P-40B Warhawk of the American Volunteer Group, attended by American and Chinese ground crew. (US National Archives)

Wreckage at the Naval Air Station, Pearl Harbor, photographed during the attack by Japanese naval aircraft. In the Pearl Harbor attack, the US Navy lost more men than in the whole of its participation in the First World War. (US Navy)

The first practical aid from the West in support of the Chinese Air Force opposing Japan in 1941, came with American Brig-Gen Claire L. Chennault's AVG (American Volunteer Group), better remembered as the Flying Tigers. With some 100 Curtiss P-40B Warhawks, the AVG first went into action on 20 December 1941, destroying six Japanese aircraft. By 4 July 1942, when it ceased to function as an independent force, it had claimed 286 enemy aircraft for the loss of 23 AVG pilots.

The first submarine to be sunk by an aircraft at night was the German U-boat U451, on 21 December 1941. Equipped with ASV radar and rockets, the attacking Fairey Swordfish was from No 812 Squadron based in Gibraltar.

The first British combined operation against Europe during the Second World War was mounted to gain knowledge of the capability of German radar installations. British air, land and sea forces were used on 27–28 February 1942 to take vital components from a radar station at Bruneval, northern France.

The first German U-boats to be destroyed by the United States Navy during the Second World War were sunk on 1 and 15 March 1942. These sinkings were achieved by Lockheed PBO-1 Hudson aircraft of the US Navy's VP-82 Squadron, based at Argentia, Newfoundland.

The first combat operation carried out by Avro Lancaster heavy bombers was a mine-laying sortie flown by No. 44 (Bomber) Squadron, based at Waddington, Lincolnshire, over the Heligoland Bight on 3 March 1942. Their first night bombing attack was recorded when two of No. 44 Squadron's aircraft took part in a raid on Essen on the night of 10–11 March 1942. The first of many famous raids involved 12 aircraft of Nos 44 and 97 Squadrons led by Sqn Ldr J. D. Nettleton, which made a low-level daylight attack on the MAN Diesel factory at Augsburg on 17 April 1942. Their first operation with the Pathfinder Force was made on the night of 18–19 August 1942.

**The first RAF aircraft to have the British H2S blind bombing radar system installed** (on 27 March 1942) was the Handley Page Halifax V9977. This radar, in conjunction with the metal foil strips known as Window which were dropped from the air to confuse enemy radar, was **first used with devastating success in an attack on Hamburg** on 24–25 July 1943.

**The first United States air attack on the Japanese mainland** was made on 18 April 1942. This occurred when 16 North American B-25 Mitchell bombers led by Lt Col James Doolittle were flown off the US Navy carrier USS *Hornet* to raid Tokyo and other targets. Unable to return to their carrier, most aircraft landed in China.

**The first naval battle in which the issue was decided by aircraft alone** was the Battle of the Coral Sea, fought on 7–9 May 1942, between US Navy Task Force 17 and Vice-Admiral Takeo Takagi's Carrier Striking Force (part of Vice-Admiral Shigeyoshi Inouye's Task Force MO). The battle was fought to prevent Japanese support of an invasion of Port Moresby and to disrupt plans to launch air strikes against the Australian mainland. In this respect the battle must be considered to have been an American victory, although the large American carrier USS *Lexington* was sunk—**the first American carrier to be lost in the Second World War**. The Japanese carrier *Shoho* was attacked and sunk by Dauntless and Devastator aircraft from the *Lexington* and *Yorktown*, becoming **the first Japanese aircraft carrier to be destroyed by American airmen**. A total of 69 American naval aircraft was lost during the battle, while the Japanese losses amounted to about 85 aircraft and some 400 naval airmen (many of whom went down with the *Shoho*). The Japanese carrier *Shokaku* was also damaged severely, but was able to limp home for repairs. The loss of experienced airmen and the absence of the *Shokaku* critically weakened Japanese naval forces that were to be involved in the vital Battle of Midway, fought 4–7 June 1942.

**The first 'thousand bomber' raid against a German target** was mounted by RAF Bomber Command. In the attack against Cologne on the night of 30–31 May 1942, 1046 aircraft were involved, of which 599 were Vickers Wellingtons.

**The first and only time a Japanese fixed-wing aircraft attacked the continental USA during** the Second World War occurred during June 1942. The aircraft, a Yokosuka E14Y1 ('Glen') light submarine-based reconnaissance floatplane launched from the Japanese submarine I-25, dropped four incendiary bombs on the wooded Oregon coast.

**First night attack on a German U-boat in which a Leigh light was used to illuminate the target** was made on the night of 3–4 June 1942 by a Vickers Wellington of No. 172 Squadron, RAF.

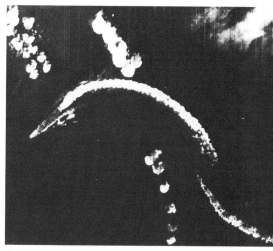

*Japanese aircraft carrier Hiryu weaves hard to avoid bombs dropped from 20 000 ft (6100 m) by US B-17 Flying Fortress bombers based on Midway, 4 June 1942. Hiryu's Aichi D3A dive-bombers later that day succeeded in crippling USS Yorktown before it was finally sunk that afternoon by aircraft from USS Enterprise. (Department of the Navy)*

**The first major naval battle of the Pacific War to confirm the lethal capability of an aircraft carrier strike force** was that known as the Battle of Midway, fought off Midway island during 3 and 4 June 1942. In a first shattering blow, dive-bomber squadrons from the USS *Enterprise* and *Yorktown*, attacking from opposite directions to confuse Japanese defences, scored lethal hits on the Japanese carriers *Akagi*, *Kaga* and *Soryu*; within minutes they were blazing and out of action. Only *Hiryu*, some miles distant, had escaped but within the next two hours was spotted by scout planes from *Yorktown* and quickly put out of action by dive-bombers from the *Enterprise*. Before this happened, however, *Yorktown* had been damaged severely by aircraft from *Hiryu*, and was later sunk by the Japanese submarine I-168 while under tow for repair in Hawaii. From that moment the Japanese fleet no longer held the initiative; not only had Japan lost four of her six first-line aircraft carriers, but very large numbers of experienced naval airmen.

**The first aerial victories claimed during the 'Continuation War' between Finland and the Soviet Union,** which broke out in June 1941, were two Soviet DB-3 bombers shot down by six Fokker D XXIs over the Riihimaki railway junction in the first air battle, which probably took place on 25 June 1942.

**The first German turbojet-powered aircraft to enter operational service** was the Messerschmitt Me 262A. The first flight of the Me 262V-1 prototype, powered by a single 1200 hp Junkers Jumo piston-engine, was made on 18 April 1941. It was not until 18 July 1942 that the first flight with two turbojet engines was recorded, these being Junkers 109-004A-0 turbojets, each of 1848 lb (840 kg) static thrust. The first production aircraft had 109-004B-1 turbojets of 1980 lb (900 kg) thrust, which provided a maximum level speed of about 539 mph (868 km/h) at 23 000 ft (7000 m).

The Me 262A-2a Sturmvogel (Stormbird) fighter-bomber variant is believed to have entered service with Kommando Schenk in early July 1944, moving to Juvincourt in France on 10 July 1944 to begin operations with six aircraft. This suggests that the Me 262 was the first turbojet-powered combat aircraft to enter operational service. The Me 262A-1a Schwalbe (Swallow) entered operational service on 3 October 1944; a test unit was expanded and renamed Kommando Nowotny under the command of the Austrian ace, Major Walter Nowotny, and became operational on that date. One of the two Staffeln of the unit was based at Achmer, the other at Hesepe.

**The first exploratory use of the RAF's Pathfinder Force** was made on the night of 16–17 August 1942 to mount an attack on Emden, Germany. The official formation of the Pathfinder Force, under the command of Air Cdre D. C. T. Bennett, had only been completed on the previous day, 15 August.

**The first Boeing B-17E to arrive in Britain** was allocated to the USAAF's 97th Bombardment Group. This unit made its first operational sortie in Europe on 17 August 1942, when 12 B-17Es attacked Rouen.

**First aircraft in the world to be equipped with crew ejection seats as standard,** and also the Luftwaffe's first operational aircraft with retractable tricycle landing gear, was the Heinkel He 219, first flown in prototype form on 15 November 1942. A twin-engined night fighter, the He 219 became operational during June 1943.

*Messerschmitt Me 262A-2a Sturmvogel jet fighter in 1944. (MBB)*

*Probably the most famous attack by RAF bombers of the Second World War was the destruction of the Eder and Möhne dams by No 617 'Dam Busters' Squadron, on 17 May 1943. Led by Wg Cdr Guy Gibson, the Lancasters dropped so-called 'bouncing bomb' mines devised by Barnes Wallis. (Imperial War Museum)*

**The first operational use of rocket-powered and remotely controlled missiles** took place on 17 August 1943, when the Luftwaffe carried out anti-shipping attacks on British vessels in the Bay of Biscay. The aircraft used for the raid were Dornier Do 217E-5s of II/KG 100, which launched Henschel Hs 293A-1 missiles. On 27 August 1943 an Hs 293 sank the Royal Navy corvette HMS *Egret* in the Bay of Biscay.

**The first air raid on a rocket research establishment** was carried out by RAF bombers on the night of 17–18 August 1943 against Peenemünde. This followed air reconnaissance that had confirmed in June the existence of large rockets at the establishment.

**The first specially designed anti-submarine patrol aircraft for the Japanese Navy** was the Kyushu Q1W Tokai, the prototype of which made its first flight in September 1943. Only a few Q1W1s entered service before the war's end, these being equipped with radar and magnetic anomaly detection (MAD) equipment.

**The first major warship to be sunk by air-launched missile** was the Italian battleship *Roma*, struck by two Ruhrstahl/Kramer Fritz X-1 radio-controlled missiles launched from Luftwaffe Do 217K-2 bombers of III/KG 100 on 9 September 1943. *Roma* was one of many ships on their way to be surrendered to the Allies, and another, the *Italia*, was damaged by a Fritz X-1. As a matter of record, III/KG 100 had flown its first operational mission with Fritz X-1s over the Mediterranean on 29 August 1943.

**The first operational use was made by the RAF of a 12 000 lb bomb**, dropped by a Lancaster bomber on the Dortmund–Ems Canal on the night of 15–16 September 1943.

**The first turbojet-powered fighter to enter operational service with the USAAF/USAF** was the Lockheed P-80 (later F-80) Shooting Star. The first XP-80 prototype (44-83020) was flown for the first time on 8 January 1944, but although the Shooting Star was too late to see service in the Second World War, it was deployed operationally with considerable success during the Korean War.

**The first night bombing attack to be made from a US aircraft carrier** was recorded on the night of 17–18 February 1944, when 12 TBF-1C Avengers from the USS *Enterprise* attacked Truk Island in the Pacific Ocean.

**Making its first major daylight attack on Berlin**, the USAAF deployed some 660 heavy bombers and escorting aircraft in this mission flown on 6 March 1944.

**The first British twin-engined aircraft to land on the deck of an aircraft carrier** was the pre-production prototype of the de Havilland Sea Mosquito (LR359) which, flown by Lt Cdr E. M. Brown, RN, landed on board HMS *Indefatigable* on 25 March 1944. Production Sea Mosquito TR33s first entered service with No. 811 Squadron at Ford, Sussex, in August 1946.

**The first German V1 missiles (Fieseler Fi 103s) launched against a capital city** were fired on 13 June 1944, from ground sites in France against London. Three reached their target. Mass attacks began on 15–16 June, with 244 launched. The last to strike London was launched on 29 March 1945, the 2419th to reach that city. V1s were also launched against other British, French and Dutch cities. Antwerp received the greatest number, at 2448. Of about 30 000 V1s built (many missing their targets or not fired), some 1200 were air-launched after the Allies destroyed or overran the ground firing sites; KG 53's Heinkel He 111s began air-launched V1 attacks on London in October 1944. Powered by an Argus 109-014 pulse-jet engine, the Fi 103 had a speed before engine cut-out of 400 mph (645 km/h), a range of 150 miles (240 km) and a 1874 lb (850 kg) warhead.

*Completed V1 flying-bombs ready for dispersal at the underground plant at Nordhausen. (Imperial War Museum)*

**The world's first operational rocket-powered fighter** was the Messerschmitt Me 163 Komet, first flown as a prototype **under full power** by Heini Dittmar at Peenemünde, Germany, on 13 August 1941. On one early flight Dittmar far exceeded what was then the official world speed record, attaining a speed of 571 mph (919 km/h); on 2 October 1941, after having been towed to altitude, he started the rocket motor and 2 min later recorded a speed of 623.85 mph (1004 km/h) in level flight. It was the success of these early trials that led to the Me 163B-1 Komet interceptor fighter, powered by a Walter 109-509A-2 rocket motor using the liquid propellants known as T-Stoff (hydrogen peroxide and water) and C-Stoff (hydrazine hydrate, methyl alcohol and water) to give a maximum static thrust of 3300 lb (1500 kg). It was armed with two 30 mm MK 108 cannon. The Komet equipped only one combat unit, Jagdgeschwader 400, which comprised eventually three Staffels. The whole unit was concentrated on Brandis in July 1944, and **the first operation** was flown against a group of B-17s on 16 August 1944, without any of the US bombers being destroyed. Although approximately 300 of these rocket-powered interceptors were built, JG 400 claimed only nine Allied aircraft destroyed and two probables before the units were disbanded in early 1945.

**The first operational use of composite combat aeroplanes was by the German Luftwaffe,** during the Allied liberation of France in June–July 1944. Devised originally under a programme designated 'Beethoven-Gerät', it was known subsequently as the 'Mistel-Programm'. The biggest problem was to develop an effective system by which the pilot of the single-seat upper aircraft could control and effect separation of the two components. Initial operational Mistel Is comprised an upper piloted Bf 109F-4 and a lower Ju 88A-4 which carried a warhead containing 3800 lb (1725 kg) of high explosive. The weapon was first issued to 2 Staffel of Kampfgeschwader 101, commanded by Hauptmann Horst Rudat, which was formed in April 1944. The first operational use of the device, known unofficially as *Vater und Sohn* (Father and Son), was on the night of 24–25 June 1944, when five Mistels were deployed against Allied shipping in the Seine Bay. Later versions of the composite had Focke-Wulf Fw 190s as the upper component.

**The first operational use of napalm incendiary material** was made on 17 July 1944 by USAAF Lockheed P-38 Lightnings making an attack on a fuel depot at Coutances, France.

**The first jet aircraft to enter operational service with the RAF** was the Gloster Meteor Mk I, powered by two 1700 lb (771 kg) thrust Rolls-Royce W2B/23 Welland I turbojet engines.

*Messerschmitt Me 163B-1 Komet with rocket motor firing. (MBB)*

Twenty Meteor Is were built, one of which was exchanged for an American-built Bell Airacomet—**the first US-designed and built jet fighter**. Three others were used for development purposes and the remainder (EE213–EE222, and EE224–EE229) were delivered to No. 616 Squadron. The first two aircraft were delivered on 12 July 1944 to the Squadron, based at Culmhead, Somerset, under the command of Wg Cdr A. McDowall. The first combat sortie was flown from Manston by the Squadron on 27 July 1944 against V1 flying bombs but was unsuccessful owing to gun-firing difficulties. **The first combat success** was scored on 4 August 1944 by Flying Officer Dean who, after his guns had jammed, flew alongside the enemy bomb and, by tipping it with his wing, forced the missile into the ground. The aircraft was EE216.

**The world's first piston-engined aircraft to attain a speed of more than 500 mph** was a specially prepared Republic XP-47J Thunderbolt (43-46952) powered by a 2100 hp Pratt & Whitney R-2800-57 engine. This occurred on 4 August 1944 when a speed of 504 mph (811 km/h) was recorded.

**The first loss of a jet aircraft in aerial combat** is thought to have taken place on 28 August 1944, when Maj Joseph Myers and Lt M. Croy of the 78th Fighter Group, US 8th Air Force, were credited with the destruction of an Me 262 operated by the Kommando Schenk.

**The first jet bomber and reconnaissance aircraft to enter operational service,** when precluding the attack-armed Messerschmitt Me

*Bomb-laden Mitsubishi Zero prepares to take off from a Philippine airfield on a kamikaze mission in October/November 1944. (US Navy)*

262A-2a, was the German Arado Ar 234B Blitz (Lightning), powered by two Junkers Jumo 004B series turbojets. The first prototype Ar 234V1 had made its first flight on 15 June 1943, powered by two 1850 lb (840 kg) thrust Jumo 004A engines. First using evaluation prototypes Ar 234 V5 and V7, 1 Staffel flew the first operational Ar 234 reconnaissance sorties during the summer of 1944. In September 1944, Sonderkommando Götz formed as the first Ar 234 'official' operational unit, equipped with Ar 234B-1s. Ar 234B-2 bombers went first to Kampfgeschwader 76, with II/KG 76 operating from Achmer and Rheine making the first combat use of the jet bomber during the Ardennes offensive, initially on 24 December (nine aircraft under the command of Hauptmann Diether Lukesch).

**The first country in the world to be subjected to an assault by ballistic rocket missiles** was France. On the morning of 8 September 1944 the first V-2 rocket was fired against Paris. At about 18.40 h on the same day the **first V-2 to land in Britain** fell in Chiswick, London, killing two people and injuring ten. The last rocket to fall in Britain was at Orpington, Kent, at 16.54 h on 27 March 1945, killing one person and injuring twenty-three. Between the two dates 1115 rockets struck Britain (of which about 500 hit London), killing 2855 and seriously injuring 6268. **The worst incident** is believed to have occurred when a V-2 fell upon a Woolworth store at Deptford, killing 160 and injuring 135. **The worst-hit**

country was, however, Belgium, more than 1500 rockets being launched against Antwerp alone.

**The first aerial victory against another piloted aircraft to be gained by the pilot of a jet aircraft** has never been identified positively, but was certainly achieved during the first week of October 1944 by a pilot of Kommando Nowotny, the target being a Boeing B-17 Flying Fortress of the US 8th Air Force.

**The first aviation unit formed specifically for suicide operations** was the *Shimpu* Special Attack Corps, a group of 24 volunteer pilots commanded by Lt Yukio Seki, formed within the 201st (Fighter) Air Group, Imperial Japanese Navy, during the third week of October 1944. The unit, equipped with Mitsubishi Zero-Sen single-seat fighters, was formed for the task of diving into the flight decks of American aircraft carriers in the Philippines area, with a 250 kg bomb beneath the fuselage of each fighter. (*Shimpu* is an alternative pronunciation of the Japanese ideographs which also represent *kamikaze*, 'Divine Wind', the name applied more generally to Japanese suicide operations.) The first successful suicide attack was made on 25 October 1944 when five Zeros, flown by members of the Special Attack Corps, sank the US escort carrier *St Lo*, and damaged the carriers *Kalinin Bay, Kitkun Bay* and *White Plains*. According to Japanese accounts the last sortie by suicide aircraft was flown on 15 August 1945, by seven aircraft of the Oita Detachment, 701st Air Group and led by Adm Matome Ugaki, commander of the 5th Air Fleet. United States records fail to confirm a *kamikaze* operation on this date, but they do list a total of 34 American naval vessels sunk and 288 damaged from the beginning of the suicide aircraft operations as mentioned above; those sunk included 3 escort aircraft carriers, 13 destroyers and a destroyer escort. The total number of suicide aircraft expended to gain these results are believed to be as follows:

|  | Sorties | Aircraft returned | Expended |
|---|---|---|---|
| Philippines area | 421 | 43 | 378 |
| Formosa area | 27 | 14 | 13 |
| Okinawa area | 1809 | 879 | 930 |
| *Totals* | 2257 | 936 | 1321 |

It has not proved possible to distinguish between actual suicide aircraft and escort fighters in the

Okinawa operations and this must necessarily invalidate the total figures to some extent. A rough estimate would show that the usual ratio of escort fighters to suicide aircraft on most sorties was about three to two, although late in the campaign many sorties were flown entirely without escort. (See also 1 April 1945.)

**The first trans-Pacific incendiary balloon attacks against the continental USA:** see Balloons and Airships (3 November 1944).

**The first jet fighter ace in the world** has not been identified positively, but it is thought that he was one of the pilots of the Kommando Nowotny. The unit was withdrawn from operations following the death in action of Maj Walter Nowotny on 8 November 1944, and later provided the nucleus for the new fighter wing, Jagdgeschwader 7 'Notwotny'; III Gruppe JG 7 became operational during December 1944. Hauptmann Franz Schall is known to have scored three aerial victories on the day of Nowotny's death, and served subsequently with 10 Staffel, JG 7; it is therefore entirely possible that he was the first pilot in the world to have achieved five confirmed aerial victories while flying jet aircraft. Other known jet aces of the Second World War are listed below. The fragmentary records which survived the final immolation of the Luftwaffe in 1945 prevent the preparation of a complete list, and the following should be regarded only as a framework for further research:

| | |
|---|---|
| Oberstleutnant Heinz Bar (JV 44) | 16 |
| Hauptmann Franz Schall (10/JG 7) | 14 |
| Major Erich Rudorffer (II/JG 7) | 12 |
| Oberfeldwebel Hermann Buchner (III/JG 7) | 12 |
| Herman Buchner (III/JG 7) | – |
| Leutnant Karl Schnorrer (II/JG 7) not fewer than | 8 |
| Leutnant Rudolf Rademacher  not fewer than (II/JG 7) | 8 |
| Major Theodor Weissenberger (Staff/JG 7) | 8 |
| Oberleutnant Walter Schuck (3/JG 7) | 8 |
| Oberst Johannes Steinhoff (Staff/JG 7, JV 44) | 6 |
| Major Wolfgang Spate (Staff/JG 7) | 5 |
| Leutnant Klaus Neumann (JV 44) | 5 |

**The first major air attack on Tokyo** was that made on 24 November 1944. This was mounted by Boeing B-29 Superfortresses of the USAAF's 21st Bomber Command, a total of 88 B-29s being despatched on this operation from their base on the Mariana Islands.

**The first widespread operational use of air-to-air rockets against aeroplanes** was by the Luftwaffe, probably by III/JG7 either in late 1944 or early 1945. The R4M unguided rockets, of which 24 were carried on racks under the wings of Messerschmitt Me 262A-1b fighters, were 55 mm folding-fin missiles aimed through a standard Revi gunsight. Fired in salvoes their effect was devastating, especially against the American formations of B-17 Flying Fortress and B-24 Liberator bombers.

**The first operational use of jet reconnaissance-bomber aircraft at night** was on the night of 31 December 1944/1 January 1945, by four Ar 234s of KG 76. Led by Diether Lukesch, they flew a reconnaissance mission and dropped bombs on Brussels and Liege.

**The first turboprop-powered aircraft to fly in the USA**, albeit with a mixed powerplant, was the Consolidated XP-81 escort fighter prototype flown on 7 February 1945. This aircraft had a conventionally mounted turboprop engine driving a tractor propeller, plus a turbojet engine mounted in the rear fuselage.

**The first interceptor designed to be piloted, rocket-powered and vertically launched** was the German Bachem Ba 349 Natter, which was first launched as an unmanned prototype on 18 December 1944. The first piloted test flight took place on 28 February 1945, which was not successful and the pilot, Oberleutnant Lothar Siebert, was killed. Three launches in March were, however, successful and the Natter was thereafter approved for deployment against Allied aircraft flying over Germany. However, no Natter was used operationally. Designed to be semi-expendable, armament was $24 \times 73$ mm unguided rockets packed into the nose.

**The first test-drop of the 22 000 lb 'Grand Slam' bomb** was made from an Avro Lancaster on 13 March 1945. This first operational drop of this bomb was made by Sqn Ldr C. C. Calder of No. 617 (Bomber) Squadron, flying Lancaster BI (Special) PD112. The bomb was dropped on the Bielefeld Viaduct on 14 March 1945, smashing two of its spans.

**The first single-seat carrier-based dive-bomber and torpedo-carrier in the US Navy**, the Douglas AD-1 Skyraider was developed too late to see operational service in the Second

World War. First flown on 18 March 1945, the Skyraider was to prove an important naval aircraft in the Korean and Vietnam conflicts. When supplied to the British Royal Navy under the MAP, it filled a unique position as an airborne early-warning aircraft. Designated AEW1 in British service, the Skyraiders were also the last piston-engined fixed-wing aircraft in first-line service with the FAA.

**The first purpose-designed suicide aircraft and the only rocket-powered aircraft to be used operationally outside Germany** was the Japanese Yokosuka MXY-7 Ohka. This single-seater was powered by three small solid fuel rocket motors, which were ignited after the aircraft had been air launched from a carrier bomber and had travelled some distance in gliding flight. The first operational sortie by Ohkas was carried out on 21 March 1945 but was not successful. The first successful Ohka missions were flown on 1 April 1945, when the American battleship USS *West Virginia*, the British aircraft carrier HMS *Indefatigable* and other ships were damaged. On 12 April an Ohka sank the American destroyer USS *Mannert L. Abele* off Okinawa.

**The first twin-engined single-seat fighter to operate from carriers of the Royal Navy** was the de Havilland Sea Hornet F20, the prototype Sea Hornet (PX212) making its first flight on 19 April 1945. Aircraft of this type equipped No. 801 Squadron, and were embarked in HMS *Implacable* in 1949, remaining in service until the squadron was re-equipped with Sea Furies in 1951. Production aircraft were powered by two 2030 hp Rolls-Royce Merlin 133s or 134s, and had a maximum speed of 467 mph (752 km/h) at 22 000 ft (6700 m).

**The first American air-to-surface radar-guided missile** and **the first self-homing missile** was the Bat, an unpowered glide-bomb developed by Hugh L. Dryden. Carrying a 1000 lb (454 kg) warload, the missile was about 12 ft (3.65 m) long and, on being launched from its carrier aircraft, used radar to home on its target. It possessed a range of about 20 miles (30 km), and in April 1945 one such missile succeeded in sinking a Japanese destroyer at this range.

**The world's first operational atomic bomb was dropped** on the Japanese city of Hiroshima on 6 August 1945, carried by the B-29 Superfortress

Above   *The Bat radar-guided air-to-surface missile. (Associated Press)*

Right   Enola Gay, *from which the first atomic bomb was dropped on Japan. (The Boeing Company)*

*Enola Gay*, captained by Col Paul W. Tibbets Jr. A second operational atomic bomb was deployed three days later, carried by the B-29 Superfortress *Bock's Car* captained by Maj Charles W. Sweeney, and dropped on the city of Nagasaki. These two devastating air attacks quickly brought an end to Japanese resistance and the signature of the surrender documents aboard the battleship USS *Missouri* (anchored in Tokyo Bay) brought an official end to the Pacific War on 2 September 1945.

**The only Japanese turbojet-powered aircraft to take off under its own power during the Second World War** was the Nakajima J8N1 Kikka (Orange Blossom). Design began in September 1944 to Naval Staff order as an attack fighter, influenced by, but not based on, the German Me 262. Powered by two underwing 1050 lb (475 kg) thrust Ne-20 turbojets, the prototype flew only twice, on 7 and 11 August 1945.

**The first American aeroplane to land under jet power on a ship** was a Ryan FR-1 Fireball compound fighter, fitted with a conventionally mounted Wright R-1820-72W radial piston-engine as well as a General Electric I-16 turbojet installed in the rear fuselage. This combination had resulted from US Navy doubts of the suitability of jet-powered aircraft for carrier operations. Flown by Ensign Jake C. West on to the escort carrier USS *Wake Island* on 6 November 1945, it had been intended to fly on using the reciprocating engine, but this failed on the approach and

West landed under jet-power. **The first US (all-) jet aircraft to land on an aircraft carrier**, on 21 July 1946, was the McDonnell FD-1 Phantom prototype, which landed on the USS *Franklin D Roosevelt*. Production aircraft were redesignated subsequently FH-1.

**The first American surface-to-air anti-aircraft guided missile** was the Western Electric SAM-A-7 Nike-Ajax, development of which was started by Bell Telephone Laboratories in 1945. Before the weapon entered service more than 1500 test rounds were fired, and by 1959 10 000 had been delivered. Its place was taken in 1959–60 by the Nike-Hercules.

**The first two post-war world absolute speed records** were established by Gloster Meteor F4 fighters. On 7 November 1945 Gp Capt H. J. Wilson established a record speed of 606 mph (975 km/k) at Herne Bay, Kent, flying the Meteor EE454 *Britannia*. On 7 September 1946 Gp Capt E. M. Donaldson raised the record to 616 mph (991 km/h) near Tangmere, West Sussex, in Meteor EE549. The three Meteors allocated to the re-formed RAF High Speed Flight (EE548-550), which was to make the attempt to set a new speed record in 1946, had their wings clipped, reducing wing span from 43 ft 0 in (13.11 m) to 37 ft 2 in (11.33 m). Unfortunately, it was discovered that this reduced their maximum speed by almost 58 mph (93 km/h) and full-span wings were used for the record attempt. Because the clipped-wing

modification improved structural integrity, as well as rate of roll, it subsequently became standard on all but the earliest F4s. In 1948 Meteor F4s superseded F3s in the RAF's first-line fighter squadrons until they, in turn, were supplanted by F8s. In May 1950, the F4s which equipped No. 222 Squadron at Leuchars became the first jet fighters to be based in Scotland. Meteor F8s first entered service with No. 245 Squadron at Horsham St Faith, Norfolk, on 29 June 1950. The Meteor F4 was powered by two 350 lb (1587 kg) thrust Rolls-Royce Derwent 5 engines, the F8 by 3600 lb (1633 kg) thrust Derwent 8s. Meteor F8s of the Royal Australian Air Force were the only British jet fighters to see action in the Korean War.

**The world's first pure jet aircraft to operate from an aircraft carrier** was a de Havilland Vampire I, the third prototype (LZ551) which had been modified for deck-landing trials. It was first landed on HMS *Ocean*, a light fleet carrier of the Colossus Class, by Lt Cdr E. M. Brown, RNVR, on 3 December 1945. The first deck landing was followed by trials in which 15 take-offs and landings were made in two days.

**The Mikoyan MiG-9 and the Yakovlev Yak-15 were the first Soviet pure jet aircraft**, both flown in prototype form on 24 April 1946. The Yak-15, designed by Alexander S. Yakovlev, was the first jet fighter to enter squadron service with the Soviet Air Forces when delivered to the IA-PVO in early 1947. Powered by a single RD-10 turbojet (a Russian adaptation of the German Jumo 004B engine) developing initially 1875 lb (850 kg) thrust, it was armed with two 23 mm Nudelman-Suranov NS-23 guns and had a top speed of 488 mph (786 km/h) at 16 400 ft (5000 m). Like the first Tupolev jet bombers, the Yak-15 was also the result of adapting a piston-engine airframe for jet propulsion. The prototype retained the wings, cockpit, tailplane and tailwheel landing gear of a Yakovlev Yak-3, the new engine being mounted in the forward fuselage. This meant that the jet efflux was below the pilot's cockpit, and production aircraft had the fuselage undersurface protected by heat-resistant stainless steel. It meant also that the first batch of production aircraft had an all-metal tail-wheel. This proved unsatisfactory, and the Yak-15 was retrofitted with tricycle landing gear. A member of the company test team in 1947 was Olga Yamschikova, **probably the first woman in history to fly a turbojet-powered fighter aircraft.**

**The first high-speed twin-engined strike aircraft designed specifically to operate from aircraft carriers of the Royal Navy** was the Short Sturgeon. Originating from a wartime requirement, to operate from *Ark Royal* and *Hermes* class carriers, the war's end resulted in the Sturgeon being completed to satisfy a gunnery training and target-towing role. The first prototype made its maiden flight on 7 June 1946.

*The FD-1 Phantom approaches USS* Franklin D. Roosevelt *on 21 July 1946, to record the first landing of a US pure jet aircraft on a carrier deck. (McDonnell Douglas)*

**The first American pure jet aeroplane to operate from a carrier** was the McDonnell FD-1 Phantom, first operating from the USS *Franklin D. Roosevelt* on 21 July 1946. It was **also the first jet fighter to serve with first-line squadrons of the US Navy and the US Marine Corps.**

**The first recorded use of an ejection seat,** to enable a man to escape from an aircraft in flight, occurred on 24 July 1946. This was the date when the first experimental live ejection was made, using a Martin-Baker ejection seat installed in a Gloster Meteor. With the aircraft travelling at 320 mph (515 km/h), 'guinea pig' Bernard Lynch ejected at a height of 8000 ft (2440 m). In subsequent tests, Lynch made successful ejections at 420 mph (675 km/h) at heights up to 30 000 ft (9145 m). It should be noted that the wartime Heinkel He 219 Uhu (Owl) **was the first operational aircraft to be equipped with ejection seats;** while no dates have been recorded, it is known that some lives were saved by this equipment in the He 219.

**The first manned test of an American ejection seat** was made by Sgt. L. Lambert, USAAF, who was ejected from a Northrop P-61 Black Widow on 17 August 1946. The two-seat aircraft was travelling at 300 mph (483 km/h) at 7800 ft (2375 m).

**The first post-war long distance record for aeroplanes** was set by a modified Lockheed P2V-1 Neptune maritime reconnaissance aircraft, the *Truculent Turtle*, which flew a distance of 11 236 miles (18 082 km) between 29 September and 1 October 1946. On 7 March 1949 a later-version P2V-2 took off from the carrier USS *Coral Sea* at the then record take-off weight from a ship of 74 000 lb (33 566 kg).

**The first six-turbojet bomber to fly in America** was the Martin XB-48. Only two prototypes were built, the first of them flown on 22 June 1947, and both were powered by six wing-mounted Allison J35 turbojet engines.

**The Soviet Union's first jet-powered bomber to fly,** on 24 July 1947, was the Ilyushin Il-22. However, early flight tests proved disappointing and its development was abandoned.

**The first Soviet jet bomber to achieve very limited production status** was the Tupolev Tu-12, little more than a Tu-2 piston-engined bomber re-engined with gas-turbines. The prototype probably flew for the first time on 27 July 1947, powered

Above   *Martin XB-48 six-jet bomber.*

Left   *One of the first two Soviet jet fighters to enter service was the Mikoyan-Gurevich MiG-9.*

Below   *Soviet operated V-2 ballistic missile.*

by two 3525 lb (1600 kg) thrust RD-10 engines, derived from the Junkers 004B. Power plant of the later aircraft consisted of RD-500 engines, the Russian equivalent of the Rolls-Royce Derwent 5, which developed 4410 lb (2000 kg) thrust.

**Free from Army control for the first time since its foundation,** the United States Army Air Force became an independent member of the new unified US armed services on 18 September 1947, receiving the title United States Air Force.

The North American F-86 Sabre, which was to become **the USAF's first sweptwing fighter, and its first fighter able to exceed a speed of Mach 1 in a shallow dive,** was flown for the first time in XP-86 prototype (NA-140) form on 1 October 1947.

**The first launch of a ballistic missile in the USSR** was made on 30 October 1947, when a reconstructed German V-2 was fired from Kazakhstan. (At the close of the Second World War, Soviet forces had captured Peenemünde, the secret German rocket research establishment,

together with missiles and technical data.) The V-2 formed the basis of the first Soviet ballistic missile, deployed with an improved missile known as Pobeda which had a range of 559 miles (900 km). The Pobeda was designed under the direction of Sergey Korolev and the first test missile was launched in 1948. It was in mass production by 1950 and subsequently was allocated the code

The first European operational swept-wing jet fighter was the Swedish Saab J-29. (Saab-Scania)

name *Shyster* by NATO. Pobeda missiles were also the first to be used in launching experiments with dogs, between 1949 and 1952. The first Soviet intercontinental ballistic missile was test launched successfully in August 1957.

**The world's first aircraft to fly on the power of a single turboprop engine** was the Boulton Paul P.108 Balliol, a three-seat advanced trainer for service with the RAF. It was first flown with its Armstrong Siddeley Mamba turboprop engine on 24 March 1948.

**The world's first turbojet-powered aircraft to exceed a speed of Mach 1** was the YP-86A prototype of the North American F-86 Sabre which, on 25 April 1948, attained supersonic speed in a shallow dive.

**The first wind tunnel with a test section having a continuous capability of 3000 mph (4828 km/h)** was that activated by the USAF at Aberdeen, Maryland, announced as being operational on 23 May 1948.

**The first deliveries of food and other supplies into West Berlin** were made on 26 June 1948 by Douglas C-47s of the USAF based near Frankfurt. This marked the beginning of the Berlin Airlift (or Operation 'Vittles' as it was known to the USAF) and also of the **first major post-war 'Cold War' confrontation between East and West.**

**The first east–west crossing of the North Atlantic by turbojet-powered aircraft** was made by six RAF de Havilland Vampire F.Mk 3s on 14 July 1948, flying via Iceland and Greenland.

**First transatlantic deployment of a USAF jet fighter unit** (the 56th Fighter Group) **and the first west–east crossing of the North Atlantic by turbojet-powered aircraft** was achieved in 9 h 20 min on 20 July 1948. This involved 16 Lockheed F-80 (formerly P-80) Shooting Stars which were *en route* to Fürstenfeldbruck, Germany via the UK.

**The USAF's first turbojet-powered all-weather interceptor** was the prototype of the Northrop XF-89 Scorpion, which recorded its first flight at Edwards AFB, California, on 16 August 1948. The Scorpion entered USAF service in 1950.

**The first European swept-wing jet fighter to enter operational service** after the Second World War was the Swedish Saab J-29. It first flew on 1 September 1948 and joined the Day Fighter Wing F13 of the Flygvapnet near Norrkoping in May 1951. Nicknamed *Tunnan* (Barrel) and powered by a British de Havilland Ghost turbojet of 4410 lb (2000 kg) thrust, the J-29B possessed a top speed of 658 mph (1059 km/h) at 5000 ft (1525 m) or Mach 0.90 at the tropopause.

**The first four-jet bomber to fly in the United States** was the North American NA-130, as the XB-45 Tornado prototype, and first joining the 47th Bombardment Group at Barksdale AFB, Louisiana in November 1948 it was **also the first operational jet bomber to serve with the USAF.**

The prototype of **the first indigenous French jet fighter** recorded its first flight on 23 January 1949. This was the Dassault MD.450 Ouragan of which

350 were delivered to the Armée de l'Air in the 1950s.

**The first non-stop round-the-world flight** was accomplished between 26 February and 2 March 1949. This was made by the Boeing B-50 *Lucky Lady II* with a crew commanded by Capt James Gallagher, USAF, and covering a distance of 23 452 miles (37 742 km) in 94 h 1 min. Taking off from and landing back at Carswell AFB, Texas, the B-50 was flight-refuelled four times.

**The first turbojet-powered all-weather interceptor to serve with the USAF's Air Defense Command** was the Lockheed F-94 Starfire, first flown in YF-94 prototype (48-356) form on 1 July 1949.

**The first use of an ejection seat by a US airman for an emergency escape from an aircraft** was recorded on 9 August 1949. This occurred when Lt J. L. Fruin of the US Navy parted company with his McDonnell F2H-1 Banshee which was travelling at some 575 mph (925 km/h) over South Carolina.

**The first aircraft in the world powered by a coupled twin-turbine engine driving contra-rotating co-axial four-blade propellers** was the Fairey Gannet, first flown on 19 September 1949. The unusual power plant was an Armstrong Siddeley Double Mamba, each of its two sections driving one propeller. Half of the engine could be shut down and its propeller feathered to provide a more economical cruise power setting.

**The first aircraft to carry more than 100 passengers in flight across the North Atlantic** was a USAF C-74 Globemaster I of MATS. Landing at Marham, Norfolk, after a non-stop flight from the US on 18 November 1949, the Globemaster had carried a total of 103 passengers and the aircraft's crew.

**First American-built aircraft to enter RAF service after the Second World War** were ex-USAF B-29 and B-29A Superfortresses, given the RAF designation Washington B1. No. 149 Squadron at Marham was the first squadron to receive these aircraft, in March 1950, and a total of 88 entered RAF service.

**Following the end of the Second World War the first major East–West military confrontation** occurred when the Communist forces of North Korea crossed the 38th Parallel to invade South Korea on 25 June 1950, marking the start of the Korean War. The USAF's Japanese-based Far Eastern Air Forces were immediately directed to the area to evacuate US nationals and provide initial support to the South Koreans.

**The first victory by an American pilot in the Korean War** occurred on 27 June 1950, when Lt William Hudson with radar observer Lt Carl Frasee in the North American F-82G Twin Mustang 46-383 shot down a North Korean Yakovlev Yak-9 north-west of Seoul.

**The first operation in the Korean War by Boeing B-29 Superfortresses** was made on 27 June 1950 when aircraft of the USAF's 19th Bombardment Group attacked railway installations and the Han river bridges at Seoul.

**The first US bomber strike into North Korea** occurred on 28 June 1950, when Douglas B-26s of the 8th Bomber Squadron, 3rd Bomb Group, made an attack on railway installations at Munsan.

*Panther jet fighters on board USS* Valley Forge *line up for take off on a strike mission against targets in North Korea, July 1950. (US Navy)*

**The first US Navy jet fighter to take part in air combat** was the Grumman F9F-2 Panther, several of which took off from the carrier USS *Valley Forge* off Korea on 3 July 1950 and went into action against North Korean forces. A US Navy pilot of a Grumman Panther shot down a MiG-15 on 9 November 1950, and thus became **the first US Navy pilot to shoot down another jet aircraft.** The Panther was the first jet fighter designed by the Grumman Corporation, and the first two XF9F-2 prototypes were powered by imported Rolls-Royce Nene turbojets of 5000 lb (2268 kg) thrust.

**The first US Marine Corps air operation in support of the South Koreans** was flown from the escort carrier USS *Sicily* on 3 August 1950. This occurred when Vought F4U-4 Corsairs of squadron VMF-214 made a rocket and bomb attack on Chinju.

**The first non-stop crossing of the North Atlantic by a turbojet-powered fighter aircraft** was recorded on 22 September 1950, when a Republic EF-84E Thunderjet with hose-and-drogue flight refuelling capability flown by Col David C. Schilling, USAF, flew from the UK to Limestone, Maine. The flight was achieved by making three in-flight refuellings *en route*.

**The first aerial victory to be gained by the pilot of one jet aircraft over another** was achieved on 8 November 1950, when Lt Russel J. Brown Jr of the 51st Interceptor Wing, USAF, flying a Lockheed F-80C, shot down a MiG-15 fighter of the Chinese People's Republic air force over Sinuiju on the Yalu River, the border between North Korea and China.

**The first turbojet-powered night fighter to enter service with the RAF**, serving with No. 29 Squadron at Tangmere, Sussex, in January 1951, was the Meteor NF11, developed by Armstrong Whitworth.

**The first jet aircraft to fly the North Atlantic non-stop and unrefuelled** was an English Electric Canberra B.Mk 2 on 21 February 1951, which was flown from Britain to Baltimore and was later purchased by the USAF to become the first Canberra to carry American markings. Canberras were the first jet bombers produced in Britain and the first to serve with the RAF. The type had the unique distinction of being the first aircraft of non-US design to enter operational service with the USAF after the end of the Second World War. USAF approval for licence-production of the Canberra by the Glenn L. Martin Company was given on 6 March 1951, leading to a pre-production batch of eight B-57As (the original USAF designation), the first of these making its first flight at Baltimore, Maryland, on 20 July 1953.

**The first west European fighter to be dived supersonically**, on 23 February 1951, was the French Dassault MD.452 Mystère prototype. When the type entered service with the Armée de l'Air in 1955, and by then powered with the SNECMA Atar turbojet, **it was the nation's first completely indigenous jet fighter**.

**The first jet bomber to be produced in the UK, and the first to serve with the RAF** when it became operational in May 1951, was the English Electric Canberra. The prototype Canberra, the A.1, was first flown in prototype form on 13 May 1949.

**The first** (and only) **use of air-dropped torpedoes during the Korean War** occurred on 1 May 1951. These were deployed by US Navy Douglas Skyraiders and Vought Corsairs flying off the USS *Princeton* to attack the flood gates of the Hwachon dam.

**The first British V-bomber** (so-called from the wing leading-edge plan-form) was the Vickers Valiant, of which the prototype (WB210) first flew on 18 May 1951. Two Mark 1 and one Mark 2 prototypes were built, and were followed by 104 production aircraft, the first of which (WP199) flew on 21 December 1953. They were powered by various versions of the Rolls-Royce Avon axial-flow turbojet, four such engines being located in the wing roots. The Valiant entered RAF service with No. 138 Squadron at Gaydon, Warwickshire, in early 1955 and afterwards equipped Nos 7, 49, 90, 148, 207, 214 and 543 Squadrons.

**The first surface-to-surface weapon to enter service with the US Air Force** was the Martin TM-61A Matador 'flying-bomb' which joined Tactical Missile Wings in the USA, Germany, Korea and Taiwan from 1951. By 1957 Martin's Baltimore factory had delivered 1000 Matadors.

The distinction of being **the world's first jet night fighter squadron** belongs to the RAF's No.

25 Squadron which, when based at West Malling (Kent) during July 1951, was equipped with de Havilland Vampire NF.Mk 10s.

**The first single-seat sweptwing interceptor jet fighter to enter service with the RAF** was the Supermarine Swift, the prototype (WJ960) of which was flown for the first time on 5 August 1951.

**The first ballistic missile to enter service in the United States** was the Firestone SSM-A-17 Corporal, a liquid-fuelled rocket-propelled (un-boosted) missile which entered service with the US Army during the early 1950s and subsequently with the British Army. It had a range of about 75–100 miles (120–160 km). Corporal had been designed in 1951 and was the first army missile with a warhead of a kiloton.

**The first standardized jet fighter to serve in FAA first-line squadrons** was the Supermarine Attacker, which was also the first aircraft powered by the Rolls-Royce Nene turbojet. The type entered service with No. 800 Squadron at Ford, Sussex, on 22 August 1951, and this was the FAA's first operational jet squadron. When withdrawn from first line service, the Attackers were transferred to RNVR air squadrons: when No. 1831 Squadron received these aircraft on 14 May 1955, it became the first jet fighter squadron of the RNVR.

**The first British delta-wing interceptor fighter, and the first twin-jet delta fighter in the world,** was the Gloster Javelin. First flight of the prototype (WD804) was made by Sqn Ldr W. A. Waterton on 26 November 1951. **The Javelin was also the RAF's first purpose-built all-weather interceptor fighter**. The use of the delta-wing posed many aerodynamic problems, early flights suffering from control surface vibration and buffeting. On the 99th flight, on 29 June 1952, both elevators were lost following violent flutter. By superb flying, Waterton managed to control the aircraft in pitch, by means of the variable incidence tailplane, and bring it in to a fast landing, which caused the landing gear to collapse. For his skill and courage in saving the aircraft and its flight recorder, Waterton was awarded the George Medal. **The first production Javelin FAW1** (XA544), powered by two 8150 lb (3697 kg) thrust Armstrong Siddeley Sapphire AS Sa6 turbojet engines, made its first flight on 22

*IM-99B Bomarc pilotless long-range ground-to-air interceptor.*

July 1954. First deliveries to No. 46 Squadron at Odiham, Hampshire, began in February 1956.

**The first operational pilotless long-range ground-to-air interceptor** was the Boeing IM-99 Bomarc. The first prototypes, designated XF-99s, were tested in 1952. Launched vertically, the Bomarc was powered by two Marquardt RJ43-MA ramjets and incorporated a Westinghouse guidance system. Its cruising speed was Mach 2.8 and maximum range varied from 200 miles (320 km) for the IM-99A to 400 miles (640 km) for the IM-99B.

**The first operational inflight refuelling of combat aircraft** was recorded on 29 May 1952. This involved 12 Republic F-84E Thunderjets of the USAF's 159th Fighter-Bomber Squadron which had taken off from Itazuke (Japan) to attack a target at Sariwon; following the attack they made a rendezvous with KB-29 tankers over Taegu, taking on sufficient fuel for the return flight to their base.

**The first turbojet-powered aircraft to complete a non-stop trans-Pacific flight** was a North American RB-45 reconnaissance aircraft of the USAF which was flown from Elmendorf AFB (Alaska) to Yokota AB (Japan) on 29 July 1952.

**The first ever double crossing of the Atlantic in one day** was achieved on 26 August 1952 by the English Electric Canberra B. Mk V (VX 185)

Right   USS Antietam, the first aircraft carrier with an angled deck.

Left   The first aircraft to cross the Atlantic twice in one day was English Electric Canberra B.Mk V VX185.

bomber prototype, crewed by Britons Wing Cdr Roland Beamont, Flt Lt Peter Hillwood and Sqn Ldr Dennis Watson. The outward leg from Aldergrove, Northern Ireland, to Newfoundland took 4 h 34 min and the inbound leg 3 h 25 min 18.13 s, giving an elapsed time (including refuelling in Newfoundland) of 10 h 3 min 29.28 s.

**The world's first large bomber to have a delta-wing plan-form** was the Avro Vulcan B.1, the prototype of which (VX770) flew for the first time on 30 August 1952. Production aircraft entered service with RAF Bomber Command in May 1956, equipping No. 230 Operational Conversion Unit at Waddington, Lincolnshire, and the type was to record more than a quarter-century of operational use with the RAF. The Vulcan was the second aircraft in the RAF's V-bomber programme, the third and last being the Handley Page Victor which was flown in prototype (WB771) form for the first time on 24 December 1952.

**The first North Korean jet aircraft to be shot down at night**, a Yakovlev Yak-15 on the night of 3 November 1952, fell to the guns of a Douglas F3D-2 Skyknight. This was a US Marine Corps aircraft crewed by Major William T. Strattio Jr with Master-Sergeant Han C. Hoglind as his radar operator.

**The oldest US fighter 'ace' of the Korean War**

was Lt Col Vermont Garrison, who, at 37, claimed ten victories while flying a North American F-86 Sabre. During the Second World War, Garrison had achieved eleven victories.

**The US Navy's first angled-deck aircraft carrier**, the USS Antietam, began operational flight testing with Navy aircraft on 12 January 1953.

**The world's first fighter aircraft capable of sustained supersonic speed in level flight**, the North American F-100 Super Sabre, was flown for the first time in YF-100A prototype form on 25 May 1953.

**The first transatlantic deployment of the USAF's Boeing B-47 Stratojet bomber** by Strategic Air Command was accomplished during the period 3–5 June 1953. This involved aircraft of the 306th Bomb Wing which staged through Limestone AFB (Maine) *en route* to RAF Fairford (Gloucestershire).

**The first British transport aircraft designed specifically to air-drop heavy loads**, and also the RAF's largest aircraft at the time of its introduction, was the Blackburn Beverley. Powered by four 2850 hp Bristol Centaurus 173 engines, the prototype (WZ889) flew for the first time on 14 June 1953. Able to carry a payload of almost 22 tons (22.4 tonnes), Beverleys began to equip No. 47 Squadron Transport Command in March 1956.

The first air disaster involving the death of more than 100 people occurred on 18 June 1953, when a USAF C-124 Globemaster II transport crashed on take-off from Tachikawa AFB (Tokyo) killing a total of 129 crew and passengers.

The world's first 'over 700 mph' speed record was set at 715.60 mph (1151.64 km/h) on 16 July 1953. This was achieved by Lt Col W. F. Barnes, USAF, flying a North American F-86D Sabre.

The RAF's first indigenous swept-wing fighter, the Supermarine Swift F.Mk 1, entered service with No. 56 Squadron at RAF Waterbeach on 13 February 1954. The aircraft was found to have a number of shortcomings and was soon withdrawn from service in the interceptor role.

The first turbojet powered all-weather fighter to serve with the Royal Navy was the de Havilland Sea Venom, which first entered service with No. 890 Squadron, which re-formed at Yeovilton, Somerset, on 20 March 1954. At the end of 1958 three Sea Venoms of No. 893 Squadron carried out the first firings of Firestreak missiles by an operational fighter squadron of the Royal Navy.

The first supersonic operational carrier-borne naval interceptor in the world was the Grumman F11F-1 Tiger of the US Navy. Designated originally F9F-9, this was changed after the first three production aircraft had been delivered and, in 1962, was designated finally F-11. The prototype, powered by a Wright J65-W-6 turbojet rated at 7800 lb (3538 kg) thrust, flew for the first time on 30 July 1954. The F-11A was capable of a speed of 890 mph (1432 km/h) in level flight at 40 000 ft (12 200 m), and was armed with four 20 mm cannon. Two or four Sidewinder missiles could be carried on underwing pylons. F11F-1s entered service with the US Navy's VA-156 Squadron in March 1957. Two F11F-1s were powered by 15 000 lb (6805 kg) thrust General Electric J79-GE-3A engines, and demonstrated Mach 2 performance in level flight.

The first supersonic single-seat fighter to serve with the RAF, the English Electric (later BAC) Lightning, designed by W. E. W. Petter, flew for the first time on 4 August 1954, piloted by Wg Cdr R. P. Beamont. Entering operational service with No. 74 Squadron at Coltishall, Norfolk, in July 1960, it was the first RAF fighter capable of speeds in excess of Mach 2, and the RAF's first integrated weapons system. During the research

*No 74 Squadron, RAF, Lightning fighters.*

which led to its construction, Britain's first transonic wind tunnel was built.

**The first man to escape from an aeroplane flying at supersonic speed and live** was George Franklin Smith, test pilot for North American Aviation Corporation, who ejected from an F-100 Super Sabre on 26 February 1955 off Laguna Beach, California. After failure of the controls in a dive, Smith fired his ejector seat at an indicated speed of Mach 1.05 or more than 700 mph (1125 km/h). After being unconscious for five days Smith made an almost complete recovery from his injuries and within nine months had been passed fit to resume flying.

**The first jet fighter in the world with a variable-incidence wing** was the Chance Vought (subsequently Ling-Temco-Vought, or LTV) F-8 Crusader supersonic air-superiority fighter of the US Navy. The operation of such a high-performance aircraft from the deck of an aircraft carrier meant that to achieve an acceptable landing speed an excessive nose-up attitude would result. The use of a variable-incidence wing provided the necessary compromise. The first of two XF8U-1 prototypes, powered by a Pratt & Whitney J57-P-11 turbojet engine, made its first flight on 25 March 1955. Deliveries of the production Crusader, under the designation F-8A, began to VF-32 (US Navy Fighter Squadron 32) on 25 March 1957, serving originally at sea aboard the USS *Saratoga*. This initial production version was powered by a J57-P-12 or -14 engine, providing a maximum level speed of 1100 mph (1770 km/h) at 40 000 ft (12 200 m). Armament comprised four 20 mm cannon and, on early models, a fuselage pack of 32 air-to-air rockets. Later F-8As carried two fuselage-mounted Sidewinder missiles.

**First US Navy unit to receive the Douglas A3D Skywarrior** carrier-based attack bomber was squadron VAH-1 based at NAS Jacksonville (Florida) on 31 March 1956. More than 30 years of operational use has given the Skywarrior an honoured place in Navy history as **its most versatile carrier-based aircraft**.

**The first operational overflight by a Lockheed U-2** reconnaissance aircraft was made on 4 July 1956. Taking off from Wiesbaden (Germany) the U-2's route took it over Moscow, Leningrad and the Soviet Baltic Sea coast.

**The first member of the RAF to survive a supersonic ejection** (and the second man in the world) was Flying Officer Hedley Molland who escaped from a Hawker Hunter fighter on 3 August 1955. Flying at 40 000 ft (12 200 m), the aircraft went into an uncontrollable dive. All of Flying Officer Molland's efforts to regain control failed, and by the time he ejected his stricken machine was travelling at an estimated Mach 1.10, its height about 10 000 ft (3050 m). Descending in the sea he was picked up by a tug, and recovered in hospital from his injuries which included a broken arm (caused by flailing in the slipstream) and a fractured pelvis.

**The world's first parachute escape from an aircraft travelling at speed on the ground** was achieved by Sqn Ldr J. S. Fifield, on 3 September 1955, at Chalgrove airfield, Oxfordshire. This occurred when he was ejected from the rear cockpit of a modified Gloster Meteor 7, piloted by Capt J. E. D. Scott, Chief Test Pilot of Martin-Baker Ltd, manufacturers of the ejection seat. The speed of the aircraft at the moment of ejection was 120 mph (194 km/h) and the maximum height reached by the seat was 70 ft (21 m) above the runway.

**The first supersonic tactical fighter-bomber to be designed as such**, and in operational form one of the USAF's most important weapons in Vietnam, the YF-105A prototype of the Republic F-105 Thunderchief was flown for the first time on 22 October 1955. Exceeding Mach 1 during this flight, the definitive F-105D had a maximum speed in excess of Mach 2 and all-weather capability resulting from its fully integrated automatic flight and fire control systems.

**The USAF's first operational delta-winged aircraft** was the Convair F-102A Delta Dagger which entered service initially with the 327th Fighter Interceptor Squadron at George AFB (California) in April 1956; it had first flown in YF-102A prototype form on 24 October 1953.

**The first air-to-air guided missile to be adopted by the US Air Force** was the Hughes GAR-1 Falcon, six of which were carried in wingtip pods on the Northrop F-89H Scorpion all-weather fighter. They entered operational service in 1956.

**The world's first known air-transportable**

Northrop F-89H Scorpion with Falcon missiles attached to the wingtip pods.

**hydrogen bomb** was dropped on 21 May 1956, from a Boeing B-52B flying at 50 000 ft (15 240 m) over Bikini Atoll in the Pacific.

**The first turbojet aircraft in the world to be used in the military transport role** was a modified version of the de Havilland Comet Series 2, the first of which was delivered to RAF Transport Command at Lyneham, Wiltshire, on 7 July 1956.

**The first-ever firing of a nuclear-tipped air-to-air missile** was carried out on 19 July 1956 when a Northrop F-89J Scorpion discharged a Douglas MB-1 Genie at 15 000 ft (4500 m) above Yucca Flat, Nevada, in the USA. This missile incorporated a warhead of about 1.5 kilotons yield and the fighter turned away sharply to avoid the missile's blast. The warhead was detonated after having travelled about 3 miles horizontally, but USAF observers standing directly below the explosion reported no immediate ill-effects from fall-out.

**The first practical steps towards the creation of the post-war Luftwaffe** came on 1 February 1956, when the West German Ministry of Defence initiated a pilot training scheme. The actual formation date of the Luftwaffe der Deutschen Bundesrepublik was on 24 September 1956.

**The first British atomic bomb** was dropped by a Vickers Valiant (WZ366) of No. 49 (Bomber) Squadron, RAF, captained by Sqn Ldr E. J. G. Flavell, over Maralinga, Southern Australia, on 11 October 1956.

**First military aircraft to land on the ice at the South Pole** was a US Navy Douglas R4D on 31 October 1956. Rear Admiral G. L. Dufek (in command) and his crew of seven were the first men to stand on that spot since January 1912.

**The first non-stop round-the-world flight by turbojet-powered aircraft**, made by three USAF Boeing B-52B Stratofortresses, was completed on 18 January 1957 after a flight of 45 hr 19 min. Commanded by Maj Gen Archie J. Old, USAF, the 24 325 mile (39 147 km) flight was made at an average speed of 537 mph (864 km/h).

B-52B Stratofortress lands back at March AFB, having made the first non-stop round-the-world flight by a turbojet aircraft.

**The first British hydrogen bomb** was dropped by a Vickers Valiant of No. 49 (Bomber) Squadron, captained by Wg Cdr Hubbard, on 15 May 1957. The bomb was detonated at medium altitude over the Pacific in the Christmas Island area.

Initial examples of the Boeing KC-135A, **the USAF's first turbojet-powered aircraft designed as a tanker/transport aircraft**, were delivered to the 93rd Air Refuelling Squadron at Castle AFB (California) on 28 June 1957.

**The world's first true stand-off bomb to achieve operational status** was the Bell GAM-63 Rascal on which, under the original designation XB-63, work started in 1946. Powered by three liquid-fuel rockets, this bomb was first delivered to the US Strategic Air Command at Pinecastle Air Force Base, Florida, on 30 October 1957, and was carried operationally under Boeing DB-47E Stratojet bombers of SAC. Its warhead was either atomic or thermonuclear, as required, and its range was about 100 miles (160 km).

**The first 'over 2000 km/h' world speed record**, later ratified at a figure of 1403 mph (2259.18 km/h), was established over Southern California on 16 May 1958 by Capt W. W. Irvin, USAF, flying a Lockheed F-104A Starfighter.

**The first swept-wing single-seat fighter to be built for the Royal Navy, and the first to be capable of low-level attack at supersonic speed**, attained in a shallow dive, was the Supermarine Scimitar. The first operational squadron, No. 803, was formed at Lossiemouth, Scotland, in June 1958. The Scimitar was also **the first British naval aircraft to have a fully power operated control system.** Prior to the introduction of the Scimitar, F.2 and subsequent versions of the Hawker Sea Hawk fighter had been given power-boosted ailerons, thereby making the Sea Hawk F.2 **the first British naval aircraft to have power operated controls.**

**The first West European aircraft to demonstrate a speed of Mach 2 in level flight**, on 24 October 1958, was the first pre-production example of the Dassault Mirage IIIA interceptor.

**The first American missile with intercontinental range** was the Northrop SM-62 Snark, an aeroplane-configured missile with a thermonuclear warhead and capable of a range of more than 6300 miles (10 140 km). Snark first became operational in 1959, with the 702nd Strategic Missile Wing, Presque Isle Air Force Base.

**Achieving his first solo flight in a turbojet-powered trainer**, on 13 March 1959, Aviation Cadet E. R. Cook became the US Navy's first student pilot to do so without previous experience in a propeller-driven aircraft.

**The first non-stop flight between the UK and Cape Town** (with two inflight refuelling contacts) was made by the Vickers Valiant B.Mk 1 XD861 of the RAF's No. 214 Squadron. Commanded by Wing Cdr M. J. Beetham, the 6060 mile (9753 km) flight was completed in 11 h 29 min on 9 July 1959.

**The first aircraft to be brought down by a surface-to-air missile (SAM) while overflying the Soviet Union**, on 1 May 1960, was a Lockheed U-2 reconnaissance aircraft piloted by Francis Gary Powers. The ability of the Soviets to intercept such a high-flying aircraft brought a major re-think in the mode of deployment of strategic aircraft.

**The USAF's first supersonic bomber aircraft**, the Convair B-58A Hustler which had a maximum speed of Mach 2, entered service on 1 August 1960 with the USAF's 43rd Bomb Wing at Carswell AFB, Texas. The Hustler had unusual self-contained emergency escape capsules that could be used at the aircraft's maximum speed and on 28 February 1962 the first manned test of one of these capsules was carried out, when Warrant Officer Edward J. Murray was ejected from a Hustler travelling at 595 mph (909 km/h) at 20 000 ft (6100 m). After a controlled time a parachute was deployed automatically to bring the capsule and its occupant safely to the ground. In a third test, on 8 June 1962, a capsule containing the chimpanzee Zena was ejected successfully at 1060 mph (1706 km/h), and this landed without causing any harm to its occupant.

**The first sortie of the 'Looking Glass' programme** was flown on 3 February 1961, a programme under which the USAF's Strategic Air Command kept an ACP (airborne command post) aircraft continuously in the air from that date. Early operations were flown by Boeing KC-135As, but specialist variants of the EC-135 were later used in this role.

**The first non-stop flight from Britain to Australia** was made in a 20 h 30 min period during

21–22 June 1961. This was achieved by the Avro Vulcan B.Mk 1A XH481 of the RAF's No. 617 Squadron, under the control of Sqn Ldr M. G. Beavis and his crew, the 11 500 mile (18 507 km) route involving flight refuelling contacts over Cyprus, Pakistan and Singapore.

**The first Soviet supersonic bomber** was the Tupolev Tu-22 'Blinder', which was first seen publicly in 1961. Some 250 were built, of which about 75 remain with the air force (but now mostly for electronic warfare and reconnaissance) and 50 serve with naval units as bombers, electronic and reconnaissance aircraft. Maximum speed is Mach 1.4.

**The world's first specially designed low-level strike aircraft** was the Blackburn NA39, subsequently named Buccaneer. The S1, powered by de Havilland Gyron Junior turbojets, first entered operational service with the FAA's No. 801 Squadron at Lossiemouth in July 1962.

**The first British aircraft designed from the outset as a long-range military transport,** and **the world's first military transport with a fully automatic landing system,** was flown in prototype (G-ASKE later XR362) form as the Short SC.5 on 5 January 1964. The type entered service as the Belfast C.Mk 1 on 20 January 1966 when the first aircraft was delivered to No. 53 Squadron at Brize Norton, Oxfordshire.

**The third and final nation to develop a supersonic strategic bomber** was France, its Dassault Mirage IV-A entering service between 1964 and 1968. Sixty-two were built, of which some 22 remain. Maximum speed is Mach 2.2.

**The first action to mark full US involvement in the Vietnam War** was made on 5 August 1964 when aircraft of the US Navy's 7th Fleet carriers USS *Constellation* and *Ticonderoga* attacked torpedo boats and their bases along the North Vietnam coastline. This was in retaliation for attacks by North Vietnam torpedo boats against the destroyer USS *Maddox* on 2 August.

**The world's first operational variable-geometry (swing-wing) combat aircraft** was the General Dynamics F-111A, which made its first flight from Fort Worth, Texas, on 21 December 1964. This was accomplished with the wings locked at a sweepback of 26°, and the first flight with the wings actuated through the full sweep

*Three B-52 Stratofortress bombers fly towards their targets in Vietnam. (US Air Force)*

from 16° to 72.5° was accomplished on 6 January 1965. Although its initial operational use in Vietnam appeared to be unsuccessful, the aircraft was developed into a valuable component of the US armed forces.

**The first massive air strike against targets in North Vietnam** was launched by the United States under Operation 'Rolling Thunder' on 2 March 1965; this first attack, on an ammunition base at Xom Ban, was carried out by 110 aircraft. The US Navy became involved in 'Rolling Thunder' operations for the first time on 26 March when aircraft from the USS *Coral Sea* and *Hancock* attacked radar stations near Vinh Son.

**The first US combat victories in the Vietnam War** (against Mikoyan MiG-17s) were gained on 17 June 1965, when pilots Cdr L. C. Page and Lt J. E. D. Batson in McDonnell Douglas Phantom IIs of US Navy squadron VF-21, flying off USS *Midway*, destroyed two of a flight of four.

**The first Boeing B-52 Stratofortress mission of the Vietnam War** was made on 18 June 1965 when 27 aircraft of the 7th and 320th Bomb Wings attacked Viet-Cong targets with conventional HE bombs.

**The first US Air Force combat victories of the Vietnam War** were gained on 10 July 1965 by two McDonnell Douglas F-4 Phantom IIs crewed by Captains K. E. Holcombe, T. C. Roberts, A. C. Clark and R. C. Anderson. Members of the USAF's 45th Tactical Fighter Squadron, they destroyed two MiG-17s over Vietnam.

**The first US attack against Hanoi**, on 29 June 1966, was by Republic F-105 Thunderchiefs of the USAF's 355th and 388th Tactical Fighter Wings, led respectively by Maj James Kasler and Lt-Col James R. Hopkins.

**A first hovering flight by a Hawker Siddeley Harrier development aircraft** was made at the company's Dunsfold (Surrey) airfield on 31 August 1966. The first production example of what had then become known as the Harrier GR.Mk 1 was flown initially on 28 December 1967, and the type was to become the world's **first jet-powered V/STOL combat aircraft to gain full operational status** when Harrier GR.Mk 1s joined the RAF's No. 1 Squadron at RAF Wittering in July 1969.

**The first** (and only) **US airborne combat assault of the Vietnam War** took place as Operation 'Junction City' on 22 February 1967, in which 845 paratroopers of the 173rd Airborne Brigade were dropped by 14 Lockheed C-130 Hercules transports.

**The first US aerial mining operation of the Vietnam War** was carried out on 26 February 1967 by Grumman A-6A Intruders of US Navy squadron VA-35.

**The first successful operational use of the Walleye guided bomb** was made on 11 March 1967 when Cdr H. Smith flying a US Navy Douglas A-4 launched one against a military barracks at Sam Son.

**The prototypes of the first two Soviet operational variable-geometry combat aircraft,** the MiG-23 and Su-17, were first displayed at Domodedovo Airport, Moscow, on 9 July 1967 as the Mikoyan Ye-231 and Sukhoi S-22I respectively. Operational deployment of production aircraft began in 1972-73.

**The first significant development of the gunship aircraft** was seen when the initial example of the Lockheed AC-130A (or Gunship II) went into action over the Ho Chi Minh trail on 27 February 1968. Armed with four 0.3-in Miniguns and four 20-mm Vulcan cannon, these aircraft played a major role by taking a heavy toll of Communist supplies and personnel.

**The first supersonic (in level flight) carrier-based interceptor fighter to serve with the Royal Navy** was the McDonnell Douglas F-4K Phantom II (RN designation Phantom FG.1), of which the first three were delivered to RNAS Yeovilton, Somerset, on 29 April 1968. The Phantom FG.1, which equipped No. 892 Squadron, was **also the FAA's last air superiority fighter**, a fact indicated by the Omega symbol on the tail fin (the last letter of the Greek alphabet). The Phantoms of No. 892 Squadron served aboard the carrier HMS *Ark Royal* until this vessel was withdrawn from service in 1978.

**The first US aircraft designed specifically for counter-insurgency (COIN) operations** was the North American OV-10A Bronco, first deployed with the US Marine Corps squadron VMO-2 at Da Nang (South Vietnam) on 6 July 1968. The OV-10A proved invaluable in this theatre, used primarily for helicopter escort, forward air control and reconnaissance missions.

**The first transatlantic crossing by a Hawker Siddeley Harrier GR.Mk 1** was recorded on 28 April 1969, this RAF aircraft flown from Northolt (Middlesex) to Floyd Bennett Field, New York.

**The first land-based pure-jet aircraft in the world to be built for anti-submarine duties and long-range maritime patrol**, the Hawker Siddeley Nimrod, developed from the de Havilland Comet 4C, entered service with RAF Strike Command on 2 October 1969. Powered by four Rolls-Royce RB.168-20 Spey Mk 250 turbofan engines, each of 12 140 lb (5507 kg) thrust, it has a typical operational endurance of 12 h.

**The first USAF mission in support of the Laotian government** was flown by Boeing B-52s during 17–18 February 1970. This attack was mounted against North Vietnamese and Pathet Lao positions on the Plain of Jars.

**Japan's first military jet transport of indigenous design and manufacture** was flown for the first time on 12 November 1970. This was the first of two XC-1 prototypes which were designed and built by the Nihon Aeroplane Manufacturing Company; C-1 production aircraft for service with the JASDF were built by Kawasaki.

**On 21 November 1970 USAF and USN aircraft made the first major air strike against North Vietnam since 1 November 1968** (when President Lyndon B. Johnson had declared an end to the bombing of targets in North Vietnam).

Enemy installations at Mu Gia and Ban Kari were attacked by some 300 aircraft.

**The world's first large variable-geometry supersonic strategic bomber** was the Soviet Tupolev Tu-22M, known to NATO as 'Backfire'. It was first observed by the West as a prototype in 1970. Two turbofan engines bestow a speed of Mach 2.

**The first VTOL fixed-wing combat aircraft to enter service with any of the US armed forces** was a Hawker Siddeley AV-8A Harrier, handed over officially to the US Marine Corps on 6 January 1971.

**Japan's first supersonic aircraft of indigenous design and manufacture** is the Mitsubishi T-2 twin-turbofan advanced trainer, in service with the JASDF. Flown initially in XT-2 prototype form on 20 July 1971, it was first flown supersonically in level flight on 19 November 1971. A single-seat close support version designated F-1 has been developed from this aircraft and the first of two prototypes was flown initially on 3 June 1975.

**The first V/STOL combat aircraft to become operational with the Soviet Navy,** and **the world's second V/STOL warplane to enter service** was the Yakovlev Yak-36MP 'Forger'. First flown in 1971, 'Forgers' were deployed on the *Baku* and three Kiev class aircraft carriers. Unlike the British-designed Harrier series, the Yak uses separate horizontal 'main' and near-vertically mounted 'lift' engines. The *Kiev*, commissioned in May 1975, was **the Soviet Navy's first aircraft carrier for fixed-wing aircraft.**

**The first jet aircraft to be built in Brazil** was the EMBRAER EMB-326GB Xavante (Servant) trainer and ground attack aircraft. Assembled under licence from Aermacchi of Italy, the first Brazilian-built example was flown initially on 3 September 1971, and the type serves with the Brazilian Air Force as the AT-26 Xavante.

**The first aircraft to be flown in the United States with a fly-by-wire control system,** on 29 April 1972, was a specially-equipped McDonnell Douglas F-4 Phantom II. Such a system replaces the conventional mechanical linkage for the operation of flight control surfaces by wires carrying electrical signals. Fly-by-wire offers many advantages, being lighter in weight, providing greater

redundancy because cable runs can be duplicated or triplicated, and is ideal for integration with computer-controlled automatic flight control systems.

**The first General Dynamics YF-16 lightweight fighter prototype** (72-01567), for competitive evaluation against the Northrop YF-17, made its official maiden flight on 2 February 1974; on 11 March 1974 this aircraft was flown at a speed of Mach 2 for the first time. Selection of this aircraft by the USAF for production as the F-16 (later named Fighting Falcon) led to **the largest single-aircraft production programme in the world** involving more than 100 major contractors and about 4000 sub-contractors; these supply assemblies and components for the General Dynamics plant at Fort Worth (Texas) as well as the production lines in Belgium, the Netherlands and Turkey. The USAF, which had ordered 2204 F-16s by 1991, saw the first example enter service with the 388th Tactical Fighter Wing at Hill AFB (Utah) on 6 January 1979, and initial operational capability was attained by this unit's 4th TFS in October 1980. The first European-built F-16s were delivered to the air forces of Belgium, the Netherlands, Norway and Denmark on 26 January 1979, 6 June 1979, 25 January 1980 and 26 January 1980 respectively. Twelve other countries have since ordered F-16s, as have the US Navy, making 3530 ordered overall by 1991.

**The first prototype of the Panavia multi-role combat aircraft** (MRCA) made its first flight at Manching, Germany, on 14 August 1974. Designed to meet the requirements of the air forces of the Federal Republic of Germany, Italy and United Kingdom, and of the German Navy, the MRCA, later named Tornado, was the **first combat aircraft to be specified to use a fly-by-wire control system.** (The first operational combat aircraft with fly-by-wire was the US General Dynamics F-16, entering service before Tornado.)

**The first operational deployment of the Grumman F-14A Tomcat** carrier-based fighter occurred on 17 September 1974, when the USS *Enterprise* with US Navy F-14 squadrons VF-1 and VF-2 included in its complement sailed from San Francisco, California. Tomcat became **the US Navy's first and so far only variable-geometry aircraft.**

**The first McDonnell Douglas F-15A Eagle fighters to be stationed in Europe** were those of the USAF's 36th Tactical Fighter Wing which left Langley AFB (Virginia) on 27 April 1977 *en route* to Bitburg, West Germany.

**Thought by many to be the most agile non-V/STOL combat aircraft in the world** is the Russian Sukhoi Su-27 'Flanker'. First flown on 20 May 1977, only the Soviet forces were operationally equipped with Su-27s in 1991.

**The first example (XZ450) of the British Aerospace Sea Harrier**, a navalized version of the RAF's Harrier, **was flown initially on 20 August 1978**. (See below.)

**The first of the ski ramp-equipped 'Invincible' class aircraft carriers**, HMS *Invincible*, began sea trials with the Royal Navy on 26 March 1979. Her intended complement of aircraft was five British Aerospace Sea Harriers and 10 Westland Sea King helicopters.

**The first British Aerospace Sea Harrier for service with the Royal Navy** was handed over on 18 June 1979. The first ship trials were carried out aboard HMS *Hermes* during November of that year. **First used in combat** during the Falkland Islands campaign (2 April to 14 June 1982), 28 Sea Harriers operating from HMS *Hermes* and HMS *Invincible* made 2380 sorties and destroyed 27 enemy aircraft in air-to-air combat without loss resulting from air-to-air combat.

**The first stage of Russian involvement in Afghanistan** began on 24 December 1979 with Mikoyan MiG-21 and MiG-23 fighters providing escort to the large numbers of transport aircraft which airlifted some 5000 troops of the 105th Airborne Guards Division into Kabul.

**The world's first operational stealth combat aircraft**, the Lockheed F-117A, was first flown on 18 June 1981. Fifty-nine were built up to July 1990, of which three have been lost. Designed to make precision attacks with two 2000 lb bombs or missiles, its multi-faceted pyramidal airframe, non-afterburning engines with special overwing air intakes and narrow slot exhaust nozzles, and avionics, ensure that its radar and infra-red signals are very low indeed against enemy detection.

**The first USAF unit to become operational with the 'Pave Tack' weapon delivery system** (on 15 September 1981) was the 494th Tactical Fighter Squadron based at RAF Lakenheath, Suffolk. A laser transmitter/receiver and a precision optical sight is incorporated in the 'Pave Tack' pod.

**The first air victories by variable geometry warplanes** were recorded on 19 August 1981, when two US Navy Grumman F-14A Tomcat fighters of Squadron VF-11 'Black Aces' destroyed two Libyan Sukhoi Su-22 'Fitters' over the Gulf of Sirte.

**The first fully automatic landing to be achieved by the McDonnell Douglas F/A-18 Hornet** was made on 22 January 1982 at the Naval Air Test Center, Patuxent River, Maryland.

**The first phase of what was to become known as the Falklands war** began on 2 April 1982 when the armed forces of Argentina began an invasion of the Falkland Islands. British reaction saw the

*RAF Harriers and Navy Sea Harriers and Sea King on board HMS* Hermes, *flagship of the Falklands Task Force. (Ministry of Defence)*

main elements of a British Task Force (including the carriers HMS *Hermes* and *Invincible*) sail from Portsmouth (Hampshire) on 5 April.

**The first air victory by a V/STOL warplane** was achieved on 1 May 1982, during the Falklands campaign. Piloting a Royal Navy Sea Harrier, Flt Lt Paul Barton of the Fleet Air Arm's No 801 Squadron shot down an Argentine Air Force Dassault Mirage IIIEA (flown by Lt Carlos Perona) with a Sidewinder AIM-9L missile. Perona ejected and survived the attack.

**The first British air attack against Argentine positions on the Falkland Islands** was made on 1 May 1982. This first of a series of 'Black Buck' operations saw the single Vulcan B.Mk 2 XM607 drop a stick of 21 1000 lb bombs diagonally across the runway of Port Stanley airfield. This attack, launched from Ascension Island and involving inflight refuelling for both the out and return flights, **takes its place in aviation history as the longest operational bombing mission.**

**The first in-strength landing of UK forces on the Falkland Islands** was made on 20 May 1982 with essential air cover provided by the Navy's Sea Harriers; little more than three weeks later, on 14 June, all Argentine forces on the islands surrendered.

**The first combat unit to become operational with the McDonnell Douglas F/A-18 Hornet** naval strike fighter, on 7 January 1983, was the US Marine Corps squadron VMFA-314 based at MCAS El Toro, California. Hornets first went into action against Libyan targets on the night of 14/15 April 1986, flying from USS *Coral Sea*.

**First service introduction of the McDonnell Douglas/British Aerospace AV-8B Harrier II V/STOL close-support aircraft** for the US Marine Corps took place on 12 January 1984. This occurred when the first of 12 preproduction aircraft was handed over officially to the USMC at Cherry Point, North Carolina. The first Harrier GR.Mk 5 was handed over to the RAF on 1 July 1987.

**The first Dassault-Breguet Mirage 2000 air-superiority fighters were declared operational** with the Armée de l'Air on 2 July 1984. This was at Dijon-Longvic where the first unit to equip with the type, Escadron de Chasse 1/2 *Cigognes*, put on a 10-aircraft demonstration flight. The French Air Force deployed 14 Mirage 2000Cs during the Gulf War, flying 508 sorties.

**The first operational test and evaluation of the USAF's new LANTIRN (Low-Altitude Navigation and Targeting Infra-Red system for Night)** was made by three General Dynamics F-16 Fighting Falcons on 15 October 1984. In tests that were regarded as 'highly successful', it was found easily possible to make night sorties at treetop height while travelling at some 500 mph (805 km/h).

**The first production example of the Rockwell B-1B Lancer long-range strategic bomber** for service with the USAF made a successful first flight at Palmdale (California) on 18 October 1984. Service entry began on 7 July 1985.

**The first airport on the Falkland Islands able to accept wide-body aircraft** was opened officially by HRH Prince Andrew on 12 May 1985. Known as Mount Pleasant airport, **the first wide-body transport to land there (on 1 May) had been an RAF Lockheed TriStar** following a proving flight from the UK via Ascension Island.

**The first destruction of a satellite in Earth orbit by a Western missile** took place on 13 September 1985, when a USAF McDonnell Douglas F-15 Eagle launched an anti-satellite missile (ASAT) which successfully destroyed an inert US satellite.

**The first Russian aircraft carrier for conventional aircraft** (rather than V/STOL or helicopters) was the *Tbilisi*, now renamed *Admiral of the Fleet Kuznetsov*. Launched on 5 December 1985 and commissioned in the early 1990s, its main aircraft strength comprises about 24 Sukhoi Su-27K 'Flanker-Ds' and Mikoyan MiG-29K 'Fulcrum-Ds'.

**The first time a Boeing B-52H Stratofortress of the USAF carried its maximum load of 20 ALCMs** (air-launched cruise missiles), a weapon load of some 64 000 lb (29 030 kg), was on 10 May 1986. This occurred during a flight from Carswell AFB (Texas) to Edwards AFB (California). During the 1991 Gulf War, B-52s flew 1624 sorties, and were the oldest combat aircraft in action with coalition forces.

**The Russian Mikoyan MiG-29** first flew as a prototype on 6 October 1977. **The first occasion**

that the MiG-29 was seen on the ground out-side of WarPac borders was on 1 July 1986, when six of these advanced fighters paid a courtesy visit to Rissala AB, Finland.

The RAF's first strategic overseas air-to-air refuelling carried out with a full passenger load occurred on 21 November 1986. As part of exercise 'Swift Sword', a VC10 Mk 1 of No 10 Squadron carrying 129 troops of the British Army's 5th Airborne Brigade undertook a non-stop flight from the UK to Oman, a distance of 4200 miles (6760 km) covered in 9½ h. The flight included an in-flight refuelling over Sicily, where 44 600 lb (20 216 kg) of fuel was taken on from a VC10K of No 101 Squadron. Captain of the VC10 Mk 1 at the time of the refuelling was Sqn Ldr D. S. Miller.

The first conventional fixed-wing aircraft to land on a Russian aircraft carrier was an experi-mental navalized version of the Sukhoi Su-27, designated T-10-24, landing on *Tbilisi* (former name of *Admiral of the Fleet Kuznetsov*) on 1 November 1989. That same day a navalized MiG-29 also landed.

The first British fighter to undertake an unrefuelled Atlantic crossing was the Panavia Tornado, on 27 September 1987.

The last pilot to fly an in-service RAF single-seat fighter was Sqn Ldr John Aldington, who flew English Electric Lightning F.Mk 6 XS925 to Cranfield on 30 June 1988, so ending the career of this jet.

The first operational use of stealth combat air-craft occurred on 21 December 1989, when two USAF Lockheed F-117As dropped 2000 lb laser-guided bombs on the Rio Hato barrack area, Panama, during Operation *Just Cause*. Later, in the 1991 coalition *Desert Storm* operations against Iraq, all 56 F-117As of the USAF's 415th and 416th TFS and 417th TFTS were used, flying 1272 sorties.

The first time air power alone caused one of the world's largest land armies to be rendered ineffective was during the Gulf War of 17 Jan-uary–28 February 1991. Coalition air forces undertook well over 110 000 sorties during oper-ation *Desert Storm*, making a major land battle unnecessary. USAF General Dynamics F-16s flew the greatest number of combat sorties of the con-flict, the 249 aircraft accounting for 13 450.

The first US Navy air victories of the Gulf War occurred on 17 January 1991, when two F/A-18C Hornets claimed two Iraqi MiG-21s. The closing speed was in excess of 1200 knots, the Hornets having been warned of the MiGs by an E-2 Hawkeye AWACS aircraft. Each Hornet was carrying four 2000 lb bombs, making this prob-ably the first time fighters had achieved air-to-air victories against enemy fighters while car-rying heavy bomb loads, which were then used to attack the appointed ground targets.

*Largest:*

The largest bombers to serve with the Russian army during the First World War were the Sikorsky *Ilya Mourometz* series, the largest of them being the IM-Ye1 (six built) with a wing span of 102 ft 10.25 in (31.35 m) and a length of 59 ft 8.5 in (18.20 m). The first true military variant was the IM-B, which entered service in 1914, and was thus the first four-engined heavy bomber to enter service with any of the world's air forces.

The largest German aeroplane to be used operationally during the First World War was the Zeppelin-Staaken R VI, a four-engined giant bomber with a wing span of 138 ft 5.4 in (42.20 m) and a length of 73 ft 6 in (22.10 m), the first of 18 entering service in June 1917. Pow-ered by four 245 hp Maybach Mb IV or 260 hp Mercedes D IVa engines, the R VI had a maximum speed of 84 mph (135 km/h).

The largest and first four-engined British bomber of the First World War was the Handley Page V/1500 biplane, first flown during May 1918, which had a wing span of 126 ft (38.40 m) and a length of 64 ft (19.50 m).

The largest aeroplane force assembled during the First World War for a single military oper-ation was that used during the battle for the Saint-Mihiel salient between 11 and 15 September 1918. In command of 1483 fighter, observation and bombing aircraft was Gen William Mitchell of the US Army Air Service.

The largest propeller ever fitted to an aero-plane was 22 ft 7½ in (6.9 m) in diameter, driven at the nose of the giant German Linke-Hofmann R.II bomber by four 260 hp Mercedes D.IVa engines. The R.II did not fly until 1919 and was fitted out as a 12 passenger airliner. The Bell-Boeing V-22 Osprey is a military tilt-rotor aircraft, first flown on 19 March 1989 and expected to join the US services from late 1991 or early 1992 for transport and other roles. The twin rotors tilt from horizontal to vertical position for high-speed horizontal flight, thereby making the rotors huge 38 ft (11.58 m) diameter propellers ('proprotors').

**The largest Japanese military aircraft built between the wars** was the Mitsubishi Ki-20, the basic design of which originated in Germany as the Junkers G 38. The first Ki-20 was completed in secrecy during 1931; by 1934 it had been joined by five others, the later examples built from Japanese components. The Japanese Army Air Force was not impressed by the aircraft, and the Ki-20s never saw action. Each had a wing span of 144 ft 4 in (44.00 m).

**The largest French bomber to enter service between the wars** was the Farman F221 which, with its derivatives, was the mainstay of the French bomber force for several years. Production began in 1934 with 12 F221s. Later versions included the F222, F222/2, F223 and F2233. The F221 had a wing span of 118 ft 1½ in (36 m) and was powered by four 800 hp Gnome-Rhône 14 Kbrs engines. Maximum speed was 185 mph (297 km/h).

**The largest number of losses suffered by an air force in a single day's offensive operations**, as a result of air combat and anti-aircraft gunfire, is believed to have been that of the Luftwaffe on 10 May 1940. On this day Germany invaded the Netherlands and Belgium and was opposed simultaneously by the air forces of Belgium, France, Great Britain and Holland. The Norwegian campaign, by then nearing its end, also claimed a small number of German victims on that day. According to its own records the Luftwaffe lost on 10 May:

|  | Destroyed | Damaged |
|---|---|---|
| Dornier Do 17 bombers | 26 | 7 |
| Dornier Do 18 flying-boat | 1 | |
| Dornier Do 215 reconnaissance aircraft | 2 | |
| Fieseler Fi 156 artillery support aircraft | 22 | |
| Heinkel He 111 bombers | 51 | 21 |
| Henschel Hs 123 dive-bomber | | 1 |
| Henschel Hs 126 reconnaissance aircraft | 1 | 3 |
| Junkers Ju 52 transports | 157 | |
| Junkers Ju 87 dive-bombers | 9 | |
| Junkers Ju 88 bombers | 18 | 2 |
| Messerschmitt Bf 109 fighters | 6 | 11 |
| Messerschmitt Bf 110 fighters | 1 | 3 |
| Other types | 10 | 3 |
| Totals | 304 | 51 |

Aircrew casualties amounted to 267 killed, 133 wounded and 340 missing; other Luftwaffe personnel casualties (Flak, engineers, etc) amounted to 326 killed or missing.

Apart from the historical interest of these figures, they indicate conclusively that the operations undertaken by the Luftwaffe on this day represented the true beginning of the *Blitzkrieg* against substantial opposition. On 10 May Germany suffered losses in excess of all previous cumulative losses since 1 September 1939, including the Polish campaign. Losses suffered by the Luftwaffe during the invasion of Poland may be summarized as follows:

*Fokker D XXI 241 was one of 9 Dutch fighters that fought 9 Messerschmitt Bf 109s on 10 May 1940, with 4 or 5 of the German aircraft shot down for the loss of 241 itself.*

| Period | Aircraft destroyed | killed | Aircrew wounded | missing |
|---|---|---|---|---|
| 1-8 Sept | 116 | 128 | 68 | 137 |
| 9-13 Sept | 34 | 15 | 15 | 15 |
| 14-18 Sept | 23 | 24 | 32 | 14 |
| 19-27 Sept | 30 | 54 | 18 | 4 |

The largest flying-boat to attain operational status during the Second World War was the German Blohm und Voss Bv 222 Wiking. Designed as a transatlantic civil transport for Lufthansa, the prototype (D-ANTE) first flew on 7 September 1940, but was quickly impressed into war service as a cargo transport. The final Bv 222C version had a wing span of 150 ft 11 in (46 m), gross weight of 108 000 lb (48 990 kg) and was powered by six Junkers Jumo 205C engines.

The largest airborne assault mounted by the Luftwaffe during the Second World War was operation 'Mercury', the landing of 22 750 men on the island of Crete beginning at 07.00 h on 20 May 1941. The Luftwaffe used 493 Junkers Ju 52/3m aircraft and about 80 DFS 230 gliders. The assault was made by 10 000 parachutists, 750 troops landed by glider, 5000 landed by Ju 52/3ms and 7000 by sea. The operation, although regarded as a brilliant success, cost Germany about 4500 men killed and some 150 transport aircraft destroyed or badly damaged, and effectively brought Luftwaffe paratroop operations to an end.

The largest military flying-boat built in Great Britain was the Short Shetland, of which only two prototypes were built. The first, designated Shetland I (DX166), flew for the first time on 14 December 1944, piloted by John Lankester Parker with Geoffrey Tyson as co-pilot. Designed for long-range maritime reconnaissance, both Shetland prototypes were powered by 2500 hp Bristol Centaurus engines, and their wing spans were 150 ft 4 in (45.82 m). The Shetland I had a maximum take-off weight of 125 000 lb (56 700 kg) and attained a maximum level speed of 263 mph (423 km/h).

The largest flying-boat to serve with the US Navy was the Martin JRM Mars. Twenty JRM-1 transports were ordered in January 1945 but only five were built, plus one heavier JRM-2. With a wing span of 200 ft (60.96 m) and gross weight of 165 000 lb (74 842 kg) in the JRM-2, the Mars flying-boat had a maximum speed of 225 mph (362 km/h). It was converted after the war for water-bombing of forest fires.

The largest military flying-boat built in Germany during the Second World War was the Blohm und Voss Bv 238. The single prototype, powered by six Daimler-Benz DB 603 engines, was first flown in March 1945. Intended to fill a long-range reconnaissance or transport role, the Bv 238 had a wing span of 197 ft 4½ in (60.17 m) and a maximum loaded weight of 176 370 lb (80 000 kg).

The largest bomber aircraft to serve with the USAF, and the largest operational bomber aircraft in the world in terms of wing span (230 ft/70.10 m) was the Convair B-36, first flown in XB-36 prototype form (42-13570) on 8 August 1946. They took part in a number of interesting experiments before the type was retired from service by Strategic Air Command on 12 February 1959.

The largest US airborne operation before the United States became actively involved in the Vietnam conflict occurred on 27 April 1964. In this action Sikorsky UH-34 helicopters of the US Marine Corps (with escorting Bell UH-1B gunships of the US Army) airlifted 420 South Vietnam troops to attack Communist positions on the Laotian border.

In early November 1967 the RAF used some 50 transport aircraft to withdraw British troops from Aden, becoming involved in its largest transport operation since the Berlin Airlift of 1948–49. This occurred when Britain gave up its sponsorship of the South Arabian Federation of Arab Emirates which had been set up in 1959.

The largest US landplane ever flown, in terms of overall dimensions and bulk, was the Lockheed C-5 Galaxy, which made its maiden flight on 30 June 1968. On 17 December 1984 a C-5A set a US national record for the greatest take-off weight, a total of 920 836 lb (417 684 kg), this including a payload of 245 731 lb (111 462 kg) which it lifted to a height of 2000 m to set an international payload-to-height record that was ratified by the FAI.

The world's largest ships are the nuclear-powered aircraft carriers of the US Navy's Nimitz class, the first of which was USS Nimitz that completed a test cruise on 14 August 1975 prior to embarking on its first overseas deployment to European waters. Each is 1092 ft (332.9 m) long. USS Abraham Lincoln has the greatest displacement of the class at 102 000 tons.

The world's largest variable-geometry bomber is the Russian Tupolev Tu-160 'Blackjack', which first entered service in 1988. This Mach 1.88

*Prototype Martin Mars flying-boat, first flown on 3 July 1942.*

strategic bomber has a wing span (spread) and length of 182 ft 9 in (55.70 m) and 177 ft (54 m) respectively.

**The largest military flying-boat in current service** is the new Russian Beriev A-40 Albatross, known to NATO as 'Mermaid'. Powered by two MKB (Perm)/Soloviev D-30 KPV turbofans, it has a wing span of 137 ft 9 in (42 m), length of 137 ft 9 in (42 m), and cruises at 497 mph (800 km/h). **The second largest flying-boat in current service** is the Chinese HAMC SH-5, with a span and length of 118 ft 1 in (36 m) and 127 ft 7½ in (38.9 m) respectively. The Japanese Shin Meiwa PS-1/US-1 is now the third largest.

**The largest military airlift ever** was recorded during Operation *Desert Shield*, in the months prior to the Gulf War. Coalition attempts to commit forces to protect Saudi Arabia began on 7 August 1990, just 18 hours after the order was given, when 2300 paratroopers of the US Army's 82nd Airborne Division were airlifted to Saudi Arabia. Over 22 days, a USAF fleet of 265 Lockheed C-141B StarLifters and 85 C-5 Galaxys, plus aircraft of the US Civil Reserve Air Fleet, recorded 4.65 billion ton-miles, with a StarLifter or Galaxy landing at Dhahran on average every seven minutes during the initial phase. Other coalition transports used to ferry equipment to the Gulf reportedly included Soviet An-124s hired to airlift British helicopters. From August 1990 to April 1991, coalition transports and flight refuelling tankers flew more missions than combat aircraft, C-130 Hercules alone flying more than 48 600.

## Heaviest

**The heaviest bomber ever built** is the Boeing B-52 Stratofortress, the B-52H version having a maximum take-off weight of over 488 000 lb (221 353 kg).

**The heaviest military transport in current service** is the Russian Antonov An-124 'Condor', with a maximum take-off weight of 892 870 lb (405 000 kg). The six-engined outgrowth of the An-124, the An-225 Mriya 'Cossack', could be made available for military operations, and this has a maximum take-off weight and payload of 1 322 750 lb (600 000 kg) and 551 150 (250 000 kg) respectively.

## Fastest:

**The fastest British and French operational combat aircraft of the First World War** appear to have been the British Airco DH4 day bomber (when Eagle VIII powered) and the French SPAD XIII fighter, with speeds of 143 mph (230 km/h) and 138 mph (222 km/h) respectively.

**The fastest Italian operational aircraft of the First World War** was probably the Ansaldo SVA 5 Primo reconnaissance and bombing biplane which was flown first during the summer of 1917. The maximum speed of this aircraft with the standard 220 hp SPA 6A engine was 143 mph (230 km/h), but variants tested with other powerplant installations achieved even higher speeds.

**The fastest operational fighter in German service during the First World War** was the Fokker D VIII parasol-wing monoplane, with a

The de Havilland DH4 was the first British aircraft produced for day bombing and proved the most successful light bomber of the First World War. First flown in August 1916, it joined operational squadrons the following year. Various engines were fitted, the largest being a 375 hp Rolls-Royce Eagle VIII which allowed a maximum speed of 143 mph (230 km/h), faster than German fighters.

Edward Rickenbacker of the 94th Aero Squadron, America's top-ranking 'ace' of the First World War, with his SPAD XIII. (US Air Force)

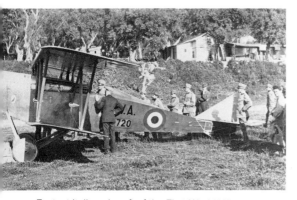

Fastest Italian aircraft of the First World War was the Ansaldo SVA 5 Primo.

maximum speed at sea level of nearly 127 mph (204 km/h).

**The fastest fighters developed by Germany during the First World War**, but flown only in prototype form, were almost certainly the AEG D I biplane and Siemens-Schuckert D VI parasol-wing monoplane, both with a maximum speed of nearly 137 mph (220 km/h).

**The fastest military biplane** was the Fiat CR 42B, a prototype based on the production CR 42 Falco fighter of 1939, but with the usual 840 hp Fiat A.74 RC-38 engine replaced by a 1010 hp Daimler-Benz DB 601A, allowing 323 mph (520 km/h) in 1941.

**The fastest aircraft in RAF Bomber Command for an entire decade**, from November 1941 until introduction of the English Electric Canberra in 1951, was the de Havilland Mosquito. Entering squadron service with No. 105 at Swanton Morley, Mosquitos made their first operational sortie on 31 May 1942, four aircraft making a surprise attack on Cologne just a few hours after the first 1000-bomber raid. The fastest variant was the Mk 35, first flown on 12 March 1945 and capable of 422 mph (679 km/h). Fighter models were also built, and on the night of 14–15 June 1944 **the first V1 flying bomb to be shot down** was destroyed over the English Channel by a Mosquito of No. 605 Squadron flown by Flt Lt J. G. Musgrave.

**The fastest piston-engined fighter designed for the Luftwaffe**, the Dornier Do 335, demonstrated a maximum speed of 474 mph (763 km/h) at 21 000 ft (6400 m). First flown in September 1943, the Do 335 Pfeil had a unique engine layout, one Daimler-Benz DB 603 being mounted conventionally in the nose, with a second DB 603 mounted in the rear fuselage and driving a pusher propeller through an extension shaft. It was developed too late to enter operational service.

**The fastest twin piston-engined combat aircraft in the world to reach operational status** was the de Havilland Hornet fighter which had a maximum speed of 485 mph (780 km/h) in 'clean' combat configuration. Powered by two 2070 hp Rolls-Royce Merlin 130 engines, the Hornet was armed with four 20 mm cannon, could carry up to 2000 lb (907 kg) of bombs or rockets on underwing pylons, and had a maximum

*RAF Mosquito B IVs of No 105 Squadron at Marham in 1942.*

range of over 2500 miles (4025 km). It was first flown by Geoffrey de Havilland Jr on 28 July 1944, but did not reach the first RAF squadron—No. 64 (Fighter) Squadron at Horsham St Faith, Norfolk—until May 1946, after the end of the Second World War. The Hornet was **the fastest piston-engined fighter to serve with the RAF** and also **the last piston-engined fighter to serve with RAF first-line squadrons.**

**The fastest flying-boat ever flown** (excluding the Convair Sea Dart flying-boat-cum-seaplane) was the US Navy's Martin P6M SeaMaster, first flown on 14 July 1955. It could attain a speed of 646 mph (1040 km/h) on the power of four J75 turbojets.

**The fastest propeller-driven aircraft** in use is the Russian Tu-95/142 'Bear', its four 14 795 shp KKBM NK-12MV engines driving eight-blade contra-rotating propellers that allow a maximum level speed of Mach 0.82 (575 mph; 925 km/h).

**The fastest military aircraft ever put into operational service** was the Lockheed SR-71A two-seat strategic reconnaissance aircraft, first flown on 22 December 1964. Relying upon height and speed to provide invulnerability from interception, the SR-71A proved capable of sustained flight at speeds of more than Mach 3 at optimum altitude. **SR-71As hold both of the world absolute speed records** (straight line and closed circuit), and one set a New York–London transatlantic record of 1 hour 54 min 56.4 s on 1 September 1974, flown by Maj James Sullivan and Maj Noel Widdifield.

SR-71A 64-17972 established four new point-to-point records on 6 March 1990, including averaging 2153 mph (3465 km/h) during a flight

between Los Angeles and Washington, a distance of 2404 miles (3869 km) covered in 1 h 8 min 17 s. Flying between St Louis, Missouri, and Cincinnati, Ohio, it flew 311 miles (500 km) in 8 min 20 s, averaging 2242 mph (3608 km/h), a higher speed than the 1976 FAI recognised achievement (see final section).

**The fastest combat aircraft in current service** is the Russian Mikoyan MiG-25 'Foxbat', reported to be capable of Mach 3.2 (2110 mph; 3395 km/h) when not carrying external weapons. The reconnaissance version is equally fast. Maximum speed reduces to Mach 2.82 in combat configuration.

**The fastest non-stop air-refuelled round-the-world flight** was that made during the period 12–14 March 1980 by two Boeing B-52H Stratofortresses of the USAF's Strategic Air Command. This circumnavigation, completed in 42 h 30 min, was an operational deployment during which reconnaissance and surveillance tasks were carried out.

**The fastest climb** was recorded by Heinz Frick of British Aerospace, who flew a McDonnell Douglas/BAe Harrier GR.Mk5 from a standing start to an altitude of 39 370 ft (12 000 m) in 2 min 6.63 s on 15 August 1989. Previously, on 17 May 1975, Alexander Fedotov (see later entry) flew the Mikoyan Ye-266M to 98 425 ft (30 000 m) in 4 min 11.7 s after take off. The fastest climbing in-service conventional aircraft is probably the Mikoyan MiG-29, with a maximum rate of climb at sea level of about 65 000 ft (19 800 m) per minute.

*Highest:*

**The highest known interception by an unpressurized aircraft**, its pilot G. W. H. Reynolds unaided by a pressure suit and breathing only a conventional oxygen supply, was that made at 49 500 ft (15 090 m) in a specially prepared Spitfire VC operating from No. 103 MU near Alexandria, in late August 1942. A Ju 86P-2 pressurized aircraft was destroyed in this interception.

**The highest altitude attained by an air-breathing aircraft**, which is also the current world absolute altitude record ratified by the FAI, is 123 524 ft (37 650 m). This was set on 31 August 1977 by Alexander Fedotov in Russia, flying the specially prepared Mikoyan Ye-266M.

*Sqn Ldr Kellett (with dog).*

*Longest:*

**The longest non-stop and unrefuelled distance flown by military aircraft prior to the Second World War** was a flight of 7158.5 miles (11 520 km) from Ismailia (Egypt) to Darwin (Australia), which also set a new world distance record. This was achieved during 5–7 November 1938 by two Vickers Wellesleys of the RAF's Long Range Flight, captained by Sqn Ldr R. G. Kellett and Flt Lt A. N. Combe.

**The longest production run of any US fighter of the Second World War** was that of the Vought F4U Corsair, first flown on 29 May 1940, at which time it was the most powerful naval fighter in the world. Initial deliveries to VF-12 (US Navy Fighter Squadron Twelve) began on 3 October 1942, the type remaining in production until December 1952.

**The longest non-stop but air-refuelled flight then made by an RAF aircraft**, set by a Vickers Valiant B.Mk 1 of No. 214 Squadron, covered a distance of 8500 miles (13 679 km) in a circuit around the UK during 2 to 3 March 1960. It was in effect a rehearsal for a UK–Singapore non-stop flight, the distance of 8110 miles (13 052 km) accomplished in 15 h 35 min during 25–26 May 1960 in a Valiant captained by Sqn Ldr J. H. Garstin.

**The longest non-stop and unrefuelled distance flown by a military aircraft** was 11 337 miles (18 245.05 km) between Okinawa (Ryukyu Islands) to Madrid (Spain) during 10–11 January

1962. Setting a new world absolute distance record, this was accomplished by a Boeing B-52H Stratofortress of the USAF captained by Maj Clyde P. Evely.

**The longest point-to-point operational sortie achieved by a bomber aircraft** was that flown by an RAF Avro Vulcan B.Mk 2 on 30 April/1 May 1982. Captained by Flt Lt Martin Withers the aircraft took off from Wideawake airfield, Ascension Island to drop its load of 21 1000 lb bombs across the runway of Port Stanley airfield, Falkland Islands. Some operational sorties flown by USAF Boeing B-52s during the Vietnam War may have been very similar in length, approaching a total distance of 8000 miles (12 875 km), but were not point-to-point operations against a single target.

**The longest non-stop air-refuelled sorties by V/STOL aircraft** occurred on 8 May 1982, when some 20 Harriers and Sea Harriers were flown from RNAS Yeovilton (Somerset) to Ascension Island, accomplished in a time of 9 hours.

**The longest serving military pilot** is believed to have been Sqn Ldr N.E. Rose, RAF (retired), who accumulated 11 539 flying hours on 54 different types of aircraft over a career lasting from 1942 to 1989.

**The longest ever fighter deployment** occurred during Operation *Desert Shield*, when on 7 August 1990, 48 McDonnell Douglas F-15C/D Eagles from the USAF's 27th and 71st TFSs were flown non-stop from Langley AFB, Virginia, to Dhahran in Saudi Arabia, each armed with Sparrow and Sidewinder missiles in case of immediate action.

**The longest continuously serving US Navy squadron** is VF-14 'Top Hatters', which was commissioned in September 1919 and currently operates Tomcats.

**The longest continuously serving US Navy fighter squadron** is VF-11 'Red Rippers', first commissioned in February 1927 and currently operating Tomcats. During its career, the squadron has flown 24 fighter types from 20 different aircraft carriers.

*Greatest:*

**The flying-boat produced in the greatest numbers** was the Consolidated PBY Catalina. Excluding production in Russia, 1196 Catalina flying-boats and 944 amphibians were built, serving with the air forces and airlines of more than 25 nations. The prototype was first flown on 28 March 1935, and the initial production version had a maximum speed of 177 mph (284 km/h).

**The greatest single-day losses suffered by the Luftwaffe during the Polish campaign** were those of 3 September 1939, when 22 German aircraft were destroyed. These comprised 4 Dornier Do 17s, 2 Fieseler Fi 156s, 1 Heinkel He 59, 2 Heinkel He 111s, 1 Henschel Hs 123, 3 Henschel Hs 126s, 1 Junkers Ju 52, 3 Junkers Ju 87s, 2 Messerschmitt Bf 109s and 3 Messerschmitt Bf 110s. One of the Messerschmitt Bf 110s was shot down accidentally by German troops near Ostrolenka. Luftwaffe personnel casualties on this day amounted to 34 killed, one wounded and 17 missing.

**The greatest single victory achieved by the Royal Netherlands Air Force during the German invasion of the Low Countries** was gained at 06.45 h on 10 May 1940 when a force of Fokker D XXIs intercepted 55 Junkers Ju 52/3m transport aircraft of KGzbV9. The Dutch pilots claimed to have shot down 37 of the formation, but German records indicate a total loss of 39 aircraft, 6 occupants killed, 41 presumed dead, 15 wounded and 79 missing.

**The greatest single loss of aircraft in any one day suffered by any nation involved in the Second World War** occurred on 22 June 1941. On that day Germany began Operation Barbarossa, its invasion of the Soviet Union, and by nightfall Soviet aircraft losses amounted to 1811, of which 1489 were destroyed on the ground.

**The Royal Air Force heavy bomber with the greatest number of operational missions** to its credit was the Avro Lancaster B Mark III, ED888, PM-M², of No. 103 (Bomber) Squadron. Mike Squared, known alternatively as 'The Mother of Them All', made its first operational sortie in a raid on Dortmund on the night of 4–5 May 1943. By the time the aircraft was retired in December 1944 it had logged 140 missions. This number of missions was, however, exceeded by the de Havilland Mosquito B Mk IX light bomber LR503, GB-F, of No. 105 Squadron and later 109 Squadron. Between 28 May 1943 and the end of the war, this aircraft completed no fewer than 213 operational sorties.

**The greatest amphibious assault in history,** preceded by air drops and Allied air force operations amounting to some 5000 sorties, the Operation 'Overlord' landings on the Normandy coast began on D-Day, 6 June 1944.

**One of the greatest technical achievements of the Second World War,** and representing the shortest elapsed time for the development of an entirely new jet fighter (which achieved combat status) was 69 days for the Heinkel He 162 Salamander. Conceived in an RLM specification issued to the German aircraft industry on 8 September 1944, the He 162 was the subject of a contract issued on 29 September 1944 for an aircraft capable of being mass-produced by semi-skilled labour using non-strategic materials. Sixty-nine days later, on 6 December 1944, the first prototype He 162V-1 was flown by Heinkel's Chief Test Pilot, Kapitän Peter, at Vienna-Schwechat. On 10 December the prototype broke up in the air and crashed before a large gathering of officials, and Peter was killed. Notwithstanding this set-back, the aircraft entered production and joined I and II Gruppen of Jagdgeschwader I at Leck/Holstein during April 1945. III Gruppe of this Geschwader was under orders to receive the new fighter but was forestalled by the end of the war. Known also as the Volksjäger, or 'People's Fighter', it was intended that large numbers would be constructed, but only 116 A-series machines were completed. The Salamander was not a pleasant machine to fly, and as a result few of these aircraft were encountered in combat. Its single BMW 003 turbojet, rated at 1760 lb (800 kg) thrust, provided a maximum speed of 522 mph (840 km/h) at 19 685 ft (6000 m).

**The greatest number of sorties flown in a period of 24 hours during the Berlin Airlift** was recorded on 16 April 1949. This was a total of 1398 flown by the international fleet of aircraft supplying West Berlin, which ferried in a total 12 940 tons (13 147 tonnes) of supplies.

**The greatest number of persons carried by a US Navy Martin Mars flying-boat** totalling 308 (301 passengers and 7 crew). This was recorded on 19 May 1949 by the *Marshall Mars* flying from Alameda (Idaho) to San Diego (California).

**The greatest bomb-load carried by an operational bomber** was that of the Boeing B-52 Stratofortress at 70 000 lb (31 751 kg); with this

US Marine Corps Lockheed KC-130F Hercules tanker makes an unassisted take-off from USS Forrestal on 21 November 1963, at a gross weight of 120 000 lb (54 430 kg). (US Navy)

warload on board the B-52 had a range of approximately 3000 miles (4928 km). Dubbed 'the big stick', the YB-52 prototype was first flown on 15 April 1952 by A. M. 'Tex' Johnson. The first of three production B-52As was delivered to the USAF's Strategic Air Command (SAC) on 27 November 1957. B-52s became subsequently the main flying deterrent of SAC and continue to have a significant strategic role in USAF planning.

**The aircraft with the greatest operating weight ever to serve as standardized equipment on board aircraft carriers** was the Douglas A3D Skywarrior carrier-based attack-bomber. The first of two XA3D-1 prototypes was flown on 28 October 1952, and initial production A3D-1s (later A-3A) were first delivered to VAH-1 (US Navy Heavy Attack Squadron One) on 31 March 1956. The definitive production version, ultimately designated A-3B, served on board carriers of the Essex and Midway classes. The A-3B Skywarrior had a span of 72 ft 6 in (22.10 m), maximum loaded weight of 82 000 lb (37 195 kg), and was powered by two 12 400 lb (5624 kg) thrust Pratt & Whitney J57-P-10 turbojets, providing a maximum level speed of 610 mph (982 km/h) at 10 000 ft (3050 m). It should also be remembered that in 1963 a USMC Lockheed KC-130F Hercules tanker made several experimental landings and take-offs from USS Forrestal (without catapult assistance for take-off) at a gross weight of 120 000 lb (54 430 kg).

**The greatest devastation to targets in North Vietnam** was caused during the 'Linebacker II' operations from 18 to 29 December 1972. In this period USAF Boeing B-52s flew more than 700 sorties, concentrating on 24 targets in the Hanoi and Haiphong areas, with such effect that the North Vietnamese asked for the resumption of peace negotiations and bringing agreement to end the Vietnam War on 27 January 1973.

**One of the greatest military aircraft designers,** Clarence L. 'Kelly' Johnson, died on 21 December 1990 at the age of 80. He had begun as a tool designer with Lockheed in 1933 and retired in 1975, having worked on such historic aircraft as the F-104 Starfighter (the first production aircraft able to fly at over Mach 2 in level flight), the U-2 and SR-71 strategic reconnaissance aircraft.

*Most:*

**The most widely used aeroplane type in military service at the beginning of the war** which was to become known as the First World War was the Etrich Taube. Designed in Austria–Hungary in 1909 it was a 'bird-winged' monoplane powered by a single engine of 85–120 hp. Maximum speed was 72 mph (116 km/h). In August 1914, about half of all the aircraft in German service were of this type and others were operated by the Austro-Hungarian air service. Intended mainly for reconnaissance and training duties, Taubes were often used for dropping light bombs. Germany alone licence-built some 500, examples of which remained in service until 1916.

**Most effective single-engined day bomber of the First World War** was considered to be the British Airco (de Havilland) DH4. The prototype first flew in August 1916, at Hendon, and production aircraft served with the RFC/RAF, RNAS and American Expeditionary Force. Various engines were fitted, including a 375 hp Rolls-Royce Eagle VIII, which gave a maximum speed of 143 mph (230 km/h); bomb load was up to 460 lb (209 kg).

**The most disastrous month in terms of losses for the RFC** was April 1917, 'Bloody April', when nearly 140 of the 365 RFC aircraft mustered for an offensive were lost in the first half of the month.

**The most successful fighter aeroplane of the First World War** was the Sopwith Camel, which achieved no fewer than 1294 victories over enemy aircraft. Production Camels were operated by the RFC and RNAS from July 1917; a total of 5490 was built. Possessing excellent manoeuvrability, the Camel had a maximum speed of 115 mph (185 km/h).

**The most successful German fighter of the First World War** was the Fokker D VII, which first became operational on the Western Front in April 1918, with Jagdgeschwader I. The type also served with several air forces after the war. Powered by a 185 hp BMW inline engine, it had a maximum speed of 124 mph (200 km/h) and excellent manoeuvrability. By the autumn of 1918, D VIIs equipped over 40 Jastas of the German air force.

**The most significant unit of the RAF** (in terms of presaging the pattern of future air warfare) was the Independent Force, established on 5 June 1918 to carry out strategic bombing raids on German industrial and military targets. It was this force which dropped the largest Allied bombs of the war, the 1650 lb (750 kg) 'block busters'. The first heavy bombers of the Force were the Handley Page O/100 and O/400, supplemented by the lighter Airco (de Havilland) DH4, DH9, DH9A and the Royal Aircraft Factory FE2b.

**The most important aircraft to the early post-war RAF** was the de Havilland DH9A which had equipped its first operational squadron (No. 110) in June 1918 and which unit arrived in France on 31 August 1918. Following their use in the closing stages of the First World War, 'Nine-Acks' saw service in Russia in their designated role as day bombers. Thereafter the DH9A is best remembered as a general-purpose aircraft, operating in Iraq and India until replaced by Westland Wapitis in 1931.

**One of the most successful French aircraft produced between the wars** was the Potez 25 reconnaissance and light bombing biplane, first flown during 1925. About 4000 examples were produced, in 87 variants, operated in France and by the armed forces of some 20 countries. Engines from several French manufacturers were installed, ranging from 450 to 600 hp. Accommodation was for two, and the Potez 25 had a maximum speed of 136 mph (219 km/h) with a 450 hp engine.

**The most extensively used Fleet Air Arm aircraft of the inter-war period** was the Fairey IIIF. The prototype made its first flight on 19 March 1926. Production totalled about 620 aircraft, of which more than 230 were operated by the RAF for general-purpose duties and some 365 by the Fleet Air Arm as spotter-reconnaissance general-purpose biplanes. The last FAA version was the Mk IIIB, powered by a 570 hp Napier Lion XIA engine and with a maximum speed of 120 mph (193 km/h). Fairey IIIFs were operated from land bases, used as seaplanes and catapulted from naval vessels. The type was pronounced obsolete by the FAA in 1940.

**Most advanced British biplane fighter to serve with the RAF and FAA** was the Gloster Gladiator which was flown as the Gloster SS.37 prototype on 12 September 1934. Entering service from February 1937 the RAF received 444 and the FAA 60 as Sea Gladiators before production ended in 1940. Only a few squadrons remained in service at the outbreak of the Second World War, but their classic exploits include operations from a frozen lake during the Norwegian campaign, participation in the surrender and capture of the Italian submarine *Galileo Galilei* on 18 June 1940, and the part played in the defence of Malta by the Sea Gladiators *Faith*, *Hope* and *Charity*.

**The most unequal conflict of the 'between-wars' years** began on 3 October 1935 when Italy declared war on Abyssinia, starting a campaign which was to last until 5 May 1936. The main Italian aircraft used in this conflict were the Caproni Ca 74, Ca 101, Ca 111 and Ca 133 bombers, and the Fiat CR20, CR30 and IMAM Ro 37 fighters.

Above *RAF Spitfires fly by Mount Vesuvius during Italian operations.*

Right *Soviet Polikarpov I-15, the most numerous fighter of the Spanish Republicans.*

**The RAF's most famous and now legendary single-seat fighter** of the Second World War was the Supermarine Spitfire, first flown as the Supermarine Type 300 prototype (K5054) on 5 March 1936. Its superb lines benefited from the experience which its designer, R. J. Mitchell, had gained during the development of racing seaplanes to compete in the Schneider Trophy Contests; its power plant derived also from the Schneider Contests, its Merlin engine a direct descendant of the Rolls-Royce 'R' that had brought Great Britain permanent possession of the coveted Trophy in 1931. The Spitfire also remained in service far longer than most of its contemporaries, the last operational sortie by the type being made in Malaya on 1 April 1954 by a photo-reconnaissance Spitfire P.R.19 (PS888) of No. 81 Squadron.

**The most significant 'between wars' use of air power was during the Spanish Civil War** which effectively began on 18 July 1936. The Spanish Republican Air Force mustered 214 obsolete aircraft at the outbreak of the Civil War. Additionally, the government had at its disposal 40 civil types of various designs. Between 1937 and 1939,

55 aircraft were built in the Republican zone. Aircraft despatched to Spain by friendly nations totalled 1947, of which 1409 came from Russia. The others included 70 Dewoitine D371, D500 and D510 fighters, Loire-Nieuport 46s and 15 S510 fighters from France; 72 aircraft, not including any fighters, from the USA; 72 aircraft from the Netherlands; 57 from Britain; and 47 from Czechoslovakia. Of these, some 400 are thought to have been destroyed other than in aerial combat, and 1520 were claimed shot down by Nationalist, German and Italian pilots.

**The first Russian aircraft to enter combat in Spain** in support of the Republican forces were the Polikarpov I-16 Type 6 fighters of General Kamanin's expeditionary command based at Santander. By September 1936, 105 of these aircraft had arrived in Spain and some 200 pilots and 2000 other personnel had also reached there from the Soviet Union. The I-16 first entered combat on 5 November 1936 and eventually a total of 475 was supplied. From March 1937 they were gathered in one formation designated Fighter Group 31, comprising seven squadrons of 15 aircraft each. More numerous was the I-15 biplane fighter, inferior to both the Fiat CR32 and Messerschmitt Bf 109, and no fewer than 415 were believed to have been lost in combat or on the ground. The most numerous Republican bomber type, the Soviet Tupolev SB-2, also fared badly; of 210 supplied, 178 were lost.

**German intervention in the Spanish Civil War** began in late July 1936 with the arrival of 20 Ju 52/ 3m bomber/transports, six Heinkel He 51 fighter biplanes and 85 volunteer air and ground crew. From this small beginning originated the Legion Condor, a balanced force of between 40 and 50-fighters, about the same number of multi-engined bombers,and about 100 miscellaneous ground-attack, reconnaissance and liaison aircraft, whose first C-in-C was Gen-Maj Sperrle. Volunteers from the ranks of the Luftwaffe served in rotation, to ensure the maximum dissemination of combat experience. Many of the major combat designs upon which Germany was to rely in the first half of the Second World War were first evaluated under combat conditions in Spain; the Heinkel He 111 bomber, Dornier Do 17 reconnaissance-bomber, Messerschmitt Bf 109 fighter, and the Henschel Hs 123 and Junkers Ju 87 ground attack aircraft were prominent. The contribution of the Legion Condor to the eventual Nationalist victory was considerable, but more important were the inferences drawn by Luftwaffe Staff planners. Valid lessons learned in Spain included the value of the dive-bomber in hampering enemy communications, and the effects of ground-strafing by fighters in the exploitation of a breakthrough by land forces. Less realistic was the impression gained of the relative invulnerability of unescorted bombers and dive-bombers, an impression based on the lack of sophisticated fighter resistance. In the field of fighter tactics, and in terms of combat experience by her fighter pilots, the Spanish Civil War put Germany at least a year ahead of her international rivals.

**Italian intervention in the Spanish Civil War** began in August 1936 with the arrival of 12 Fiat CR32 biplane fighters. CR32s were later to become the Nationalists' main fighters, superseding the slower Heinkel He 51s. The eventual strength of the Italian Aviacion del Tercio in Spain was some 730 aircraft, all supplied by Italy and including Fiat CR32s, SM81s, SM79s, BR20s,

Ro37s, Ba65s and a squadron of Fiat G50s. Of these, 86 aircraft were lost on operations and 100 from other causes, and 175 flying personnel were killed. A total of 903 enemy aircraft was claimed destroyed in combat, and a further 40 on the ground.

**One of the most unusual fighter aircraft to serve with the US Army Air Force during the Second World War** was Lockheed's P-38 Lightning. Of distinctive twin-boom configuration, it was first flown in XP-38 prototype form on 27 January 1939.

**One of the Soviet Union's most outstanding combat aircraft** of the Second World War was the Petlyakov Pe-2, the VI-100 prototype of which was first flown on 7 May 1939. In production form more than 11 000 were built; they formed the backbone of Soviet tactical operations on the Eastern Front, but were used also in fighter, reconnaissance and trainer roles.

**The Polish fighter most widely used at the time of the German invasion** in September 1939 was the PZL P11, of which 128 were on strength on 1 September 1939. They equipped Nos 111, 112, 113 and 114 Squadrons of the 1st Air Regiment based at Warsaw, Nos 121 and 122 Squadrons of the 2nd Air Regiment based at Krakow, Nos 131 and 132 Squadrons of the 3rd Air Regiment at Poznan, Nos 141 and 142 Squadrons of the 4th Air Regiment at Torun, No. 152 Squadron of the 5th Air Regiment in the Wilno/Lida area, and No. 161 Squadron of the 6th Air Regiment based at Lwow. The P11/I prototype was flown for the first time during August 1931, and the first production P11as entered service in 1934. Definitive version was the P11c, powered by a PZL-built Mercury VI S2 radial engine of 645 hp, giving it a maximum level speed of 242 mph (390 km/h) at 18 000 ft (5485 m). Armament consisted of four 7.7 mm machine-guns, and two 12 kg fragmentation bombs could be carried beneath the wings.

**The most famous Japanese bomber aircraft of the Second World War,** one of the outstanding aircraft of that war **and the most extensively-built Japanese bomber,** was the Mitsubishi G4M Navy Type 1 Attack Bomber. First flown on 23 October 1939, the G4M—known by the Allied codename *Betty*—was first used operationally in May 1941 in an attack on Chungking. In service throughout the entire Pacific War, the last operational flight of two G4M1s carried the Japanese surrender delegation to Ie-Shima on 19 Aug 1945.

**The most extensively built American aircraft of the Second World War**, the Consolidated B-24 Liberator of which more than 18 000 were produced, was flown for the first time in XB-24 prototype form on 29 December 1939.

**The French military aeroplane most widely used at the beginning of the Battle of France** on 10 May 1940 belonged to the Potez 630 series, of which a total of 1250 were built. The main variants were the 630 and 631 fighters and the 63/II reconnaissance aircraft. First flown in April 1936, the three-seat Potez 630 fighter, powered by two 640 hp Hispano-Suiza HS 14AB 10/11 engines, had a maximum speed of 280 mph (450 km/h) at 13 000 ft (3960 m). Standard armament comprised two nose-mounted Hispano 9 or 404 cannon, plus one MAC machine-gun for rear defence. Shortage of cannon made it necessary to arm many 630/631s with four machine-guns and when, in February 1940, it was decided to increase the fire power of these fighters, the cannon were supplemented by six machine-guns mounted beneath the wings.

**One of the most gallant torpedo attacks made by aircraft during the Second World War,** and also the last torpedo attack launched by the Fairey Swordfish, was on 12 February 1942, when six unescorted aircraft of No. 825 Squadron, led by Lt Cdr Eugene Esmonde, FAA, attempted to torpedo the German battleships *Gneisenau* and *Scharnhorst* and the heavy cruiser *Prinz Eugen*. This was in an attempt to prevent these warships from escaping through the English Channel, but without fighter escort the Swordfish faced a hopeless task, and all six were shot down by the protective umbrella of German fighter aircraft. Only five of the 18 crew members survived: all were decorated and a posthumous Victoria Cross was awarded to Lt Cdr Esmonde, the first to be won by a member of the Fleet Air Arm.

**The most successful US Navy fighter aircraft of the Second World War** was the Grumman F6F Hellcat, the prototype of which flew for the first time on 26 June 1942. US Navy statistics record that almost 75 per cent of all Navy wartime combat victories were achieved with Hellcats, of which 12 275 had been built when production ended in November 1945.

**The most convincing proof of the sinking of a U-boat by an attack from the air** was provided by the aircraft which sank it, a Consolidated Liberator IIIA of RAF Coastal Command which, captained by Sqn Ldr D. M. Sleep, was engaged in an anti-submarine patrol on 20 October 1942. Attacking the U-boat from low level, the explosion from the aircraft's bombs damaged the Liberator severely and it was a major feat for the crew to fly it some 800 miles (1287 km) back to base where it crashed on landing. It was discovered subsequently that a small piece of the submarine, identified by the Admiralty, had imbedded itself in the Liberator's tailplane.

**The most successful destroyer of V1 flying-bombs in flight** was Sqn Ldr Joseph Berry, RAF, who shot down 60 of these weapons during 1944.

**The most enemy aircraft destroyed by a US Navy pilot in the course of a single sortie** was achieved on 24 October 1944, when Cdr David McCampbell, accompanied by one other aircraft, attacked a formation of 60 land-based Japanese aircraft approaching the US Fleet. Cdr McCampbell destroyed nine enemy aircraft and for this action, the destruction of seven enemy aircraft on 19 June 1944 and his inspired leadership of Air Group 15, he was awarded the Congressional Medal of Honor.

**Most important fighter aircraft of the FAA at the outbreak of the Korean War** was the Hawker Sea Fury, which also proved to be the last piston-engined fighter in FAA squadrons. First flown on 21 February 1945, the type entered service with No. 807 Squadron in August 1947 and operated with distinction throughout the Korean War. The Sea Fury flown by Lt P. Carmichael of No. 802 Squadron destroyed the squadron's first MiG-15 on 9 August 1952.

**The only combat aircraft of canard configuration to be the subject of a production contract during the Second World War** was the Japanese Kyushu J7W Shinden, which was intended as a heavily armed high-performance interceptor for use by the Navy. Powered by a 2130 hp Mitsubishi MK9D 18-cylinder supercharged radial engine, driving a six-blade pusher propeller, the prototype made its first flight on 3 August 1945. Only two more short flights were made before the Japanese surrender.

The most combat victories in the Korean War was achieved by Capt Joseph McConnell of the USAF's 39th Fighter Interceptor Squadron. On 18 May 1953 he destroyed three North Korean Mikoyan MiG-15s, bringing his total score to 16 confirmed victories.

The US Navy's most effective 'dogfighter' during the Vietnam War, and the type with the best 'kill' record over Soviet-built MiG fighters was the Vought F8U Crusader. It had entered US Navy service almost a decade earlier, the first of them delivered to Squadron VF-32 at Cecil Field (Florida) on 25 March 1957.

The most used landing airstrip was the Bien Hoa Air Base in South Vietnam, which recorded about one million take-off/landing movements in 1970.

The most powerful turboprop engine in the world is the Russian KKBM (formerly Kuznetsov) NK-12MA, at 15 000 shp. Four engines power the Antonov An-22 transport.

The safe ejection of the four-man crew of a US Navy Grumman EA-6B Prowler of Sqn VAQ-141 from USS *Theodore Roosevelt*, on 31 December 1990, brought the number of lives saved by Martin-Baker ejection seats to 6000.

The most expensive aircraft must be the new USAF Northrop B-2 strategic 'flying-wing' bomber, expected (in 1991) to cost US $776 million for each of the first 15 aircraft. The first B-2 flew on 17 July 1989.

## Youngest and Oldest

The youngest person to qualify as a military pilot was Sgt Thomas Dobney, born on 6 May 1926, who became an RAF pilot at the age of 15 years 5 months, having kept his true age a secret on entry.

The oldest bombers in current military strength are 15 or more Tupolev Tu-4 'Bulls', Soviet copies of the Boeing B-29 Superfortress, still in the inventory of the Chinese Air Force of the People's Liberation Army. They are used, however, as UAV (unmanned air vehicle) carriers.

The oldest US Air Force aircraft in first-line service are the Boeing B-52 Stratofortress bombers, averaging 30 years in mid-1991.

## Formation Dates of Air Arms

### ABU DHABI
Air Wing, Abu Dhabi Defence Forces, 1968
Abu Dhabi Air Force, 1972. Joined with Dubai Police Air Wing in 1976 to form United Arab Emirates Air Force

### AFGHANISTAN
Afghan Military Air Arm, 1924
Afghan Air Force, 1937
Royal Afghan Air Force, 1948
Afghan Republican Air Force, 1973

### ALBANIA
Albanian People's Army Air Force, 1947

### ALGERIA
Armée de l'Air Algérienne, 1962
Al Quwwat al-Jawwiya al Jaza'eriya

### ANGOLA
Fôrça Aérea Populare de Angola, 1976

### ARGENTINA
*Air Force*
Servicio Aeronautico del Ejército, 10 August 1912
Fuerza Aérea Argentina, 4 January 1945
*Army Aviation*
Comando de Aviación del Ejército, 3 November 1959
*Naval Aviation*
Comando de Aviación Naval Argentina, 17 October 1919

### AUSTRALIA
*Air Force*
Army Aviation Corps, September 1912
Australian Flying Corps, January 1913
Australian Air Corps, 1920
Australian Air Force, 31 March 1921
Royal Australian Air Force, June 1921
*Army Aviation*
16 Army Light Aircraft Squadron, RAAF, 1960
1st Aviation Regiment (Divisional), 1966
Australian Army Aviation Corps, 1 July 1968
*Naval Aviation*
Fleet Air Arm, Royal Australian Navy, 1948

### AUSTRIA
K.u.K. Militär-äronautische Anstalt, 1892
K.u.K. Luftschifferabteilung, 1909
Kommando der Luftstreitkräfte, 1928
Fliegertruppen des Österreichischen Bundesheeres, 1 June 1935

Österreichische Heeresfliegerkräfte, 1955
Österreichische Luftstreitkräfte


BAHAMAS
Royal Bahamas Defence Force, 1973

BAHRAIN
Bahrain Amiri Air Force, 1977

BANGLADESH
Mukti Bahini Air Wing, 1971
Bangladesh Biman Bahini, 1972

BELGIUM
Air Force
Compagnie des Ouvriers et Aérostiers, 5 March
    1911
Compagnie des Aviators, 16 April 1913
Aviation Militaire, 20 March 1915
Aéronautique Militaire, 1925
Force Aérienne Belge-Belgische Luchtmacht,
    1 October 1946
Army Aviation
Aviation Légere de la Force Terrestre-Licht
    Vliegwezen van de Landmacht

BELIZE
Belize Defence Force, Air Wing, 1983

BENIN
Force Aérienne de Dahomey, 1961
Force Aérienne du Benin, 1975
Force Armées Popular du Benin

BOLIVIA
Cuerpo de Aviación, August 1924
Fuerza Aérea Boliviana, 1940

BOPHUTHATSWANA
Bophuthatswana Defence Force, Air Wing, 1981
Tshireletso ya Bophuthatswana, 1990

BOTSWANA
Botswana Defence Force, Air Arm, 1977

BRAZIL
Air Force
Brazilian Army Balloon Corps, 1908
Brazilian Army Air Service, 1918
Fôrça Aérea Brasileira, 20 January 1940
Army Aviation
Aviaco do Exercito Brasiléiro, 1986
Naval Aviation
Naval Aviation School, 26 August 1916
Brazilian Naval Air Service, 1922

Absorbed into Air Force, 20 January 1941 until
    formation of Fôrça Aeronaval de Marinha do
    Brasil, 26 January 1965

BRUNEI
Royal Brunei Armed Forces, Air Wing, 1965

BULGARIA
Army Aviation Corps, 1912
Royal Bulgarian Air Force, 1937
Bulgarski Vozdusny Vojski, 1946

BURKINA FASO (formerly Upper Volta)
Force Aérienne de Burkina Faso, 4 August 1984

BURMA (MYANMAR)
Union of Burma Air Force, 1955
Tamdaw Lay

BURUNDI
Force Armée du Burundi, 1966
Armée Nationale du Burundi


CAMBODIA
Royal Khmer Aviation, 1953
Aviation Nationale Khmere, 1954
Air Force of Kampuchea Liberation Army, 1975
Cambodian Air Force, 1985?

CAMEROUN
L'Armée de l'Air du Cameroun, 1960

CANADA
Canadian Aviation Corps, 1914 until February
    1915
Canadian Naval Air Service, 1918–19
Canadian Air Force, November 1918 until
    February 1920
Royal Canadian Air Force, 1 April 1924
Canadian Armed Forces—Air Command, 1968

CAPE VERDE ISLANDS
Força Aérea Caboverdaine

CENTRAL AFRICAN REPUBLIC
Force Aérienne Centrafricaine, 1961
Escadrille Centrafricaine

CHAD REPUBLIC
Escadrille Nationale Tchadienne, 1961

CHILE
Air Force
Escuela de Aeronautica Militar, 11 February
    1913
Chilean Army Aviation Company, 1918
Fuerza Aérea de Chile, 21 March 1930

*Army Aviation*
Comando de Aviación, Ejercito de Chile, 1948
*Naval Aviation*
Naval Aviation Service, 1919; united with
    Fuerza Aérea Chilena, 21 March 1930
Servicio de Aviación de la Armada de Chile,1948

CHINA (Chinese People's Republic)
*Air Force*
Air Force of the People's Liberation Army, 1950
*Naval Aviation*
Aviation of the People's Navy, 1950

CISKEI
Ciskei Defence Force, 1982

COLOMBIA
*Air Force*
Colombian Army Air Arm, April 1922
Fuerza Aérea Colombiana, 1943
*Naval Aviation*
Armada de Colombia, 1984

COMORES
Comores Military Aviation, 1976

CONGO
Force Aérienne Congolaise, 1961

COSTA RICA
Guardia Civil Seccion Aérea, 1949

CÔTE D'IVOIRE (IVORY COAST)
Force Aérienne de la Côte d'Ivoire, 1962

CUBA
Cuerpo de Aviación, 1917
Fuerza Aérea Ejercito de Cuba, 1955
Fuerza Aérea Revolucionaria, 1959

CZECHOSLOVAKIA
Czechoslovak Army Air Force, 29 October 1918
Slovak Air Force, 1939
Ceskoslovenské Letectvo, 1945
Czech and Slovakian Air Force, 1990


DENMARK
*Air Force*
Army Flying School, 2 July 1912
Army Flying Corps, 1 February 1923
Haerens Flyvertropper, 1932
Kongelige Danske Flyvevåbnet, 1 October 1950
*Army Aviation*
Haerens Flyvetjaeneste, July 1971
*Naval Aviation*
Navy Flying School, 1912

Sovaernets Flyvetjaeneste, 1971

DJIBOUTI
Force Aérienne Djiboutienne, 1978

DOMINICAN REPUBLIC
Dominican Army Aviation Company, 1939
El Cuerpo de Aviación Militar, 1948
Fuerza Aérea Dominicana, 1955

DUBAI
Air Wing, Union Defence Force, 1971
Dubai Police Air Wing, 1973. Joined with Abu
    Dhabi Air Force in 1976 to form United Arab
    Emirates Air Force

ECUADOR
*Air Force*
Cuerpo de Aviadores Militares, 1920
Fuerza Aérea Ecuatoriana, 1935
*Army Aviation*
Aviación del Ejército Ecuatoriana
*Naval Aviation*
Aviación Naval Ecuatoriana

EGYPT
Egyptian Army Air Force, May 1932
Royal Egyptian Air Force, 1939
Al Quwwat al-Jawwiya Ilmisriya, 1953

EL SALVADOR
Army Aviation Service, 1923
Fuerza Aérea Salvadorena, 1948

EQUATORIAL GUINEA
Equatorial Guinea National Guard

ESTONIA
Air Defence Command (pre-Second World
    War title).
Present situation unclear at time of writing.

ETHIOPIA
Imperial Ethiopian Aviation, 1924
Imperial Ethiopian Air Force, 1946
Ye Ethiopia Ayer Hail, 1974

FIJI
Fiji Military Forces, 1989

FINLAND
Ilmailuvoimat, March 1918
Ilmavoimat, 1920

FRANCE
*Air Force*
Service Aéronautique, April 1910

Aviation Militaire, October 1910
L'Armée de l'Air, August 1933
French Vichy Air Force, 1940
Forces Aériennes Françaises Libres, 1941
L'Armee de l'Air, 1943
*Army Aviation*
Aviation Légère de l'Armée de Terre, November
   1952
*Naval Aviation*
Service de l'Aéronautique de la Marine,
   12 March 1912
Aéronautique Maritime, 1925
Aéronautique Navale, 1945

*GABON REPUBLIC*
Force Aérienne Gabonaise, 1961

*GERMANY*
*Air Force*
Military Aviation Service, 1 October 1912
Luftwaffe, March 1935
Volkspolizei-Luft (of former East Germany),
   March 1950
Luftstreitkräfte und Luftverteidigung (of former
   East Germany), 1955
Luftwaffe der Deutschen Bundesrepublik (of
   former West Germany), 24 September 1956
Luftwaffe, 3 October 1990
*Army Aviation*
Heeresfliegertruppen, 1957
*Naval Aviation*
Marineflieger, 1957

*GHANA*
Ghana Air Force, 1959

*GREECE*
*Air Force*
Air Squadron of Royal Hellenic Army,
   September 1912
Hellenic Army Air Force, 1917
Hellenic Combat Air Force, December 1929
Royal Hellenic Air Force, November 1935
Elliniki Aeroporia
*Army Aviation*
Elliniki Aeroporia Stratou
*Naval Aviation*
Elliniki Pterix Naftica

*GUATEMALA*
Cuerpo de Aéronautica Militar, 1929
Fuerza Aérea Guatemalteca, 1945

*GUINEA-BISSAU*
Force Aérienne de Guinea-Bissau, 1978

*GUINEA REPUBLIC*
Force Aérienne de Guineé, 1959

*GUYANA*
Air Wing, Guyana Defence Force, 1968
Air Command, Guyana Defence Force, 1970

*HAITI*
Corps d'Aviatión d'Haiti, 1943

*HONDURAS*
Aviación Militar Hondureña, 1933
Fuerza Aérea Hondureña, 1954

*HONG KONG*
Air Arm, Hong Kong Defence Force, 1 May
   1949
Air Arm, Royal Hong Kong Defence Force,
   1951
Royal Hong Kong Auxiliary Air Force, 1970

*HUNGARY*
Hungarian Air Arm, 1936
Magyar Királyi Légierö, 1938
Magyar Légierö, 1957

*INDIA*
*Air Force*
Bharatiya Vayu Sena, 1 April 1933
*Army Aviation*
Army Aviation Corps, November 1986
*Naval Aviation*
Indian Naval Aviation, 1950

*INDONESIA*
*Air Force*
Netherlands East Indies Army Air Corps, 1940
Netherlands East Indies Air Arm, 1945
Tentara Nasional Indonesia—Angkatan Udara,
   1950
*Army Aviation*
Tentara Nasional Indonesia—Angkatan Darat,
   1959
*Naval Aviation*
Tentara Nasional Indonesia—Angkatan Laut,
   1958

*IRAN*
Air Office of the Imperial Iranian Army, 1924
Imperial Iranian Air Force, 1932
Islamic Republic of Iran Air Force, 1979

*IRAQ*
Royal Iraqi Air Force, 1931
Al Quwwat al-Jawwiya al-Iraqiya, 1958

IRISH REPUBLIC (Eire)
Irish Air Corps, 1922

ISRAEL
Sherut Avir, November 1947
Chel Ha'Avir, 27 May 1948
Heyl Ha'Avir, 1951

ITALY
*Air Force*
Battaglione Aviatori, 27 June 1912
Servizio d'Aviazione Coloniale, 19 November 1912
Flotta Aerea d'Italia, 28 November 1912
Corpo Aeronautico Militare, 7 January 1915
Regia Aeronautica, 23 March 1923
Aeronautica Militare Italiana, 13 October 1943
*Army Aviation*
Aviazione Leggera dell'Esercito, 1951
*Naval Aviation*
Aviazione per la Marina Militare, 1943

JAMAICA
Jamaica Defence Force, Air Wing, July 1963

JAPAN
*Air Force*
Provisional Committee for Military Balloon Research, 30 July 1909
Air Battalion of the Army Transport Command, December 1915
Army Aviation Department, April 1919
Army Air Corps, 1 May 1925
Japan Air Self-Defence Force (Koku Jiei-tai), 1 July 1954
*Army Aviation*
Japanese Army Air Force, 1911
Japan Ground Self-Defence Force (Rikujye Jiei-tai), 1 July 1954
*Naval Aviation*
Naval Committee for Aeronautical Research, 26 June 1912
Japanese Naval Air Service, 1912
Naval Air Corps, April 1916
Japan Maritime Self-Defence Force (Kaijoh Jiei-tai), 1 July 1954

JORDAN
Arab Legion Air Force, 1949
Al Quwwat al-Jawwiya Almalakiya al-Urduniya, 1956

KENYA
Kenya Air Force, 1 June 1964
The '82 Air Force, August 1982

KOREA, NORTH
North Korean Aviation Society, September 1945
North Korean Army's Aviation Division, 1946
Korean People's Armed Forces Air Corps, 1948
Korean People's Army Air Force, May 1955

KOREA, SOUTH
Republic of Korea Air Force (Hankook Kong Goon), May 1949

KUWAIT
Kuwait Air Force, 1960

LAOS
Laotian Army Aviation Service, 1955
Royal Lao Air Force, August 1960
Air Force of the People's Liberation Army, April 1975

LATVIA
Aviation Regiment (pre-Second World War title)
Present situation unclear at time of writing.

LEBANON
Al Quwwat al-Jiwwiya al-Lubnania, 1949

LESOTHO
Police Mobile Unit (Air Wing), 1978
Lesotho Royal Defence Force—Air Squadron, 20 June 1986

LIBERIA
Liberian Army Air Reconnaissance Unit, 1976

LIBYA
*Air Force*
Royal Libyan Air Force, 1959
Al Quwwat al-Jawwiya al-Libiyya, 1970
*Army Aviation*
Aviation Section of Army, 1970
*Naval Aviation*
Naval section

LITHUANIA
Lithuanian Air Force (pre-Second World War title)
Present situation unclear at time of writing.

MADAGASCAR
Armée de l'Air Malgache, 24 April 1961

MALAWI
Malawi Army Air Wing, 1966

MALAYSIA
*Air Force*
Malayan Volunteer Air Force, September 1940

Malayan Auxiliary Air Force, 1 October 1950
Royal Malayan Air Force, 1 June 1958
Tentara Udara Diraja Malaysia, 16 September 1963
*Naval Aviation*
Naval Air Wing

MALDIVE
Maldives Defence Force, 1990

MALI REPUBLIC
Force Aérienne de la République du Mali, 1962

MALTA
Armed Forces of Malta, Helicopter Flight, 1971

MAURITANIA
Force Aérienne Islamique de Mauritanie, 1961

MAURITIUS
Mauritius Defence Forces, Air Arm, 1990

MEXICO
*Air Force*
Mexican Aviation Corps, 1915
Fuerza Aérea Mexicana, 1924
*Naval Aviation*
Aviación de la Armada de Mexico, 1944

MONGOLIA
Air Force of the Mongolian People's Republic, 1966

MOROCCO
Aviation Royale Chérifienne, 19 November 1956
Force Aérienne Royale Marocaine, 1961

MOZAMBIQUE
Fôrça Populare Aérea de Libertaçāo de Moçambique, 1975


NEPAL
Royal Nepalese Army Air Wing, early 1960s
Royal Nepal Air Force, 1979

NETHERLANDS
*Air Force*
Army Balloon Unit, 1886
Luchtvaartafdeling, 1 July 1913
Wapen der Militaire Luchtvaart, 1 November 1938
Koninklijke Luchtmacht, 27 March 1953
*Naval Aviation*
Marine Luchtvaartdienst, 18 August 1917

*NEW ZEALAND*
New Zealand Permanent Air Force, June 1923
Royal New Zealand Air Force, 1 April 1937

*NICARAGUA*
Army Air Arm, 1923
Fuerza Aérea de la Guardia Nacional, 9 June 1938
Fuerza Aérea Guardia de Nicaragua, 1947
Fuerza Aérea Sandinista, 19 July 1979

*NIGER*
Force Aérienne de Niger, 1961
Escadrille Nationale du Niger

*NIGERIA*
*Air Force*
Federal Nigerian Air Force, January 1964
*Naval Aviation*
Federal Nigerian Fleet Air Arm

*NORWAY*
*Air Force*
Haerens Flyvåpen, 1915
Kongelige Norske Luftforsvaret, early 1944
*Naval Aviation*
Marinens Flevevaesen, 1915, but combined with Haerens Flyvåpen in early 1944 to form Kongelige Norske Luftforsvaret


*OMAN*
Al Quwwat al-Jawwiya al-Sultanat Oman, 1958


*PAKISTAN*
*Air Force*
Royal Pakistan Air Force, 14 August 1947
Pakistan Air Force, 23 March  1956
*Army Aviation*
Air Observation Flight of RPAF, 1947
Pakistan Army Aviation Corps, 1958
*Naval Aviation*
Pakistan Navy Air Arm, 1973

*PANAMA*
Fuerza Aérea Panamena, January 1969

*PAPUA NEW GUINEA*
Papua New Guinea Defence Force, Air Transport Squadron, 14 November 1974

*PARAGUAY*
*Air Force*
Fuerzas Aéreas Nacionales, 1935
Fuerza Aérea Paraguaya, 1949

*Naval Aviation*
Aviacion de la Armada Nacional Paraguay

PERU
*Air Force*
Peruvian Army Aviation Service, 1919
Cuerpo de Aeronautica del Perú, 20 May 1929
Fuerza Aérea Peruana, July 1950
*Army Aviation*
Aviación del Ejército Peruano, 1965
*Naval Aviation*
Peruvian Naval Air Service, 1924, but combined
  into Cuerpo de Aeronautica del Perú on 20
  May 1929
Servicio Aeronaval de la Marina Peruana, 1965

PHILIPPINES
*Air Force*
Philippine Army Air Corps, 2 May 1935
Philippine Air Force, 3 July 1947
*Army Aviation*
Air Battalion, Philippine Army, 1980
*Naval Aviation*
Philippine Naval Aviation, 1975

POLAND
*Air Force*
1st Polish Aviation Unit, 19 August 1917
Aviation of the 1st Polish Corps, March 1918
1st Aviation Unit of the Polish Forces,
  15 October 1918
Polskie Wojska Lotnicze, 29 September 1919
Pulk Lotnictwa Mysliwskiego Warszawa,
  10 August 1944
Polskie Wojska Lotnicze, 1945
Wojska Lotnicze i obrony Powietrznej, 1990
*Naval Aviation*
Morskie Lotnictwo Wojskowe, 1945

PORTUGAL
*Air Force*
Campo de Seixcal, 1912
Arma da Aeronáutica, 1917
Fôrça Aérea Portuguesa, 1 July 1952
*Naval Aviation*
Aviaçao Maritima, 1917, but merged into Fôrça
  Aérea Portuguesa on 1 July 1952

QATAR
Qatar Public Security Forces Air Wing, March
  1968
Qatar Emiri Air Force, 1974

ROMANIA
Corpul Aerian Româna, 1915

Divisia I-a Aerianá, 1919
Fortelor Regal ale Aeriene Româna, 1936
Fortele Aeriene ale Republicii Populare
  România, 1947
Fortele Aeriene ale Republicii Socialiste
  România, 1966

RUSSIA
*Air Force*
Imperial Russian Flying Corps, 1910
Chief Directorate, Workers' and Peasants' Red
  Air Fleet, 24 May 1918
Sovietskaya Voyenno-Vozdushniye Sily, 1924,
  currently part of armed forces of
  Commonwealth of Independent States, 1991
*Naval Aviation*
Naval Aviation School, 1910
Volga Military Flotille, 1918
Voyenno-Morskoy Flot, 1924

RWANDA
Force Aérienne Rwandaise, 1972

SAUDI ARABIA
*Air Force*
Al Quwwat al-Jawwiya Assa'udiya, 1950
*Army Aviation*
Royal Saudi Land Forces
*Naval Aviation*
Royal Saudi Navy, Air Arm

SENEGAMBIA
Armée de l'Air du Sénégal, 1960
Armée de l'Air du Sénégambia, December 1981

SEYCHELLES
Seychelles Defence Force Air Wing, 1980
Seychelles People's Air Force

SHARJAH
Amiri Guard Air Wing, 20 December 1984

SIERRA LEONE
Sierra Leone Defence Force, 1973

SINGAPORE
Singapore Air Defence Command, September
  1971
Republic of Singapore Air Force, 1 April 1975

SOMALIA
Somalian Aeronautical Corps, 1961

SOUTH AFRICA
South African Aviation Corps, early 1915
No. 26 (South African) Squadron, Royal Flying
  Corps, 1915–18

Suid Afrikaanse Lugmag, 1 February 1920

## SPAIN
*Air Force*
Servicio Militar de Aerostación, 1896
Aeronáutica Militar Española, March 1911
Servicio de Aeronáutica Militar Española,
　February 1913
Ejército del Aire Español, 9 November 1939
Fuerza Aérea Española, 1980
*Army Aviation*
Aviación Ligera del Ejército de Tierra, July 1965
Fuerzas Aeromoviles del Ejército de Tierra,
　March 1973
*Naval Aviation*
Aeronáutica Naval, 1917, but integrated into
　Ejército del Air Español on 9 November 1939
Arma Aérea de la Armada, June 1954

## SRI LANKA
Royal Ceylon Air Force, 10 October 1950
Sri Lanka Air Force, 1971

## SUDAN
Silakh al-Jawwiya as-Sudaniya, 1955

## SURINAME
Suriname Air Force, 1982

## SWAZILAND
Umbutfo Swaziland Defence Force, Air Wing,
　June 1979

## SWEDEN
*Air Force*
Svenska Flygvapnet, 1 July 1926
*Army Aviation*
Armeflygkar, 1954
*Naval Aviation*
Svenska Marinen, 1957

## SWITZERLAND
Fliegertruppe, 31 July 1914
Militär-Flugwesen, 1919
Schweizerische Flugwaffe, a component of the
　Kommando der Flieger- und Flieger-
　abwehrtruppen, 19 October 1936

## SYRIA
*Air Force*
Al Quwwat al-Jawwiya al Arabiya as-Souriya,
　1946
*Naval Aviation*
Naval Air Arm

## TAIWAN
Army Air Arm, 1914
Chinese Aviation Service, 1919
Central Government Air Force, 1934
Chinese Air Force, 1946
Republic of China Air Force (Chung-Kuo Kung
　Chuan), 1949

## TANZANIA
Tanzanian People's Defence Force, Air Wing,
　1964

## THAILAND
*Air Force*
Royal Siamese Flying Corps, 23 March 1914
Royal Aeronautical Service, 1919
Royal Siamese Air Force, April 1937
Royal Thai Air Force, 1939
*Army Aviation*
Royal Thai Army, Air Arm, early 1950s
*Naval Aviation*
Royal Thai Navy, Air Arm, early 1950s

## TOGO
Force Aérienne Togolaise, 1964

## TONGA
Tonga Air Force, mid-1986

## TRANSKEI
Transkei Defence Force, Air Arm, late 1986

## TRINIDAD & TOBAGO
Trinidad & Tobago Defence Force, Air Arm,
　1974

## TUNISIA
Al Quwwat al-Jawwiya al-Djoumhouria al-
　Tunisia, 1960

## TURKEY
*Air Force*
Army Aviation Section, 1912
Turkish Flying Corps, 1914
Turkish Army Air Service, 1917
Türk Hava Kuvvetleri, 1928
*Army Aviation*
Turk Kara Kuvvetleri, 1950
*Naval Aviation*
Turk Cumhuriyet Bahrya, 1971

## UGANDA
Uganda Army Air Force, 1964

## UNITED ARAB EMIRATES
United Arab Emirates Air Force, May 1976

## UNITED KINGDOM
*Air Force*
Air Battalion of the Royal Engineers, 1 April 1911
Royal Flying Corps, 13 May 1912
Royal Air Force, 1 April 1918
*Army Aviation*
Army Air Corps, 1 September 1957
*Naval Aviation*
Royal Flying Corps Naval Wing, 13 May 1912
Royal Naval Air Service, 1 July 1914, but integrated into Royal Air Force on 1 April 1918
Fleet Air Arm of RAF, April 1924
Naval Aviation (Air Branch of the Royal Navy), May 1939
Fleet Air Arm of Royal Navy, 1953

## UNITED STATES OF AMERICA
*Air Force*
Aeronautical Division, US Signals Corps, 1 August 1907
Aviation Section, US Signals Corps, 18 July 1914
United States Air Service, 24 May 1918
United States Army Air Service, 4 June 1920
United States Army Air Corps, 2 July 1926
United States Army Air Force, 20 June 1941
United States Air Force, 18 September 1947
*Army Aviation*
US Army Air Forces, 1948
*Naval Aviation*
Naval Flying Corps, 29 August 1916, with naval aviation subsequently being carried out by US Navy and US Marine Corps air arms

## URUGUAY
*Air Force*
Escuela Militar de Aéronautica, 20 November 1916
Aéronautica Militar, 1919
Fuerza Aérea Uruguaya, 4 December 1953
*Naval Aviation*
Aviación Naval Uruguaya, 1965

## VENDA
Venda Defence Force, 1983

## VENEZUELA
*Air Force*
Venezuelan Military Air Service, 17 April 1920
Regimiento de Aviación Militar, January 1936
Fuerza Aérea Venezolanas, 1949

*Army Aviation*
Aviación del Ejercito Venezolana, 1974
*Naval Aviation*
Naval Aviation Centre, early 1920s
Servicio de Aviación Naval Venezolana, 1974
Aviación de la Marina Venezolana

## VIETNAM
Observation, Communications, and Liaison Squadrons of the Vietnam Armed Forces (South Vietnam), 1951
Vietnam Democratic Republic Air Force (North Vietnam), 1954–5
Vietnam Air Force (South Vietnam), July 1955
Vietnamese People's Army Air Force, 2 July 1976

## YEMEN, NORTH
Yemen Arab Republic Air Force, 1962

## YEMEN, SOUTH
Air Force of the People's Democratic Republic of Yemen, 1969

## YUGOSLAV FEDERATION
Serbian Military Air Service, 1913
Aviation Department, Yugoslav Army, 1918
Jugoslovensko Ratno Vazduhoplovstvo, 1930, but disbanded 1941
Croatian Air Force, 1941–4
Jugoslovensko Ratno Vazduhoplovstvo, 5 January 1945
Current position unclear at time of writing (early 1992) with former Yugoslavia now split into smaller states

## ZAÏRE
Force Aérienne Katangaise, 1961
Force Aériennes Congolaises, 1962
Force Aérienne Zaïroise, 1973

## ZAMBIA
Zambian Air Wing, 1964
Zambian National Defence Forces, 1968
Zambian Air Force and Air Defence Command

## ZIMBABWE
Southern Rhodesia Air Section, 1936
Southern Rhodesian Air Force, 1939
Royal Rhodesian Air Force, October 1954
Rhodesian Air Force, 1969
Zimbabwe–Rhodesia Air Force, 1979
Air Force of Zimbabwe, 1980

# Research,
# Experimentation
# and Spaceflight

Research has been fundamental to progress and achievement in aviation from the outset, whether the outcome of such work led to initial failure or established the foundations for subsequent demonstrable, commercial production or military successes. It is ironic that the names of many enlightened scientists, inventors and forward-thinkers who contributed to man's understanding of flight during the 16th–19th centuries, without themselves having demonstrated any form of workable flying machine, have largely been forgotten. Yet, without their contributions, both theoretical and practicable, the Wright Brothers, Santos-Dumont, Blériot and many others would have found their own research so much the harder. And once manned and powered flying was a reality, so the amount of research only increased, not least to meet the demands of war.

The United States of America can be said to have enjoyed the first lengthy period of technological superiority in manned heavier-than-air flying, through the research and experiments of pioneers like the Wright Brothers. However, by the close of the first decade of the 20th century, Europe, and especially France, had regained the initiative it had enjoyed in the previous two centuries, having more or less moved away from lighter-than-air experimentation and forged ahead in aeroplane design at a time of US complacency.

For a time after the First World War, there was still talk of the 'war to end wars'; but it did no such thing. Rather, the manner of its victories, and the

*Gloster E.28/39 in developed form.*

conditions imposed upon the vanquished under the peace agreements which followed, made a Second World War inevitable, and Germany brilliantly forged ahead of the rest of the world in rocketry, jet propulsion and other military orientated technologies during the 1930s through huge research programmes.

In the early post-Second World War years, when inventiveness and engineering skill held the key to progress, Britain set the pace in many ways. The United States was first to prove that the 'sound barrier' could be penetrated by the brute force of rocket power allied to human courage; it was the Fairey Delta 2 which combined British leadership in jet propulsion with design genius that demonstrated that passing the speed of sound, Mach 1, need result in nothing more alarming than the flicker of a needle or two on the instrument panel. British money began to run out by the time the Fairey Rotodyne pioneered the whole new field of vertical take-off and landing (VTOL) for commercial operations. It dried up completely before the British Aircraft Corporation's TSR.2 could keep Britain in the military 'big league' with its supersonic bombing capabilities.

The United States, on the other hand, launched into new generations of aviation research which investigated every kind of technique for achieving VTOL, without producing anything better than the relatively simple helicopter; and poured countless millions of dollars into a giant Mach 3 bomber that became only a research prototype. In a last fling at more reasonable economic levels, Britain produced the first thoroughly practical VTOL combat aircraft as the Harrier, which America decided it had to buy and later further develop as a partner. With its French neighbours, Britain then evolved the Concorde supersonic airliner, unbeaten as a technological triumph.

Meanwhile, the United States progressed relentlessly from the Mach 1.015 of 'Chuck' Yeager's little Bell X-1 of 1947 to Mach 6.72 with the North American X-15A-2, and then to 17 600 mph (28 325 km/h) orbital speed with its Space Shuttle Orbiter reusable transportation system. The US broke entirely new ground in the pursuit of 'low observable' or stealth technology, which led to production of the world's first true stealth combat aircraft, the Lockheed F-117A and Northrop B-2. Its space programme had also put several Apollo crews on the Moon, still the only nation to have achieved manned landings.

*Firsts:*

**The first gyroscopic automatic stabilizer was successfully demonstrated** by the Americans, Lawrence B. Sperry and Lt Patrick Nelson Lynch Bellinger, in a Curtiss F flying-boat in 1913. The aircraft was longitudinally and laterally stabilized.

**The first experiments with a pressurized cabin** were made on a de Havilland DH4 at Wright Field in the USA during 1922.

**The first full-size rocket-powered aeroplane in the world** was the sailplane *Ente* (Duck), powered by two Sander slow-burning rocket motors and built by the Rhön-Rossitten Gesellschaft of Germany. Piloted by Friedrich Stamer, it made a flight of just over 0.75 mile (1.2 km) near the Wasserkuppe Mountain in about 1 min on 11 June 1928. The rocket-powered glider flown by Fritz von Opel at Rebstock, near Frankfurt, is often stated as being the world's first rocket aeroplane, but this did not fly until 30 September 1929. Known as the Opel-Hatry Rak-1, it however flew for more than 1.1 miles (1.8 km) and attained a speed of 100 mph (160 km/h). (It is worth noting here that Max Valier had demonstrated rocket propulsion in Germany in 1928 and had received backing from Fritz von Opel for his work. Further, in 1929 Prof Hermann Oberth built a liquid-fuelled rocket while in Berlin.)

**The first work in Germany on the development of an aircraft turbojet engine** began at Heinkel's Marienehe plant on 15 April 1936, when the German engineer Dr Hans Joachim Pabst von Ohain and Dipl Ing Max Hahn began work on such a power plant at the instigation of Ernst Heinkel.

**The first aircraft turbojet engine in the world** was bench-tested for the first time on 12 April 1937. This was the W/U Type with centrifugal compressor, designed by Briton Frank Whittle (later Sir Frank) for Power Jets and built by the British Thomson-Houston Company at Rugby. In March 1938 Whittle received an Air Ministry contract for a production engine, and on 15 May 1941 the Gloster E.28/39, powered by this W1 engine, took off at Cranwell on a 17 minute flight, flown by Flt Lt P. E. G. Sayer. **This was the first British turbojet powered aeroplane.** Interestingly, a non-airworthy version of the W1 engine that had been built simultaneously using spare parts and rejected components, known as the W1X, had been fitted to the E.28/39 for taxiing trials, during which (on 8 April 1941) the aircraft had made a few 'hop' flights.

**The first aircraft with a completely successful pressurized cabin** was the Lockheed XC-35. Built for research at high altitude, it was flown for the first time on 7 May 1937.

**The first known project to develop a specifically designed rocket-powered manned aeroplane** was begun in Germany as *Projekt X* by Dr Alexander Lippisch at the German DFS in July 1937. Though experimental, the resulting aircraft was the DFS 194, forerunner of the operational Messerschmitt Me 163 Komet rocket plane (see below).

**The Heinkel HeS 3b turbojet engine designed by Pabst von Ohain was flown for the first time** during June 1938, a Heinkel He 118 serving as a testbed aircraft.

**The first specifically designed rocket-powered and piloted aeroplane** was the Heinkel He 176, which made its maiden flight at the secret German research establishment at Peenemünde on 20 June 1939. Piloted by Erich Warsitz, the He 176 was powered by a single Walter HWK R.I-203 motor.

**The first aircraft in the world to fly solely on the power of a turbojet engine** was the German Heinkel He 178, which made its first true flight at Heinkel's Marienehe airfield on 27 August 1939. It was powered by a Heinkel HeS 3b engine designed by Dr Pabst von Ohain.

**The first successful liquid-fuel rocket aircraft in the world** was the German DFS 194 which, having been conceived by a team under Dr Alexander Lippisch, was taken over by Messerschmitt A.G. at Augsburg and flown in August 1940 by Heini Dittmar. It was powered by a 600 lb (272 kg) thrust Walter rocket motor.

**The first design for a Mach 2+ delta-winged combat aircraft** was produced by Dr Alexander Lippisch at the LFA in Vienna in late 1944. As the LP-13a and eventually intended for Luftwaffe service if developed successfully, it had delta wings of elliptical section and a triangular fin incorporating the cockpit. Power was to be provided by a ramjet engine enclosed in the centre section of the wings and fuelled by powdered coal, ignited only after a rocket motor had taken the aircraft to the necessary speed for the ramjet to operate. Only the DM-1 manned glider was almost completed for airframe aerodynamic testing by the end of the Second World War, and this was captured by US forces and taken back to the USA. Next stages in the development of the LP-13a would have been the turbojet powered DM-2 and rocket DM-3.

**The first research aircraft to be designed for flight at 1000 mph (1600 km/h) was the Miles M-52.** Development began in 1943, and by February 1946 the detail design was virtually completed. Construction was underway when the project was cancelled due to economic problems and the belief that it should have been designed with swept instead of very thin bi-convex wings. However, models of the M-52 flown during 1947–8 showed that the aircraft could have achieved its aim. Power for the M-52 was to have been provided by one Power Jets W2/700 turbojet engine, with augmentor and afterburner, developing up to 4100 lb (1860 kg) thrust.

**The first American rocket-powered military aircraft** was the Northrop MX-324, which was first flown under rocket power by Harry Crosby on 5 July 1944. It was powered by an Aerojet XCAL-200 motor, fuelled by monoethylaniline. It had originally flown as a glider in October 1943.

**The world's first flying-wing jet fighter to fly** was the Northrop XP-79B, which made its one and only test flight of 15 minutes' duration (before going out of control) on 12 September 1945. Powered by two 1150 lb (522 kg) thrust Westinghouse J30 turbojet engines, it was thought to be capable of 510 mph (821 km/h) and was intended to cut off the tails of enemy bombers using its welded magnesium wing. The pilot lay prone in the cockpit so as to withstand the impact.

**The first British jet-powered aircraft to exceed a speed of Mach 1** was the de Havilland DH108, three examples of which were built to investigate the stability and control problems of swept wings, so providing information for the design of the de Havilland Comet I airliner. The first DH108 made its maiden flight on 15 May 1946, using a standard de Havilland Vampire fighter fuselage and powered by one 3750 lb (1700 kg) thrust Goblin 4 turbojet engine. This first aircraft was used to provide data on the slow-flying characteristics of the swept wings; the second and third were used for high-speed flying. The last aircraft recorded a speed between Mach 1.0 and 1.1 on 6 September 1948 while in a dive from 40 000 ft (12 200 m).

**The first French aircraft to be designed specifically for stratospheric flight research** was the Aérocentre Belphégor, which flew for the first time on 6 June 1946. Powered by a single Daimler-Benz DB 610 engine, developing 3000 hp, it had pressurized accommodation for five persons in its bulbous fuselage, including two research members; the pilot was situated in a cupola above the main cabin. With an all-up weight of 22 050 lb (10 000 kg), the Belphégor could fly to an altitude of 42 000 ft (12 800 m).

**The first flying-boat in the world capable of a maximum level speed of over 500 mph (805 km/h)** was the British Saunders-Roe SR A/1 jet fighter flying-boat which first flew on 16 July 1947. Powered by two Metrovick Beryl axial-flow turbojets, the SR A/1, **which was also the world's first jet-powered flying-boat,** had a top speed of 512 mph (824 km/h) and had an armament of four 20 mm guns. Three prototypes were built, but the project was abandoned when flight

Above  *de Havilland DH 108, the first British supersonic jet aircraft.*

Left  *Northrop XP-79B flying-wing fighter. (Northrop)*

Right  *The world's first jet flying-boat was the Saunders-Roe SR A/1.*

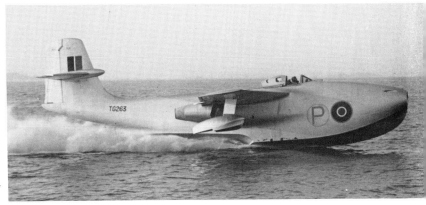

tests showed that the large flying-boat hull compromised both speed and manoeuvrability.

**The first manned supersonic aeroplane in the world** was the rocket-powered American Bell X-1. The second prototype made its first powered flight on 9 December 1946, piloted by Chalmers Goodlin, after being air-launched from a Boeing B-29 Superfortress. Flown by Capt Charles 'Chuck' Yeager, USAF, the X-1 was taken progressively nearer to 'the speed of sound' and finally, on 14 October 1947, escaped from the buffeting of near-sonic compressibility into the smooth airflow of supersonic flight. The speed recorded on that historic occasion was 700 mph (1126 km/h) at a height of 45 000 ft (13 715 m), the equivalent Mach* number being 1.06.

*The use of the Mach scale for aircraft speeds was introduced by Prof Ackeret of Zürich, Switzerland. The Mach number is the ratio of the velocity of a moving body to the local velocity of sound. This ratio was first employed by Dr Ernst Mach (1838–1916) of Vienna, Austria, in 1887. Thus Mach 1.0 equals 760.98 mph (1224.67 km/h) at sea-level at 15°C, and is assumed, for convenience, to fall to a constant 659.78 mph (1061.81 km/h) in the stratosphere, i.e. above 36 089 ft (11 000 m).

**The first piloted aircraft to be flown at twice the speed of sound** was the Douglas Skyrocket, which flew for the first time on 4 February 1948. Designed to investigate sweptback wings, it was powered by one Reaction Motors XLR-8 rocket motor of 6000 lb (2720 kg) thrust and one Westinghouse J34 turbojet engine of 3000 lb (1360 kg) thrust. The wings were of conventional

subsonic configuration with a 35° sweepback. Altogether three Skyrockets were built, and on 31 August 1953 one reached an altitude of 83 235 ft (25 370 m). However, the most memorable flight of a Skyrocket was made on 20 November of the same year when the aircraft attained a speed of Mach 2.005 after being launched from a Boeing 'motherplane' at 32 000 ft (9750 m).

**The first jet-powered fighter to be designed specifically as a parasite aircraft** was the McDonnell XF-85 Goblin, which made its first flight on 23 August 1948. Designed to be carried inside the forward bomb-bay of the Consolidated Vultee B-36 long-range bomber, the Goblin had an extremely short and stubby fuselage, with swept short-span wings and multiple tail surfaces. It was launched and picked up via a retractable 'skyhook' on the Goblin which hooked on to a retractable trapeze on the bomber. Following one abortive attempt to hook back on to the B-36, which nearly ended in disaster, the first successful hook-on was made on 14 October 1948. Although several more hook-ons were achieved, and the Goblin demonstrated a speed of 520 mph (837 km/h), the project was cancelled after only two Goblins had been built. One of them remains on view at the USAF Museum at Dayton, Ohio. The length of the Goblin was only 14 ft 10½ in (4.53 m); power was provided by a Westinghouse J34 engine of 3000 lb (1360 kg) thrust.

**The Northrop X-4 Bantam** was designed to investigate the subsonic flight characteristics of

*McDonnell Goblin parasite fighter approaches the lowered trapeze on the Boeing B-29 Superfortress used for the experiments.*

aircraft with swept wings but without a tailplane. Two X-4s were produced, the first flying on 15 December 1948. The programme was completed successfully in April 1954, after some 60 flights had been made.

**The first British delta-wing research aircraft** was the Avro 707, which made its first flight on 4 September 1949. Designed to gain data on the flight characteristics of delta wings at low speeds, the Type 707 was basically a scale model of the then-projected Vulcan bomber. Following its destruction in an accident, the Type 707B was produced to continue low-speed research, first flying in September 1950. Two Type 707As then followed for research into high-speed flight; and the series was completed by a single Type 707C, a two-seat version built to give pilots training in flying delta-wing aircraft. The 707C first flew in mid-1953, powered by a Rolls-Royce Derwent engine of 3600 lb (1635 kg) thrust.

**The Douglas X-3** was built to investigate the effectiveness of turbojet engines and short-span double-wedge wing and tail surfaces at very high altitudes, and to study thermodynamic heating at speeds up to Mach 2. Construction of the aircraft caused many problems, as it was built primarily of then little used titanium. To measure the pressure on the airframe during flight, a huge number of pin-hole orifices were positioned strategically over the airframe, and temperature and stress were also measured at many locations. Powered by two Westinghouse J34 turbojets, the X-3 made its unofficial maiden flight on 15 October 1952 and its official first flight on the 20th. Unfortunately, the X-3 proved barely capable of supersonic flight, managing Mach 1.21 in a dive during the manufacturer's tests but Mach 0.95 being the normal maximum level speed. The programme was terminated in May 1956, after 20 flights had been made by NASA.

**Built as an experimental ramjet-powered aircraft**, the French Leduc 0.10 made its first powered flight on 21 April 1949 after being released over Toulouse from a Languedoc motherplane. This carried the 0.10 above its fuselage on special mounting struts, providing the stream of air to flow into the engine which was necessary for the ramjet to work. On this occasion the 0.10 reached a speed of 422 mph (680 km/h) on 50 per cent power. Maximum speed achieved during a later

*From the Leduc 0.10 was developed the Leduc 0.21, seen above the Languedoc motherplane. First flown on 16 May 1953, it was completely successful and tested components for the proposed 0.22 interceptor.*

flight was Mach 0.84. Three 0.10s were produced; each had a tubular double-skinned fuselage, the outer shell forming the annular ramjet duct and the inner shell accommodating the cockpit for the crew of two.

**The first aircraft to have variable-geometry wings that could be adjusted in flight** was the Bell X-5, first flown on 20 June 1951. Its development stemmed from the capture of the wartime **German Messerschmitt P.1101** prototype jet fighter, which had been found by the US forces in incomplete form in the Tyrol region of Austria. The Bell X-5 that was developed from studies of the P.1101 differed mainly in engine type and its ability to vary wing angle in flight (between 20°– 60° sweepback); the P.1101 could have its wings altered between 35° and 45° only on the ground and was never intended to have 'swing-wings' if put into production.

**The first French supersonic aircraft and the first French rocket/turbojet mixed power research aircraft**, designed to provide data for future interceptors of similar concept, was the Sud-Ouest SO 9000 Trident, which first flew on 2 March 1953. Power was provided initially by two wingtip-mounted Turboméca Marboré II turbojet engines. These were replaced later by Dassault Viper turbojet engines of nearly double the power, and an SEPR 481 rocket motor of 9920 lb (4500 kg) thrust was installed subsequently in the rear fuselage. Testing of the rocket power unit began in April 1955, and the Trident eventually attained a speed of 1055 mph (1700 km/h).

Sud-Ouest SO 9000 Trident mixed-power research aircraft.

Convair Sea Dart using skis to gain hydrodynamic lift. (General Dynamics)

**The Convair Sea Dart** was an experimental seaplane fighter fitted with delta wings and hydroskis. It set several 'firsts', being **the first delta-winged seaplane** and **the first seaplane to exceed the speed of sound.** The original aircraft was designated XF2Y-1 and made its first flight on 9 April 1953. It was joined subsequently by the development version, designated YF2Y-1, which exceeded Mach 1 on 3 August 1954 in a dive, shortly before being destroyed in an accident. Whereas the XF2Y-1 was powered by two Westinghouse J34 turbojet engines, each of 3400 lb (1542 kg) thrust, the later aircraft had two J46 engines of 6000 lb (2720 kg) thrust each, both with afterburning. The YF2Y-1 proved sufficiently promising for the US Navy to order three more similar aircraft, but the whole concept of a seaplane fighter was soon abandoned.

**The first aircraft to test the practicability of the aero-isoclinic wing** was the Short SB4 Sherpa, which made its maiden flight on 4 October 1953. The wing was designed as a partially flexible structure, with all-moving tips which were used as both ailerons and elevators. Flight testing showed that the handling characteristics of the aircraft were very satisfactory.

**The first French, and European, aircraft to exceed Mach 1 in level flight without the use of an afterburner or rocket power** was the Nord Gerfaut 1A, a small delta-winged research aircraft intended to gather information on high-speed flight useful to future fighter design. It first flew on 3 August 1954. The improved Gerfaut II, of 1956 appearance, attained Mach 1.3 on the power of a 9700 lb (4400 kg) thrust SNECMA Atar 101G turbojet engine.

**The first aircraft to set a world speed record of over 1000 mph (1600 km/h)** was the Fairey Delta 2, the first example of which made its maiden flight on 6 October 1954. Built originally to investigate the problems encountered during transition from subsonic to supersonic speeds, each Delta 2 was powered by a Rolls-Royce Avon turbojet engine. The first aircraft had an Avon RA5 which gave 12 000 lb (5445 kg) thrust, the second an RA28 which developed 1000 lb (450 kg) more thrust. The record was set on 10 March 1956, off the Sussex coast between Ford and Chichester, Lt Cdr L. Peter Twiss flying the first aircraft (WG774) at an FAI accredited speed of 1131.76 mph (1821.39 km/h), the fastest of two runs made at 1147 mph (1846 km/h). Subsequently, this aircraft was converted into the BAC 221, with new delta wings and control surfaces, new landing gear, longer fuselage and a hydraulically actuated drooping nose. Data gained with it were used in the development of the Concorde SST airliner.

**The first aircraft to carry an airborne nuclear reactor** was the Convair NB-36H, a modified B-36H strategic bomber that first flew with the reactor operating in September 1955. In total, this aircraft completed 47 flights with the reactor in the aft bomb bay, intended not to power the engines but to test shielding in preparation for the two actual X-6 aircraft (again modified B-36Hs) that would have General Electric P-1 nuclear turbojet engines fitted. In the event, the X-6s were never completed.

**The first aircraft to fly at over Mach 3 in level flight** was the Bell X-2, two examples of which were built for continued research at transonic and supersonic speeds. Built with a K-monel metal fuselage, and stainless steel swept wings and tail unit, the first X-2 was destroyed after an explosion in its B-50 motherplane which resulted in the research aircraft being jettisoned. The second X-2 made its maiden flight on 18 November 1955, but after several successful flights this too was destroyed, on 27 September 1956, at the end of a test in which it recorded Mach 3.2.

**The Ryan X-13 Vertijet** first flew on 10 December 1955 as a turbojet-powered vertical take-off and landing aircraft, although on this occasion it flew in conventional aeroplane mode. Vertical flights, with the aircraft resting on its tail and pointing upward, began on 28 May 1956. On 28 November 1956, an X-13 (two built) completed **the world's first transition by a pure jet aircraft from horizontal to vertical flight and vice versa,** and then on 11 April 1957 **the first full transition from vertical to horizontal flight and back again for a vertical descent** and hook-on landing to its special trailer.

**Built to test a turbo-ramjet engine, which was designed to form the bulk of the aircraft's air-frame,** the French Nord 1500-02 Griffon II was a direct development of the earlier Griffon I, which had been powered by a conventional turbojet only. The Griffon had a turbojet mounted inside the ramjet, to propel it to the speed at which the ramjet could ignite and provide power. It flew for the first time on 23 January 1957, and exceeded Mach 1 on 17 May, with its ramjet power on. Over 200 flights were made by the aircraft, culminating in a flight during which Mach 2.19 was attained on 13 October 1959, at which speed the ramjet developed four-fifths of the aircraft's total thrust.

**The first artificial satellite launched into Earth orbit** was the Soviet *Sputnik 1* (Fellow Traveller), launched from the Baikonur Cosmodrome at Tyuratam on 4 October 1957, on an SS-6 (ICBM) launcher. With a diameter of 22.8 in (58 cm) and weighing 184.3 lb (83.6 kg), it is believed to have remained active until 4 January 1958.

**The first American artificial satellite launched into Earth orbit** was *Explorer I*, on 1 February 1958. Launched on a Jupiter-C rocket from Cape

Above    *Fairey Delta 2, the first aircraft to fly at over 1000 mph. (Shell)*

Below    *Convair NB-36H with a nuclear reactor on board.*

Canaveral, its transmitted data led to the discovery of the Van Allen radiation belts.

**One of the first French research aircraft to give an effective STOL demonstration of the 'blown-wing' or 'deflected-slipstream' technique,** the Breguet 940 Integral research aircraft, was flown for the first time on 21 May 1958. It led to production of the similar Breguet 941S, four of which served with the Armée de l'Air.

**The first full transitions from vertical to horizontal flight, and vice versa, by a British jet aeroplane, and the world's first transitions with the aeroplane itself remaining in flat horizontal attitude,** were made by the Short SC.1 VTOL research aircraft on 6 April 1960. The aircraft was powered by four Rolls-Royce RB.108 turbojet engines mounted to give vertical jet lift, and a fifth engine mounted horizontally to give forward flight.

**The world's first fully successful experimental V/STOL fighter** was the Hawker Siddeley P1127. The first of two prototypes made its initial tethered hovering flight on 21 October 1960. In September 1961 the first transition flights from vertical to horizontal were made, and in 1963 the type was tested on board HMS *Ark Royal*. Several other development and evaluation models were built, with the name Kestrel, leading subsequently to the production Harrier. Power for the Kestrel was provided by one Bristol Siddeley Pegasus 5 vectored-thrust turbofan engine of 15 200 lb (6895 kg) thrust.

**The first human to enter space** was the Soviet cosmonaut Flt Maj Yuriy Alexeyevich Gagarin (aged 27, born Friday 9 March 1934 near Gzatsk, died in a jet crash on Wednesday, 27 March 1968). Launched at 09.07 h, Moscow time, on 12 April 1961, from Baikonur, East Kazakhstan, in the 10 417 lb (4725 kg) *Vostok 1* spacecraft, Gagarin completed a single orbit of the Earth, landing safely near Smelovka 1 h 48 min later.

**The first full-throttle test flight of the North American X-15A** was made on 21 April 1961, piloted by Maj Robert White, USAF, when a speed of 3074 mph (4947 km/h) was attained. (See also *Fastest*.)

**The first American to enter space** was Alan B. Shepard who, on 5 May 1961, was launched in a sub-orbital trajectory of 297 miles (478 km). In

*The first hero of spaceflight, Major Yuriy Gagarin. (Soviet Weekly)*

his 15 min 22 s journey in the *Mercury* capsule *Freedom 7*, Shepard had attained a height of 118 miles (190 km) and travelled at a speed of 5188 mph (8350 km/h). (The third man into space was also an American, Virgil Grissom, who travelled in sub-orbital flight on 21 July 1961.) Shepard's flight was **the shortest successful manned mission so far.**

**The first manpowered aircraft to be built and flown under the Royal Aeronautical Society rules** established for the Kremer Competition was completed by a group of postgraduate students as the Southampton University Manpowered Aircraft (SUMPA). Under muscular power, it attained a distance of 70 yards (68 m) at a height of six feet (1.83 m) on 9 November 1961, at Lasham Airfield, Hampshire, England. Pilot was Derek Piggott, the Chief Flying Instructor at the Lasham Glider Centre.

**The first American astronaut to go into Earth orbit** was Lt Col John H. Glenn who, on 20 February 1962, completed three orbits in *Mercury* capsule 6 *Friendship 7*. The flight lasted 4 h 55 min 23 s.

**First pilot of a fixed-wing aircraft to gain 'astronaut's wings',** for having attained an altitude of more than 50 miles (80 km) above the Earth's surface, was NASA test pilot Joe Walker. They were awarded after he had flown the North

Above   *North American XB-70A Valkyrie Mach 3 research bomber.*

Left   *Alan B. Shepard in the Mercury capsule just before his 5 May 1961 sub-orbital spaceflight. (NASA)*

American X-15A to a height of 271 000 ft (82 600 m) on 17 January 1963.

**The first woman to enter space** was the Soviet cosmonaut Jr Lt Valentina Vladimirovna Tereshkova, aged 26, who, in *Vostok* 6, was placed in Earth orbit on 16 June 1963 and completed 48 orbits during the 70 h 50 min mission.

**The largest research aircraft ever built** was the North American XB-70A Valkyrie, which was designed originally as a Mach 3 strategic bomber for the USAF, but modified subsequently into an aerodynamic test vehicle. Two Valkyries were built, the first flying on 21 September 1964. Each had large delta wings, with hydraulically drooping wingtips and 12 elevons and canard foreplanes. Power was provided by six General Electric YJ93 turbojet engines, each giving a thrust of 31 000 lb (14 050 kg) with afterburning. Mach 3 was achieved for the first time on 14 October 1965. One of the Valkyries was destroyed at a later date after colliding with its accompanying chase aircraft, and the programme was completed in 1969 after the surviving aircraft had made more than 70 flights.

**The first multi-crew space mission** was achieved by the Soviet Union, following the launch of the three-man *Voskhod* 1 on 12 October 1964. Crewed by cosmonauts Vladimir Komarov, Konstantin Feoktistov and Boris Yegorov, the mission (without use of spacesuits) lasted 1 d 17 min and covered 16 Earth orbits.

**The first ever EVA (Extravehicular Activity) or 'spacewalk'** was accomplished by Soviet cosmonaut Alexei Leonov who, with Pavel Belyayev, crewed *Voskhod* 2. Launched on 18 March 1965, the flight lasted 1 d 2 h 2 min, during which Leonov spent 23 min 41 s in a spacesuit outside the craft but tethered to it by a 16 ft (5 m) line.

**The first American multi-crew mission and the first mission to perform manned orbital manoeuvres** was *Gemini* 3, a two-man spacecraft, with astronauts Virgil Grissom and John Young on board. The first mission to begin with a launch using a huge Titan II booster, it was made on 23 March 1965 and lasted 4 h 53 min.

**The first American 'spacewalk'** was performed by Edward White who, with James McDivitt, crewed *Gemini* 4. Launched on 3 June 1965, the mission lasted 4 d 1 h 56 min, during which White made a 21 minute 'spacewalk'.

**The first recognized manoeuvred rendezvous in space** was achieved by American spacecraft *Gemini* 6 and *Gemini* 7, launched on 15 December and 4 December 1965 respectively. During the mission, which lasted 13 d 18 h 35 min for *Gemini* 7, *Gemini* 6 was manoeuvred to within 6 ft (1.8 m) of *Gemini* 7. *Gemini* 6 and 7 were crewed by Walter Schirra and Thomas Stafford and Frank Borman and James Lovell respectively.

**The first docking of spacecraft in space** was achieved by America's *Gemini* 8 and an Agena docking target. Launched on 16 March 1966,

*Gemini 8* was crewed by Neil Armstrong and David Scott. The docking, however, had to be terminated almost immediately as the spacecraft began spinning uncontrollably.

**The first unpowered flight of the Northrop/ NASA M2-F2 lifting-body re-entry research vehicle** was made on 12 July 1966, following launch at 45 000 ft (13 710 m) from a B-52 'motherplane'. Representing one of the stages in development of NASA's Space Shuttle, it had a fuselage structure D-shaped in cross-section with the straight side of the 'D' forming the upper surface. After five unpowered flights it was dismantled for examination and then rebuilt, as the M2-F3, with power provided by an 8000 lb (3629 kg) thrust Thiokol XLR-11 rocket engine. The M2-F3 made its first powered flight on 25 November 1970, achieving a speed of Mach 0.8 at 53 000 ft (16 150 m). When the programme terminated in December 1972, a total of 20 powered flights had been made.

**The world's first experimental space bomb** was launched on 25 January 1967 as Cosmos K-139 by the Soviet Union. A version of the SS-9 *Scarp* intercontinental ballistic missile, it became known as FOBS (Fractional Orbital Bombardment System). It is believed that this system did not become operational.

**The first spaceflight fatality** was Soviet cosmonaut Col Vladimir Mikhailovich Komarov. Launched on board *Soyuz 1* on 23 April 1967, he met his death after being in orbit for more than 25 h, when his craft impacted on the final descent due to parachute failure.

**The first manned flight around the Moon** was performed by American spacecraft *Apollo 8*, launched on 21 December 1968 with astronauts Frank Borman, James Lovell and William Anders on board. Flying around the Moon on 24 December, they returned to Earth on the 27th. Mission time was 6 d 3 h 1 min.

**The first manned spacecraft to go into lunar orbit** was *Apollo 10*. Launched on 18 May 1969 with astronauts Thomas Stafford, Eugene Cernan and John Young on board, this was a Moon landing rehearsal, during which Stafford and Cernan made two descents to within 8.7 miles (14 km) of the Moon's surface in the Lunar Module. The mission lasted for 8 d 3 min.

*Edwin Aldrin stands by the deployed Solar Wind Composition during the first mission to the Moon. (NASA)*

**The first human to set foot on the Moon** was the American astronaut Neil A. Armstrong, aged 38 (born on Tuesday 5 August 1930 at Wapakoneta, Ohio). At 02.56 h 20 s GMT on Monday 21 July 1969 Armstrong stepped on to the Moon's surface from the lunar module *Eagle*, an event watched through television by 600 million viewers 232 000 miles away on Earth. Shortly afterwards his colleague Edwin E. A. Aldrin joined him on the Moon, while Michael Collins remained in Moon orbit in the command module *Columbia*. The entire flight to the Moon by *Apollo 11* had been a complete success, having begun on 16 July, and the safe return to Earth was terminated with splash-down at 16.49 h GMT on 24 July, 940 miles (1510 km) south-west of Honolulu in the Pacific Ocean.

In his Special State of the Union Message of 25 May 1961, eight years earlier, the late President John F. Kennedy had addressed to Congress a request for additional funds to accelerate space research:

'I believe this nation should commit itself to achieving the goal before this decade is out, of landing a man on the Moon and returning him to Earth. No single space project in this period will be more exciting, or more impressive, or more important for the long-range exploration of space; and none will be so difficult or expensive to accomplish. Including necessary sup-

*The first men to reach the Moon, Neil Armstrong, Michael Collins and Edwin Aldrin. (NASA)*

porting research, this objective will require an additional $531 000 000 this year and still higher sums in the future. We propose to accelerate development of the appropriate lunar space craft. We propose to develop liquid and solid boosters much larger than any now being developed. . . . We propose additional funds for other engine development and for unmanned explorations, which are particularly important for one purpose which this nation will never overlook—the survival of the man who first makes this daring flight. But in a very real sense, it will not be one man going to the Moon—it will be an entire nation. For all of us must work to put him there.'

After the expenditure of $24 000 000 000 Neil Armstrong brought success to the President's proposal.

**The first powered flight of the Martin Marietta SV-5P Pilot (X-24A)** was made on 19 March 1970. A lifting-body research aircraft to expand and complement the work of the Northrop/NASA HL-10 and M2-F2, it was designed for use to prove that NASA's planned Space Shuttle would be able to re-enter the Earth's atmosphere, fly under control like any other fixed-wing aircraft, and land on a conventional runway for subse-

quent re-use. Powered by an 8000 lb (3629 kg) thrust Thiokol XLR11 rocket engine and two Bell rockets each of 500 lb (227 kg) thrust, it completed a successful 28-flight programme as the X-24A, before being rebuilt as the X-24B. First flown in this latter form on 1 August 1973, it made its final powered flight on 23 September 1975.

**The first two-crew man-powered aircraft to fly,** on 23 December 1972 at Radlett, Herts, was the Hertfordshire Pedal Aeronauts Toucan. Its best flight, of 2100 ft (640 m), was made on 3 July 1973. It was superseded by the modified Toucan 2 which, with a wing span of 139 ft (42.37 m), was **the largest man-powered aircraft built**.

**The first electrically powered manned aircraft to fly** was the Austrian Militky MB-E1. Derived from the airframe of a Brditschka HB-3 sailplane, and powered by a Bosch electric motor driven by rechargeable batteries, it was flown for the first time at Linz on 21 October 1973.

**The first combined US and USSR space mission** was the ASTP (Apollo-Soyuz Test Project), during which the crews of *Soyuz 19* and the *Apollo ASTP* docked in orbit for astronaut/cosmonaut exchanges and combined experiments. *Soyuz* was launched on 15 July 1975 with Alexei Leonov and

Valeri Kubasov on board, and the same day America launched the *Apollo* with astronauts Thomas Stafford, Vance Brand and Donald Slayton. The mission ended on the 24th.

**The first 1-mile (1.6-km) figure-of-eight flight by a man-powered aircraft** was achieved on 23 August 1977. This was accomplished in the *Gossamer Condor* aircraft, designed by a team in the United States under the leadership of Dr Paul MacCready. Spanning 96 ft 0 in (29.26 m) and having a gross weight of 207 lb (94 kg) including its pilot/power unit racing cyclist Bryan Allen, the 7 min 27.5 s flight between and around two pylons half a mile apart was made at Shafter, California, winning the £50 000 Kremer Prize.

**The world's first known aircraft designed to test the feasibility of 'low observable' or stealth technology** was the Lockheed XST, two of which were built under USAF Flight Dynamics Laboratory contract in the secret *Have Blue* programme. Resembling small versions of the subsequent F-117A but with inward-canted ruddervators, the first was flown initially to test the multi-faceted airframe in December 1977, at Groom Lake, Nevada.

**Claimed to be the first flight by a solar-powered aircraft**, the Solar One designed by Freddie To and David Williams made its first brief hop in the UK on 19 December 1978. A flight covering a distance of almost three-quarters of a mile (1200 m) was made from Lasham Airfield, Hampshire, on 13 June 1979. In this aircraft batteries were used to store the electricity generated by 750 solar cells, and as a result purists have argued that this was an electric- rather than solar-powered aircraft.

**The first manpowered aircraft crossing of the English Channel,** to win the £100 000 Kremer Prize, was achieved by Dr Paul MacCready's *Gossamer Albatross* on 12 June 1979. Taking off from Folkestone, Kent, at 05.51 hours, pilot Bryan Allen landed 22.26 miles (35.82 km) distant at Cap Griz Nez, France, at 08.40 hours. This flight also established a world distance in a straight line record of 22.26 miles (35.82 km) and a duration record for human-powered aircraft of 2 h 49 min. However, on 22 January 1987, the distance flown by a manpowered aircraft was increased (though this time in a closed circuit over Edwards Air Force Base) to 36.452 miles (58.664 km) by the

Massachusetts Institute of Technology's (MIT) *Michelob Light Eagle*, flown by Glenn Tremml. The MIT *Daedalus* has since flown 74 miles (119 km) – see *Longest*.

**The MacCready Gossamer Penguin,** an interim solar-powered aircraft converted from a three-quarter scale version of the *Gossamer Albatross*, made its first purely solar-powered flight on 7 August 1980. Piloted by Janice Brown, weighing 99 lb (45 kg), a straight flight of about 2 miles (3 km) was recorded. The *Gossamer Penguin* had flown earlier under solar power, on 18 May 1980, when a short climbing flight was made following an assisted take-off.

**A first short-duration pure solar-powered test flight** was made by the MacCready *Solar Challenger* on 20 November 1980. On 7 July 1981, piloted by Steve Ptacek (USA), the *Solar Challenger* became the first aircraft of this category to achieve a crossing of the English Channel. Taking off from Cormeilles-en-Vexin, near Paris, the aircraft was flown a distance of 163 miles (262 km) to make a landing at Manston aerodrome, Kent, 5 h 23 min later. Power for the *Challenger* was provided by no fewer than 16 128 solar cells on the upper surfaces of the wings and tailplane, providing maximum power of 3 hp to the electric motor power unit.

**The world's first reusable spacecraft** was America's NASA Space Shuttle Orbiter *Columbia*, which was launched on its first mission (STS-1) on 12 April 1981. Crewed by John Young and Robert Crippen, *Columbia* took off under the power of its own engines and those of two jettisonable boosters and made 37 orbits before landing 2 d 6 h 21 min later as an unpowered aircraft on the dry bed of Rogers Lake, Edwards Air Force Base, California, on the 14th. Having achieved a speed of 16 600 mph (26 715 km/h) in space when the engine was cut off, *Columbia* became the fastest fixed wing craft of all time.

**The first untethered 'spacewalk'** was performed by American Capt Bruce McCandless on 7 February 1984. A crew member of Space Shuttle Orbiter *Challenger*, he used an MMU (Manned Manoeuvering Unit) while 164 miles (264 km) above Hawaii.

**The first 'spacewalk' by a woman** was made on 25 July 1984, by Soviet cosmonaut Svetlana

Savitskaya, a crew-member of Soyuz T12/Salyut 7. Savitskaya also became **the first woman to make two spaceflights.** Sally Ride became **the first American woman to make two spaceflights,** on 5 October 1984, during space shuttle mission STS 41-G using *Challenger*, while Kathryn Sullivan on the same mission became **the first American woman to perform a 'spacewalk'.**

**The worst accident to a spacecraft** occurred on 28 January 1986, when US Space Shuttle Orbiter *Challenger* exploded 75 seconds after lift-off during mission STS 51-L. The crew of seven were killed.

**The first Russian Space Shuttle** was named *Buran*, and was first launched on 15 November 1988. Payload and overall design are similar to the US Shuttle, except that all the main lift-off engines are contained in the separate *Energiya* rocket booster.

*Largest:*

**The largest crew of a spacecraft** was the eight members of US Space Shuttle Orbiter *Challenger* during mission STS 61-A, begun on 30 October 1985 and lasting 7 days and 45 min. The crew comprised Bluford, Buchli, Dunbar, Furner, Hartsfield, Nagel, Messerschmid and Ockels.

*Fastest:*

**The fastest aeroplane ever flown** is the rocket-powered North American X-15A-2 research aircraft. Three X-15s were built during the late 1950s and the first free flight was made on 8 June 1959. Just over three months later, on 17 September, the second craft made the first powered flight. Because the 60 000 lb (26 215 kg) thrust Thiokol XLR99-RM-2 rocket engine was not ready, two XLR11-RM-5 engines powered X-15 No. 2. Despite the fact that these gave a combined thrust of only 33 000 lb (15 000 kg), a speed of Mach 2.3 was recorded. By December 1963, then powered by the XLR99, speed had climbed to Mach 6.06, and a surface skin temperature of 1320°F (715.6°C) had confirmed yet another problem associated with very high-speed flight. Following a landing accident to No. 2, it was rebuilt and various modifications introduced, becoming the X-15A-2. The highest altitude the X-15 attained was 354 200 ft (67.08 miles) on a flight by J. A. Walker on 22 August 1963, and the highest speed

was 4534 mph (Mach 6.72) by W. J. Knight on 3 October 1967. A list of the progressive speeds achieved by these aircraft is given at the end of the book.

**The fastest aerospace craft intended for civil and military applications** is the US NASP (National Aero-Space Plane), which is expected to take-off and land on runways and cruise at between Mach 5 and 15 at a height of about 105 000 ft (32 000 m). Power will be provided by hydrogen fuelled ramjet/scramjet engines with small rocket motors. A NASP airliner could cover the distance between the capital cities of the USA and Japan in under two hours. As an initial phase in its development, the USAF/NASA are directing the construction of two X-30 scale research craft of about 150–200 ft (45.7–61.0 m) length, which will fly towards the end of the 1990s.

*Longest:*

**The world distance in a straight line record for human-powered flight** was set on 23 April 1988, when the Massachusetts Institute of Technology (MIT) *Daedalus* was piloted by Kanellos Kanellopoulos from Crete to the island of Santorini – a distance of 74 miles (119 km). Flight speed averaged 18.5 mph (29.7 km/h). This beat the previous record of 22.26 miles (35.82 km), established during the cross-Channel flight of the MacCready *Gossamer Albatross* on 12 June 1979.

**The longest manned space mission** was achieved by 'Soviet' cosmonauts Col Vladimir Georgeyevich Titov and Flt Engineer Musa Khiramanovich Manarov, who were carried to the *Mir* space station on board *Soyuz TM4* on 21 December 1987, and returned to Earth on board *Soyuz TM6* on 21 December 1988, landing near Dzhezkazgan, Kazakhstan. The mission time was 365 days 22 h 39 min and 47 s. Manarov's subsequent 175-day mission on *Soyuz TM11/Mir*, that ended on 26 May 1991, means that he has spent **the longest period in space** of any cosmonaut/astronaut, at 541 days 31 min 10 s. In all, 20 cosmonauts from nations of the former Soviet Union have spent more than 100 days in space. **The longest period for an American astronaut** is 84 days 1 h 15 min, established by Gerald Carr, Edward Gibson and William Pogue during a Skylab mission from 16 November 1973 to 8 February 1974.

# Valour and Achievement

Valour is described by the Oxford English Dictionary as 'the quality of mind which enables a person to face danger with boldness or firmness', and achievement as something which is 'finished, carried out successfully, or brought to an end'. They are clearly closely related, bound together by the words of John Milton: 'And courage never to submit or yield: And what is else not to be overcome?'

The pages which follow provide many instances of the bravery of men and women of all nations in both war and peace. Inevitably, courage abounds in plenty during times of conflict, but it is also an essential ingredient of so many tasks that are faced frequently by those engaged in all aspects of aviation. Test pilots still face many hazards as routine, but civilian pilots may be called upon to deal with crises beyond normal expectation. And for those who set out to establish new records, whether for speed, altitude or distance, great courage is almost invariably an essential ingredient for achievement.

Happily, humans are still capable of great courage and achievements and it is good to know that the world of aviation still has more than its fair share of such people. The following section of this book records just some of their entries on the pages of aviation history.

*Firsts:*

**The first gallantry decoration to be 'earned' by a marine aviator** was the Distinguished Flying Cross awarded posthumously to Eugene B. Ely, who was killed while flying on 14 October 1911. The award of the DFC was made 25 years later in recognition of his outstanding contributions to marine aviation during 1910 and 1911. His sole reward during his life was an award of $500 made by the US Aeronautical Reserve during 1911.

**The first true fighter leader of the First World War** was Hauptmann Oswald Boelcke. He became interested in aviation during army manoeuvres, and gained his Pilot's Certificate at the Halberstadt Flying School on 15 August 1914. He was posted to La Ferte to join Feldfliegerabteilung Nr 13 in September and, with his brother Wilhelm as observer, soon amassed a considerable number of sorties in Army Co-operation Albatros B II biplanes. By early 1915 he had 42 missions in his log-book, and had been awarded the Iron Cross, Second Class. The visit of Leutnant Parschau to his unit to demonstrate the Fokker M8 monoplane scout fired him with enthusiasm; and in April, having received the Iron Cross, First Class, he secured a posting to Hauptmann Kastner's Feldfliegerabteilung Nr 62, where he flew an armed machine for the first time—an Albatros C I, number 162/15. Before long, he was selected to fly early examples of Fokker's E-series armed monoplane scouts; few were available, and Boelcke, Kastner and Leutnant Max Immelmann at first took turns to fly them. After a tour of other fronts in early 1916, Boelcke returned to the West and was given command of the new Jagdstaffel Nr 2 (Jasta 2) which was equipped with Albatros D I and D II scouts. Boelcke was killed on 28 October 1916 during an engagement in which one of his colleagues, Leutnant Boehme, who was flying close to him, banked sharply. Boehme's undercarriage struck the wing of his Albatros, which spiralled to the ground. He was 25 years old, a holder of the Ordre Pour le Mérite and numerous other decorations, the victor of 40 aerial combats, and the idol of his country.

*Svetlana Savitskaya, who holds the current record for extra-vehicular duration in space, set on 25 July 1984 at 3 hours 33 min 4 secs while at Salyut-7 (Novosti)*

**The first air Victoria Cross** was awarded posthumously to Lt W. B. Rhodes Moorhouse, pilot of a BE2c of No. 2 Squadron, RFC, for gallantry in a low-level bombing attack on Courtrai railway station on 26 April 1915.

**The first Victoria Cross for gallantry in air fighting** was awarded to Captain Lanoe George Hawker, RFC, for courageous air combat over a period, culminating in the shoot-down of two Aviatik C-types and an Albatros while flying a Bristol Scout C on 25 July 1915. Patrolling in an Airco DH.2 on 23 November 1916, at which time Hawker was commanding officer of No. 24 Squadron and had a total of nine confirmed victories, he had a prolonged combat with Manfred von Richthofen. This ended in his death, marking the German ace's eleventh victory, when a single bullet from more than 500 discharged by Richthofen's guns hit him in the head.

**One of Germany's first two great fighter aces** was Leutnant Max Immelmann, 'The Eagle of Lille'. He was serving with Feldfliegerabteilung No. 62 at Douai when the first Fokker monoplane scouts became available. Hauptmann Kastner instructed Boelcke in the subtleties of the new machine, and Boelcke taught Immelmann. On 1 August 1915 Immelmann was responsible for the first victory by a Fokker E.I fighter with synchronized machine-gun, but he met his death on 18 June 1916 when an FE2b of No. 25 Squadron, RFC, shot him down near Lens. Immelmann had, by then, gained 15 'air victories'.

**The first great British ace**, Capt Albert Ball, joined No. 13 Squadron, RFC, in France on 15 February 1916, his first operational squadron. His first mount was a BE2c used on artillery-spotting flights. In May he was posted to No. 11 Squadron, equipped with Nieuport scouts. His first two air victories came on 22 May, when he drove down an Albatros D I and forced an LVG two-seater to land. Only the latter was confirmed. His last squadron was No. 56, which flew the new SE5 fighter and the Nieuport Ball loved to fly. As Flt Cdr, Ball gained his 47th and last victory on 6 May 1917. The following evening he dived an SE5 into dense cloud while chasing a German two-seater near Lens and was never seen alive again. His wrecked aircraft and his body were found by the Germans. His Victoria Cross was gazetted on 3 June 1917.

Max Immelmann, 'The Eagle of Lille'.

Albert Ball in a Royal Aircraft Factory SE5, his final mount. (Imperial War Museum)

**The first British gallantry decorations to be gazetted in the Second World War**, on 10 September 1939, were two Distinguished Flying Crosses awarded to Flying Officer A. McPherson and Flt Lt K. C. Doran. McPherson, from the RAF's No. 139 Squadron, had been captain of the first British aircraft to cross the German frontier, on 3 September 1939; and Doran, from No. 110 Squadron, had led a formation of five aircraft which were the first British aircraft to drop bombs on enemy targets during the Second World War.

**One of the first members of the Royal Air Force to be awarded the George Cross** was Aircraftsman Vivian ('Bob') Hollowday who, in July 1940, at Cranfield, Bedfordshire, entered a crashed and blazing bomber and extricated the pilot, and in so doing suffered severe burns to his hands. One month later, at the moment of returning from hospital, he again dashed into a blazing aircraft three times amongst exploding ammunition, and brought out three crew members. He survived his near-fatal burns despite having been on the danger list for 27 days.

**The first Victoria Cross to be won during the Battle of Britain** was awarded posthumously to Acting Seaman J. F. (Jack) Mantle, RN, who was operating an anti-aircraft gun aboard HMS *Foyle Bank* in Portland Harbour, Dorset, on 4 July 1940. The ship, the only one in port with an anti-aircraft gun, became the focus of an enemy raid and was hit by a bomb which cut the power supply. Jack Mantle, though severely wounded, continued to fire the gun, operating it manually; despite another direct hit upon the ship, which severed his left leg, he remained at his post until the end of the raid but succumbed to his terrible wounds almost immediately afterwards. His Victoria Cross was only the second to be awarded for an action in or over Great Britain, the first having been awarded to Lt W. Leefe Robinson of No. 39 Home Defence Squadron, RFC, for his destruction of a Schütte-Lanz airship on the night of 2–3 September 1916 at Cuffley, Hertfordshire.

**The first Victoria Cross awarded to a pilot of RAF Bomber Command** was that won by Flt Lt R. A. B. Learoyd. The award was made for gallantry when, on the night of 12–13 August 1940, Flt Lt Learoyd was flying Hampden P4403, as one of a force of five from Nos 49 and 83 Squadrons which dropped delayed action bombs on an aqueduct of the Dortmund–Ems Canal.

**The first American aircraft to be shot down by an aircraft of the Imperial Japanese Navy Air Force** during the Second World War, over the Phillipines on 8 December 1941, fell to the guns of an aircraft flown by Lieutenant (jg) Saburo Sakai. He had scored 60 victories before being seriously wounded and almost losing sight and becoming 'permanently' grounded in 1944. In the closing stages of the war, with Japan desperately in need of experienced pilots, Sakai at his own request took to the air again (though completely blind in one eye) and succeeded in adding four more victories to his score. He survived the war as Japan's fourth-ranking ace.

**The first jet fighter pilot to achieve five confirmed aerial victories over jet aircraft** was Capt James Jabara, an F-86 Sabre pilot of the 4th Fighter Interceptor Wing, USAF, who shot down his fifth MiG-15 on 20 May 1951. Capt Jabara later went on to destroy a total of 15 MiG-15s, thereby becoming the second most successful Allied pilot of the Korean War.

**The first US Navy pilot to achieve five air victories over Korea** was Lt Guy Bordelon who, flying a piston-engined Vought F4U Corsair, shot down his fifth victim on 17 July 1953.

**The first US aces of the Vietnam war** were the two-man team of Lt Randy Cunningham and his RIO (Radio Intercept Officer) Lt (Jg) William Driscoll of the US Navy's Squadron VF-96 flying off the USS *Constellation*. In a dramatic action on 10 May 1972 they destroyed their third, fourth and fifth North Vietnamese MiG fighters to achieve their ace status, an action which terminated in Cunningham and Driscoll ejecting from their battle-damaged F-4J Phantom II over the Gulf of Tonkin and their rescue by a US Marine Corps Boeing Vertol HH-46A Sea Knight.

**The US Air Force's first aces of the Vietnam War** were Capt Richard S. Richie and Lt Charles DeBellevue (RIO) of the 555th Tactical Fighter Squadron, who recorded their fifth 'kill' on 28 August 1972 while flying a combat patrol in their McDonnell Douglas F-4C Phantom II.

## Highest:

**The highest-scoring Allied pilot during the Battle of Britain** was Sergeant Josef Frantisek, a Czech pilot who served with No. 303 (Polish) Squadron, RAF. His confirmed score of 17 enemy aircraft shot down was achieved entirely during September 1940; he was killed on 9 October 1940. The only British gallantry decoration awarded to Frantisek was the Distinguished Flying Medal, but he had been awarded previously the Czech War Cross and the Polish Virtuti Militari.

Major Marie T. Rossi, female pilot of a US Army Boeing Vertol CH-47D Chinook, was but one of the many pilots involved in ferrying troops of the 101st Airborne Division into battle on 24 February 1991. Asked at the time about her feelings as she went into action, she admitted that piloting such a large helicopter at low level posed some risks. Ironically, she died on 1 March 1991, soon after the Gulf War cease-fire, when her Chinook hit a microwave tower while engaged on a low-level mission. Major Rossi was **the highest ranking American to die during Operation Desert Storm.**

## Greatest:

**The greatest Allied ace of the First World War** was Capitaine René Paul Fonck, who served with Escadrille SPA103, one of the units of the famous Groupe de Combat No. 12 'Les Cigognes'. Officially Fonck is credited with 75 victories; his own personal estimate, including aircraft destroyed but not confirmed by Allied ground observers, was 127. His first victory came on 6 August 1916, when he forced down a Rumpler while flying a Caudron G IV reconnaissance and bombing biplane. His second victory, gained on 17 March 1917, was against one of five attacking Albatros fighters. This second confirmed victory led to his transfer to the 'Cigognes' group a month later. On 9 May 1918 he achieved no fewer than six confirmed 'kills'—including three two-seaters destroyed in 45 s, the three wrecks being found in a radius of 1200 ft (365 m). On 26 September he again shot down six aircraft, comprising a two-seater, four Fokker D VIIs, and an Albatros D V. Fonck's last victory was over a leaflet-dropping two-seater on 1 November 1918. Fonck died peacefully in his sleep at his Paris home on 18 June 1953.

**The greatest ace of the First World War**, in terms of confirmed aerial victories, was Rittmeister (Cavalry Captain) Manfred, Freiherr von Richthofen—the so-called 'Red Baron'. The eldest son of an aristocratic Silesian family, he was born on 2 May 1892 and was killed in action on 21 April 1918, by which time he had been credited with 80 victories, had been awarded his country's highest decoration, commanded the élite unit of the Imperial German Air Service (Luftstreitkräfte), and was the object of great adulation in his homeland and an ungrudging respect among his enemies. Early in the war, Richthofen served on the Eastern Front as an officer in Uhlan Regiment Nr 1 'Kaiser Alexander III, and transferred to the Air Service in May 1915. His first operational posting was to Feldfliegerabteilung Nr 69; with this unit he flew two-seater reconnaissance machines in the East – without apparently any unusual skill. In September 1916 he was selected for Jagdstaffel 2, the scout squadron led by Oswald Boelcke (q.v.). His first officially recognized victory was over an FE2b of No. 11 Squadron, RFC; Richthofen, flying an Albatros D II scout, shot down this aircraft on 17 September 1916; the crew, 2nd Lt L. B. F. Morris and Lt T. Rees, lost their lives. Richthofen continued to score steadily, and in January 1917 was awarded the coveted 'Blue Max', the Ordre pour le Mérite. He was given command of Jagdstaffel 11, and characteristically maintained a collection of silver cups, each engraved with the particulars of a victim. The silversmith's most lucrative month was 'Bloody April' of 1917, when Richthofen shot down 21 aircraft. In June 1917 he was given command of a new formation, Jagdgeschwader Nr 1, comprising Jastas 4, 6, 10 and 11; this group of squadrons became known to the Allies as 'Richthofen's Flying Circus', because of the bright colours of their aircraft. Contrary to popular legend Richthofen did not invariably fly a personal all-red aircraft but a variety of Albatros D IIIs and Fokker Dr Is, some of which were painted blood-red all over and some only partially red. Richthofen's death on 21 April 1918 has been the subject of controversy ever since. He was flying Fokker Dr I number 425/17 when he became engaged in combat with Sopwith Camels of No. 209 Squadron, RAF, over Sailly-le-Sec. At one point, 2nd Lt W. R. May was flying at low altitude with Richthofen in pursuit and the aircraft of Capt A. Roy Brown, DSC, diving to attack the German. Brown opened fire in an attempt to save the inexperienced May from the enemy ace, and Richthofen's triplane was then seen to break away and crash-land. Richthofen was found dead in his cockpit with a bullet wound in the chest. At about the same time as Brown attacked, machine-gunners of an Australian Field Artillery battery fired at Richthofen's aircraft. Although Brown was officially credited with the 'kill', it has never been established who fired the fatal shot.

During the Second World War the greatest altitude from which anyone jumped without a parachute and survived was 22 000 ft (6705 m). In January 1942 Lt I. M. Chisov of the USSR fell from an Ilyushin Il-4 which had been

badly damaged. He struck the ground a glancing blow on the edge of a snow-covered ravine and slid to the bottom, sustaining a fractured pelvis and severe spinal damage. It is estimated that the human body reaches 99 per cent of its low-level terminal velocity after falling 1880 ft (573 m); this is 117–125 mph (188–201 km/h) at normal atmospheric pressure in a random posture, but up to 185 mph (298 km/h) in a head-down position. **The British record** stands at 18 000 ft (5490 m) set by Flt Sgt Nicholas Stephen Alkemade, RAF, who jumped from a blazing Lancaster bomber over Germany on 23 March 1944. His headlong fall was broken by a fir tree, and he landed without a broken bone in an 18 in (46 cm) snow-bank.

**The greatest decoration for gallantry to be given to a member of the Royal Canadian Navy during the Second World War** was the Victoria Cross awarded posthumously to Lt Robert Hampton Gray of the RCN Volunteer Reserve. Attached to the Fleet Air Arm, and as the pilot of a Vought Corsair fighter-bomber, he was killed on 9 August 1945 while making an attack on a Japanese destroyer in the bay of Onagawa Wan. This occurred after the two atomic bomb attacks on Japan and only a few days before the Japanese surrender; Gray was thus the recipient of the last Victoria Cross to be won during the Second World War, and his was also the only one of the war awarded to a member of the RCN.

**The greatest altitude from which anyone has fallen without a parachute and survived** is 33 330 ft (10 160 m). This occurred on 26 January 1972 when a Douglas DC-9 airliner of Jugoslovenski Aerotransport exploded and was destroyed over the Czechoslovak village of Serbska Kamenice. Air hostess Vesna Vulovic survived the fall, suffering a 27 day coma and many broken bones which enforced a 16 month stay in hospital.

*Most:*

**France's second most successful pilot of the First World War** was Capitaine Georges Marie Ludovic Jules Guynemer, who served in the 'Cigognes' group with Escadrille MS3/N3/SPA3 and achieved the first of his 54 confirmed victories on 19 July 1915 while in a Morane-Saulnier Parasol. He failed to return from a flight over Poelcapelle (Belgium) on 11 September 1917 and

Georges Marie Ludovic Jules Guynemer at Verdun in 1916.

he has no known grave. However, although it is often asserted that no trace of his body or aircraft has ever been found, the records of the 413th Württemberg Regiment, which held that section of the German line on the date in question, show that both were indeed found and identified and that various papers on Guynemer at the time were removed. There is some question as to the identity of the pilot who shot down Guynemer, although usually Leutnant Kurt Wisseman, Jagdstaffel 3, is credited. Wisseman himself was shot down and killed on 28 September 1917.

**The third of France's great trio of First World War aces** was Lt Charles Eugène Jules Marie Nungesser of Escadrilles VB. 106 and N. 65, with which he scored 45 confirmed victories and survived all that conflict could offer. After joining a Hussar regiment at the beginning of the war he later transferred to the *Service Aéronautique*, being posted to VB. 106 on 8 April 1915. His first combat victory was not scored until the autumn of 1915, and shortly after that event he joined Escadrille N. 65. The first victory in his new unit came on 28 November, and the remainder of his wartime career was a mixture of brilliant successes and long periods in hospital. Many of his total of 45 kills were gained during a period when he was in intense pain, unable to walk, and had to be carried to and from his aircraft. In 1927 he attempted an East–West Atlantic crossing, in the Levasseur P.L.8 *Le Oiseau Blanc*. On 8 May he took off for the transatlantic attempt, together with his navigator Capitaine Coli, crossing over Le Havre at 06.48 hours, but neither of the men was ever seen again.

**Britain's most successful fighter pilot in the First World War** was Major Edward 'Mick'

Mannock. His score of combat victories stands at 73, but he is known to have insisted that several additional victories justly attributable to him should be credited to other pilots. Born on 24 May 1887, the son of a soldier, Mannock was working in Constantinople when the war broke out, and was interned by the Turks. He was repatriated in April 1915 on health grounds and rejoined the Territorial Army medical unit to which he had belonged before leaving the country. He was commissioned in the Royal Engineers on 1 April 1916 and finally transferred to the Royal Flying Corps in August 1916. His acceptance for flying duties was remarkable as he suffered from astigmatism in the left eye, and must have passed his medical by a ruse. He gained his Pilot's Certificate on 28 November 1916, and was posted to No. 40 Squadron, France, on 6 April 1917, the unit being equipped at that time with Nieuport scouts. He shot down a balloon on 7 May, and on 7 June scored his first victory over an aeroplane. Returning from leave in July he shot down two-seaters on the 12th and 13th of that month, and his Military Cross was gazetted. He was promoted Captain, and took command of a flight. His score grew rapidly, as he was possessed by a bitter and ruthless hatred of the enemy, uncommon among his contemporaries. His care of the pilots under his command, however, was irreproachable, and he has been judged the greatest patrol leader of any combatant air force. In January 1918 he returned to England to take enforced leave, by which time his score stood at 23. He returned to France in March as a Flt Cdr in the newly formed No. 74 ('Tiger') Squadron, equipped with the SE5a, and in his three months with the unit added 39 to his score. He was promoted Major in mid-June, and was given leave before taking command of No. 85 Squadron. With No. 85 he raised his score to 73 before being shot down on 26 July by German ground fire that hit his petrol tank. His grave has never been found and it was nearly a year later that he was awarded a posthumous Victoria Cross.

**The second most successful British and Empire pilot** of the war was a Canadian, William Avery Bishop, born on 8 February 1894 in Ontario. While in England as a cavalry subaltern in the Canadian Mounted Rifles in 1915, Bishop decided he would see more action as a pilot, and transferred to the Royal Flying Corps in July of that year. He flew in France as an observer with

No. 21 Squadron for several months, and was hospitalized as the result of a crash-landing and frostbite. He trained subsequently as a pilot and joined No. 60 Squadron in March 1917. The squadron was at that time equipped with Nieuport 17 scouts, an aircraft which Bishop was to handle brilliantly. On 25 March he scored his first victory over an Albatros and subsequently gained many honours including the Victoria Cross for his action over an enemy airfield on 2 June. When his score reached 45, Bishop was promoted Major and awarded a Bar to his DSO. Late in 1917 and early in 1918 he carried out a number of non-combat duties, including recruiting drives in Canada and instructing at an aerial gunnery school. He was subsequently given command of No.85 Squadron, flying SE5as, and went back to France on 22 May 1918. After gaining 27 more victories, he was recalled to England, and never flew operationally again. His DFC was gazetted on 2 July. Bishop remained in the service, rising to the rank of Honorary Air Marshal in the Royal Canadian Air Force. He died in Florida, USA, in September 1956.

**The most successful fighter pilot of the Royal Naval Air Service** during the First World War, and, with 60 confirmed victories, third in the overall British and Empire aces' list, was Raymond Collishaw. A member of No. 3 Wing, RNAS, he gained his first air victory on 12 October 1916. In February 1917 he joined a scout unit, No. 3 (Naval) Squadron, and in April was posted to No. 10 (Naval) Squadron as commander of 'B' Flight. Equipped with Sopwith Triplanes, the 'Black Flight' of 'Naval Ten' earned a reputation as one of the most formidable Allied units of the war. The Flight was composed entirely of Canadians; their aircraft were decorated with black paint, and named *Black Maria* (Collishaw), *Black Prince*, *Black Sheep*, *Black Roger* and *Black Death*. Between May and July 1917 the Flight destroyed 87 enemy aircraft, and during June Collishaw himself shot down 16 in 27 days. After the Armistice, Collishaw commanded No. 47 Squadron in the Russian campaign of 1919–20, where he destroyed two more aircraft. He remained in the Royal Air Force, serving in the Second World War and reaching the rank of Air Vice-Marshal, CB, with the DSO and Bar, DSC, DFC and Croix de Guerre, as well as both military and civil grades of the OBE.

**The most successful American pilot of the First World War** was Capt Edward Vernon Rickenbacker, with 26 confirmed aerial victories. Born on 8 October 1890 in Columbus, Ohio, Rickenbacker made a considerable name for himself between 1910 and 1917 as one of America's leading racing motorists. While in England in 1917, he became interested in flying and when America entered the war he returned home and advanced the idea of a squadron composed entirely of racing drivers. The idea did not arouse official interest, but a meeting with Gen Pershing in Washington led to Rickenbacker's enlistment and sent him to France as the General's chauffeur. In August 1917 he transferred to the Aviation Section, and his mechanical expertise led to a posting to the 3rd Aviation Instruction Center at Issoudun as Chief Engineering Officer. In his own time he completed advanced flying and gunnery courses, and on 4 March 1918 finally secured a transfer to the 94th Aero Squadron—the 'Hat-in-the-Ring' squadron commanded by Raoul Lufbery, the Escadrille Lafayette ace. With Lufbery and Douglas Campbell, Rickenbacker flew **the first American patrol over enemy lines** on 19 March, and on 29 April he shot down his first victim, an Albatros scout. On 30 May his fifth victory qualified him as an ace, but it was to be his last for four months. An ear infection put him in hospital and convalescence until mid-September, when he returned to the squadron as a Captain and Flight Commander. He took over command of the 94th on 25 September, and continued to score heavily until the Armistice. Capt Rickenbacker was active in the automobile and airline industries between the wars, and was largely responsible for building up Eastern Air Lines, of which corporation he became Chairman in 1953. During the Second World War he toured widely, visiting Air Force units abroad and undertaking various missions for his Government. In the course of a flight over the Pacific his aircraft was forced to ditch, and Rickenbacker survived 21 days on a life-raft before being picked up. He remained active in various public fields until his death on 23 July 1973, at the age of 82. His many American and foreign decorations included his country's highest award for gallantry, the Congressional Medal of Honor.

**Following a most courageous action on 16 August 1940, Flt Lt James Brindley Nicholson, RAF, became the recipient of the only Victoria**

Cross awarded to a member of RAF Fighter Command. A flight commander of No. 249 (Hurricane) Squadron, Nicholson was leading a section of three fighters on patrol near Southampton, Hampshire, when he sighted enemy aircraft ahead. Before he could complete the attack his section was 'bounced' from above and behind by German fighters which shot down one Hurricane and set Nicholson's aircraft ablaze. With flames sweeping up through his cockpit, the British pilot remained at his controls long enough to complete an attack on an enemy aircraft which had flown into his sights, and then baled out. Meanwhile, a detachment of soldiers on the ground, seeing Nicholson and his wingman descending on parachutes and believing them to be enemy paratroops, opened fire with rifles. Nicholson was hit but survived his wounds and burns; but his colleague was dead when he reached the ground (whether or not he was killed by rifle-fire has never been established).

**The most successful fighter pilot of the Imperial Japanese Navy Air Force** during the Second World War was Warrant Officer Hiroyoshi Nishizawa who, before he was ironically killed as a passenger in a military transport aircraft on 25 October 1944, had accumulated a total of 87 combat victories.

**The most successful fighter pilot of the Japanese Army Air Force** during the Second World War was Master Sergeant Satoshi Anabuki. At the war's end his victories totalled 51, 35 of them gained over Burma during the first five months of 1943. Then, on 8 October 1943, he destroyed five aircraft, shooting down two Lockheed P-38s and two Consolidated B-24s, and destroying a third B-24 by ramming it, an action which he survived.

**The most successful fighter pilot of the United States Marine Corps** during the Second World War was Lt Colonel Gregory Boyington, formerly with Brigadier-General Claire Chennault's 'Flying Tigers' defending the Burma Road. As commander of Marine Squadron VMF-214 he added 22 victories to the six gained with the 'Flying Tigers' before being shot down on 3 January 1944. He survived crashing into the sea, was picked up by a Japanese submarine, and remained a prisoner of war until VJ-Day.

**Almost certainly the most unusual response to a valorous action** was that given to Lt Michael

Devyatayev, a Soviet fighter pilot shot down by the Luftwaffe over Lvov on 13 July 1944, who is the only known pilot who has been both gaoled and awarded his country's highest gallantry decoration for the same exploit. Taken prisoner by the Germans, Devyatayev escaped, seized a Heinkel He 111 bomber and flew nine other escapees back to Soviet-held territory. On regaining his freedom, the 23-year-old pilot was gaoled under the USSR criminal code which labelled him a traitor for having been taken prisoner. Nine years later, in 1953, he was freed under an amnesty prevailing at the time, and in 1958 was made Hero of the Soviet Union and awarded the Order of Lenin and Gold Star Medal.

**The most successful fighter pilot in the world, and Germany's leading ace in the Second World War**, was Maj Erich Hartmann of Jadgeschwader 52. The first of only two fighter pilots in the world to score 300 victories, the achievement brought him into a select band of men—numbering 27 only—who wore the Diamonds to the Knight's Cross, the award being made on 25 July 1944. Hartmann eventually surrendered to American forces in Czechoslovakia during May 1945, by which time he had scored a total of 352 victories.

**The most successful German fighter pilot in combat against the Western Allies during the Second World War** was Hauptmann Hans-Joachim Marseille. In April 1941 he was posted to I Gruppe Jagdgeschwader 27 in Libya, and it was in desert warfare that he became a master. On 2 September 1942 he received the Diamonds to his Knight's Cross. Known as the 'Star of Africa', he died on 30 September 1942 when he baled out of his Messerschmitt Bf 109G but his parachute failed to open. Then only 22 years old, he had been credited with 158 victories, all of them gained in combat against the RAF and Commonwealth air forces.

**The most successful English fighter pilot of the Second World War** was Gp Capt James Edgar 'Johnnie' Johnson, credited with 38 confirmed aerial victories over German aircraft. Johnson remained in the RAF after the war, retiring finally with the rank of Air Vice-Marshal in 1966.

**The most successful American fighter pilot of the Second World War** was Maj Richard Ira Bong, whose 40 confirmed aerial victories are unsurpassed by any American military pilot of any war. Born at Superior, Wisconsin, on 24 September 1920, Bong enlisted as a Flying Cadet on 29 May 1941. After flying training at Tulare and Gardner Fields, California, and Luke Field, Arizona, he received his 'wings' and a commission (all American military pilots were automatically commissioned) on 9 January 1942. In May he was posted to Hamilton Field, California, for combat training on the Lockheed P-38 Lightning twin-engined fighter, and subsequently joined the 9th Fighter Squadron of the 49th Fighter Group, then based in Australia. All of his 40 victories had been scored by late 1944, in the Pacific theatre of war. General George C. Kenney, his commanding officer, ordered him back to the United States in December 1944, with a recommendation for the Congressional Medal of Honor—which award was subsequently granted. Bong became a test pilot for Lockheed at Burbank, California; on 6 August 1945, the day the world's first atomic bomb was dropped on Hiroshima, he died when the engine of his P-80 jet failed. Many of his victories were gained while flying the P-38J *Marge* named after his fiancée.

**The most successful Soviet woman fighter pilot of the Second World War,**[*] and thus presumably the most successful woman fighter pilot in the world, served with the mixed-sex 73rd Guards Fighter Regiment. She was Jr Lt Lydia Lityvak, who was killed in action on 1 August 1943 at the age of 22, with a total of 12 confirmed victories while flying Yak fighters.

[*]During the Second World War, most Russian women combat pilots served with the 122nd Air Group of the Soviet Air Force. This all-female unit comprised the 586th Fighter Air Regiment, the 587th Bomber Air Regiment and the 588th Night Bomber Air Regiment. The 586th IAP (Istebitelnyi aviatsionnyi polk = fighter air regiment) was formed at Engels, on the Volga River, in October 1941; it was commanded by Maj Tamara Aleksandrovna Kazarinova. The pilots of this unit flew a total of 4419 operational sorties, took part in 125 air combats, and were credited with 38 confirmed victories. The unit flew Yak-1, -7B and -9 fighters. During the Second World War, 30 Russian airwoman received the gold star of a Hero of the Soviet Union. It is believed that 22 of them served with the 588th/46th Guards Night Bomber Air Regiment, which was equipped with Po-2 biplanes.

**During the Korean War one of the most courageous and self-sacrificing actions** was that of Maj George A. Davis Jr of the USAF. On 10 February 1952 Davis was flying a North American F-86 Sabre, in company with a wingman, when he

Maj Richard Ira Bong. (US Air Force)

spotted a formation of 12 Mikoyan MiG-15s preparing to 'jump' a force of USAF fighter-bombers at lower level. Without hesitation he attacked the enemy formation, destroying two of their number before being hit and crashing to his death. This courageous action proved sufficient to prevent the MiGs from attacking the fighter-bombers, which completed their mission successfully, and the self-sacrifice of Davis was recognized by the posthumous award of the Medal of Honor.

**The most successful US Marine Corps pilot of the Korean War** was Maj John Bolt who on 11 July 1953, while flying a North American F-86 Sabre of the USAF's 39th Fighter Interceptor Squadron, destroyed two MiG-15s to bring his total score to six. He thus became the Marine Corps' only ace of the Korean War. The US Navy's only ace of this war was Lt Guy P. Bordelon who gained his 'ace' status by the destruction of his fifth enemy aircraft, a Yakovlev Yak-18, on 27 July 1953.

## *The Great Air Fighters of the First World War*

### The six most successful British and Empire pilots of the First World War
*Bar to award

| | |
|---|---|
| Maj Edward Mannock, VC, DSO**, MC .. | 73 |
| Maj W. A. Bishop, VC, DSO*, MC, DFC, LD'H, CDEG ..................... | 72 |
| Maj R. Collishaw, DSO*, DSC, DFC, CDEG .......................... | 60 |

Maj J. T. B. McCudden, VC, DSO*, MC*,
MM, C D E G . . . . . . . . . . . . . . . . . . . . . .  57
Capt A. W. Beauchamp-Proctor, VC, DSO,
MC*, DFC  . . . . . . . . . . . . . . . . . . . . . .  54
Capt D. R. MacLaren, DSO, MC*, DFC,
L D'H, C D E G  . . . . . . . . . . . . . . . . . .  54

*In addition to the above*
8 pilots gained between 40 and 52 victories
11 pilots gained between 30 and 39 victories
57 pilots gained between 20 and 29 victories
226 pilots gained between 10 and 19 victories
476 pilots gained between  5 and  9 victories
Thus by the 'five victory' convention, the British
and Empire air forces of the First World War produced 784 aces.

## The six most successful German pilots of the First World War

Rittmeister Manfred, Freiherr von
Richthofen . . . . . . . . . . . . . . . . . . . . . .  80
Oberleutnant Ernst Udet . . . . . . . . . . . . . .  62
Oberleutnant Erich Loewenhardt . . . . . . . .  53
Leutnant Werner Voss  . . . . . . . . . . . . . . .  48
Leutnant Fritz Rumey  . . . . . . . . . . . . . . .  45
Hauptmann Rudolph Berthold . . . . . . . . . .  44
All of these pilots were decorated with the Ordre
Pour le Mérite.

*With his head in bandages, Rittmeister Manfred Freiherr von Richthofen is honoured by the Kaiser.*

*In addition to the above*
6 pilots gained between 40 and 43 victories
21 pilots gained between 30 and 39 victories
38 pilots gained between 20 and 29 victories
96 pilots gained between 10 and 19 victories
196 pilots gained between  5 and  9 victories
Thus by the 'five victory' convention, the Imperial
German air force of the First World War produced 363 aces.

## The four most successful French pilots of the First World War

Capitaine René P. Fonck . . . . . . . . . . . . . .  75
Capitaine Georges M. L. J. Guynemer . . . . .  54
Lieutenant Charles E. J. M. Nungesser . . . . .  45
Capitaine Georges F. Madon . . . . . . . . . . .  41

*In addition to the above*
2 pilots gained between 30 and 39 victories
8 pilots gained between 20 and 29 victories
39 pilots gained between 10 and 19 victories
105 pilots gained between  5 and  9 victories
Thus the French air forces of the First World War
produced 158 aces.

## The four most successful American pilots of the First World War

Capt Edward V. Rickenbacker, CMH, DSC,
L D'H, C D E G . . . . . . . . . . . . . . . . . . . .  26
2nd Lt Frank Luke Jr, CMH, DSC, C D E G  21
Maj G. Raoul Lufbery, L D'H, MM, C D E G,
MC . . . . . . . . . . . . . . . . . . . . . . . . . . .  17
Lt G. A. Vaughn Jr, DSC, DFC . . . . . . . . . .  13

*In addition to the above*
84 pilots gained between 5 and 12 victories; thus
America produced 88 aces during the First World
War. (It should be noted that the above figures
include pilots who served with foreign air forces
only, pilots who served with the American forces
only, and pilots with mixed service, and all
victories gained by these pilots irrespective of
service.)

## The four most successful Italian pilots of the First World War

Maggiore Francesco Baracca . . . . . . . . . . .  34
Tenente Silvio Scaroni . . . . . . . . . . . . . . .  26
Tenente-Colonnello Pier Ruggiero Piccio . .  24
Tenente Flavio Torello Baracchini . . . . . . .  21

*In addition*
39 pilots gained between 5 and 20 victories; thus Italy produced 43 aces during World War I.

## The four most successful Austro–Hungarian pilots of the First world War
Hauptmann Godwin Brumowski . . . . .    35–40
Offizierstellvertreter Julius Arigi . . . . . .    26–32
Oberleutnant Frank Linke-Crawford . .    27–30
Oberleutnant Benno Fiala, Ritter von
    Fernbrugg . . . . . . . . . . . . . . . . . . .    27–29

(It should be noted that Austrian, Hungarian and Italian sources disagree as to the absolute accuracy of these pilots' scores.)

*In addition to the above*
Approximately 26 pilots gained between 5 and 19 victories. Thus it can be stated with reasonable certainty that the Austro–Hungarian Imperial air forces produced between 25 and 30 aces during the First World War.

## The four most successful Imperial Russian pilots of the First World War
Staff Capt A. A. Kazakov, DSO, MC, DFC,
   L D'H. . . . . . . . . . . . . . . . . . . . . . . . . .    17
Capt P. V. d'Argueeff. . . . . . . . . . . . . . . .    15
Lt Cdr A. P. Seversky . . . . . . . . . . . . . . . .    13
Lt I. W. Smirnoff . . . . . . . . . . . . . . . . . . . .    12

*In addition to the above*
Either 14 or 15 pilots gained between 5 and 11 victories; thus the Imperial Russian air forces produced either 18 or 19 known aces during the First World War. Other Russian pilots became aces, but the records are incomplete.

## The four most successful Belgian pilots of the First World War
2nd Lt Willy Coppens, DSO . . . . . . . . . . .    37
Adj André de Meulemeester . . . . . . . . . . .    11
2nd Lt Edmond Thieffry . . . . . . . . . . . . . .    10
Capt Fernand Jacquet, DFC . . . . . . . . . . .    7

Confirmation of aerial victories during the First World War was subject to the most stringent regulations, and this has led to confusion over the actual number of victories achieved by various pilots. The figures quoted earlier are, with certain exceptions, those accepted officially as accurate in the countries of origin, and refer only to confirmed victories within the letter of the regulations. They are thus more liable to err on the side of under rather than overstatement.

**The numbers of aircraft shot down by fighter pilots of the Second World War** varied much more widely than was the case in the First World War, due to the enormous differences in conditions and standards of equipment in the various combat areas. Comparison of the lists of national top-scoring fighter pilots reveals the almost incredible superiority of German pilots in terms of confirmed victories—i.e. Major Erich Hartmann, the Luftwaffe's leading ace, is credited with nearly nine times as many victories as the leading British and American pilots, and 35 Germans are credited with scores in excess of 150.

Since the end of the war there have been persistent attempts to discredit these scores; but by any reasonable criterion, the figures must now be accepted as accurate. The Luftwaffe's confirmation procedure was just as rigorous as that followed by Allied air forces, and the quoted figures are those prepared at unit level and were not subject to manipulation by the Propaganda Ministry. The main reasons for the gulf between German and Allied scores were the different conditions of service and the special circumstances which existed on the Russian Front in 1941 and 1942. In Allied air forces an operational tour by a fighter pilot was almost invariably followed by a posting to a second-line establishment for several months. This process of rotating pilots to areas where they could recover from the strain of prolonged combat operations was unknown in the Luftwaffe; apart from very short periods of leave, a German fighter pilot was effectively on combat operations from the day of his first posting until the day his career ended—in death, serious injury or capture. The Luftwaffe fighter pilot's career was thus, in real terms, about twice as long as his RAF or USAAF counterpart.

When Germany invaded the Soviet Union in June 1941, the Russian Air Forces were equipped with very large numbers of obsolescent aircraft. They had no fighter whose speed and armament approached the performance of the Messerschmitt Bf 109E and Bf 109F, and their bombers in squadron service were markedly inferior to contemporary European designs. Thus, the Luftwaffe was presented with large numbers of easy targets—the perfect environment for the development of a fighter pilot's skill and confidence. The situation did not become significantly more challenging for many months, by which time many of the Jagdflieger had learned their trade so well that they retained the initiative. Despite this factor, one is left with the inescapable conclusion that Germany produced a group of officers who were fighter pilots of exceptional skill and determination.

The pilots who scored **100 or more victories against the Western Allies** in northern Europe, southern Europe, the Mediterranean area and North Africa were as follows (Western victories only, in cases of mixed service):

Hauptmann Hans-Joachim Marseille . . . . .   158
Oberstleutnant Heinz Bär . . . . . . . . . . . .   124
Oberstleutnant Kurt Bühligen . . . . . . . . .   112
Generalleutnant Adolf Galland . . . . . . . . .   104
Major Joachim Müncheberg . . . . . . . . . .   102
Oberstleutnant Egon Mayer . . . . . . . . . .   102
Major Werner Schroer  . . . . . . . . . . . . . .   102
Oberst Josef Priller . . . . . . . . . . . . . . . . .   101

These figures become even more impressive if one reflects on the fact that Marseille achieved 151 of his victories between April 1941 and September 1942; and that Galland did virtually no combat flying between November 1941 and the end of 1944, while he occupied the post of General of Fighters.

Two categories of victories in northern Europe are worthy of special attention; those scored over heavy bombers, and those scored while flying jet aircraft. The achievements of the world's first generation of jet combat pilots are described elsewhere in this chapter. The Luftwaffe placed great value on the destruction of the very heavily armed four-engined Boeing Fortress and Consolidated Liberator bombers which formed the United States 8th Air Force's main equipment in the massive daylight bombing offensive of 1943–5. Usually flying in dense formations protected by an enormous combined firepower—and, in the later months, by superb escort fighters—these large aircraft were obviously far more difficult to destroy than smaller ones. The leading 'heavy bomber specialists' among Germany's daylight home defence pilots included:

Oberleutnant Herbert Rollwage . . . . . . . . .   44
Oberst Walther Dahl . . . . . . . . . . . . . . . . .   36
Major Werner Schroer  . . . . . . . . . . . . . . .   26
Hauptmann Hugo Frey . . . . . . . . . . . . . . .   26
Oberstleutnant Egon Mayer . . . . . . . . . . .   25
Oberstleutnant Kurt Bühligen . . . . . . . . . .   24
Oberstleutnant Heinz Bär . . . . . . . . . . . . .   21
Hauptmann Hans-Heinrich König . . . . . . .   20
Hauptmann Heinz Knoke . . . . . . . . . . . . .   19

## The Great Air Fighters of the Second World War

**The most successful fighter pilots of the Second World War, by nationality,** are listed below: all scores are levelled down to the nearest unit: British Gallantry decorations are quoted:

| Country of origin | | Aircraft destroyed in combat |
|---|---|---|
| Australia | Gp Capt Clive R. Caldwell, DSO, DFC* . . . . . . . . . . . . | 28 |
| Austria | Maj Walter Nowotny . . . . . . . | 258 |
| Belgium | Flt Lt Vicki Ortmans, DFC . . . | 11 |
| Canada | Sqn Ldr George F. Buerling, DSO, DFC, DFM* . . . . . . . | 31 |
| Czecho-slovakia | Sgt Josef Frantisek, DFM . . . . | 28 |
| Denmark | Gp Capt Kaj Birksted . . . | either 8 or 10 |
| Finland | F/Mstr E. I. Juutualainen . . . . | 94 |
| France | Sqn Ldr Pierre H. Clostermann, DFC* . . . . . . . . . . . . . . . . . . | 19 |
| Germany | Maj Erich Hartmann . . . . . . . | 352 |
| Hungary | 2nd Lt Dezjö Szentgyörgyi . . . | 43 |
| Ireland | Wg Cdr Brendan E. Finucane, DSO, DFC** . . . . . . . . . . . . | 32 |
| Italy | Maj Adriano Vinconti . . . . . . | 26 |
| Japan | Sub-Officer Hiroyoshi Nishizawa . . . . . . . . . . . . . . | 103 |
| Netherlands | Lt Col van Arkel . . . . | 12 V-1s and 5 |
| New Zealand | Wg Cdr Colin F. Gray, DSO, DFC** . . . . . . . . . . | 27 |
| Norway | Flt Lt Svein Heglund . . . . | either 14 or 16 |
| Poland | Jan Poniatowski (rank unknown) . . . . . . . . . . . . | 36 |
| Romania | Capt Prince Constantine Cantacuzino . . . . . . . . . . . . | 60 |
| South Africa | Sqn Ldr M. T. St J. Pattle, DFC* . . . . . . . . . . . . . . . . | 41 |
| United Kingdom | Gp Capt James E. Johnson, DSO**, DFC* . . . . . . . . . . | 38 |
| United States | Maj Richard I. Bong . . . . . . . | 40 |
| USSR | Guards Col Ivan N. Kozhedub | 62 |

*Bar to award.

**Fighter pilots serving with the Royal Air force during the Second World War who achieved 25 or more confirmed aerial victories** (countries of origin indicated in parentheses):

Sqn Ldr M. T. St J. Pattle, DFC*  . . . . . 41   (SA)

Gp Capt J. E. Johnson, DSO**,
DFC* ...................... 38   (UK)
Gp Capt A. G. Malan, DSO*, DFC* .. 35   (SA)
Wg Cdr B. E. Finucane, DSO, DFC** . 32   (Ir)
Sqn Ldr G. F. Buerling, DSO, DFC,
DFM* ...................... 31   (Ca)
Wg Cdr J. R. D. Braham, DSO**
DFC**, AFC .................. 29   (UK)
Wg Cdr R. R. S. Tuck, DSO, DFC** .. 29   (UK)
Sqn Ldr N. F. Duke, DSO, DFC**,
AFC ...................... 28   (UK)
Gp Capt C. R. Caldwell, DSO, DFC* . 28   (Au)
Gp Capt F. H. R. Carey, DFC**, AFC,
DFM ...................... 28   (UK)
Sqn Ldr J. H. Lacey, DFM* ......... 28   (UK)
Wg Cdr C. F. Gray, DSO, DFC** .... 27   (NZ)
Flt Lt E. S. Lock, DSO, DFC* ....... 26   (UK)
Wg Cdr L. C. Wade, DSO, DFC** ... 25   (US)

*Bar to award.

**Fighter pilots serving with the United States air forces during the Second World War who achieved 25 or more confirmed aerial victories:**

USAAF:

Maj Richard I. Bong (CMH) ............   40
Maj T. B. McGuire (CMH) .............   38
Col F. S. Gabreski ..................   31
Lt Col R. S. Johnson..................   28
Col C. H. MacDonald .................   27
Maj G. E. Preddy .....................   26

USN:

Capt D. McCampbell..................   34

USMC:

Maj J. J. Foss........................   26
Lt R. M. Hanson......................   25
Lt Col G. Boyington ..................   22

(Lt Col Boyington is known to have destroyed an additional six enemy aircraft while serving with the Air Volunteer Group under Chinese command.)

*Luftwaffe fighter pilots with 150 or more confirmed victories during the Second World War and the Spanish Civil War*

✠🦅✂◆ = Knight's Cross with Oak Leaves, Swords and Diamonds
✠🦅✂ = Knight's Cross with Oak Leaves and Swords
✠🦅 = Knight's Cross with Oak Leaves
✠ = Knight's Cross of the Iron Cross

| Name, rank, decorations | Units | Total score | Day/Night | Fronts | Four engined | With jet a/c |
|---|---|---|---|---|---|---|
| Major Erich Hartmann ✠🦅✂◆ | JG 52 | **352** | 352/0 | 352 E | 0 | 0 |
| Major Gerhard Barkhorn ✠🦅✂ | JG 52, 6, JV 44 | **302** | 301/1 | 301 E | 0 | ? |
| Major Günther Rall ✠🦅✂ | JG 52, 11, 300 | **275** | 275/0 | 3 W, 272 E | ? | 0 |
| Oberleutnant Otto Kittel ✠🦅✂ | JG 54 | ***267** | 267/0 | 267 E | 0 | 0 |
| Major Walter Nowotny ✠🦅✂◆ | JG 54, Kdo. Nowotny | **258** | 258/0 | 255 E, 3 W | *1 | 3 |
| Major Wilhelm Batz ✠🦅✂ | JG 52 | **237** | 237/0 | 232 E, 5 W | 2 | 0 |
| Major Erich Rudorffer ✠🦅✂ | JG 2, 54, 7 | **222** | 222/0 | 136 E, 60 W, 26 Afr | 10 | 12 |
| Oberstleutnant Heinz Bär ✠🦅✂ | JG 51, 77, 1, 3, JV 44 | **220** | 220/0 | 96 E, 79 W, 45 Afr | *21 | 16 |
| Oberst Hermann Graf ✠🦅✂◆ | JG 51, 52, 50, 11, 52 | **212** | 212/0 | 202 E, 10 W | 10 | 0 |
| Major Theodor Weissenberger ✠🦅 | JG 77, 5, 7 | **208** | 208/0 | 175 E, 33 W | ? | 8 |
| Oberstleutnant Hans Philipp ✠🦅✂ | JG 76, 54, 1 | **206** | 206/0 | 177 E, 29 W | 1 | 0 |
| Oberleutnant Walter Schuck ✠🦅 | JG 5, 7 | **206** | 206/0 | 198 E, 8 W | 4 | 8 |
| Major Heinrich Ehrler ✠🦅 | JG 5, 7 | ***204** | 204/0 | 204 E? | ? | ? |
| Oberleutnant Anton Hafner ✠🦅 | JG 51 | **204** | 204/0 | 184 E, 20 Afr | 5 | 0 |
| Hauptmann Helmut Lipfert ✠🦅 | JG 52, 53 | **203** | 203/0 | majority E, *4 W | 2 | 0 |
| Major Walter Krupinski ✠🦅 | JG 52, 5, 11, 26, JV 44 | **197** | 197/0 | 177 E, 20 W | 1 | ? |
| Major Anton Hackl ✠🦅✂ | JG 77, 11, 26, 300, 11 | **192** | 192/0 | 105 E, 87 W | 32 | 0 |
| Hauptmann Joachim Brendel ✠🦅 | JG 51 | **189** | 189/0 | 189 E | 0 | 0 |
| Hauptmann Max Stotz ✠🦅 | JG 54 | **189** | 189/0 | 173 E, 16 W | 0 | 0 |
| Hauptmann Joachim Kirschner ✠🦅 | JG 3, 27 | **188** | 188/0 | 167 E, 13 Gr, 6 W, 2 Malta | *2 | 0 |
| Major Kurt Brändle ✠🦅 | JG 53, 3 | **180** | 180/0 | 160 E, 20 W | 0 | 0 |
| Oberleutnant Günther Josten ✠🦅 | JG 51 | **178** | 178/0 | majority E | 1 | 0 |
| Oberst Johannes Steinhoff ✠🦅✂ | JG 26, 52, 77, 7, JV 44 | **176** | 176/0 | 148 E, 28 W & Afr | 4 | 6 |
| Oberleutnant Ernst-Wilhelm Reinert ✠🦅✂ | JG 77, 27 | **174** | 174/0 | 103 E, 51 Afr, 20 W | 2 | 0 |
| Hauptmann Günther Schack ✠🦅 | JG 51, 3 | **174** | 174/0 | 174 E | 0 | 0 |
| Hauptmann Emil Lang ✠🦅 | JG 54, 26 | **173** | 173/0 | 148 E, 25 W | ? | 0 |
| Hauptmann Heinz Schmidt ✠🦅 | JG 52 | **173** | 173/0 | 173 E | 0 | 0 |
| Major Horst Ademeit ✠🦅 | JG 54 | **166** | 166/0 | 165 E, 1 W | 0 | 0 |
| Oberst Wolf-Dietrich Wilcke ✠🦅✂ | JG 53, 3 | **162** | 162/0 | 137 E, 21 W, 4 Malta | 4 | 0 |
| Hauptmann Hans-Joachim Marseille ✠✂🦅◆ | JG 52, 27 | **158** | 158/0 | 151 Afr, 7 W | 0 | 0 |
| Hauptmann Heinrich Sturm ✠ | JG 52 | **157** | 157/0 | 157 E | 0 | 0 |
| Oberleutnant Gerhard Thyben ✠🦅 | JG 3, 54 | **157** | 157/0 | 152 E, 5 W | ? | 0 |
| Oberleutnant Hans Beisswenger ✠🦅 | JG 54 | **152** | 152/0 | 152 E | 0 | 0 |
| Leutnant Peter Düttmann ✠ | JG 52 | **150** | 150/0 | 150 E | 0 | 0 |
| Oberst Gordon Gollob ✠🦅✂◆ | ZG 76, JG 3, 77 | **150** | 150/0 | 144 E, 6 W | 0 | 0 |

E = Eastern Front; W = Europe; Afr = North Africa; Gr = Greece; * = at least

*Progressive world absolute speed records achieved by man in the atmosphere*

| Speed | | Pilot | Nationality | Aircraft | Location of achievement | Date |
|---|---|---|---|---|---|---|
| mph | km/h | | | | | |
| 34.03 | 54.77 | Paul Tissandier | France | Wright biplane | Pau, France | 20 May 1909 |
| 43.34 | 69.75 | Glenn Curtiss | USA | Herring-Curtiss biplane | Reims, France | 23 Aug 1909 |
| 46.17 | 74.30 | Louis Blériot | France | Blériot monoplane | Reims, France | 24 Aug 1909 |
| 47.84 | 76.99 | Louis Blériot | France | Blériot monoplane | Reims, France | 28 Aug 1909 |
| 48.20 | 77.57 | Hubert Latham | France | Antoinette monoplane | Nice, France | 23 Apr 1910 |
| 66.18 | 106.50 | Léon Morane | France | Blériot monoplane | Reims, France | 10 Jul 1910 |
| 68.18 | 109.73 | Alfred Léblanc | France | Blériot monoplane | Belmont Park, Long Island, USA | 29 Oct 1910 |
| 69.46 | 111.79 | Alfred Léblanc | France | Blériot monoplane | | 12 Apr 1911 |
| 74.40 | 119.74 | Édouard Nieuport | France | Nieuport biplane | | 11 May 1911 |
| 77.67 | 124.99 | Alfred Léblanc | France | Blériot monoplane | | 12 Jun 1911 |
| 80.80 | 130.04 | Édouard Nieuport | France | Nieuport biplane | Châlons, France | 16 Jun 1911 |
| 82.71 | 133.11 | Édouard Nieuport | France | Nieuport biplane | Châlons, France | 21 Jun 1911 |
| 90.18 | 145.13 | Jules Védrines | France | Deperdussin monoplane | Pau, France | 13 Jan 1912 |
| 100.21 | 161.27 | Jules Védrines | France | Deperdussin monoplane | Pau, France | 22 Feb 1912 |
| 100.99 | 162.53 | Jules Védrines | France | Deperdussin monoplane | Pau, France | 29 Feb 1912 |
| 103.64 | 166.79 | Jules Védrines | France | Deperdussin monoplane | Pau, France | 1 Mar 1912 |
| 104.32 | 167.88 | Jules Védrines | France | Deperdussin monoplane | Pau, France | 2 Mar 1912 |
| 106.10 | 170.75 | Jules Védrines | France | Deperdussin monoplane | | 13 Jul 1912 |
| 108.16 | 174.06 | Jules Védrines | France | Deperdussin monoplane | Chicago, Illinois, USA | 9 Sep 1912 |
| 111.72 | 179.79 | Maurice Prévost | France | Deperdussin monoplane | | 17 Jun 1913 |
| 119.22 | 191.87 | Maurice Prévost | France | Deperdussin monoplane | Reims, France | 27 Sep 1913 |
| 126.666 | 203.85 | Maurice Prévost | France | Deperdussin monoplane | Reims, France | 29 Sep 1913 |

The final entry above was the last world absolute speed record to be ratified by the FAI until 1920, more than a year after the end of the First World War.

*Louis Blériot. (Air Force)*

*Progressive world absolute speed records achieved by man in the atmosphere*

| mph | km/h | Pilot | Nationality | Aircraft | Location of achievement | Date |
|---|---|---|---|---|---|---|
| 171.01 | 275.22 | Sadi Lecointe | France | Nieuport-Delage 29 | Villacoublay, France | 7 Feb 1920 |
| 176.12 | 283.43 | Jean Casale | France | Blériot monoplane | Villacoublay, France | 28 Feb 1920 |
| 181.83 | 292.63 | Baron de Romanet | France | Spad biplane | Buc, France | 9 Oct 1920 |
| 184.51 | 296.94 | Sadi Lecointe | France | Nieuport-Delage 29 | Buc, France | 10 Oct 1920 |
| 187.95 | 302.48 | Sadi Lecointe | France | Nieuport-Delage 29 | Villacoublay, France | 20 Oct 1920 |
| 191.98 | 308.96 | Baron de Romanet | France | Spad biplane | Buc, France | 4 Nov 1920 |
| 194.49 | 313.00 | Sadi Lecointe | France | Nieuport-Delage 29 | Villacoublay, France | 12 Dec 1920 |
| 205.20 | 330.23 | Sadi Lecointe | France | Nieuport-Delage 29 | Villesauvage, France | 20 Sep 1922 |
| 211.89 | 341.00 | Sadi Lecointe | France | Nieuport-Delage 29 | Villesauvage, France | 21 Sep 1922 |
| 222.93 | 358.77 | Brig Gen W. A. Mitchell | USA | Curtiss HS D-12 | Detroit, Michigan, USA | 13 Oct 1922 |
| 233.00 | 374.95 | Sadi Lecointe | France | Nieuport-Delage 29 | Istres, France | 15 Feb 1923 |
| 236.54 | 380.67 | Lt R. L. Maughan | USA | Curtiss R-6 | Wright Field, Ohio, USA | 29 Mar 1923 |
| 255.40 | 411.04 | Lt A. Brown | USA | Curtiss HS D-12 | Mitchell Field, NY, USA | 2 Nov 1923 |
| 267.16 | 429.96 | Lt Alford J. Williams | USA | Curtiss R-2 C-1 | Mitchell Field, NY, USA | 4 Nov 1923 |
| 278.47 | 448.15 | Adj Chef A. Bonnet | France | Ferbois V-2 | Istres, France | 11 Dec 1924 |
| 297.83 | 479.21 | Maj Mario de Bernardi | Italy | Macchi M-52 | Venice, Italy | 4 Nov 1927 |
| 300.931 | 484.304 | Maj Mario de Bernardi | Italy | Macchi M-52bis | Venice, Italy | 22 Oct 1927 |
| 318.57 | 512.69 | Maj Mario de Bernardi | Italy | Macchi M-52bis | Venice, Italy | 30 Mar 1928 |
| 406.94 | 654.90 | Flt Lt G. H. Stainforth AFC | GB | Supermarine S6B | Ryde, IoW, England | 29 Sep 1931 |
| 423.82 | 682.078 | Warrant Officer F. Agello | Italy | Macchi-Castoldi 72 | Lago di Garda, Italy | 10 Apr 1933 |
| 440.60 | 709.07 | Lt F. Agello | Italy | Macchi-Castoldi 72 | Lago di Garda, Italy | 23 Oct 1934 |
| 463.82 | 746.45 | Flugkapitän Hans Dieterle | Germany | Heinkel He 100V-8 | Oranienburg, Germany | 30 Mar 1939 |
| 469.22 | 755.138 | Flugkapitän Fritz Wendel | Germany | Messerschmitt Me 209 | Augsburg, Germany | 26 Apr 1939 |

The final entry above was the last world absolute speed record to be ratified by the FAI until November 1945, more than six years later.

| mph | km/h | Pilot | Nationality | Aircraft | Location of achievement | Date |
|---|---|---|---|---|---|---|
| 606.25 | 975.67 | Gp Capt H. J. Wilson, AFC | GB | Gloster Meteor F4 | Herne Bay, Kent, England | 7 Nov 1945 |
| 615.65 | 990.79 | Gp Capt E. M. Donaldson, DSO, AFC | GB | Gloster Meteor F4 | Rustington, Sussex, England | 7 Sep 1946 |
| 623.61 | 1003.60 | Col Albert Boyd | USA | Lockheed P-80R Shooting Star | Muroc, California, USA | 19 Jun 1947 |
| 640.60 | 1030.95 | Cdr T. F. Caldwell, USN | USA | Douglas D-558 Skystreak | Muroc, California, USA | 20 Aug 1947 |
| 650.78 | 1047.33 | Maj M. E. Carl, USMC | USA | Douglas D-558 Skystreak | Muroc, California, USA | 25 Aug 1947 |
| 670.84 | 1079.61 | Maj R. L. Johnson USAF | USA | North American F-86A Sabre | Muroc, California, USA | 15 Sep 1948 |
| 698.35 | 1123.89 | Capt J. Slade Nash, USAF | USA | North American F-86D Sabre | Salton Sea, California, USA | 19 Nov 1952 |

| mph | km/h | Pilot | Nationality | Aircraft | Location of achievement | Date |
|---|---|---|---|---|---|---|
| 715.60 | 1151.64 | Lt Col W. F. Barnes, USAF | USA | North American F-86D Sabre | Salton Sea, California, USA | 16 Jul 1953 |
| 727.48 | 1170.76 | Sqn Ldr Neville Duke, DSO, OBE, DFC, AFC | GB | Hawker Hunter 3 | Littlehampton, Sussex, England | 7 Sep 1953 |
| 735.54 | 1183.74 | Lt Cdr M. Lithgow, OBE | GB | Supermarine Swift 4 | Libya | 25 Sep 1953 |
| 752.78 | 1211.48 | Lt Cdr J. B. Verdin, USN | USA | Douglas F4D-1 Skyray | Salton Sea, California, USA | 3 Oct 1953 |
| 754.99 | 1215.04 | Lt Col F. K. Everest, USAF | USA | North American YF-100A Super Sabre | Salton Sea, California, USA | 29 Oct 1953 |
| 822.09 | 1323.03 | Col H. A. Hanes, USAF | USA | North American F-100C Super Sabre | Edwards Air Force Base, California, USA | 20 Aug 1955 |
| 1131.76 | 1821.39 | Lt P. Twiss, OBE, DSC | GB | Fairey Delta 2 | Chichester, Sussex, England | 10 Mar 1956 |
| 1207.34 | 1943.03 | Maj Adrian Drew, USAF | USA | McDonnell F-101A Voodoo | Edwards Air Force Base, California, USA | 12 Dec 1957 |
| 1403.79 | 2259.18 | Capt W. W. Irvin, USAF | USA | Lockheed F-104A Starfighter | Edwards Air Force Base, California, USA | 16 May 1958 |
| 1483.51 | 2387.48 | Col G. Mosolov | USSR | Mikoyan Type E-66 | Sidorovo, Tyumenskaya, USSR | 31 Oct 1959 |
| 1525.93 | 2455.74 | Maj J. W. Rogers, USAF | USA | Convair F-106A Delta Dart | Edwards Air Force Base, California, USA | 15 Dec 1959 |
| 1606.51 | 2585.43 | Lt Col R. B. Robinson | USA | McDonnell F4H-1F Phantom II | Edwards Air Force Base, California, USA | 22 Nov 1961 |
| 1665.89 | 2681.00 | Col G. Mosolov | USSR | Mikoyan Type E-166 | Sidorovo, Tyumenskaya, USSR | 7 Jul 1962 |
| 2070.10 | 3331.51 | Col R. L. Stephens | USA | Lockheed YF-12A | Edwards Air Force Base | 1 May 1965 |
| *2193.17 | 3529.56 | Capt E. W. Joersz Maj G. T. Morgan Jr | USA | Lockheed SR-71A | Edwards Air Force Base | 28 Jul 1976 |

* See Lockheed SR-71A entry for 22 Dec 1964 in *Air Warfare & Military Aviation*.

*Progressive (selected) maximum speeds achieved by the North American X-15 rocket-powered research aircraft*

The record speed achieved by Captain Joersz and Major Morgan on 28 July 1976 represents the highest ratified speed record attained by an aeroplane which took off under its own power from the earth's surface. Between 1960 and 1967, however, the US Air Force conducted a substantial programme of manned flight trials with the North American X-15 and X-15A-2. Powered by a liquid oxygen and ammonia rocket engine, the X-15 was carried to altitude by a Boeing B-52 before embarking upon ultra-high-speed and high altitude flights, as summarized next.

| mph | km/h | Mach No. | Pilot | Date |
|---|---|---|---|---|
| 2111 | 3397 | 3.19 | J. A. Walker | 12 May 1960 |
| 2196 | 3534 | 3.31 | J. A. Walker | 4 Aug 1960 |
| 2275 | 3661 | 3.50 | R. M. White | 7 Feb 1961 |
| 2905 | 4675 | 4.43 | R. M. White | 7 Mar 1961 |
| 3074 | 4947 | 4.62 | R. M. White | 21 Apr 1961 |
| 3307 | 5322 | 4.95 | J. A. Walker | 25 May 1961 |
| 3603 | 5798 | 5.27 | R. M. White | 23 Jun 1961 |
| 3647 | 5869 | 5.21 | R. M. White | 11 Oct 1961 |
| 3900 | 6276 | 5.74 | J. A. Walker | 17 Oct 1961 |
| 4093 | 6587 | 6.04 | R. M. White | 9 Nov 1961 |
| 4104 | 6605 | 5.92 | J. A. Walker | 27 Jun 1962 |
| 4250 | 6840 | 6.33 | W. J. Knight | 18 Nov 1966 |
| 4534 | 7297 | 6.72 | W. J. Knight | 3 Oct 1967 |

*Progressive world absolute height records achieved by man in the atmosphere*

| Height ft | m | Pilot | Nationality | Aircraft | Location | Date |
|---|---|---|---|---|---|---|
| 508 | 155 | H. Latham | GB | Antoinette | Reims, France | 29 Aug 1909 |
| 984 | 300 | Comte Charles de Lambert | France | Wright | Paris, France | 18 Oct 1909 |
| 1486 | 453 | H. Latham | GB | Antoinette | Châlons, France | 1 Dec 1909 |
| 3281 | 1000 | H. Latham | GB | Antoinette | France | 7 Jan 1910 |
| 3966 | 1209 | L. Paulhan | France | Henry Farman | Los Angeles, USA | 12 Jan 1910 |
| 4380 | 1335 | W. Brookins | USA | Wright | Indianapolis, USA | 14 Jun 1910 |
| 4540 | 1384 | H. Latham | GB | Antoinette | Reims, France | 7 Jul 1910 |
| 6234 | 1900 | W. Brookins | USA | Wright | Atlantic City, USA | 10 Jul 1910 |
| 6601 | 2012 | A. Drexel | USA | Blériot | Lanark, Scotland | 11 Aug 1910 |
| 8471 | 2582 | Léon Morane | France | Blériot | Deauville, France | 3 Sep 1910 |
| 8488 | 2587 | G. Chavez | France | Blériot | Issy-les-Moulineaux, France | 8 Sep 1910 |
| 9120 | 2780 | H. Wynmalen | France | Henry Farman | Mourmelon, France | 1 Oct 1910 |
| 9449 | 2880 | A. Drexel | USA | Blériot | Philadelphia, USA | Oct 1910 |
| 9711 | 2960 | R. Johnston | USA | Wright | Belmont Park, USA | 31 Oct 1910 |
| 10170 | 3100 | G. Legagneux | France | Blériot | Pau, France | 8 Dec 1910 |
| 10423 | 3177 | M. Loridan | France | Henry Farman | Châlons, France | 8 July 1911 |
| 10466 | 3190 | Capt Félix | France | Blériot | Etampes, France | 9 Aug 1911 |
| 12828 | 3910 | Roland Garros | France | Blériot XI | St-Malo, France | 4 Sep 1911 |
| 16076 | 4900 | Roland Garros | France | Blériot XI | Houlgate, France | 6 Sep 1912 |
| 17880 | 5450 | G. Legagneux | France | Morane-Saulnier | Corbeaulieu, France | 17 Sep 1912 |
| 18405 | 5610 | Roland Garros | France | Morane-Saulnier | Tunis | 11 Dec 1912 |
| 19291 | 5880 | M. Perreyon | France | Blériot XI | Buc, France | 11 Mar 1913 |
| 20079 | 6120 | G. Legagneux | France | Nieuport | St-Raphael, France | 28 Dec 1913 |

The final entry above was the last world absolute height record to be ratified by the FAI until 1920, more than a year after the end of the First World War.

| Height ft | Height m | Pilot | Nationality | Aircraft | Location | Date |
|---|---|---|---|---|---|---|
| 33 113 | 10 093 | Maj R. W. Schroeder | USA | Lepere | Dayton, USA | 27 Feb 1920 |
| 34 508 | 10 518 | Lt J. A. MacReady | USA | Lepere | Dayton, USA | 18 Sep 1921 |
| 35 242 | 10 742 | Sadi Lecointe | France | Nieuport | Villacoublay, France | 5 Sep 1923 |
| 36 565 | 11 145 | Sadi Lecointe | France | Nieuport | Issy-les-Moulineaux, France | 30 Oct 1923 |
| 38 418 | 11 710 | Lt C. C. Champion | USA | Wright Apache | Washington, USA | 25 Jul 1927 |
| 39 140 | 11 930 | Lt Apollo Soucek | USA | Wright Apache | USA | 8 May 1929 |
| 41 795 | 12 739 | W. Neuenhofen | Germany | Junkers W34 | Dessau | 26 May 1929 |
| 43 166 | 13 157 | Lt Apollo Soucek | USA | Wright Apache | Washington, USA | 4 Jun 1930 |
| 43 976 | 13 404 | Capt C. F. Uwins | GB | Vickers Vespa | Filton, England | 16 Sep 1932 |
| 44 820 | 13 661 | G. Lemoine | France | Potez 50 | Villacoublay, France | 28 Sep 1933 |
| 47 352 | 14 433 | Cdr R. Donati | Italy | Caproni 161 | Rome, Italy | 11 Apr 1934 |
| 48 698 | 14 843 | G. Détré | France | Potez 50 | Villacoublay, France | 14 Aug 1936 |
| 49 944 | 15 223 | Sqn Ldr S. R. Swain | GB | Bristol 138 | Farnborough, England | 28 Sep 1936 |
| 51 362 | 15 655 | Lt Col M. Pezzi | Italy | Caproni 161 | Montecelio, Italy | 8 May 1937 |
| 53 937 | 16 440 | Flt Lt M. J. Adam | GB | Bristol 138 | Farnborough, England | 30 Jun 1937 |
| 56 046 | 17 083 | Lt Col M. Pezzi | Italy | Caproni 161 bis | Montecelio, Italy | 22 Oct 1938 |

The final entry above was the last world absolute height record to be ratified by the FAI until March 1948, more than nine years later.

| Height ft | Height m | Pilot | Nationality | Aircraft | Location | Date |
|---|---|---|---|---|---|---|
| 59 445 | 18 119 | J. Cunningham | GB | de Havilland Vampire I | Hatfield, England | 23 Mar 1948 |
| 63 668 | 19 406 | W. F. Gibb | GB | English Electric Canberra | England | 4 May 1953 |
| 65 889 | 20 083 | W. F. Gibb | GB | English Electric Canberra | England | 29 Aug 1955 |
| 70 308 | 21 430 | M. Randrup | GB | English Electric Canberra | England | 28 Aug 1957 |
| 76 932 | 23 449 | Lt Cdr G. C. Watkins | USA | Grumman F11F-1 Tiger | USA | 18 Apr 1958 |
| 79 452 | 24 217 | R. Carpentier | France | SO9050 Trident (F-ZWUM) | France | 2 May 1958 |
| 91 243 | 27 811 | Maj H. C. Johnson | USA | Lockheed F-104A Starfighter | USA | 7 May 1958 |
| 94 659 | 28 852 | Maj V. Ilyushin | USSR | Sukhoi T431 | USSR | 14 Jul 1959 |
| 98 556 | 30 040 | Cdr L. Flint | USA | McDonnell Douglas F-4 Phantom II | USA | 6 Dec 1959 |
| 103 389 | 31 513 | Capt J. B. Jordan | USA | Lockheed F-104C Starfighter | USA | 14 Dec 1959 |
| 113 891 | 34 714 | Col G. Mosolov | USSR | Mikoyan E-66A | USSR | 28 Apr 1961 |
| 118 898 | 36 240 | A. Fedotov | USSR | Mikoyan E-266 | USSR | 25 Jul 1973 |
| 123 524 | 37 650 | A. Fedotov | USSR | Mikoyan E-266M | USSR | 31 Aug 1977 |

*Progressive world absolute distance records achieved by man in the atmosphere*

| Distance (miles) | km | Pilot | Nationality | Aircraft | Location of start | Date |
|---|---|---|---|---|---|---|
| 722 ft | 220 m | A. Santos-Dumont | Brazil | Santos-Dumont 14 bis | Bagatelle, France | 12 Nov 1906 |
| 2530 ft | 771 m | H. Farman | France | Voisin | Issy-les-Moulineaux, France | 26 Oct 1907 |
| 0.62 | 1 | H. Farman | France | Voisin | Issy-les-Moulineaux, France | 13 Jan 1908 |
| 1.25 | 2.004 | H. Farman | France | Voisin | Issy-les-Moulineaux, France | 21 Mar 1908 |
| 2.44 | 3.925 | L. Delagrange | France | Voisin | Issy-les-Moulineaux, France | 11 Apr 1908 |
| 7.92 | 12.75 | L. Delagrange | France | Voisin | Centocelle | 30 May 1908 |
| 14.99 | 24.125 | L. Delagrange | France | Voisin | Issy-les-Moulineaux, France | 17 Sep 1908 |
| 41.38 | 66.60 | Wilbur Wright | USA | Wright | Auvours, France | 21 Sep 1908 |
| 62 | 99.8 | Wilbur Wright | USA | Wright | Auvours, France | 18 Dec 1908 |
| 77.48 | 124.7 | Wilbur Wright | USA | Wright | Auvours, France | 31 Dec 1908 |
| 83.26 | 134 | Louis Paulhan | France | Voisin | Betheny | 25 Aug 1909 |
| 96.08 | 154.62 | H. Latham | GB | Antoinette | Betheny | 26 Aug 1909 |
| 111.8 | 180 | H. Farman | France | Farman | Betheny | 27 Aug 1909 |
| 145.53 | 234.21 | H. Farman | France | Farman | Mourmelon | 4 Nov 1909 |
| 244 | 392.75 | Jan Olieslagers | Belgium | Blériot | Mourmelon | 20 July 1910 |
| 289.4 | 465.72 | M. Tabuteau | France | Maurice Farman | Etampes, France | 28 Oct 1910 |
| 320.6 | 515.9 | G. Legagneux | France | Blériot | Pau, France | 11 Dec 1910 |
| 363.35 | 584.75 | M. Tabuteau | France | Maurice Farman | Buc, France | 30 Dec 1910 |
| 388.4 | 625 | Jan Olieslagers | Belgium | Nieuport monoplane | Kiewit | 16 Jul 1911 |
| 449.21 | 722.94 | Fourny | France | Maurice Farman | Buc, France | 1 Sep 1911 |
| 460 | 740.3 | Gobé | France | Nieuport monoplane | Pau, France | 24 Dec 1911 |
| 628.1 | 1010.9 | Fourny | France | Maurice Farman | Etampes, France | 11 Sep 1912 |
| 634.5 | 1021.2 | A. Seguin | France | Henry Farman | Buc, France | 13 Oct 1913 |

The final entry above was the last world absolute distance record to be ratified by the FAI until 1925.

| Distance (miles) | km | Pilot | Nationality | Aircraft | Location of start | Date |
|---|---|---|---|---|---|---|
| 1967 | 3166 | Capts L. Arrachart and H. Lemaître | France | Breguet 19 | Etampes, France | 3–4 Feb 1925 |
| 2675 | 4305 | Capt L. Arrachart and Adj Arrachart | France | Potez 550 | Le Bourget, France | 26–7 Jun 1926 |

| Distance miles | km | Pilot | Nationality | Aircraft | Location of start | Date |
|---|---|---|---|---|---|---|
| 2930 | 4715.9 | Capt L. Girier and Lt Dordilly | France | Breguet 19 | Le Bourget, France | 14–15 Jul 1926 |
| 3215 | 5174 | Lt Challe and Capt Weiser | France | Breguet 19 | Le Bourget, France | 31 Aug–1 Sep 1926 |
| 3353 | 5396 | Capts D. Costes and J. Rignot | France | Breguet 19 | Le Bourget, France | 28–9 Oct 1926 |
| 3609.5 | 5809 | Charles Lindbergh | USA | Ryan monoplane | New York to Paris | 20–1 May 1927 |
| 3911 | 6294 | C. D. Chamberlin and A. Levine | USA | Bellanca | New York, USA | 4–6 Jun 1927 |
| 4466.6 | 7188.25 | A. Ferrarin and D. Prete | Italy | Savoia-Marchetti S64 | Rome, Italy | 3–5 Jul 1928 |
| 4912 | 7905 | Capt D. Costes and M. Bellonte | France | Breguet 19 | Le Bourget, France | 27–9 Sep 1929 |
| 5011 | 8065 | R. N. Boardman and J. Polando | USA | Wright J6 | Brooklyn, USA | 28–30 Jul 1931 |
| 5309 | 8544 | Sqn Ldr O. Gayford and Flt Lt G. Nicholetts | GB | Fairey Special monoplane | Cranwell, England | 6–8 Feb 1933 |
| 5657 | 9104 | Rossi and P. Codes | France | Blériot Zapata | New York, USA | 5–7 Aug 1933 |
| 6306 | 10148 | Col M. Gromov, Ing S. Daniline and Cmdt A. Youmachev | USSR | ANT-25 | Moscow to San Jacinto | 12–14 Jul 1937 |
| 6658.3 | 10715.5 | Flt Lts H. A. V. Hogan and Mosson | GB | Vickers Wellesley | Ismailia to Koepang | 5–7 Nov 1938 |
| 7158.4 | 11520.4 | Sqn Ldr R. Kellett and Flt Lt Gething | GB | Vickers Wellesley | Ismailia to Darwin | 5–7 Nov 1938 |
| 7158.4 | 11520.4 | Flt Lt A. N. Combe and Bornett | GB | Vickers Wellesley | Ismailia to Darwin | 5–7 Nov 1938 |

The final entry above was the last world absolute distance record to be ratified by the FAI until 1945.

| Distance miles | km | Pilot | Nationality | Aircraft | Location of start | Date |
|---|---|---|---|---|---|---|
| 7916 | 12739.6 | Col Irving and Lt Col Stawley | USA | Boeing B-29 Superfortress | Northwest to Washington | 12 Nov 1945 |
| 11235.6 | 18081.99 | Cdr T. Davis and E. P. Rankin | USA | Lockheed P2V Neptune | Perth to Columbus, Ohio | 29 Sep–1 Oct 1946 |
| 12532.3 | 20168.78 | Maj Clyde P. Evely | USA | Boeing B-52H | Okinawa to Madrid, Spain | 10–11 Jan 1962 |
| 24986.66 | 40212.14 | Dick Rutan and Jeana Yeager | USA | Voyager | Round-the-world non-stop flight | 14–23 Dec 1986 |

# Index

III (see Walden)
IIIC (see Fairey)
IIID (see Fairey)
IIIF (see Fairey)
IV (see Antoinette)
VI *Libellule* (see Blériot)
VII (see Blériot)
X (see Voisin)
XI (see Blériot)
XII (see Blériot)
XIII (see Blériot)
XIII (see SPAD)
XIX (see Breguet)
1MF1 (see Mitsubishi)
4-AT Trimotor (see Ford)
'14-bis' (see Santos-Dumont)
19 (see Breguet)
25 (see Potez)
28 (see Nieuport)
29 (see Nieuport-Delage)
46 (see Loire-Nieuport)
130 Clipper (see Martin)
172 (see Cessna)
180 (see Cessna)
184 (see Short)
194 (see DFS)
221 (see BAC)
230 (see DFS)
260B Comanche (see Piper)
342 (see Doblhoff/WNF)
504K (see Avro)
534 Baby (see Avro)
581 Avian (see Avro)
600 (see Verville-Packard)
630 series (see Potez)
940 Integral (see Breguet)
941S (see Breguet)
990 Coronado (see Convair)
1500-02 Griffon II (see Nord)

## A

A-1 Triad (see Curtiss)
A3D Skywarrior (see Douglas)
A-4 (see Douglas)
A4N1 (see Nakajima)
A5M (see Mitsubishi)
A-6 Intruder (see Grumman)
A6M Zero (see Mitsubishi)
A-7/-7Za autogyro: 47
A-11 (see Aero)
A-40 Albatross (see Beriev)
A 129 Mangusta (see Aeritalia)
A-140 (see Cameron)
A300 *et seq* (see Airbus Industrie)
AB (see Curtiss)
AB Aerotransport: 101
*Abraham Lincoln*, USS: 186
Abruzzo, B. L.: 21, 23
AC-130 (see Lockheed)
AD-1 Skyraider (see Douglas)
Adams, J.: 16
Ader, C.: 76, 131
Ader
  *Avion III*: 76
  *Éole*: 76

*Admiral of the Fleet Kuznetsov*: 183, 184
AEG D.I.: 188
Aerial Carriage (see Cayley)
Aerial Derby (UK): 95
Aerial Experimental Association *Silver Dart*: 81
*Aerial Steam Carriage*: 74
*Aerial Steamer*: 76
Aeritalia A 129 Mangusta: 58
Aero A 11: 148
Aérocentre Belphégor: 209
Aero Club (UK): 77, 80, 81, 85
Aéro Club de France: 76, 78, 86, 132, 133
Aero Club of America: 78
Aero Club of California: 85
*Aerodrome* (see Langley)
Aeroflot: 115, 120, 124
Aerolineas Argentinas: 116
Aeromarine West Indies Airways: 96
Aeronautical Society of GB: 75, 80
*Aéronave*: 75
Aero Spacelines
  B-377PG Pregnant Guppy: 116
  Super Guppy: 116
Aérospatiale
  Alouette III: 58
  SA 315B Lama: 61
*Africa*, HMS: 134
AF-WRI-1: 20, 21
Agello, F.: 125
AH-1 Cobra (see Bell)
AH-1G HueyCobra (see Bell)
AH-58 Warrior (see Bell)
AH-64 Apache (see McDonnell Douglas Helicopters)
Aichi D3A: 160
Airacomet (see Bell)
**Air Arms of the World** (formation dates): 197–205
Airbus Industrie
  Airbus A300: 116, 122
  Airbus A310: 119
  Airbus A320: 119
  Airbus A321: 119
  Airbus A330: 119
  Airbus A340: 119
  Airbus A350: 129
Airco (see de Havilland)
Aircraft Transport & Travel Ltd: 92–4, 96, 128
Air France: 118, 119, 129
Air India: 116
Air League Challenge Cup Race: 98
Airship Guarantee Company R-100: 35, 36
Airship Industries
  Skyship 500: 37, 38
  Skyship 600: 38
Airspeed
  Courier: 109
  Horsa: 68
*Akagi*: 160
*Akitsu Maru*: 47
*Akron*, USS: 36–39
*Alabama*, USS: 146, 147
Alabaster, Capt R. C.: 114
Albatros
  B.II: 220

C.I: 221
D.I: 142, 221
D.II: 221, 224
D.III: 33, 224
D.V: 146, 223
Albatross, A-40 (see Beriev)
Albrecht, F.: 106
Alcock, Capt J.: 95, 97, 118
Aldington, Sqn Ldr J.: 184
Aldrin, E. E. A.: 216, 217
Alfeurov, G. V.: 56
Alkemade, Flt Sgt N. S.: 224
Allen, B.: 218
Allen, Brig-Gen J.: 131
Alouette III (see Aérospatiale)
Altair (see Lockheed)
*Altmark*: 154
American Airlines: 111, 117
American Volunteer Group (AVG): 159
Amundsen, R.: 34
An-2 'Colt' *et seq* (see Antonov)
Anabuki, M/Sgt S.: 227
Anders, W.: 216
Anderson, Capt O.: 20
Anderson, Capt R. C.: 179
Anderson, M. L.: 21
Anderson, R.: 62
Andreani, Chevalier P.: 13
Andreasson BA-4B: 124
Andrée, S. A.: 10, 19
Andreev, E.: 70
ANEC monoplane: 99
Ansaldo SVA 5 Primo: 187, 188
Anson (see Avro)
ANT-1 (see Tupolev)
ANT-2 (see Tupolev)
*Antietam*, USS: 174, 175
Antoinette IV: 82–4
Antonov
  An-2 'Colt': 129
  An-22: 197
  An-124 'Condor': 123, 124, 127, 187
  An-225 Mryia 'Cossack': 73, 124, 129, 187
Aoki, R.: 23
Apache, AH-64 (see McDonnell Douglas Helicopters)
*Apollo 8*: 216
*Apollo 10*: 216
*Apollo 11*: 216
*Apollo ASTP*: 217, 218
Aquila Airways: 115
Ar 68 (see Arado)
Ar 234B Blitz (see Arado)
Arado
  Ar 68: 151
  Ar 234B Blitz: 164, 165
Archdeacon, E.: 79, 80
Archdeacon Prize: 78
Archduke Léopold Salvator of Austria: 87
Archimedes of Syracuse: 9
Archytas of Tarentum: 75
Argosy (see Armstrong Whitworth)
*Argus*, HMS: 143
*Ark Royal*, HMS: 140, 156, 157, 130, 214
'Ark Royal' class carrier: 168
Armstrong, N. A.: 216, 217

Armstrong, R.: 126
Armstrong Whitworth
  Argosy: 105, 106
  AW 23: 112
  SS dirigible: 31
  SS Z dirigible: 31
  Whitley: 155–9
Arnold, Lt L. P.: 100
Arrowsmith, Cpl V.: 155
AS 56 (see Colt)
AS 261 (see Thunder & Colt)
ASH-25 (see Schleicher)
Astir CS (see Grob)
Astra-Torres AT 1 to AT 4: 31, 138
ASW-12 (see Schleicher)
AT 1 to AT 4 (see Astra-Torres)
AT-26 Xavante (see EMBRAER)
Attacker (see Supermarine)
Aubrun, E.: 85
Aushza, VK-8 (see Kensgaila)
Australasian: 17
Autogiro (see Cierva)
AV-8A Harrier (see Hawker Siddeley)
AV-8B Harrier II (see McDonnell Douglas/
  BAe)
Avenger, TBF (see Grumman)
Avian, 581 (see Avro)
Avian III (see Avro)
Avianca (Aerovias Nacionales de Colombia
  SA): 126
Aviasud Sirocco: 120, 121
Aviatik C type: 140, 221
Avions III (see Ader)
Avro
  504: 95, 137, 139
  534 Baby: 95
  581 Avian: 103
  Anson: 156
  Avian III: 103
  Lancaster: 159, 161, 162, 165, 191
  Lancastrian: 113
  Rota: 44
  Type 707: 211
  Type F: 89
  Vulcan: 174, 179, 183, 190, 211
AW23 (see Armstrong Whitworth)
Ayling, J. R.: 109
Aztec D (see Piper)

B

B.II (see Albatros)
B-1 (see Boeing)
B-1 (see Goodyear)
B-1B Lancer (see Rockwell)
B-2 (see Northrop)
B-8 Gyro-Copter (see Bensen)
B-8B Gyro-Boat (see Bensen)
B-17 Flying Fortress (see Boeing)
B-24 Liberator (see Convair)
B-25 Mitchell (see North American)
B-26 (see Douglas)
B-29 Superfortress (see Boeing)
B-36 (see Convair)
B-47 Stratojet (see Boeing)
B-50 (see Boeing)
B-52 Stratofortress (see Boeing)
B-57 (see Martin)
B-58 Hustler (see Convair)
B-377PG Pregnant Guppy (see Aero
  Spacelines)

BA-4B (see Andreasson)
Ba 65 (see Breda)
Ba 349 Natter (see Bachem)
Babington, Flt Cdr J. T.: 139
Baby (see Porte)
Baby, 534 (see Avro)
Baby Bird (see Stits)
BAC
  221: 212
  TSR.2: 207
BAC/Aérospatiale Concorde: 117–19, 129,
  207, 212
Bachem Ba 349 Natter: 165
Bachstelze, Fa 330 (see Focke-Achgelis)
'Backfire' (see Tupolev Tu-22M)
Baden-Powell, Maj B. F. S.: 80
BAe Sea Harrier: 182, 183, 190
Bager, R.: 98
Bailey, Lady: 104
Baker, T.: 87
Baku: 181
Balbo, Gen I.: 150
Balchen, B.: 105
Baldwin, Capt T.: 132
Baldwin, F. W. ('Casey'): 83
Baldwin, Sgt I: 20
Ball, Capt A.: 221, 222
Balliol, P.108 (see Boulton Paul)
Balloon or Aerostatic Magazine, The: 17
Banshee, F2H (see McDonnell)
Bantam, X-4 (see Northrop)
Barber, H.: 88
Barling XNBL-1: 148
Barlow, R. K.: 137
Barnard, Capt F. F.: 99
Barnes, Lt-Col W. F.: 175
Barreswil, M.: 19
Barton, Flt Lt P.: 183
Batson, Lt J. E. D.: 179
Batten, J: 105, 110, 120
Battle (see Fairey)
Baumgarten, Herr: 26
BE1 (see Farnborough)
BE2 (see Farnborough)
BE2c/e (see Royal Aircraft Factory)
BEA (British European Airways): 50, 51,
  113–16
Beamont, Wg Cdr R. P.: 174, 175
'Bear' (see Tupolev Tu-95/-142)
Beardmore Wee Bee: 101
Béarn: 148
Beaumont, Capt F.: 19
Beavis, Capt F.: 19
Beavis, Sqn Ldr M. G.: 179
Beck, Lt P.: 132
Beech Bonanza: 120
Beetham, Wg Cdr M. J.: 178
Beiking No. 1: 115
Belfast (see Short)
Bell, G.: 137
Bell, H. ('Dinger'): 82
Bell
  AH-1 Cobra: 54, 60
  AH-1G HueyCobra: 55, 60
  AH-58 Warrior: 60
  Airacomet: 163
  GAM-63 Rascal: 178
  H-13 Sioux: 54
  JetRanger III: 58
  Model 47: 50, 52

Model 206L LongRanger II: 57, 58, 61
Model 207 Sioux Scout: 54
Model 209 HueyCobra: 55, 56
Model B: 62
  UH-1: 186
  X-1: 207, 210, 219
  X-2: 213, 219
  X-5: 211
  XV-3: 53
Bell-Boeing V-22 Osprey: 62, 185
Bell/NASA XV-15: 62
Bellinger, Lt (Jg) P. N. L.: 137, 207
Belphégor (see Aérocentre)
Belyayev, P.: 215
Ben-My-Chree, HMS: 140, 141
Bennett, Capt D. C. T.: 126, 161
Bennett, F.: 102
Benoist flying-boat: 92
Bensen
  B-8 Gyro-Copter: 62
  B-8B Gyro-Boat: 53
Bentley, Lt R. R.: 103
Beriev A-40 Albatross: 124, 187
Berlin Airlift: 170, 186, 191
Berry, Capt A.: 66
Berry, J.: 20
Berry, Sqn Ldr J.: 196
Berson, Professor: 20
Beta: 28, 29
Bettington, Lt C. A.: 135
'Betty' (see Mitsubishi G4M)
Beverley (see Blackburn)
Bf 109 (see Messerschmitt)
Bf 110 (see Messerschmitt)
Biard, H.: 97
Bienvenu, M.: 41
Biggin, G.: 15
Bikle, P. F.: 70
Biplane No. 2 (see Short)
Birmingham, USS: 133, 137
Birch, Lt W. C.: 140
Bishop, Maj W. A.: 225
Bismarck: 155
Black, T. C.: 109
Black, W. van L.: 103
Blackburn, R.: 129
Blackburn
  Beverley: 174
  Bluebird IV: 106
  Buccaneer: 179
  Dart: 148
  Monoplane: 129
  Roc: 157
  Skua: 154, 156
Black Hawk, UH-60 (see Sikorsky)
'Blackjack' (see Tupolev Tu-160)
Black Widow, P-61 (see Northrop)
Blair, C.: 114
Blanchard, J.-P.: 14–17, 65
Blanchard, Mme: 17
Blenheim (see Bristol)
Blenheim IV (see Bristol)
Blériot, L.: 78, 81–3, 129, 134, 206, 234
Blériot
  VI Libellule: 78
  VII: 78
  XI: 81, 83, 90, 129
  XII: 82, 83
  XIII: 83
'Blinder' (see Tupolev Tu-22)
Blitz, Ar 234B (see Arado)

Blohm und Voss
  Bv 222 Wiking: 186
  Bv 238: 186
  Ha 139: 111
Bluebird IV (see Blackburn)
BN-2A Islander (see Britten-Norman)
BOAC (British Overseas Airways
  Corporation): 112, 114, 116, 125, 128
*Bodensee*: 33
Boehme, Lt: 221
Boeing
  B-1: 97
  B-17 Flying Fortress: 112, 158, 160, 161,
    163–5, 231
  B-29 Superfortress: 113, 165, 166, 171,
    197, 210
  B-47 Stratojet: 174
  B-50: 171
  B-52 Stratofortress: 177, 179, 180, 183,
    187, 189–92, 197, 216
  Bomarc: 173
  DB-47: 178
  EC-135: 178
  GA-1: 146
  KB-29: 173
  KC-135: 178
  Model 200: 105, 106
  Model 247: 107, 108
  Model 307 Stratoliner: 112
  Model 314 Clipper: 112
  Model 367-80: 15
  Model 707: 115–17, 120, 128, 129
  Model 727: 119, 121, 127
  Model 737: 127
  Model 747: 7, 117, 118, 125, 127–9
  Model 767: 124, 127, 129
  Model 777: 129
  Model CL-4S: 94
  P-26: 150
  Washington: 171
  XP-936: 150
  Y1B-9A: 150
  YB-52: 192
Boeing Air Transport: 105
Boeing Vertol
  CH-47 Chinook: 60, 223
  HH-46A Sea Knight: 223
Boelcke, Hauptmann O.: 142, 220, 221, 224
Bogan, B.: 21
Bolt, Maj J.: 228
Bomarc (see Boeing)
Bonanza (see Beech)
Bong, Maj I.: 227, 228
Bonney, L.: 106, 111
Boothman, Flt Lt J. N.: 150
Bordelon, Lt G. P.: 223, 228
Borgward Kolibri I: 54
Borman, F.: 215, 216
Borton, Brig-Gen A. E.: 93
Bossoutrot, L.: 93, 94
Boulet, J.: 61
Boulton Paul
  Defiant: 154
  Overstrand: 151, 152
  P.108 Balliol: 170
Bourgeois, D.: 13
*Bournemouth* airship: 37
Bowser, Lt-Cdr R.: 39
Boxkite (see Bristol)
Boyce, Flt Lt: 148
Boyington, Lt-Col G.: 227

BR (see Fiat)
BR 20 (see Fiat)
Brabazon I (see Bristol)
Brancker, Maj-Gen Sir S.: 35
Brand, Sqn Ldr C. Q.: 97
Brand, V.: 218
Brandon, 2nd Lt A.: 31
Brandt, Deck Off P.: 142
Branson, R.: 7, 22
Breda Ba 65: 195
Breguet, L.: 45, 128
Breguet
  XIX: 103, 147
  940 Integral: 214
  941S: 214
Breguet-Dorand *Gyroplane Laboratoire*: 45
Breguet-Richet Gyroplane 1: 42
Brennan, L.: 43
Brett, Mrs S.: 71
Brewer, G.: 80
Brewster
  F2A Buffalo: 154
  XF2A-1: 154
Briggs, Sqn Ldr E. F.: 139
Bright, Capt W. J.: 118
Brink, E.: 23
Brink, H.: 23, 24
Bristol
  Blenheim: 110, 156
  Blenheim IV: 155
  Boxkite: 87, 133
  Brabazon I: 219
  Britannia: 115
  F2B Fighter: 145, 147
  Monoplane: 135
  Scout C: 140, 142, 221
  Sycamore: 50
  Type 142: 110
  Type 170 Freighter: 113
  Type 173: 52
Britannia (see Bristol)
Britannia Airways: 129
British Aerospace (see BAe)
British Airways (pre-1940): 111
British Airways (post-March 1972): 118, 120,
  129
*British Army Aeroplane No. 1* (see Cody)
British Marine Air Navigation Co.: 100
British Overseas Airways Corporation (see
  BOAC)
Britten-Norman BN-2A Islander: 118, 127
Broadwick, G. ('Tiny'): 67
Brock, W. L.: 92
Bronco, OV-10 (see North American)
Brookins, W.: 125
Brown, Capt A. R.: 224
Brown, J.: 218
Brown, Lt A. W.: 95, 118
Brown, Lt-Cdr E. M.: 162, 167
Brown, Mr: 17
Brown, Jr, Lt R. J.: 172
Browning, J.: 65
Bruce, Hon Mrs V.: 106
BS1 (see Farnborough)
Buccaneer (see Blackburn)
'Bull' (see Tupolev Tu-4)
*Bumble Bee Two* (see Starr)
*Buran* space shuttle: 219
Burattini, T. L.: 74
Butler, F. H.: 20, 80
Butler, J. W.: 75

Buxton, Capt F. L.: 118
Bv 222 Wiking (see Blohm und Voss)
Bv 238 (see Blohm und Voss)
Byrd, Lt-Cdr R. E.: 102, 105

C

C (see Halberstadt)
C.I (see Albatros)
CI (see Hansa-Brandenburg)
C.V (see DFW)
C-1 (see Goodyear)
C-1 (see Kawasaki)
C-2 (see Fokker)
C.4 (see Cierva)
C-5 Galaxy (see Lockheed)
C.6 (see Cierva)
C.6D (see Cierva)
C-7 (see Goodyear)
C.8L (see Cierva)
C11 (see LVG)
C.30A (see Cierva)
C-47 (see Douglas)
C-74 Globemaster I (see Douglas)
C-124 Globemaster II (see Douglas)
C-130 Hercules (see Lockheed)
C-141B StarLifter (see Lockheed)
C200 (see Macchi)
Ca 32 *et seq* (see Caproni)
Cabral, Capt S.: 98
Calder, Sqn Ldr C. C.: 165
'Camber' (see Ilyushin Il-86)
Camel (see Sopwith)
Camerman, Lieutenant: 132
Cameron, Capt J.: 50
Cameron, D.: 21, 23
Cameron
  A-140: 21
  D-38: 39
  D-96: 37
  DP-70: 38
  *Endeavour*: 23
  N-850 *Nashua Number One*: 24
  Roziere R-60: 22
  ULD-1: 23
Camm, Sydney: 101, 150
Campbell, Ist Lt D.: 146, 226
Canadair CL-44D-4: 116
Canadian Pacific Airlines: 115
Canberra (see English Electric)
Candelaria, Lt L. C.: 93
Canning, C.: 120
Capper, Col J. C.: 20, 27, 28
Capper, Mrs: 20
Caproni
  Ca32: 141
  Ca 74: 193
  Ca 101: 193
  Ca 111: 193
  Ca 133: 193
  Ca 161*bis*: 125
Caproni-Campini CC.2: 157, 158
Caravelle, S.E.210 (see Sud-Est Aviation)
Carmichael, Lt P.: 196
Carr, R. H.: 67
Castoldi, Dr M.: 154
Catalina, PBY (see Consolidated)
*Cathedral* (see Cody)
Caudron G IV: 223
Cavallo, T.: 11
Cavendish, H.: 9, 11

Cayla, Lt: 135
Cayley, Sir G.: 41, 64, 65, 74, 75
Cayley Aerial Carriage: 41
CC.2 (see Caproni-Campini)
C-class Empire flying-boat (see Short)
Celebi, H.: 64
Centre NC 223.4: 157
Cernan, E.: 216
Césari, Lieutenant: 137
Cessna, C.: 124
Cessna
    172: 127
    180: 117
    Skylane: 69
    Turbo Centurion: 120
CFM Shadow: 73, 121
CG-4 (see Waco)
CH-47 Chinook (see Boeing Vertol)
CH-53 (see Sikorsky)
CH-53E Super Stallion (see Sikorsky)
Challenger, SSO: 218, 219
Chamberlin, C.: 102
Chambers, Capt W. I.: 136
Chandler, R. J.: 126
Chanute, Dr O.: 71, 72
Chapman, V. E.: 142
Charabanc (see Grahame-White)
Charles, Prof J. A. C.: 10, 12, 13
Chavez, G.: 87
Chennault, Brig-Gen C. L.: 159, 227
Chinook, CH-47 (see Boeing Vertol)
Chisholm, J.: 120
Chisov, Lt I. M.: 224
Christiaen, M.: 87
Church, E.: 105, 106
Churchill, Rt Hon W. S.: 112
Cierva
    C.4 Autogiro: 44
    C.6: 44
    C.6D: 44
    C.8L: 44
    C.30A: 44, 45
CL-44D-4 (see Canadair)
Clark, Capt A. C.: 179
Clark, J.: 89
Clark, R.: 23
Clément-Bayard Type II: 29
Clipper, 130 (see Martin)
Clipper, Model 314 (see Boeing)
Clydesdale, Marquess of: 108
Coanda, H.: 87
Cobham, A.: 101, 109, 112
Cobra, AH-1 (see Bell)
Coburn, J. W.: 57, 58, 61
Cochran, Miss J.: 115
Cocking, R.: 17, 63, 65
Cody, Mrs: 83
Cody, S. F.: 28, 66, 83, 91, 132, 135
Cody
    British Army Aeroplane No. 1: 83, 132
    Cathedral: 135
Coiffard, Sous-Lt M.: 24
Coli, Capitaine: 225
Collett, Flight Lieutenant: 138
Collins, M.: 216, 217
Collishaw, R.: 226
Colmore, Lt G. C.: 133
'Colossus' class fleet carrier: 167
'Colt' (see Antonov An-2)
Colt AS 56: 38, 39
Columbia, SSO: 218

Comanche, 260B (see Piper)
Combe, Flt Lt A. N.: 190
Comet, DH88 (see de Havilland)
Comet 1, DH106 (see de Havilland)
Comet 4 (see de Havilland)
Concorde (see BAC/Aérospatiale)
Condor: 123
'Condor' (see Antonov An-124)
Condor (see Curtiss)
Condor, Fw 200 (see Focke-Wulf)
Coney, Lt W. D.: 98
Connecticut Aircraft Company DN-1 (A-1):
    32
Conrad, M.: 128
Conran, Capt E. L.: 140
Consolidated
    B-24 Liberator: 165, 196, 227, 231
    PBY Catalina: 113, 190, 191
    NY-2: 150
    XP-81: 165
    XB-24: 196
Constellation (see Lockheed)
Constellation, USS: 179, 223
Constitution: 18
Conte Rosso: 143
Conti, Cardinal (Pope Innocent III): 11
Convair
    990 Coronado: 116
    B-36: 186, 210, 212
    B-58 Hustler: 178
    CV-340: 115
    F-102 Delta Dagger: 176
    NB-36H: 212, 213
    XB-36: 186
    XF2Y-1 Sea Dart: 189, 212
    YF2Y-1: 212
Cook, Cadet E. R.: 178
Cook, D.: 120
Cook, J.: 127
Cook, Miss E. M.: 85
Coral Sea, USS: 168, 179, 183
Cordner, Mr: 65
Cornu, P.: 42
Coronado, 990 (see Convair)
Corporal (see Firestone)
Corsair, F4U (see Vought)
Cosmos K-139 FOBS: 216
'Cossack' (see Antonov An-225 Mryia)
Costes, Capt D.: 103
Coutelle, Capitaine: 16
Coutinho, Capt G.: 98
Cover, C. A.: 111
Coxwell, H. T.: 17, 18
C.R.1 (see Fiat)
CR20 et seq (see Fiat)
Crippen, R.: 218
Crissy, Lt M. S.: 134
Crocco, G. A.: 42
Crooks, W. G.: 126
Crosbie, R.: 15
Crosby, H.: 209
Croy, Lt M.: 163
Crusader: 19
Crusader, F8U (F-8) (see Vought)
CSA (Ceskoslovenske Statni Aerolinie): 99
C type (see Aviatik)
Cub (see Piper)
Cuckoo (see Sopwith)
Culleu, Flt Sub-Lt S.: 146
Cunningham, Lt R.: 223

Curtiss, G. H.: 79, 80, 126, 132-4
Curtiss
    A-1 Triad: 134, 136
    AB: 136, 137, 141, 143
    Biplane: 133, 134
    Condor: 109
    F flying-boat: 207
    F9C-2 Sparrowhawk: 36, 37
    JN-4 ('Jenny'): 33, 93, 96
    June Bug: 80
    Large America: 144
    P-40 Warhawk: 159
    SBC Helldiver: 151
    XF12C-1: 151
CV-340 (see Convair)
Cygnet (see Hawker)


                    D

D.I (see AEG)
D.I (see Albatros)
D.II (see Albatros)
D.III (see Albatros)
D.IIIa (see Pfalz)
D.V (see Albatros)
D.VI (see Siemens-Schuckert)
D.VII (see Fokker)
D.VIII (see Fokker)
D.XXI (see Fokker)
D3A (see Aichi)
D-38 (see Cameron)
D-96 (see Cameron)
D371 et seq (see Dewoitine)
Dacre, Flt Lt G. B.: 141
Daedalus (see MIT)
Daigle, D.: 62
Daily Mail: 78, 110
Daily Mail prizes: 78, 81, 82, 84-6, 91, 99
Daily Mail Translatlantic Air Race: 118
Daimler Airways: 99, 100
Dakota (see Douglas)
d'Arlandes, Marquis: 13
Dart (see Blackburn)
d'Ascanio, M.: 62
Dassault
    MD.450 Ouragan: 170, 171
    MD.454 Mystère: 172
    Mirage III: 178, 183
    Mirage IV: 179
    Mirage 2000: 183
Daucourt, M.: 92
Dauntless, SBD (see Douglas)
Davey, C.: 23
da Vinci, L.: 40, 41, 64
Da Vinci III: 58
Davis, Lt-Cdr B.: 118
Davis Jr, Maj G. A.: 228
Dawes, Capt G. W. P.: 133
Dayton-Wright RB racer: 97
DB-3 (see Ilyushin)
DB-47 (see Boeing)
DC-1 (see Douglas)
DC-2 (see Douglas)
DC-3 (see Douglas)
DC-6B (see Douglas)
DC-8 (see Douglas)
DC-9 (see McDonnell-Douglas)
Dean, F/O: 163
Dean, Mr: 17
DeBellevue, Lt C.: 223
de Caxias, Marquis: 18

Defiant (see Boulton Paul)
de Forest Chandler, Capt C.: 135
Defries, C.: 84
Degen, J.: 41
de Gusmão, B. L.: 9, 11
de Havilland, G.: 134
de Havilland
    Comet 4: 115, 116, 120, 180
    DH2: 140, 221
    DH4: 93, 95, 145, 148, 187, 188, 193, 207
    DH6: 94
    DH9: 94, 97, 147, 193
    DH16: 93, 94, 96, 128
    DH18: 99
    DH34: 100
    DH50: 101, 104
    DH60 Moth: 101–6, 111
    DH66 Hercules: 105
    DH80 Puss Moth: 107
    DH82 Tiger Moth: 126
    DH88 Comet: 109, 110
    DH106 Comet 1/2: 113–15, 120, 177, 209
    DH108: 208
    Dominie: 129
    Dragon: 109
    Hornet: 188, 189
    Mosquito: 188, 189, 191
    Sea Hornet: 166
    Sea Mosquito: 162
    Sea Venom: 175
    Vampire: 167, 170, 173, 209
de Havilland Canada U-1A Otter: 53, 54
de Havilland Jr, G.: 189
de la Cierva, J.: 44
Delag: 29, 30, 33
de Lagarde, Mlle: 14
Delagrange, L.: 79, 80, 83, 126
de la Loubères, M.: 64
de Lana-Terzei, F.: 9, 11
de Laroche, Mme la Baronne: 85
de Louvrie, C.: 75
Delta 2 (see Fairey)
Delta Air Lines: 99, 119, 128
Delta Dagger, F-102 (see Convair)
de Montalembert, Marchioness: 14
de Pateras Pescara, Marquis: 44
de Podenas, Countess: 14
de Rozier, F. P.: 12, 13, 15, 22
de Salis, Flt Lt J.: 70
Destroyer EFB 1 (see Vickers)
Deutsch de la Meurthe, H.: 79
Deutsche Lufthansa: 111, 115
Deutsche Luft-Reederei: 93, 99
Deutschland: 26
Devastator, TBD (see Douglas)
Devyatayev, Lt M.: 227
de Witt Milling, Lt T.: 135
Dewoitine
    D371: 194
    D500: 151, 194
    D501: 151
    D510: 151, 194
de Zeven Provincien: 30
DFS
    194: 208
    230: 186
DFW C.V.: 143
DH2 et seq (see de Havilland)
di Bernardi, Maj M.: 148, 157
Dickson, B.: 133
Diener, N.: 109

Dittmar, H.: 162, 208
Dixmude: 34
Dixon, Capt B.: 133
DN-1 (A-1) (see Connecticut Aircraft Co.)
Do 11 et seq (see Dornier)
Doblhoff/WNF 342: 48
Dobney, Sgt T.: 197
Dobrolet: 99
Dominie (see de Havilland)
Doolittle, Lt J. H.: 99, 102, 103, 123, 149, 160
Donaldson, Gp Capt E. M.: 167
Doran, Flt Lt K. C.: 156, 222
Dorand, R.: 45
Dornier
    Do 11: 150
    Do 17: 154, 156, 191, 195
    Do 18: 156
    Do 217: 161, 162
    Do 335 Pfiel: 188
    Do X: 122, 123
    Komet: 99
    Wal: 101, 106
Double Eagle II: 21
Double Eagle V (see Raven)
Douglas
    A3D Skywarrior: 176, 192
    A-4: 180
    AD-1 Skyraider: 165, 166, 172
    B-26: 171
    C-47: 170
    C-74 Globemaster I: 171
    C-124 Globemaster II: 175
    Dakota: 67
    DC-1: 108, 111
    DC-2: 108, 109, 111
    DC-3: 108, 111, 114, 116
    DC-6B: 115
    DC-8: 128
    DWC: 100
    F3D Skyknight: 174
    MB-1 Genie: 177
    R4D: 177
    SBD Dauntless: 160
    Skyrocket: 210, 219
    TBD Devastator: 152, 160
    XA3D: 192
    X-3: 211
Do X (see Dornier)
DP-70 (see Cameron)
Dr.I (see Fokker)
Drache, Fa 223 (see Focke-Achgelis)
Dragonfly (see Westland/Sikorsky)
Drake, B.: 69
Driscoll, Lt (Jg) W.: 223
Dryden, H. L.: 166
Dufek, Rear Adm G. L.: 177
Duigan, J. R.: 86
Duke, R.: 99
Duncan, H.: 70
Dunkerque: 157
Dunning, Sqn Cdr E. H.: 143–5
Dupuy-de-Lôme: 30
Duroug, J.: 19
du Temple de la Croix, F.: 75
Dux-1 biplane: 136
DWC (see Douglas)

E

E.I (see Fokker)
E.III (see Fokker)

E-2 Hawkeye (see Grumman)
E14 submarine: 140
E14Y1 'Glen' (see Yokosuka)
E.28/39 (see Gloster)
EA-6B Prowler (see Grumman)
Eagle: 18
Eagle, F-15 (see McDonnell Douglas)
Earhart, A.: 104, 107, 110
Eastern Air Lines: 46, 226
EC-135 (see Boeing)
Eckener, Dr H.: 35, 39
Edmonds, Flt Cdr C. H.: 140
Edwards, E.: 75
EF-84 (see Republic)
Effimov, M.: 85
Efremov, E.: 61
Egginton, T.: 61
Egret, HMS: 161
EH 101 Heliliner (see EH Industries)
EH Industries EH 101 Heliliner: 58
Eielson, Lt C. B.: 104
Eindecker (see Fokker)
El Al (Israeli Airlines): 7, 128
Ellehammer, J. C. H.: 42, 43, 78, 80
Ellehammer No. IV: 80
Elliott, A. B.: 101
Ellsworth, L.: 34
Ellyson, Lt T. C.: 136
Ely, E. B.: 133, 134, 220
EMB-326GB Xavante (see EMBRAER)
EMBRAER
    AT-26 Xavante: 181
    EMB-326GB Xavante: 181
Empire flying-boat, C-class (see Short)
Endeavour (see Cameron)
Engadine, HMS: 142
Engelhardt, Captain: 85
England–Australia Commemorative Air Race:
    118
English Electric
    Canberra: 70, 172–4, 188
    Lightning: 175, 184
    Wren: 99, 100
Ente rocket-plane: 207
Enterprise: 17
Enterprise, USS: 160, 162, 181
Entreprenant: 16
Éole (see Ader)
Erbslön, O.: 29
Esmonde, Lt Cdr E.: 196
Esnault-Pelterie, R.: 78
España: 28
'Essex' class carrier: 192
Etrich, I.: 91
Etrich Taube: 81, 192
Euler, A.: 133
Eurocopter Tiger: 58, 59
Evely, Maj C. P.: 190
Everett, Lt R. W. H.: 158
Excelsior: 18
Explorer I: 213

F

F flying-boat (see Curtiss)
F.VIIa (see Fokker)
F.VIIA-3m (see Fokker)
F.VIIB-3m (see Fokker)
F-1 (see Mitsubishi)
F2A Buffalo (see Brewster)
F2B Fighter (see Bristol)

F2H Banshee (see McDonnell)
F3D Skyknight (see Douglas)
F-4 Phantom II (see McDonnell Douglas)
F4U Corsair (see Vought)
F6F Hellcat (see Grumman)
F8U (F-8) Crusader (see Vought)
F9C-2 Sparrowhawk (see Curtiss)
F9F Panther (see Grumman)
F11F (F-11) Tiger (see Grumman)
F13 (see Junkers)
F-14A Tomcat (see Grumman)
F-15 Eagle (see McDonnell Douglas)
F-16 Fighting Falcon (see General Dynamics)
F60 Goliath (see Farman)
F-80 (see Lockheed P-80)
F-82 Twin Mustang (see North American)
F-84 Thunderjet (see Republic)
F-86 Sabre (see North American)
F-89 Scorpion (see Northrop)
F-94 Starfire (see Lockheed)
F-100 Super Sabre (see North American)
F-102 Delta Dagger (see Convair)
F-104 Starfighter (see Lockheed)
F-105 Thunderchief (see Republic)
F-111 (see General Dynamics)
F-117A (see Lockheed)
F/A-18 Hornet (see McDonnell Douglas)
F221 et seq (see Forman)
Fa 223 Drache (see Focke-Achgelis)
Fa 266 Hornisse (see Focke-Achgelis)
Fa 330 Bachstelze (see Foche-Achgelis)
Fabre, H.: 85, 87
Fabre Hydravion: 85–7
Fairey
  IIIC: 94, 98
  IIID: 98, 100
  IIIF: 193
  Battle: 156
  Delta 2: 207, 212, 213
  Fulmar: 157
  Gannet: 171
  Hendon: 150
  Long Range Monoplane: 105
  Rotodyne: 54, 62, 207
  Swordfish: 156–9, 196
Falco, CR 42 (see Fiat)
Falcon, GAR (see Hughes)
Farban, M. F.: 17
Farfadet, SO 1310 (see Sud-Ouest)
Farman, H.: 78–81, 83, 125, 126, 133
Farman
  Biplane: 133, 134, 137, 138
  F60 Goliath: 93, 99
  F221 et seq: 185
Farnborough
  BE1: 134, 135
  BE2: 135
  BS1: 134
Farquhar, Sqn Ldr D.: 157
FB5 Gunbus (see Vickers)
FD-1 (FH-1) Phantom (see McDonnell)
FE2b (see Royal Aircraft Factory)
Fédération Aéronautique Internationale
  (FAI): 21, 59–62, 70, 78, 82, 84, 90, 125,
  127, 189, 212
Fedotov, A.: 189
Feoktistov, K.: 215
Féquant, Lieutenant: 133
Ferber, Captain: 84
Ferguson, H. G.: 85
Ferry, R. G.: 62

FF-1 (see Grumman)
FF 29 (see Friedrichshafen)
Fi 156 (see Fieseler)
Fiat
  BR: 96
  BR20: 195
  C.R.1: 148
  CR20: 193
  CR30: 193
  CR32: 195
  CR42 Falco: 188
  CR42B: 188
  G50: 195
Fickel, Lt J. E.: 133
Fieseler Fi 156: 191
Fifield, Sqn Ldr J. S.: 69, 176
Fighter, F2B (see Bristol)
Fighting Falcon, F-16 (see General Dynamics)
Finn, F.: 129
Finnair: 118
Finter, Lt C. V.: 34
Fireball, FR-1 (see Ryan)
Firestone Corporal: 173
Fischer, M.: 89
Fiske, P/O W. M. L.: 157
Fitzmaurice, Capt J.: 104
Fl 282 Kolibri (see Flettner)
'Flanker' (see Sukhoi Su-27)
Flavell, Sqn Ldr E. J. G.: 177
Flesselles: 22
Flettner Fl 282 Kolibri: 47
Fleurant, M.: 14
Fleurus: 30
Flyer (see Wright brothers)
Flyer II (see Wright brothers)
Flying Doctor Service: 104
Flying Fortress, B-17 (see Boeing)
Flynn, Rev J.: 104
Focke, Prof H.: 45, 54
Focke-Achgelis
  Fa 223 Drache: 46, 49, 50
  Fa 266 Hornisse: 46
  Fa 330 Bachstelze: 47, 48
Focke-Wulf
  Fw 61: 45, 46
  Fw 190: 154, 163
  Fw 200 Condor: 112, 156, 158
Fokker
  C-2: 103
  D.VII: 193, 223
  D.VIII: 187, 188
  D.XXI: 156, 161, 185, 191
  Dr.I: 145, 224
  E.I: 140, 221
  E.III: 141
  Eindecker: 140, 141
  F.VIIa: 103, 104
  F.VIIA-3m: 102
  F.VIIB-3m: 104, 105
  M5K: 140
  M8: 140, 221
  T-2: 99
'Fokker Scourge': 140
Fonck, Capt R.: 223
Fontana, J.: 75
Ford, Henry: 101
Ford 4-AT Trimotor: 102, 105
'Forger' (see Yakovlev Yak-36MP)
**Formation dates of World Air Arms**: 197–
  205
Forrestal, USS: 192

Foucault: 142
Fournier, R.: 82
'Foxbat' (see Mikoyan MiG-25)
Foyle Bank, HMS: 222
FR-1 Fireball (see Ryan)
Franceschi, P.: 121
Franco, Commandante: 101
Franklin D. Roosevelt, USS: 55, 167, 168
Frantisek, Sgt J.: 223
Frantz, Sgt J.: 138
Frasee, Lt C.: 171
Freedom 7: 214
Freighter, Type 170 (see Bristol)
Fresson, E. E.: 109
Frick, H.: 189
Friedrichshafen FF 29: 139
Friendship 7: 214
Fritz X-1 (see Ruhrstahl/Kramer)
Frohwein, Leutnant: 143
'Fulcrum' (see Mikoyan MiG-29)
Fulmar (see Fairey)
Furious, HMS: 143–5, 148, 158
Furnas, C. W.: 80
Fury I (see Hawker)
Fw 61 (see Focke-Wulf)
Fw 190 (see Focke-Wulf)
Fw 200 Condor (see Focke-Wulf)

G

G IV (see Caudron)
G4M 'Betty' (see Mitsubishi)
G 23 (see Junkers)
G 38 (see Junkers)
G 50 (see Fiat)
G102 (see Grob)
GA-1 (see Boeing)
Gagarin, Flt Maj Y. A.: 214
Gager, O. A.: 17
Gakkel, Y. M.: 81
Gakkel Gakkel-3: 81
Galaxy, C-5 (see Lockheed)
Galileo Galilei: 193
Gallagher, Capt J.: 171
GAM-63 Rascal (see Bell)
Gamecock (see Gloster)
Gamma: 28
Gannet (see Fairey)
GAR-1 Falcon (see Hughes)
Garnerin, A. J.: 63, 65
Garrison, Lt-Col V.: 174
Garros, R.: 90, 92, 140
Garstin, Sqn Ldr J. H.: 190
Gatty, H.: 106
Gaudron, A. F.: 23
Gauntlet (see Gloster)
Gavotti, 2nd Lt G.: 134
Gayford, Sqn Ldr O. R.: 105
Gee Bee Super Sportster: 123
Gelber Hund: 30, 133
Gellatly, Sqn Ldr W. R.: 62
Gemini 3: 215
Gemini 4: 215
Gemini 6: 215
Gemini 7: 215
Gemini 8: 215, 216
General Aircraft Hamilcar: 68
General Dynamics
  F-16 Fighting Falcon: 181, 183, 184
  F-111: 179
  YF-16: 181

Genie, MB-1 (see Douglas)
Georgeson, S. H. ('Dick'): 69
*George Washington Parke Custis*: 18
Gerfaut 1A (see Nord)
Gerfaut II (see Nord)
Gerli, A.: 13
Gerli, C.: 13
Geysendorffer, Capt G. J.: 103
Gibson, Wg Cdr G.: 161
Giffard, H.: 25
Gigant, Me 321 (see Messerschmitt)
Gladiator (see Gloster)
Glaisher, J.: 20
'Glen' (see Yokosuka E14Y1)
Glenn, Lt-Col J. H.: 214
Gliders 1 to 3 (see Wright brothers)
Globemaster I, C-74 (see Douglas)
Globemaster II, C-124 (see Douglas)
Gloster
    E.28/39: 206–8
    Gamecock: 148
    Gauntlet: 110, 149
    Gladiator: 193
    Grebe: 148
    Javelin: 173
    Meteor: 69, 112, 163, 166, 168, 172
    Sea Gladiator: 193
*Gneisenau*: 154, 196
Gnu (see Sopwith)
Gobeil, Sqn Ldr F.: 67
Goble, Wg Cdr S. J.: 100
Goblin, XF-85 (see McDonnell)
Godard, E.: 19
Godard, L.: 17
Goliath, F60 (see Farman)
Golubev, I. N.: 76
Gontermann, Lt H.: 24
Goodlin, C.: 210
Goodyear
    B-1: 32
    C-1: 33
    C-7: 33
    K-1: 36
    ZPG 2: 39
    ZPG 3-W: 38, 39
Gordon, S.: 105
Gordon Bennett, J.: 20
Gordon Bennett Aviation Cup Race: 97
Gordon Bennett Trophy: 20
Gorrell, F.: 22
*Gossamer Albatross* (see MacCready)
*Gossamer Condor* (see MacCready)
*Gossamer Penguin* (see MacCready)
Gotha bomber: 144, 145
Goupy, A.: 80
Goupy
    Goupy I: 80, 81
    Goupy II: 80
Grade, H.: 80, 81
*Graf Zeppelin*: 35, 39
*Graf Zeppelin II*, LZ 130 (see Zeppelin)
Graham, R.: 43
Grahame-White, C.: 86
Grahame-White Charabanc: 67
Gran, T.: 92
Grands Express Aériens: 99
Gray, Lt R. H.: 224
Gray, T.: 73
**Great Air Fighters**
    First World War: 228–30
    Second World War: 231–3

*Great Nassau Balloon*: 17, 63, 65
Grebe (see Gloster)
Green, C.: 17
Griffin, Lt V. C.: 148
Griffith-Jones, Sqn Ldr: 158
Grissom, V.: 214, 215
Grob
    Astir CS: 70
    G102: 70
Grosse, H.-W.: 68
Grosse, K.: 68
Grosvenor Challenge Cup: 99
Grumman
    A-6 Intruder: 180
    E-2 Hawkeye: 184
    EA-6B Prowler: 197
    F6F Hellcat: 196
    F9F Panther: 171, 172
    F11F (F-11) Tiger: 175
    F-14 Tomcat: 181, 182, 190
    FF-1: 151
    Gulfstream II: 117
    TBF Avenger: 158, 162
    XF9F: 172
    XFF-1: 151
    XTBF-1: 158
Guardian Angel parachute: 67
Guidoni, Capitano: 134
Guille, C.: 65
Gulfstream II (see Grumman)
Gull (see Percival)
Gull (see Slingsby)
Gunbus, FB5 (see Vickers)
Guynemer, Capt G. M. L. J.: 224, 225
Gyro-Boat, B-8B (see Bensen)
Gyro-Copter, B-8 (see Bensen)
Gyrodyne QH-50A: 54
Gyroplane 1 (see Breguet-Richet)
*Gyroplane Laboratoire* (see Breguet-Dorand)

**H**

H4 Hercules (see Hughes)
H-13 Sioux (see Bell)
H-21 Shawnee/Workhorse (see Piasecki-Vertol)
Ha 139 (see Blohm und Voss)
Hack, F.: 106
Hafner, A.: 45
Hageman, W.: 23
Hahn, Dipl Ing M.: 207
Haile Jr, F.: 120
Halberstadt, C.: 140
Halifax (see Handley Page)
'Halo' (see Mil Mi-26)
HAMC SH-5: 187
Hamel, G.: 88, 90
Hamilcar (see General Aircraft)
Hampden (see Handley Page)
*Hancock*, USS: 179
Handcock, T.: 24
Handley Page
    Halifax: 68, 160
    Hampden: 157, 222
    Hinadai: 149
    HP38 Heyford: 148, 149
    HP45: 111
    O/10: 97
    O/100: 193
    O/400: 93, 94, 98
    V/1500: 184

Victor: 174
W8b: 100
W.10: 109
Handley Page AirTransport: 94, 96, 100
Han Hsin: 131
Hänlein, Paul: 26
Hanlon, Lt D. R.: 140
*Hansa*: 30
Hansa-Brandenburg CI: 93
Harding Jr, Lt J.: 100
Hargrave, L.: 63, 65, 66
Harper, H.: 78
*Harpon*: 82
Harrier (see Hawker Siddeley)
Harrier, AV-8A (see Hawker Siddeley)
Harrier II, AV-8B (see McDonnell Douglas/BAe)
Harris, Lt H. R.: 67
Harris, R. R.: 70
Hartmann, Maj E.: 227, 230
Harvey, 1st Off I.: 126
Harvey-Kelly, Lt H. D.: 137
Hastings, Colonel: 15
'Havoc' (see Mil Mi-28)
Hawker, Capt L. G.: 140, 221
Hawker, H.: 91
Hawker
    Cygnet: 101
    Furi I: 150
    Hunter: 176
    Hurricane: 153, 156, 227
    Sea Fury: 196
    Sea Hawk: 178
    Sea Hurricane: 158
    Typhoon: 158
Hawker Siddeley
    AV-8A Harrier: 181
    Harrier: 180–2, 190, 207, 214
    Nimrod: 180
    P.1127/Kestrel: 214
    Trident I: 120
Hawkeye, E-2 (see Grumman)
He 51 *et seq* (see Heinkel)
Hearst, W. R.: 89
Heath, Lady: 103
Hedren, W. G.: 120
Hegenberger, Lt A. F.: 103, 150
Heinkel, E.: 207
Heinkel
    He 51: 151, 195
    He 59: 191
    He 111: 154, 157, 162, 191, 195, 227
    He 118: 208
    He 162 Salamander: 191
    He 176: 208
    He 178: 208
    He 219 Uhu: 161
    He 280: 158
Heliliner, EH 101 (see EH Industries)
Hellcat, F6F (see Grumman)
Helldiver, SBC (see Curtiss)
Hendon (see Fairey)
Henschel
    Hs 123: 191, 195
    Hs 126: 191
    Hs 293: 161
Henson, W. S.: 74
Hercules, C-130 (see Lockheed)
Hercules, DH66 (see de Havilland)
Hercules, H4 (see Hughes)
*Hermes*, HMS: 182, 183

'Hermes' class carrier: 168
Herndon Jr, H.: 107
Herring, A.: 132
Herring, A. M.: 72
Hervé, Captain: 136
'Hewitt-Sperry biplane': 142
Hewlett, Mrs H. B.: 88
Heyford, HP38 (see Handley Page)
HH-3 (see Sikorsky)
HH-46A Sea Knight (see Boeing Vertol)
Hibernia, HMS: 135
Hicks, Lt G. R.: 95
Hicks, Sgt L.: 70
Highland Airways: 109
Hiller
    HJ-1 Hornet: 50, 51
    XH-44: 49
Hillwood, Flt Lt P.: 174
Hinadai (see Handley Page)
'Hind' (see Mil Mi-24)
Hindenburg, LZ 129 (see Zeppelin)
Hinkler, Sqn Ldr H. J. L. ('Bert'): 103
Hiryu: 160
Hitchcock, US Postmaster General: 88, 89
Hitler, A.: 156
HJ-1 Hornet (see Hiller)
HL-10 (see Northrop/NASA)
Hoglind, M/Sgt H.: 174
'Hokum' (see Kamov)
Holcombe, Capt K. E.: 179
Holland, R.: 17
Holloway, Ac V.: 222
Hooke, R.: 74
Hopkins, Lt Col J. R.: 180
Hornet (see de Havilland)
Hornet, F/A-18 (see McDonnell Douglas)
Hornet, HJ-1 (see Hiller)
Hornet, USS: 55, 160
Hornisse, Fa 226 (see Focke-Achgelis)
Horsa (see Airspeed)
Hosho: 147, 148, 154
Hotchkiss, 2nd Lt E.: 135
Hoy, Capt E. C.: 96
HP38 Heyford (see Handley Page)
HP45 (see Handley Page)
HPA Toucan 1/2: 217
HRP-1 (see Piasecki)
Hs 123 (see Henschel)
Hs 126 (see Henschel)
Hs 293 (see Henschel)
HTK-1 (see Kaman)
Hubbard, Wg Cdr: 178
Hubbard Air Service: 94
Hudson (see Lockheed)
Hudson, Lt W.: 171
Huerta, General: 136
HueyCobra, AH-1G (see Bell)
HueyCobra, Model 209 (see Bell)
Hughes, H.: 123
Hughes
    GAR-1 Falcon: 176
    H4 Hercules: 123
    NOTAR: 57
    OH-6: 57, 62
    XH-17: 59
Humber biplane: 88
Humber monoplane: 133
Hunt, Cdr J. R.: 39
Hunter (see Hawker)
Hurricane (see Hawker)
Hustler, B-58 (see Convair)

Hydravion (see Fabre)
Hydro-Aeroplane Trial: 91

I

I-1 (Il-400) (see Polikarpov)
I-15 (see Polikarpov)
I-16 Ishak (see Polikarpov)
I-25 submarine: 160
I-168 submarine: 160
Ibis: 28
Il-4 et seq (see Ilyushin)
Ilyushin
    DB-3: 161
    Il-4: 224
    Il-22: 168
    Il-86 'Camber': 120
    Il-96-300: 128
Ilya Mourometz (see Sikorsky)
IMAM Ro 37: 193, 195
Immelman, Lt M.: 140, 221, 222
Imperial Airways: 99, 100, 105, 106, 110–13
Implacable, HMS: 166
Indefatigable, HMS: 162, 166
Indian National Airways: 109
Indian Trans-Continental Airways: 110
Inouye, Vice-Adm S.: 160
Instone Airlines: 100
Integral, 940 (see Breguet)
Intrepid: 18
Intruder, A-6 (see Grumman)
Invincible, HMS: 182, 183
'Invincible' class carrier: 182
Irvin, Capt W. W.: 178
Irvin, L. L.: 67
Ishak, I-16 (see Polikarpov)
Islander, BN-2A (see Britten-Norman)
Italia airship: 34, 35
Italia ship: 162

J

J1 (see Junkers)
J7W Shinden (see Kyushu)
J8N1 Nikka (see Nakajima)
J 29 (see Saab)
Jabara, Capt J.: 223
Jackintell, S.: 70
Jackson, E.: 73, 121
Jahnow, Oberleut R.: 137
James, J. H.: 99
Janello, G.: 96
Jannus, A.: 67, 92
JAT (Jugoslovenski Aerotransport): 224
Jatho, K.: 74
Javelin (see Gloster)
Jefferson, T.: 16
Jeffries, Dr J.: 14
Jenkins, Flt Lt N. H.: 105
Jensen, V.: 126
JetRanger III (see Bell)
JN-4 ('Jenny') (see Curtiss)
Johnson, A.: 105, 107
Johnson, A. M. ('Tex'): 192
Johnson, C. L. ('Kelly'): 192
Johnson, Gp Capt J. E. ('Johnnie'): 227
Johnson, Pres L. B.: 180
Jones, Capt O. P.: 113
Jones Williams, Sqn Ldr A. G.: 105
Jordan, Capt: 148
Joubert de la Ferté, Capt P.: 137

JRM Mars (see Martin)
Ju 52/3m et seq (see Junkers)
June, H.: 105
June Bug (see Curtiss)
Junkers, H.: 95
Junkers
    F13: 95–7
    G23: 101
    G38: 185
    J1: 141, 144
    Ju 52/3m: 101, 154, 155, 186, 191, 195
    Ju 86: 189
    Ju 87: 155, 191, 195
    Ju 88: 156, 163
    W33: 104
Jupiter, USS: 146

K

K-1 (see Goodyear)
K-225 (see Kaman)
Ka-1 (see Kayaba)
Ka-22 Vintokryl et seq (see Kamov)
Kaga: 160
Kalinin Bay, USS: 164
Kaman
    HTK-1: 51
    K-225: 51
kamikaze attacks: 164, 165
Kamov, N.: 44
    'Hokum': 62
    Ka-22 Vintokryl: 61
    Ka-26: 58
    Ka-118: 58
Kamov-Skrzhinskii KaSkr-1: 44
Kanellopoulos, K.: 219
Karapetyan, G. P.: 56
Karel, E. K.: 69
KaSkr-1 (see Kamov-Skrzhinskii)
Kasler, Maj J.: 180
Kästner, Oberleutnant: 140, 221
Kauper, H. A.: 91
Kawasaki
    C-1: 180
    XC-1: 180
Kayaba K-1: 47
KB-29 (see Boeing)
KC-1A (see Kellett)
KC-130 (see Lockheed)
KC-135 (see Boeing)
KD-1 (see Kellett)
Keane, Sgt P. P.: 70
Kellett
    KC-1A: 47
    KD-1: 45, 46
    KH-15: 53
    XH-8: 49
    YG-1: 45
Kellett, Sqn Ldr R. G.: 190
Kelly, Lt O. G.: 99
Kennedy, Pres J. F.: 216, 217
Kenney, Gen G. C.: 228
Kensgaila, V.: 124
Kensgaila VK-8 Aushza: 124
Keys, Lt R. E.: 34
KH-15 (see Kellett)
Khaled, L.: 128
Ki-20 (see Mitsubishi)
Ki-27 (see Nakajima)
Kidd, Flt/Sgt A. K.: 70
Kiev: 181

'Kiev' class carrier: 181
Kikka, J8N1 (see Nakajima)
King, Capt W. A. C.: 27, 28
King George V: 89, 97, 135
King John V (Portugal): 11
King Khalid International Airport: 124
King Louis XVI (France): 12
King's Cup Air Race: 99
King Wladyslaw IV (Poland): 74
*Kitkun Bay*, USS: 164
Kittinger, Col J. W.: 22, 70
KLM (Royal Dutch Airlines): 96, 109, 116, 128
Knabe, Herr: 26
Knight, J.: 95
Knight, W. J.: 219
Köhl, H.: 104
Kolibri, Fl 282 (see Flettner)
Kolibri I (see Borgward)
*Köln*: 47
Komarov, Col V. M.: 215, 216
Komet (see Dornier)
Komet, Me 163 (see Messerschmitt)
Korolev, S.: 169
Krebs, Lt A.: 26
Kremer Prize: 218
Kress, W.: 77
Kubasov, V.: 218
Kukkonen, Sgt: 156
Kuparanto, R. J.: 16, 65
Kyushu
    J7W Shinden: 196
    Q1W Tokai: 162

**L**

L1 *et seq* (see Zeppelin)
L.1011 TriStar (see Lockheed)
Lacy, Capt C.: 125
*La Foudre*: 135
*La France*: 26
Lahm, Lt Frank P.: 20, 132
Lama, SA 315B (see Aérospatiale)
Lamb, D. I.: 136
Lambert, Sgt L.: 168
La Mountain, J.: 17
Lancashire Aero Club: 84
Lancaster (see Avro)
Lancastrian (see Avro)
Lancer, B-1B (see Rockwell)
Langhoff, Leutnant: 140
Langley, S. P.: 76
*Langley*, USS: 146–8
Langley *Aerodrome*: 76, 77
Languedoc (see Sud-Est)
Large America (see Curtiss)
Latham, H.: 82–4, 124, 125
Launoy, M.: 41
Lavoisier, M.: 9, 16
Learoyd, Flt Lt R. A. B.: 222
Lebaudy brothers: 26
Lebaudy brothers
    *Lebaudy* : 26
    *Lebaudy II*: 27
Le Breton, Lt: 135
le Bris, J. M.: 65
Le Brix, Lt-Cdr: 103
Lecointe, S.: 146, 147
Leduc
    O.10: 211
    O.21: 211

Lee, Capt H. P.: 19
Leete, B. S.: 102
Lefebvre, E.: 84
Legagneux, G.: 81, 83
*Le Grand* (see Sikorsky)
*Le Gustav*: 14
le Normand, S.: 64
Leonov, A.: 215, 217
Letchford, Sgt F.: 156
Letov
    S1: 146
    S2: 146
    SH-1: 146
Levasseur P.L.8: 225
Levine, C.: 102
*Lexington*, USS: 160
Liberator, B-24 (see Consolidated)
Lightning (see English Electric)
Lightning, P-38 (see Lockheed)
Lilienthal, O.: 8, 66, 71, 72
Lilienthal No. 11 glider: 66
Lillywhite, R. J.: 92
Lindbergh, Capt C.: 102, 103
Lindstrand, P.: 7, 22, 23
Lindström, O.: 38, 39
Link, E. A.: 149
Link Trainer: 149
Linke-Hoffmann R.II: 184
Lippisch, Dr A.: 208
Lippisch LP-13a: 208
Lischak, W.: 127
Lityvak, Jr Lt L.: 228
*Ljebedy*: 28
Loader, Y.: 70
Lockheed
    AC-130: 180
    Altair: 110
    C-5 Galaxy: 123, 186, 187
    C-130 Hercules: 56, 180, 187
    C-141B StarLifter: 187
    Constellation: 113
    F-94 Starfire: 171
    F-104 Starfighter: 178, 192
    F-117A: 182, 184, 207, 218
    Hudson: 154–6, 159
    KC-130: 192
    L.1011 TriStar: 128, 183
    P2V Neptune: 168
    P-38 Lightning: 163, 195, 227, 228
    P-80 (F-80) Shooting Star: 113, 162, 170, 172, 228
    PBO-1: 159
    SR-71A: 189, 192
    U-2: 176, 178, 192
    Vega: 104, 106, 107, 109, 110
    XC-35: 208
    XP-38: 195
    XP-80: 162
    XST: 218
    YF-94: 171
Loganair: 127
Löhner flying-boat: 142
Loire-Nieuport 46: 194
Lomonosov, M. V.: 41
*London Evening News*: 94
Long, Capt E. M.: 119
Long, J. E.: 128
Longmore, Sqn Cdr A.: 137
Long Range Monoplane (see Fairey)
LongRanger II, Model 206L (see Bell)
Longton, Flt Lt W. H.: 99

López, F. S.: 18
Loraine, R.: 87, 88
*Los Angeles*, USS (ZR-3): 33, 34
Los Angeles Airways: 50
Lovell, J.: 215, 216
Lowe, F/O P.: 70
Lowe, T. S. C.: 17, 18
LP-13a (see Lippisch)
LS-3 (see Rolladen-Schneider)
Lufbery, R.: 226
Lufthansa: 123, 186
Luke, 2nd Lt F.: 24
Lukesch, Haupt D.: 164, 165
*Luna Habitabilis*: 73
Lunardi, V.: 14, 15
Luukkanen, Lt E.: 156
LVG C11: 142
Lynch, B.: 168
Lynx (see Westland)
Lyon, H.: 104
LZ 1 *et seq* (see Zeppelin)

**M**

M1 (see Motor-Luftfahrzeug)
M2-F2 (see Northrop/NASA)
M2-F3 (see Northrop/NASA)
M5K (see Fokker)
M8 (see Fokker)
M-52 (see Miles)
M.52bis (see Macchi)
Macchi
    C200: 154, 155
    M.52bis: 148
    MC72: 125
MacCready, Dr P.: 218
MacCready
    *Gossamer Albatross*: 218, 219
    *Gossamer Condor*: 218
    *Gossamer Penguin*: 218
    *Solar Challenger*: 218
MacLaren, Maj A. S.: 93
Macmillan, Capt N.: 99
*Macon*, USS: 38
Macreadie, Lt J. A.: 99
MacRobertson England–Australia Air Race: 109
*Maddox*, USS: 179
Madison, J.: 16
Magennis, C. S.: 84
Maitland, Lt L. J.: 103
Majendie, Capt A. M.: 114
Malibu, PA-46-310P (see Piper)
Malloy, H. ('Bud'): 126
Maloney, D.: 66
*Mammoth*: 23
Manarov, Flt Eng M. K.: 7, 219
Mangin, M.: 19
Mangusta, A 129 (see Aeritalia)
Manly, C. M.: 76
*Mannert L. Abele*, USS: 166
Mannock, Maj E. ('Mick'): 225
Mantle, Acting Seaman J. F.: 222
Manpowered aircraft: 214
*Maplin*, HMS: 158
Mappleback, Lt G.: 137
Marie-Antoinette: 12
Marix, Flt Lt R. L. G.: 138
Mars, JRM (see Martin)
Marsden, Capt J. T. A.: 114
Marseille, Haupt H.-J.: 227

Martens, Herr: 67
Martin, G.: 67
Martin
130 Clipper: 111
B-57: 172
JRM Mars: 186, 187, 191
MB-1: 98
MB-2: 146, 147
P6M SeaMaster: 189
TM-61 Matador: 172
XB-48: 168, 169
Martin Marietta
SV-5P Pilot: 217
X-24: 217
Mason, M.: 17
Masson, D.: 136
Matador, TM-61 (see Martin)
Mathers, Corp: 93
Maxim, Sir H.: 122
May, 2nd Lt W. R.: 224
Mayo, Maj R. H.: 113
MB-1 (see Martin)
MB-1 Genie (see Douglas)
MB-2 (see Martin)
MB-3 (see Thomas Morse)
MB-E1 (see Militky)
MC-4 (see McCulloch)
MC72 (see Macchi)
McCallion, Mr: 107
McCampbell, Cdr D.: 196
McCandless, Capt B.: 218
McClean, F. K.: 82, 89–91
McClellan, General: 18
McConnell, Capt J.: 197
McCulloch MC-4: 52
McCullough, P.: 20
McCurdy, J. A. D.: 81, 83, 86
McDivitt, J.: 215
McDonnell
F2H Banshee: 171
FD-1 (FH-1) Phantom: 167, 168
XF-85 Goblin: 210
McDonnell Douglas
DC-9: 117, 224
F-4 Phantom II: 118, 179-81, 223
F-15 Eagle: 182, 183, 190
F/A-18 Hornet: 182-4
McDonnell Douglas/BAe AV-8B Harrier II:
183, 189
McDonnell Douglas Helicopters
AH-64 Apache: 60
MD 520N: 58
MD 530N: 58
McDowall, Wg Cdr A.: 163
McIntosh, Wg Cdr R. H.: 107
McIntyre, Flt Lt D. F.: 108
McIntyre, F/O I. E.: 100
McKinley, A.: 105
McMaster, Sir F.: 98
McNeil, G.: 58
McPherson, F/O A: 155, 222
MD.450 Ouragan (see Dassault)
MD.452 Mystère (see Dassault)
MD 520N (see McDonnell Douglas
Helicopters)
MD 530N (see McDonnell Douglas
Helicopters)
Me 163 Komet et seq (see Messerschmitt)
Meagher, Capt A.: 115
Mellin (see Spencer-Moering)
Merritt, C. E.: 69

Messenger (see Sperry)
Messerschmitt
Bf 109: 152, 153, 156, 163, 185, 191, 195,
227, 230
Bf-110: 191
Me 163 Komet: 162, 163, 208
Me 262: 158, 161, 163-6
Me 321 Gigant: 69
Me 323: 69
P.1101: 211
Messiha, Dr K.: 64
Metallballon (see Schwartz)
Meteor (see Gloster)
Meurisse, M.: 84
Meusnier, Lt J.-B. M.: 25
Meyer, D.: 62
MH-53E Sea Dragon (see Sikorsky)
Mi-12 et seq (see Mil)
Michelob Light Eagle (see MIT)
Midway, USS: 179
'Midway' class carrier: 192
Mier, M.: 99
MiG-9 et seq (see Mikoyan)
Mikoyan
MiG-9: 167, 169
MiG-15: 172, 196, 197, 223, 228
MiG-17: 179
MiG-21: 182
MiG-23: 180, 182
MiG-25 'Foxbat': 189
MiG-29 'Fulcrum': 183, 184, 189
Ye-231: 180
Ye-266M: 189
Mil
Mi-12: 59
Mi-24 'Hind': 56, 57
Mi-26 'Halo': 56, 57
Mi-28 'Havoc': 58
Milbank, Maj C.: 58
Miles M-52: 208
Militky MB-E1: 217
Miller, B.: 117
Miller, Sqn Ldr D. S.: 184
Millichap, Capt R. E.: 116
Milling, Lt T. D.: 136
Mir space station: 219
Mirage III (see Dassault)
Mirage IV (see Dassault)
Mirage 2000 (see Dassault)
Miss Champagne: 24
Mississippi, USS: 137
Missouri, USS: 166
'Mistel-Programm': 163
MIT
Daedalus: 218, 219
Michelob Light Eagle: 218
Mitchell, B-25 (see North American)
Mitchell, Brig-Gen W. ('Billy'): 147, 184
Mitchell, R. J.: 96, 97, 194
Mitsubishi
1MF1: 146, 148
A5M: 154
A6M Zero: 157
F-1: 181
G4M 'Betty': 195, 196
Ki-20: 185
T-2: 181
XT-2: 181
Mock, J.: 117
Model 47 (see Bell)
Model 200 (see Boeing)

Model 206L LongRanger II (see Bell)
Model 207 Sioux Scout (see Bell)
Model 209 HueyCobra (see Bell)
Model 247 (see Boeing)
Model 307 Stratoliner (see Boeing)
Model 314 Clipper (see Boeing)
Model 367-80 (see Boeing)
Model 707 (see Boeing)
Model 727 (see Boeing)
Model 737 (see Boeing)
Model 747 (see Boeing)
Model 767 (see Boeing)
Model 777 (see Boeing)
Model A (see Short-Wright)
Model A (see Wright)
Model B (see Bell)
Model B (see Wright)
Model CL-4S (see Boeing)
Model J (see Standard)
Moisant, J. B.: 86
Moll, J. J.: 109
Molland, F/O H.: 176
Mollison, J. A.: 107, 108
Monoplane (see Blackburn)
Monroe, J.: 16
Montgolfier, E.: 10, 12
Montgolfier, J.: 10, 11, 22
Montgolfier balloon: 10-14, 16, 22
Montgolfier brothers: 9–12
Moore, Lt L. A.: 39
Moore-Brabazon, J. T. C.: 81, 84, 85
Moorhouse, Lt W. B. R.: 89, 221
Morane Type M: 137
Morane-Saulnier
M-S 405: 153
M-S 406: 153
Parasol: 224
Type L: 31
Type N: 140, 141
Morehouse, M.: 88
Morris, Lt L. B. F.: 224
Morrish, Flt Sub-Lt C. R.: 144
Morton, J. G.: 62
Moseley, Capt C. C.: 98
Mosquito (see de Havilland)
Moth, DH60 (see de Havilland)
Motor Luftfahrzeug M1: 28
Mould, P/O P. W.: 156
Moy, T.: 76
Mozhaiski, A. F.: 76
MRCA (see Panavia)
Mryia, An-225 (see Antonov)
M-S 405 (see Morane-Saulnier)
M-S 406 (see Morane-Saulnier)
Mullikin, Capt W. H.: 118
Multiplane: 76, 78
Murphy, Lt A. W.: 97
Murray, W/O E. J.: 178
Musgrave, Flt Lt J. G.: 188
Mustang, P-51 (see North American)
Mustin, Lt-Cdr H.: 141
MX-324 (see Northrop)
MXY-7 Ohka (see Yokosuka)
Myers, Maj J.: 163
Mystère, MD.452 (see Dassault)


N

N.1 Norge: 34, 35
N-850 Nashua Number One (see Cameron)

NACA (National Advisory Committee for Aeronautics): 92
Nakajima
    A4N1: 154
    J8N1 Kikka: 166
    Ki-27: 154
Nashua Number One, N-850 (see Cameron)
National Aero-Space Plane: 219
Natter, BA 349 (see Bachem)
Navajo (see Piper)
Navy/Curtiss NC: 94, 95
NB-36H (see Convair)
NC (see Navy/Curtiss)
NC 223.4 (see Centre)
Nelson, D.: 70
Nelson, Lt E.: 100
Nemer, Cdr H.: 124
Neptune, P2V (see Lockheed)
Nesterov, Lt P. N.: 91, 137
Nettleton, Sqn Ldr J. D.: 159
Newell, W.: 67
Newman, Larry M.: 21, 23
New York Daily Graphic: 19
Nicholetts, Flt Lt G. E.: 105
Nicholson, Flt Lt J. B.: 226, 227
Nieuport
    28: 146
    Scout: 221, 225
    Type IV: 91
Nieuport-Delage 29: 146, 147
Nimbus 2 (see Schempp-Hirth)
Nimitz, USS: 186
'Nimitz' class carrier: 186
Nimrod (see Hawker Siddeley)
Nishizawa, W/O H.: 227
No. IV (see Ellehammer)
No. 1 airship (see Yamada & Heraka)
No. 2 helicopter (see Oehmichen)
No. 3 helicopter (see Pescara)
No. 6 (see Santos-Dumont)
No. 11 glider (see Lilienthal)
No. 15 (see Santos-Dumont)
Nobile, U.: 34
Nord
    1500-02 Griffon II: 213
    Gerfaut 1A: 212
    Gerfaut II: 212
Nordair: 118
Norge (see N.1)
North American
    B-25 Mitchell: 160
    F-82 Twin Mustang: 171
    F-86 Sabre: 115, 169, 174, 175, 223, 228
    F-100 Super Sabre: 174, 176
    OV-10 Bronco: 180
    P-51 Mustang: 114
    RB-45: 173
    X-15A: 214, 215
    X-15A-2: 207, 219
    XB-45 Tornado: 170
    XB-70A Valkyrie: 215
    YF-100A: 174
    YP-86A: 170
North Carolina, USS: 141, 143
Northrop
    B-2: 6, 197, 207
    F-89 Scorpion: 176, 177
    MX-324: 209
    P-61 Black Widow: 168
    SM-62 Snark: 178
    X-4 Bantam: 210, 211

XF-89 Scorpion: 170
XP-79B: 208, 209
YF-17: 181
Northrop/NASA
    HL-10: 217
    M2-F2: 216
    M2-F3: 216
Norton, Capt R.: 121
NOTAR (see Hughes)
Nott, J.: 23
Nowotny, Maj W.: 161, 165
Nulli Secundus: 27
Nungesser, Lt C. E. J. M.: 225
Nurr, M.: 70
NY-2 (see Consolidated)
NYP Monoplane (see Ryan)

O

O/10 (see Handley Page)
O.10 (see Leduc)
O.21 (see Leduc)
O/100 (see Handley Page)
O/400 (see Handley Page)
Oberth, Prof H.: 207
Obregon, Gen A.: 136
Ocean, HMS: 167
Oehmichen, E.: 43, 44
Oehmichen No. 2 helicopter: 43, 44
OH-6 (see Hughes)
Ohka, MXY-7 (see Yokosuka)
Old, Maj Gen A. J.: 177
Oliver of Malmesbury: 64
Onofrio, C.: 113
Opel-Hatry Rak-1: 207
Operation
    Barbarossa: 191
    Black Buck: 183
    Colossus: 158
    Desert Sabre: 60
    Desert Shield: 187, 190
    Desert Storm: 130, 184, 223
    Downfall: 131
    Junction City: 180
    Just Cause: 184
    Linebacker II: 192
    Mercury: 186
    Overlord: 191
    Rolling Thunder: 179
    Solomon: 128
    Vittles: 170
Omen: 10
Osprey, V-22 (see Bell-Boeing)
Ostfriesland: 147
Otter, UH-1A (see de Havilland Canada)
Otto, N.: 76
Ouragan, MD.450 (see Dassault)
OV-10 Bronco (see North American)
Overstrand (see Boulton Paul)
Ovington, E. L.: 88, 89
Oxford v. Cambridge Air Race: 98

P

P2V Neptune (see Lockheed)
P6M SeaMaster (see Martin)
P.7 (see PZL)
P11 (see PZL)
P24 (see PZL)
P-26 (see Boeing)
P-35 (see Seversky)

P-38 Lightning (see Lockheed)
P-40 Warhawk (see Curtiss)
P-51 Mustang (see North American)
P-61 Black Widow (see Northrop)
P-80 Shooting Star (see Lockheed)
P.108 Balliol (see Boulton Paul)
P.1101 (see Messerschmitt)
P.1127/Kestrel (see Hawker Siddeley)
PA-46-310P Malibu (see Piper)
Page, Cdr L. C.: 179
Pålson Type 1: 92
Pan American Airways: 103, 110, 112, 116–18, 120, 128, 129
Panavia
    MRCA: 181
    Tornado: 181, 184
Pangborn, C. E.: 107
Panther, F9F (see Grumman)
Papin, M.: 43
Parasol (see Morane-Saulnier)
Parke, Lt W.: 135
Parker, J. L.: 111, 186
Parmalee, P. O.: 87, 134
Parmentier, K. D.: 109
Parnall Pixie: 99
Parschau, Leutnant: 220
Parseval PL4 Type B: 28
Passarola: 9
Patoka, USS: 33
Patteson, C.: 96
Paulhan, L.: 86, 89, 132
'Pave Tack' weapons delivery: 182
Pavlova, T.: 69
PBO-1 (see Lockheed)
PBY Catalina (see Consolidated)
Pe-2 (see Petlyakov)
Pearse, R. W.: 77
Peck, Capt B. A.: 93
Pégoud, A.: 91
Peltier, Mme T.: 80
Pennsylvania, USS: 134
Pequet, H.: 88
Percival Gull: 110
Perona, Lt C.: 183
Perot Jr, R.: 57, 58, 61
Pershing, General: 226
Pescara No. 3 helicopter: 44
Peter, Kapitän: 191
Peter, Lt: 143
Petlyakov Pe-2: 195
Petter, W. E. W.: 175
Pfalz D.IIIa: 146
Pfiel, Do 335 (see Dornier)
Phantom, FD-1 (FH-1) (see McDonnell)
Phantom II, F-4 (see McDonnell Douglas)
Phillips, W. H.: 40, 41, 76, 78
Piantanid, N.: 23
Piasecki
    HRP-1: 49
    PV-3: 49
Piasecki-Vertol H-21 Shawnee Workhorse: 52–4
Piazza, Capitano: 134, 135
Piccard, Prof A.: 20
Piercy, Mr: 101
Piggot, D.: 214
Pike, Capt T.: 58
Pilcher, P. S.: 71, 72
Pioneer: 19
Piper
    260B Comanche: 117

Aztec D: 118
Cub: 113
Navajo: 119
PA-46-310P Malibu: 121
Pitcairn, H.: 44
Pixie (see Parnall)
Pixton, H.: 92
PKZ-1 (see von Karman-Zurovec)
PL4 Type B (see Parseval)
P.L8 (see Levasseur)
Platt-Le-Plage XR-1: 49
Pocock, G.: 71
Pohle, Haupt: 156
Polikarpov
    I-1 (Il-400): 148
    I-15: 151, 194, 195
    I-16 Ishak: 151, 152, 154, 194
Polo, M.: 63, 64
Ponche, M.: 89
Ponche-Primard *Tubavion*: 89
Pond, Capt C. F.: 134
Porte Baby: 142
Post, W.: 106, 108, 109
Potez
    25: 193
    630 series: 196
Powers, F. G.: 178
Prather, Lt Cdr V. A.: 23
Pregnant Guppy, B-377PG (see Aero
    Spacelines)
Prévost, M.: 90, 125
Prier, P.: 88
Primard, M.: 89
Primo, SVA 5 (see Ansaldo)
Prince Andrew: 183
Prince of Wales: 132
*Princeton*, USS: 172
*Prinz Eugen*: 154, 196
*Progress in Flying Machines*: 72
Prowler, EA-6B (see Grumman)
Prudhommeau, Corp: 137
PS-1/US-1 (see Shin Meiwa)
Ptacek, S.: 218
Pulitzer Trophy Race: 98
Pup (see Sopwith)
Puss Moth, DH80 (see de Havilland)
PV-3 (see Piasecki)
PV-3 (see Westland)
PZL
    P.7: 149
    P11: 195
    P24: 157

Q

Q1W Tokai (see Kyushu)
Qantas: 127
QANTAS (Queensland and Northern
    Territory Aerial Service): 98, 104
Qantas Empire Airways: 110, 116
QH-50A (see Gyrodyne)
Quénault, Corporal: 138
Quimby, H.: 88

R

R.II (see Linke-Hoffman)
R VI (see Zeppelin-Staaken)
R1 *Mayfly* (see Vickers)
R-4 (see Sikorsky)
R4D (see Douglas)

R-23 airship: 33
R-34 airship: 33
R-38 (see Short)
R-100 (see Airship Guarantee Co.)
R-101 (see Royal Airship Works)
Rader, P.: 136
Radley-England Waterplane: 91
Rak-1 (see Opel-Hatry)
Rankin, Lt-Col W. H.: 68
Rascal, GAM-63 (see Bell)
Raven *Double Eagle V*: 22, 23
Rawlinson, A.: 85
Raynham, F.: 87
RB-45 (see North American)
RB Racer (see Dayton-Wright)
*Redoubt*, HMS: 146
Rees, Lt T.: 224
Reid, L. G.: 109
Reitsch, H.: 46
Renard, Capt C.: 26
Republic
    EF-84: 172
    F-84 Thunderjet: 173
    F-105 Thunderchief: 176, 180
    XP-47J: 163
    YF-105: 176
Reynolds, G. W. H.: 189
RH-53D (see Sikorsky)
Richey, H.: 110
Richie, Capt R. S.: 223
Richter, Lt J. P.: 148
Rickenbacker, Capt E. V.: 188, 226
Riddick, Mr: 13
Ride, S.: 219
Ro 37 (see IMAM)
Robert brothers: 13, 25
Roberts, Capt T. C.: 179
Robertson, G.: 71
Robertson, Sir MacPherson: 109
Robinson, Lt W. L.: 32, 142, 222
Robinson, R.: 68
Roc (see Blacburn)
Rockwell, Lt K.: 142
Rockwell B-1B Lancer: 183
Rodgers, C. P.: 89
Roe, A. V.: 78, 82, 83, 89
Roe
    Roe 1: 82, 83
Roëland, M.: 136
Rogers, W.: 109
Rohlfs, E.: 45, 54
Rolladen-Schneider LS-3: 69
Rolls, Hon C. S.: 80, 86
*Roma*: 162
Romain, J.: 15
Rose, Sqn Ldr N. E.: 190
Rosetti, C.: 121
*Rosie O'Grady*: 22
Ross, Cdr M. D.: 23
Rosseau, Mr: 14
Rossi, Maj M. T.: 223
Rota (see Avro)
Rotachute: 47
Rothermere, Lord: 110
Rotodyne (see Fairey)
Rouilly, M.: 43
Roux, M.: 92
Rowe, L/Cpl R.: 32
Royal Aero Club of GB: 77, 81, 84, 85, 99,
    101, 137
Royal Aeronautical Society: 24

Royal Aircraft Factory
    BE2c: 31, 97, 137, 140, 142, 221
    FE2b: 144, 193, 221, 224
    SE5a: 98, 221, 222, 225, 226
Royal Airship Works R-101: 35, 38
Royal Brunei Airlines: 127
Royal Society: 11
*Royal Vauxhall Balloon, The*: 17
Roziere R-60 (see Cameron)
Rudat, Haupt H.: 163
Ruhrstahl/Kramer Fritz X-1: 162
Rutan, D.: 122
Rutland, Flt Lt F.: 142
Ryan
    FR-1 Fireball: 166
    NYP monoplane: 102, 103
    X-13 Vertijet: 213
Rymer, Capt R.: 114

S

S1 (see Letov)
S2 (see Letov)
S.6B (see Supermarine)
S.16 (see Sikorsky)
S20 *Mercury* (see Short)
S21 *Maia* (see Short)
S-221 (see Sukhoi)
S.26 (see Short)
S.33 (see Short)
S.38 (see Short)
S-51 (see Sikorsky)
S55 (see Savoia-Marchetti)
S-55 (see Sikorsky)
S-58 (see Sikorsky)
S-65 (see Sikorsky)
S.68 (see Short)
SA 315B Lama (see Aérospatiale)
Saab J 29: 170
Sabena: 52, 53
Sabre, F-86 (see North American)
Sadler, J.: 14, 16
Sadler, W.: 16
Sage, Mrs L. A.: 15
Sakai, Lt (jg) S.: 222, 223
Salamander, He 162 (see Heinkel)
Salmond, Maj-Gen W.: 93
Samson, Lt C. R.: 134, 135, 137, 146
Santos-Dumont, A.: 26, 63, 78, 82, 206
Santos-Dumont
    '14-bis': 78, 79
    No. 6: 26
    No. 15: 26, 27
Saracen of Constantinople: 64
*Saratoga*, USS: 176
SAS (Scandinavian Airlines System): 115
Saunders-Roe SR A/1: 209
Savitskaya, S.: 219, 221
Savoia-Marchetti
    S55: 150
    SM 79: 195
    SM 81: 195
Sayer, Flt Lt P. E. G.: 207
SB-2 (see Tupolev)
SB4 Sherpa (see Short)
SBC Helldiver (see Curtiss)
SBD Dauntless (see Douglas)
SC.1 (see Short)
SC.5 (see Short)
Schall, Haupt F.: 165
*Scharnhorst*: 154, 196

Schempp-Hirth Nimbus 2: 69, 70
Schiegg, U.: 13
Schilling, Col D. C.: 172
Schimpf, C. M.: 128
Schirra, W.: 215
Schleicher
    ASH-25: 68
    ASW-12: 68
Schneider Trophy Contest: 90, 92, 96, 97,
    125, 131, 136, 150, 194
Schütte-Lanz
    SL1: 29
    SL2: 29
    SL3: 31
    SLXI: 32, 142
*Schwaben*: 30
Schwartz *Metallballon*: 26
Schweizer
    SGS 1-23E: 70
    SGS 2-32: 70
*Scientific American* trophy: 80
Scimitar (see Supermarine)
Scorpion, F-89/XF-89 (see Northrop)
Scott, B.: 87
Scott, Capt J. P. D.: 176
Scott, C. W. A.: 109
Scott, D.: 216
Scott, J.: 132
Scott, S.: 117, 119, 120
Scott, Sqn Ldr G. H.: 33
Scout (see Nieuport)
Scout C (see Bristol)
SE5a (see Royal Aircraft Factory)
SE.210 Caravelle (see Sud-Est Aviation)
Sea Dart, XF2Y-1 (see Convair)
Sea Dragon, MH-53E (see Sikorsky)
Sea Eagle (see Supermarine)
Sea Fury (see Hawker)
Sea Gladiator (see Gloster)
Seagrave Trophy: 121
Sea Harrier (see BAe)
Sea Hawk (see Hawker)
Sea Hornet (see de Havilland)
Sea Hurricane (see Hawker)
Sea King (see Westland)
Sea King, SH-3 (see Sikorsky)
Sea Knight, HH-46A (see Boeing Vertol)
Sea Lion (see Supermarine)
Seaman, K.: 69
SeaMaster, P6M (see Martin)
Sea Mosquito (see de Havilland)
Sea Otter (see Supermarine)
Sea Venom (see de Havilland)
Seki, Lt Y.: 164
Selfridge, Lt T. E.: 130, 132
Sentinel 500 (see Westinghouse Airships)
Seversky P-35: 152, 153
Seys, Sqn Ldr R. G.: 67
SGS 1-23E (see Schweizer)
SGS 2-32 (see Schweizer)
SH-1 (see Letov)
SH-3 Sea King (see Sikorsky)
SH-5 (see HAMC)
Shackleton, E. A.: 129
Shadow (see CFM)
Sharman, H.: 7
Shaw, H. ('Jerry'): 116, 128
Shawnee/Workhorse, H-21 (see Piasecki-
    Vertol)
Shepard, A. B.: 214, 215
Sherman, Lt T. C.: 136

Sherpa, SB4 (see Short)
Shetland (see Short)
Shinden, J7W (see Kyushu)
Shin Meiwa PS-1/US-1: 187
Shoecroft, J.: 22
*Shoho*: 160
*Shokaku*: 160
Shooting Star, P-80 (see Lockheed)
Short, E.: 81
Short brothers: 8
Short
    184: 140, 141
    Belfast: 179
    C-class Empire flying-boat: 111, 112, 125
    No. 2 biplane: 81, 84, 85
    R-38: 33
    S20 *Mercury*: 112, 126
    S21 *Maia*: 112
    S.26: 133
    S.33: 89
    S.38: 134
    S.68: 91
    SB4 Sherpa: 212
    SC.1: 214
    SC.5: 179
    Shetland: 186
    Stirling: 158
    Sturgeon: 168
Short-Mayo Composite: 112, 113
Short-Wright Model A: 82, 84
Shuttleworth Collection: 129
*Sicily*, USS: 172
Siebert, Oberleut L.: 165
Siemens-Schuckert D VI: 188
Sikorsky, I. I.: 46, 47, 58, 90
Sikorsky
    CH-53: 55, 62
    CH-53E Super Stallion: 60
    HH-3: 55, 56
    *Ilya Mourometz*: 90, 97, 139, 184
    *Le Grand*: 90, 91
    MH-53E Sea Dragon: 55, 56
    R-4: 48
    RH-53D: 55
    S.16: 139
    S-51: 50
    S-55: 50, 52, 53
    S-58: 54
    S-65: 55
    SH-3 Sea King: 55
    UH-34: 186
    UH-60 Black Hawk: 60
    XR-4: 48
Silver City Airways 113, 117
*Silver Dart* (see Aerial Experimental
    Association)
Simon, Corp: 146
Simonet, Mlle: 15
Simons, Maj D. G.: 20, 21
Sioux, H-13 (see Bell)
Sioux Scout, Model 207 (see Bell)
Sippé, Flt Lt S. V.: 139
Sirocco (see Aviasud)
Skene, 2nd Lt R. B.: 137
Skrzhinskii, N.: 44
Skua (see Blackburn)
Skyknight, F3D (see Douglas)
Skylane (see Cessna)
Skyraider, AD-1 (see Douglas)
Skyrocket (see Douglas)
Skyship 500 (see Airship Industries)

Skyship 600 (see Airship Industries)
Skyship 500/600 (see Slingsby Aviation)
Skywarrior, A3D (see Douglas)
SL1 (see Schütte-Lanz)
SL2 (see Schütte-Lanz)
SL3 (see Schütte-Lanz)
SL XI (see Schütte-Lanz)
Slayton, D.: 218
Sleep, Sqn Ldr D. M.: 196
Slingsby Gull: 69
Slingsby Aviation
    Skyship 500: 11
    Skyship 600: 11
SM-62 Snark (see Northrop)
SM 79 (see Savoia-Marchetti)
SM 81 (see Savoia-Marchetti)
Smith, Capt C. K.: 104, 105, 110
Smith, Capt L. H.: 148
Smith, Capt R. M.: 93, 96, 97, 118
Smith, Cdr H.: 180
Smith, D.: 58
Smith, G. F.: 176
Smith, H.: 146
Smith, Lt K.: 97, 118
Smith, Lt L. H.: 100
Snark, SM-62 (see Northrop)
Snipe (see Sopwith)
SO 1310 Farfadet (see Sud-Ouest)
SO 9000 Trident (see Sud-Ouest)
SOCATA TB 10 Tobago: 120
*Solar Challenger* (see MacCready)
Solar One (see To-Williams)
Sommer, R.: 128
Sopwith
    Camel: 33, 145, 146, 193, 224
    Cuckoo: 143
    Gnu: 99
    Pup: 143–5
    Snipe: 147
    Tabloid: 92, 136, 138
    Triplane: 142, 226
    *Soryu*: 160
South African Airways: 118
Sowrey, 2nd Lt: 32
*Soyuz 19*: 217
*Soyuz T12/Salyut 7*: 219
*Soyuz TM4*: 219
Space Shuttle Orbiter: 207, 218, 219
SPAD XIII: 187, 188
Sparrowhawk, F9C-2 (see Curtiss)
Speight, D.: 69
Spencer, S.: 27
'Spencer Kavanagh', Miss: 85
Spencer-Moering Mellin: 27
Spenser-Grey, Sqn Cdr D. A.: 138
Sperrle, Maj-Gen: 195
Sperry, L. B.: 207
Sperry Messenger: 34
Spitfire (see Supermarine)
Sportsman, VJ-22 (see Volmer)
*Sputnik 1*: 213
SR-71A (see Lockheed)
SR A/1 (see Saunders-Roe)
SS dirigible (see Armstrong-Whitworth)
SS Twin (see Vickers)
SS Z dirigible (see Armstrong-Whitworth)
Stack, T. N.: 102
Stafford, T.: 215, 216, 218
Stainforth, Flt Lt G. H.: 150
Stamer, F.: 207
Standard Model J: 93

Starfighter, F-104 (see Lockheed)
Starfire, F-94 (see Lockheed)
StarLifter, C-141B (see Lockheed)
Starr, R. H.: 124
Starr *Bumble Bee Two*: 124
Steill, B.: 17
Stephenson, G.: 69
Stevens, Capt A.: 20
Stirling (see Short)
Stits, D.: 124
Stits *Baby Bird*: 124
*St Lo*, USS: 164
Stoney, Capt T. B.: 116
St Petersburg–Tampa Airboat Line: 92
Stratofortress, B-52 (see Boeing)
Stratojet, B-47 (see Boeing)
Stratoliner, Model 307 (see Boeing)
*Stratoquest* (see Thunder & Colt)
Strattio Jr, Maj W. T.: 174
Stringfellow, J.: 74, 75
Stultz, W.: 105
Sturgeon (see Short)
Stuwer, J.: 14
*Su-17 et seq* (see Sukhoi)
Sud-Est Aviation
    Languedoc: 211
    SE.210 Caravelle: 115
Sud-Ouest
    SO 1310 Farfadet: 52, 53
    SO 9000 Trident: 211, 212
Sukhoi
    S-22I: 180
    Su-17: 180
    Su-22 'Fitter': 182
    Su-27 'Flanker': 182-4
Sullivan, K.: 219
Sullivan, Maj J.: 189
*Superchicken III*: 22
Superfortress, B-29 (see Boeing)
Super Guppy (see Aero Spacelines)
Supermarine
    Attacker: 173
    S.6B: 150
    Scimitar: 178
    Sea Eagle: 100
    Sea Lion: 97
    Sea Otter: 154
    Spitfire: 154, 156, 157, 189, 194
    Swift: 175
    Type 300: 194
Super Sabre, F-100 (see North American)
Super Sportster (see Gee Bee)
Super Stallion, CH-53E (see Sikorsky)
Suring, Professor: 20
SV-5P Pilot (see Martin Marietta)
SVA 5 Primo (see Ansaldo)
Swallow biplane: 102
Swedenborg, E.: 74
Sweeney, Maj C. W.: 166
Swift (see Supermarine)
Swingwing, VJ-23 (see Volmer)
Swissair: 128
Swiss Air Transport: 109
Swordfish (see Fairey)
Sycamore (see Bristol)

T

T-2 (see Fokker)
T-2 (see Mitsubishi)
T-18 Tiger (see Thorpe)

Taaffe, R. W.: 38
**Tables of Progressive World Records**
    Absolute speed: 234-7
    Absolute height: 237-8
    Absolute distance: 239-40
Tabloid (see Sopwith)
Takagi, Vice-Adm T.: 160
*Taube* (see Etrich)
Taylor, Capt P. G.: 110
Taylor, D.: 120
Taylor, F.: 66
Taylor, G. A.: 66
TB-3 (ANT-6) (see Tupolev)
TB 10 Tobago (see SOCATA)
TBD Devastator (see Douglas)
TBF Avenger (see Grumman)
*Tbilisi*: 183, 184
TC-3 dirigible: 34
Teesdale, K. J.: 70
Templer, Capt J. L. B.: 19
Tereshkova, Jr Lt V.: 215
Terski, V.: 127
Testu-Brissy, P.: 16
*The République*: 28, 29
*Theodore Roosevelt*, USS: 197
*Thetis Bay*, USS: 53
Thible, Mme: 14
Thirtle, Sqn Ldr J.: 70
Thomas, G. H.: 92
Thomas Morse MB-3: 146
Thompson, Commander: 155
Thompson, Lt S. W.: 145
Thomson, Lord: 35
Thorpe T-18 Tiger: 120
Thunder & Colt
    AS 261: 38
    *Stratoquest*: 23
    Type 300A: 22
    *Virgin Atlantic Flyer*: 22, 23
    *Virgin Otsuka Pacific Flyer*: 8, 22, 23
Thunderchief, F-105 (see Republic)
Thunderjet, EF-84/F-84 (see Republic)
Tibbets Jr, Col P. W.: 166
*Ticonderoga*, USS: 179
Tiger (see Eurocopter)
Tiger, F11F (F-11) (see Grumman)
Tiger, T-18 (see Thorpe)
Tiger Moth, DH82 (see de Havilland)
Timm, R.: 127
Tissandier, G.: 19, 26
Tissandier, P.: 82
Titov, Col V. G.: 219
TM-61 Matador (see Martin)
To, Freddie: 218
Tobago, TB 10 (see SOCATA)
Tokai, Q1W (see Kyushu)
Tomcat, F-14 (see Grumman)
Tornado (see Panavia)
Tornado, XB-45 (see North American)
Toucan 1/2 (see HPA)
Tournachon, F.: 17
Towers, Cdr H.: 94, 95, 136
To-Williams Solar One: 218
Townsend, E. C.: 71
Transcontinental & Western Air: 106, 112
Trans-Mediterranean Airways: 119
Transom, A.: 17
Tremml, G.: 218
*Trent*, SS: 28
Trewin, G. S.: 142
Triad, A-1 (see Curtiss)

Trident, SO 9000 (see Sud-Ouest)
Trident I (see Hawker Siddeley)
Triplane (see Sopwith)
*Tripoli*, USS: 55
TriStar, L. 1011 (see Lockheed)
Trouvé, G.: 75
TSR. 2 (see BAC)
*Tu-12 et seq* (see Tupolev)
*Tubavion* (see Ponche & Primard)
Tudor, L.: 70, 71
Tupolev
    ANT-1: 98
    ANT-2: 101
    SB2: 156, 195
    TB-3 (ANT-6): 150
    Tu-4 'Bull': 197
    Tu-12: 168, 169
    Tu-22 'Blinder': 179
    Tu-22M 'Backfire': 181
    Tu-95/-142 'Bear': 189
    Tu-104: 115
    Tu-144: 117
    Tu-154: 122
    Tu-155: 122
    Tu-156: 122
    Tu-160 'Blackjack': 186, 187
Turbo Centurion (see Cessna)
Turnbull, Mr: 99
TWA (Trans World Airlines) 108, 128
Twin Mustang, F-82 (see North American)
Twiss, Lt Cdr L. P.: 212
Type I (see Voisin-Farman)
Type II (see Clément-Bayard)
Type IV (see Nieuport)
Type IX U-boat: 47
Type 1 (see Pålson)
Type 142 (see Bristol)
Type 170 Freighter (see Bristol)
Type 173 (see Bristol)
Type 300 (see Supermarine)
Type 300A (see Thunder & Colt)
Type 707 (see Avro)
Type F (see Avro)
Type L (see Morane-Saulnier)
Type M (see Morane-Saulnier)
Type N (see Morane-Saulnier)
Typhoon (see Hawker)
Tyson, G.: 186
Tytler, J.: 14

U

U-1A Otter (see de Havilland Canada)
U-2 (see Lockheed)
*U-36* submarine: 144
*U-206* submarine: 159
*U-451* submarine: 159
*U-570* submarine: 155
Ugaki, Adm M: 164
UH-1 (see Bell)
UH-34 (see Sikorsky)
UH-60 Black Hawk (see Sikorsky)
Uhu, He 219 (see Heinkel)
ULD-1 (see Cameron)
Ulm, C. T. P.: 104, 105
*Union*: 18
United Air Lines: 105, 125, 127
*United States*: 18
US National Air Races: 123

**V**

V-1 flying-bomb: 152, 162, 188, 196
V-2 (A-4) rocket: 152, 164, 169
V12 (see Zodiac)
V-22 Osprey (see Bell-Boeing)
V/1500 (see Handley Page)
Valiant (see Vickers)
Valier, M.: 207
Valkyrie, XB-70A (see North American)
Valkyrie monoplane: 88
*Valley Forge*, USS: 172
Vampire (see de Havilland)
van de Hagen, Oberleut O.: 31
van Deman, Mrs R.: 84
van Ryneveld, Lt Col P.: 97
Varney Speed Lines: 102
VC10 (see Vickers)
VE-7SF (see Vought)
Védrines, J.: 92
Vega (see Lockheed)
Vening, J. M.: 124
Ventry, Lord: 37
Veranzio, F.: 64
Vernon (see Vickers)
Vertijet, X-13 (see Ryan)
Verville-Packard 600: 98
Vickers
    Destroyer EFB 1: 136
    FB5 Gunbus: 140
    R1 *Mayfly*: 29
    SS Twin: 33
    Valiant: 172, 177, 178, 190
    VC10: 128, 184
    Vernon: 147
    Victoria: 149
    Viking: 113
    Viking amphibian: 97
    Vimy: 95–7, 100
    Viscount: 113–15, 120
    Wellesley: 36, 190
    Wellington: 36, 156, 158, 160
Victor (see Handley Page)
Victoria (see Vickers)
Viking (see Vickers)
Viking amphibian (see Vickers)
*Ville d'Orléans*: 19
Vimy (see Vickers)
Vintokryl, Ka-22 (see Kamov)
'Viola Spencer': 85
*Virgin Atlantic Flyer* (see Thunder & Colt)
*Virgin Otsuka Pacific Flyer* (see Thunder & Colt)
Viscount (see Vickers)
VJ-22 Sportsman (see Volmer)
VJ-23 Swingwing (see Volmer)
VK-8 Aushza (see Kensgaila)
Vlaicu, A.: 86
Vlaicu *Vlaicu I*: 86
Voisin, C.: 79
Voisin, G.: 79, 80
Voisin brothers: 63, 66
Voisin
    biplane: 81, 83, 85, 140
    X: 138
Voisin-Farman Type I: 78–80
Volmer
    VJ-22 Sportsman: 26
    VJ-23 Swingwing: 120
von Gronau, Capt W.: 106
von Guericke, Otto: 9

von Hiddessen, Lt F: 138
von Hunefeld, Baron: 104
von Karman, Dr Ing T.: 43
von Karman-Zurovec PKZ-1: 43
von Ohain, Dr H. J. P.: 207, 208
von Opel, F.: 207
von Parseval, A.: 19
von Petroczy, Oberstleut S.: 43
von Richthofen, M.: 221, 223, 224, 229
von Rosenthal, Leut Baron: 137
von Sigsfeld, B.: 19
von Tiedemann, Lt R.: 133
von Zeppelin, Count F.: 26, 29, 39
*Voskhod 1*: 215
*Voskhod 2*: 215
Voss, Lt W.: 145
*Vostok 1*: 214
*Vostok 6*: 215
Vought
    F4U Corsair: 172, 190, 223, 224
    F-8 Crusader: 176
    F8U Crusader: 68, 197
    VE-7SF: 148
    XF8U-1: 176
Vought-Sikorsky VS-300: 47
*Voyager* (see Voyager Aircraft)
Voyager Aircraft *Voyager*: 121, 122
VS-300 (see Vought-Sikorsky)
Vulcan (see Avro)
Vulovic, V.: 224

**W**

W8b (see Handley Page)
W. 10 (see Handley Page)
W33 (see Junkers)
WA-116 (see Wallis)
WA-116/F (see Wallis)
WA-121/Mc (see Wallis)
Waco CG-4: 67
*Wakamiya Maru*: 138
Wakefield, Sir C.: 32
*Wake Island*, USS 166
Wal (see Dornier)
Walden, Dr H. W.: 84
Walden III: 84
Walker, J.: 214, 219
Wallace (see Westland)
Walleye guided bomb: 180
Wallis, N. B.: 36, 161
Wallis, Wg Cdr K. H.: 60, 61
Wallis
    WA-116: 61
    WA-116/F: 60
    WA-121/Mc: 61
Walsh, V. C.: 88
Walters, Sgt B.: 67
Wapiti (see Westland)
Warchalovski brothers: 87
Warhawk, P-40 (see Curtiss)
Warneford, Flt Sub-Lt R. A. J.: 31
Warner, J.: 104
Warrior, AH-58 (see Bell)
Warsitz, E.: 208
*Washington*: 18
Washington (see Boeing)
Washington, Pres G.: 16
Wasp (see Westland)
*Wasp*, USS: 62
Waterfall, Lt V.: 137
Waterplane (see Radley-England)

Waterton, Sqn Ldr W. A.: 173
Watson, Sqn Ldr D.: 174
Watts, B.: 62
WDL 1B airship: 38
Webb, T. H.: 93
Wee Bee (see Beardmore)
Wellesley (see Vickers)
Wellington (see Vickers)
Wellman, W: 28
Welsh, Dr K. H. V.: 104
Wenham, F. W.: 65
Wessex (see Westland)
West Australian Airways: 98
Westenra, Hon Mrs R.: 107
West, Ensign J. C.: 166
Westinghouse Airships Sentinel 5000: 11, 38
Westland
    Lynx: 60, 61
    PV-3: 108
    Sea King: 182
    Wallace: 108
    Wapiti: 193
    Wasp: 55
    Wessex: 54
Westland/Sikorsky Dragonfly: 50, 51
*West Virginia*, USS: 166
Wheeler, Dr J.: 71
White, E.: 215
White, Maj R.: 214
Whitehead, G.: 77
*White Plains*, USS: 164
Whitley (see Armstrong Whitworth)
Whitlock, Capt A: 126
Whittle, F.: 207
Widdifield, Maj N.: 189
Wiking, Bv 222 (see Blohm und Voss)
Wilkins, Capt G. H.: 104
William, D.: 71
Williams, D.: 218
Willows, E. T.: 29
Willows Willow III *City of Cardiff*: 29
Wills Wing: 70
Wilson, D. C.: 89
Wilson, Gp Capt H. J.: 167
Windham, Capt W. G.: 88
'Window': 160
Wing (see Wills)
Winslow, 2nd Lt A.: 146
Wintgens, Lt K.: 140
Winton, E. S.: 125
Wise, J. C.: 17, 19
Wisner, B. C.: 120
Wisner, W. H.: 120
Wisseman, Leut K.: 225
Withers, Flt Lt M.: 190
Wolf, Ms C.: 23
Wölfert, Dr K.: 26
**World Air Arms**, Formation dates of: 197–205
Wren (see English Electric)
Wright, O.: 63, 66, 73, 77, 79, 80, 130-2
Wright, W.: 63, 66, 73, 77, 79–81, 84, 125, 126, 131
Wright brothers: 66, 72, 77, 131, 132, 206
Wright
    Biplane: 81, 82, 84, 86, 125, 132-4
    *Flyer*: 63, 66, 73, 77, 79, 86, 131
    *Flyer II*: 78
    Gliders 1 to 3: 63, 66
    Model A: 84, 132
    Model B: 87, 135

Wrigley, Capt H. N.: 97
Wronieki, Sgt Maj: 146

## X

X-1 (see Bell)
X-1, Fritz (see Ruhrstahl/Kramer)
X-2 (see Bell)
X-3 (see Douglas)
X-4 Bantam (see Northrop)
X-5 (see Bell)
X-13 Vertijet (see Ryan)
X-15A (see North American)
X-15A-2 (see North American)
X-24 (see Martin Marietta)
XA3D (see Douglas)
Xavante, AT-26 & EMB-326GB (see
    EMBRAER)
XB-24 (see Consolidated)
XB-36 (see Convair)
XB-45 Tornado (see North American)
XB-48 (see Martin)
XB-70A Valkyrie (see North American)
XC-1 (see Kawasaki)
XC-35 (see Lockheed)
XF2A-1 (see Brewster)
XF2Y-1 Sea Dart (see Convair)
XF8U-1 (see Vought)
XF9F (see Grumman)
XF12C-1 (see Curtiss)
XF-85 Goblin (see McDonnell)
XF-89 Scorpion (see Northrop)
XFF-1 (see Grumman)
XH-8 (see Kellett)
XH-17 (see Hughes)
XH-44 (see Hiller)
XNBL-1 (see Barling)
XP-38 (see Lockheed)
XP-47J (see Republic)
XP-79B (see Northrop)
XP-80 (see Lockheed)
XP-81 (see Consolidated)
XP-936 (see Boeing)
XR-1 (see Platt-Le-Page)
XR-4 (see Sikorsky)

XST (see Lockheed)
XT-2 (see Mitsubishi)
XTBF-1 (see Grumman)
XV-3 (see Bell)
XV-15 (see Bell/NASA)

## Y

Y1B-9A (see Boeing)
Yak-3 et seq (see Yakovlev)
Yakovlev, A. S.: 167
Yakovlev
    Yak-3: 168
    Yak-9: 171
    Yak-15: 167, 168, 174
    Yak-18: 228
    Yak-36MP 'Forger': 181
Yamada & Heraka No. 1: 29
Yamschikova, O.: 168
Yarry, M.: 21
YB-52 (see Boeing)
Ye-231 (see Mikoyan)
Ye-266M (see Mikoyan)
Yeager, Capt C. ('Chuck'): 207, 210
Yeager, J.: 122
Yegorov, B.: 215
YF2Y-1 (see Convair)
YF-16 (see General Dynamics)
YF-17 (see Northrop)
YF-94 (see Lockheed)
YF-100A (see North American)
YF-105 (see Republic)
YG-1 (see Kellett)
Yokosuka
    E14Y1 ('Glen'): 160
    MXY-7 Ohka: 166
Yokoyama, Lt T.: 157
*Yorktown*, USS: 160
Young, J.: 215, 216, 218
YP-86A (see North American)

## Z

Z1 (see Zeppelin LZ 3)
Zambeccari, Count F.: 13

Zeppelin
    L3: 30
    L6: 30
    L35: 33
    L53: 146
    LZ 1: 26, 27
    LZ 2: 27
    LZ 3 (Z1): 27
    LZ 5: 29
    LZ 6: 28
    LZ 14 (L1): 29
    LZ 18 (L2): 30
    LZ 25 (Z9): 138
    LZ 27 (L4): 30
    LZ 32 (L7): 139
    LZ 36 (L9): 31
    LZ 37: 31
    LZ 38: 31
    LZ 39: 31
    LZ 48 (L15): 31, 32
    LZ 50 (L16): 33
    LZ 74 (L32): 32
    LZ 76 (L33): 32
    LZ 85 (L45): 32
    LZ 89 (L50): 33
    LZ 93 (L44): 32, 33
    LZ 96 (L49): 32
    LZ 101 (L55): 33
    LZ 114 (L72): 34
    LZ 126: 34
    LZ 129 *Hindenburg*: 36, 37, 39
    LZ 130 *Graf Zeppelin II*: 37, 38
Zeppelin-Staaken R VI: 145, 184
Zero, A6M (see Mitsubishi)
Zimmer, E.: 106
Zodiac V12: 36
ZPG 2 (see Goodyear)
ZPG 3-W (see Goodyear)
ZR-1 *Shenandoah*: 34
Zurovec, W.: 43
Zvonariev, Capt: 154